# The Education of Teachers
## in Britain

# The Education of Teachers in Britain

*Edited by*
## DONALD E. LOMAX

**Department of Education**
**University of Manchester**

## JOHN WILEY & SONS
London · New York · Sydney · Toronto

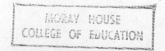

Library of Congress catalog card number
72-8607

ISBN 0 471 54380 2

Made and printed in Great Britain by
The Garden City Press Limited
Letchworth, Hertfordshire SG6 1JS

## Preface

Higher education has been the prerogative of small elite groups ever since the establishment of universities in medieval times. The last decade, however, witnessed unprecedented world-wide expansion of educational opportunities and saw the emergence in rich nations such as the United States, the Soviet Union and Japan of new concepts of mass higher education. A continuing high demand for places in universities and colleges has been ensured by the widely implemented policy of expanding secondary education. The expansion of educational opportunities has produced economic, social, political and administrative problems which governments have sometimes been slow to solve.

In Britain full secondary education will soon be open to all and more people will consequently be qualified to seek places in universities, polytechnics and colleges of education. This expansion of educational opportunity has made it essential that both the quality and quantity of the teaching force should be increased by making wider provision for their adequate personal and professional education. The British have traditionally indulged in piecemeal reform and have often been credited with a genius for compromise in the face of inadequately foreseen developments. While plans for the construction of a better future society are always likely to founder in a sea of change over which there is little human control, there is nevertheless the need to seek to formulate rational policies for future growth.

In 1972 the James Report provided recommendations for the further development of teacher education in England and Wales which ensured that discussions on the future of teacher education would gather momentum. This book is written as a further contribution to a debate which is certain to continue for many years. The twenty educationists who have contributed to this volume all have a deep personal interest in various aspects of teacher training. Most of the chapters may be read separately or in any order by the reader seeking information on specific topics. The book as a whole, however, is somewhat arbitrarily organized into sections in an effort to present a coherent perspective of both the historical background to our present problems and the concepts which underlie our future aspirations.

Part 1 is intended to serve as an introduction to the study of teacher education in Britain. The editor's opening chapter attempts briefly to outline some of the themes which are developed in detail later in the book. In the following chapter Brian Holmes provides a comparative study of teacher education in which he describes the recent international expansion of higher education before going on to discuss the development of teacher training in Europe and the United States. He ends by taking an optimistic view of the opportunities offered by the Government's broad acceptance of the James Report proposals. Next James Scotland outlines the Scottish tradition in teacher education and reviews current developments which reflect changes in this tradition. He analyses the ways in which the Scottish approach has differed from the English, and discusses possible future changes in the system currently operating 'north of the border'. The section concludes with a paper by Sir Ronald Gould on the nature of the teaching profession. He maintains that teaching is a high grade non-manual job which performs a definite social service and allows the individual a substantial measure of freedom in his work. In future, however, it will demand a more rigorous study of the theory and practice of education from its members. Unfortunately the profession does not enjoy self-government and is unlikely, he believes, to do so in the near future.

In Part 2 detailed studies are provided by John Tuck and Eric Robinson of the historical development of the university departments of education and of the relatively new expanding polytechnics. Both authors critically assess the significance of the James Report proposals. Similar treatment is given in Part 3 to the colleges of education. Alec Ross, having reviewed their early history, turns his attention to the development of the teacher training curriculum and ends by analysing the future role of colleges within a binary system of higher education. John Turner provides a different perspective by giving a clear account of the creation of the Area Training Organizations. The final part of his chapter provides a detailed evaluation of the James Report. Gerald Collier brings this section to a close by giving an insightful technical analysis of the administrative problems encountered in individual colleges.

Part 4 directs attention to the teacher education curriculum and its underlying values. After David Aspin has given a rigorous philosophical interpretation of the basic problems, Peter Renshaw in the following chapter provides some interesting suggestions for curriculum development. Edith Cope next surveys the practical teaching element of the curriculum and after reviewing research in the field, gives a report of her own recent studies in Bristol. Gerald Collier then gives added relevance to the other chapters by extending the discussion into the area of teaching methods. Part 5 holds special interest for anyone who is familiar with the 'James' proposal to extend in-service training. After John Taylor and Ian Dale report their recent study of the probationary year, Tom Hollins reviews the problems and potentialities of in-service training. The section ends with Allan Rudd's description of recent work in Manchester that has examined the implications of certain new ideas in curriculum, teaching methods and classroom organization which may illustrate changing concepts of in-service training.

Part 6 is devoted to a study of the economics of teacher education. As Keith Drake points out, in theory economics should be a good paradigm for rational decision-making about teacher education, but unfortunately little is known about the costs and benefits of training in any occupation. Part 7 opens with the editor's introduction to research in education. Two chapters by Louis Cohen then review research into student characteristics and the impact of the college course. John McLeish starts the next chapter by giving a thorough account of research on college environments before going on to provide an outline of his well-known large-scale study in the Cambridge Institute. The section closes with a discussion by John Garner of the nature of teaching and recent studies of teaching effectiveness.

It is the hope of all contributors to this book that it will help to stimulate further study of important problems in teacher education.

DONALD E. LOMAX

Department of Education,
University of Manchester
June, 1972

# Contributors

DR D. N. ASPIN — *Lecturer in Education, University of Manchester*

DR L. COHEN — *Lecturer in Education, University of Bradford*

K. G. COLLIER — *Principal, Bede College of Education, Durham*

MISS EDITH COPE — *Lecturer in Education, University of Bristol*

I. R. DALE — *Lecturer in Education, The Open University, Bletchley, Buckinghamshire*

K. B. DRAKE — *Lecturer in Education, University of Manchester*

DR J. GARNER — *Lecturer in Education, University of Armidale, Australia*

SIR RONALD GOULD — *Former General Secretary, National Union of Teachers*

PROFESSOR T. H. B. HOLLINS — *The Institute of Education, University of Leeds*

DR B. HOLMES — *Reader in Education, University of London Institute of Education*

DR D. E. LOMAX — *Lecturer in Education, University of Manchester*

PROFESSOR J. MCLEISH — *Department of Educational Psychology, University of Alberta, Canada*

P. RENSHAW — *Lecturer in Education, University of Leeds*

E. E. ROBINSON — *Deputy Director, North East London Polytechnic*

PROFESSOR A. M. ROSS — *Department of Educational Research, University of Lancaster*

DR W. G. A. RUDD — *Senior Lecturer in Education, University of Manchester*

J. Scotland                 *Principal, Aberdeen College of Education*

J. K. Taylor                *Research Fellow, University of Bristol*

Professor J. P. Tuck        *Department of Education, University of Newcastle*

Professor J. D. Turner      *The School of Education, University of Manchester*

# Contents

# Part 1

# THE DEVELOPMENT OF TEACHER EDUCATION

# CHAPTER 1

# Some Aspects of Teacher Education in Britain

## D. E. LOMAX

It seems likely that by the beginning of the next century British schools will require over half a million teachers to educate the ten million children who will then be within the school system (Wilson, 1969). Within this system children and teachers alike will need increased opportunities for personal growth (Taylor, 1968). It therefore seems clear that the teaching profession will continue to experience that rapidity of expansion and development which has been its dominant characteristic for at least a hundred years. Although rudimentary attempts were made to organize the training of British teachers in the early nineteenth century (Dent, 1971), the three great periods of growth in the teaching profession were initiated by the Education Acts of 1870, 1902 and 1944 (Floud and Scott, 1961). The concept of a qualified teaching profession, which found support following the first of these acts, has provided a focus for debate ever since. At many times during the last hundred years it has seemed that the expansion of the teaching force rather than the professional quality of its members has been the major concern of central government. Although, as Vaizey (1969) has pointed out, problems of the supply and training of teachers are inextricably intertwined, in recent years increasing attention has been paid to the programmes by means of which teachers are prepared for their vocation.

Unlike most other highly selected professional groups, teachers are numerically large and relatively less well organized. In Chapter 4 of this book, Sir Ronald Gould argues that teachers may not in fact be described as learned professionals in all senses of the term. He believes that teaching is a high-grade, non-manual job which performs a definite social service. It emphasizes duties as well as rights and allows the individual practitioner a substantial degree of freedom in his work. Increasingly, he believes, the profession will demand of its members a rigorous study of the theory and practice of education, but he sees no sign that it will enjoy an increased measure of self-government in the near future. Gould argues that the most distinctive mark of elitist professional groups is that they are largely or wholly self-governing. They control entrance to their groups and exercise discipline over their members. These powers are denied to teachers. It is not only British teachers who face these restrictions, however, for in all developed countries teacher training is subjected to varying degrees of control by central government. Gould does not believe that the self-government of the teaching profession will be raised as a real issue in Britain in the near future. Now, as in the past, the teachers' case is weakened by the conflicts existing between their various unions.

The diversity of opinion found between different sections of the teaching profession has to some degree been exacerbated by the different forms of education and training which are available. It is frequently maintained that the differences which exist between the institutions responsible for teacher training have serious unfortunate consequences (Willey and Maddison, 1971). Until recent times the universities provided places for students of higher social class than those found in the training colleges, whose recruits often saw teaching as an important route to social advancement. The training colleges were also essentially female preserves while men filled the majority of places available in the universities. This sexual distinction is still maintained in the colleges of education where women heavily outnumber men, and in the universities where women still take up far fewer places than might be expected at a time when many assume sexual and social equality to be obviously established. The career prospects for the university graduates have been so clearly superior that it is not surprising to find high levels of disenchantment amongst college students.

To understand the existing differences between the institutions entrusted with the education and training of our teachers, it is necessary to trace their development during the last hundred years. Aspects of this development have been well described by Binns (1908), Jones (1924), Rich (1933), Barnard (1961), Curtis (1967) and Scotland (1969). However, as Ross says in Chapter 8 of this volume, it is usual to tell the story of the colleges of education separately from that of the university departments of education. The training college tradition, which may be traced back to the early years of the nineteenth century, has its roots in the need to provide sufficient education for a minority of the poor to enable them in their turn to pass on a limited amount of instruction to other members of their depressed and under-nourished class. The university graduate teacher has, however, invariably been educated to take his place in those secondary schools which mainly cater for the needs of the middle and upper classes.

Tuck, in Chapter 5, stresses that the university departments of education were originally founded as the second phase of the public provision of institutions for the training of teachers for elementary schools. During the nineteenth century voluntary residential colleges had been founded which based their training programmes on the pupil teacher system. Most of the forty-three voluntary colleges which existed towards the end of this first phase in 1890 were religious foundations, while the pupil teachers who applied for entry to them were usually those who had been apprenticed in elementary church schools. The School Boards found this system, which gave little opportunity for teacher training to pupils in Board Schools, to be unsatisfactory. At this time the final examination for pupil teachers also served as the entrance examination for the training colleges. About half of the candidates were successful in the examination and entered the colleges, leaving the rest in the schools where, after serving for a period as teachers, they could eventually take their certificate examination. The steady increase in the number of pupils in the schools, however, created a demand for teachers which the hard-pressed colleges could not meet. In 1886 the Cross Commission was established and empowered to investigate 'the working of the Elementary Education Acts, England and Wales'. As at this period about half the teaching force was composed of pupil teachers, and as the voluntary colleges were seriously overworked, it would seem that there was an urgent need for reform. The Commission, however, was cautious in its report. They believed that the pupil teacher system should be retained, although they were aware of its failings. Although they held the view that residential colleges were better, they suggested that some experiments might be made with day training colleges. This work, however, was only to be entrusted to the universities. The newly-founded university colleges had already indicated their interest in this work and shrewdly grasped their opportunity. In the early days they were usually able to offer students a three-year concurrent certificate and degree course and a one-year postgraduate certificate course, but in 1911 the Board of Education issued new regulations for four-year courses (Tibble, 1971). The first three years were to be occupied by degree studies, while the final year was to be devoted to professional training. The unpopular three-year concurrent course was now destined to disappear from the universities. By the end of the First World War the four-year course was well established in the universities, and a pattern of training had been created which was to persist for some years. Most secondary school teachers, however, entered the profession as soon as they secured their degree, holding the traditional belief that expert knowledge of subject matter gave them licence to teach.

When the 1902 Education Act promised increased opportunities for secondary education it seemed that the university elementary teacher training departments should undertake the education of the additional secondary school teachers who would be needed. By the outbreak of the First World War eighteen institutions were already providing facilities for small groups of intending secondary school teachers. The subsequent confusing relationship between elementary and secondary training has been carefully analysed by Tuck in Chapter 5. As the years passed the number of students engaged in secondary training steadily increased whilst standards rose. Eventually it became possible to make the possession of a degree obligatory for students following secondary training programmes. The years leading up to the Second World War, however, saw the steady increase in student numbers halted by the drab economic misfortunes suffered by the nation in the 1930s.

The 1902 Act had also created other opportunities for further radical expansion in teacher training by sanctioning the establishment of local education authority colleges. From this point onwards the number of LEA colleges steadily increased. By the time of the 1944 Education Act twenty-nine of the eighty-three recognized training colleges were under the control of the LEAs. Throughout the years of rapid expansion of teacher training in the 1960s this trend was maintained. By 1968 out of a total of 166 colleges of education, which were then in existence, no less than 113 were provided by local education authorities (Taylor, 1969).

As the years of the late nineteenth and early twentieth century passed the academic study of education became increasingly respectable, and acquired such status that important Chairs of Education were established. In general, university departments expanded and acquired status. Similar success was denied the training colleges. As Turner indicates in Chapter 9, the two distinguishing characteristics of the colleges in 1944 were their small size and their poverty. Sixty-four of the eighty-three colleges had less than 150 students, and in at least half of the colleges the training facilities were seriously inadequate. Although the 1925 Board of Education Report had recommended that the colleges should be brought together under Joint Examination Boards in a working relationship with the universities, the plan in operation failed to create the stimulating, desirable associations which might have been anticipated. It is only fair to add that the Joint Boards came into being in times of great anxiety, when the economic depression was imposing seriously inhibiting restrictions upon many aspects of life. However, by the time that the President of the Board of Education, Mr R. A. Butler, established the McNair Commission in 1942, it was clear that changes in the organization of teacher education were urgently needed.

When the McNair Committee reported in 1944 it was divided in its recommendations for the structure and co-ordination of the national teacher training system. It was nevertheless united in its belief that all the institutions concerned with the education of teachers should be grouped to produce an integrated service by means of which teachers might be provided to assist the anticipated expansion of the nation's educational system. Turner, in Chapter 9, has described in full the deliberations which eventually led to the creation of the Area Training Organizations. It was hoped that the ATOs would bring together the various claimants to the control of teacher education, and thereby enable a coherent policy to emerge. The extent to which this hope has been disappointed has been a matter for debate for some years. It is probably fair to say that there has been disappointment over the way in which relationships have sometimes failed to develop, either between the constituent colleges of the ATOs or between these colleges and the universities. The feeling that the majority of teachers are being trained in institutions which are markedly inferior in status to universities has roused considerable indignation in some sections of the teaching profession. These, of course, are not purely British problems. As Holmes points out in Chapter 2, problems of status are endemic in Europe. Where status has been attained by teacher training institutions, it has resulted from successful academic competition with the universities. In his analysis of teacher education in Europe, Holmes suggests that in all countries there are found similar origins for two distinct systems. Alongside the closed systems, within which a relatively small number of grammar schools (or their equivalents) prepared their pupils for university studies, and recruited their teachers from these same universities, there existed parallel systems of teacher training which provided teachers for that expansion of elementary education made necessary by economic and industrial development.

It is sometimes argued that over the last century there is evidence of these different systems of teacher education slowly coming together (Tibble, 1971). There can be little argument about the slow pace of this movement. Although the McNair Report drew attention to the fact that many secondary school teachers lacked professional training, this situation will not be remedied until 1973. As Turner comments, the delay of some thirty years is remarkable even in educational reform. Even after 1973 graduates will not be required necessarily to undergo professional training before seeking positions in the independent English schools. Some people therefore still consider such training to be irrelevant. Generally speaking, however, it seems that both universities and colleges have shared an interest in the professional training of teachers. It may also be argued that the two traditions of teacher training have drawn closer together as the gap between the academic quality of their work has narrowed. The training college curriculum in the early days of teacher education attempted the superficial coverage of a wide range of subjects. Such studies had only remote associations with the needs of people outside the colleges. Of course much had to be done within a short period of time. For over a century the training period was only two years. At last in 1961 the course was extended to three years. The slow progress towards this important objective had created much frustration in training colleges and schools. The eventual establishment of the three-year course has been described by Sir Ronald Gould as the most significant professional event in the whole of his career. 'It made', he says, 'training more meaningful and efficient.'

Progress towards 'meaningful' and 'efficient' training for teachers has certainly been slow. By the mid-1920s, the raising of the school leaving age to eighteen for intending teachers, and the demand that college applicants must have obtained the School Certificate, led to the disappearance of the pupil-apprenticeship system. Given students with better basic qualifications, colleges no longer needed to attempt coverage of the whole range of subjects in the elementary curriculum. Henceforth they would have the opportunity to encourage the study of fewer subjects in greater depth, and would be able to focus more attention on professional training. The fact that colleges still had to provide both education and training at the same time ensured that the debate about the advantages and evils of what is now referred to as 'concurrency' would continue. The progress of this lengthy debate is discussed by Ross later in this book (Chapter 8). Most recently the Committee of Enquiry reported in 1972 on the 'virtues and weaknesses' of concurrent courses. The 'radical solution' proposed in the James Report was based on the belief that, on the whole, it would be better if a 'consecutive' pattern of training were adopted in colleges. The consecutive pattern caters first for the students' personal educational needs before providing a further course of concentrated professional training. These proposals have merited lengthy discussion. Tuck (Chapter 6) points out, the assumption that college of education courses should be based on the consecutive principle is in some ways odd. The original three-year university course was based on the principle of concurrency. It was only when the university course was extended to four years that a consecutive pattern was adopted for students who were studying for degrees. Tuck believes experience to reveal that one-year professional training is appropriate only for the ablest students, and that the most effective pattern for three-year college courses should be based on the principle of concurrency. In his chapter he thoroughly describes and analyses the background against which these arguments must be seen.

After the Second World War there was a gradual run down of the four-year course in university departments of education, and by 1950 the last four-year students had been admitted. Student numbers had increased rapidly until the early 1950s, and had then remained relatively steady for some years. Following the Robbins Report (1963), there was another period of rapid expansion in the numbers of graduates in training. It was at this point that the opportunity to become more deeply involved in graduate training was offered to the colleges of education. It was an opportunity which they did not miss. For some time there had been those who had argued that all graduate teaching should be concentrated in the colleges. The James Report (1972) gave support to this point of view by recommending that the expansion of student numbers in university departments of education should in future be restricted. The expected expansion of graduate training, which may therefore take place in the colleges, may produce in England and Wales a system more closely resembling that currently seen in Scotland. Tuck (Chapter 6) has described the far-reaching developments which have taken place in university postgraduate courses in recent years. It would seem regrettable if this vital area of growth were in any way stunted, especially as it is uncertain whether the colleges are equipped to carry this additional responsibility.

As James Scotland indicates in Chapter 3 of this book, the Scottish education system has always been distinctly different from the English even though the two structures have tended to move closer in recent years. In Scotland the training of virtually all teachers is conducted by the colleges of education. In contrast to the English pattern the universities play no part in basic teacher training. However, almost all the Scottish universities are now involving themselves in teacher training by helping to establish academic standards for the colleges. It seems that on both sides of the border changes are inevitable. In England and Wales, Tuck argues that it might be better to develop larger graduate training departments in the colleges, which could have the status of university departments of education. Chairs of Education might be established and the existing relationship between colleges and universities could be strengthened. If radical changes of this kind are eventually made, then those who believe that the different systems of teacher education are drawing together will have grounds for optimism. But these developments do demand change in the universities, and many will agree with Holmes (Chapter 2) who argues that some of the problems which beset teacher training stem from the dominance of universities and their reluctance to change. Holmes believes that the James Report assumed that the universities do not welcome radical change. Without change university interests may continue to dominate teacher training. In his discussion of developments in Europe and the United States of America, he illustrates the unreasonable ways in which the universities may be said to have dominated secondary education. This point is again made by Robinson in Chapter 7, who also has a word of criticism for the unfortunate conservatism of some sectors of the teaching profession.

Although the polytechnics have so far played little part in the education of teachers, Robinson sees their development as being of major importance for the future of teacher training, for it is they, and not the universities, who are the experts in professional education. The universities, he argues, have paid attention to only a small group of professions and have been ambivalent in their attitudes towards the teaching profession. During the 1970s the polytechnics will increase and widen their contribution to teacher education. They will take advantage of the more liberal attitude towards entry qualifications held by the CNAA to open to all qualified teachers new courses leading to new qualifications. These new courses will differ from traditional university courses in having a curriculum 'purpose-built' for experienced teachers, with the emphasis being placed more on professional studies in education and less on academic studies. Robinson believes that a national network of 'compatible' courses may be established to enable a teacher to continue his studies uninterrupted, should a change of job force him to move to another part of the country. Although there is not yet complete agreement as to how change is to be implemented in teacher education, there is a general feeling that a fuller measure of integration with other areas of higher education is desirable. Some believe that the necessary radical changes in teacher education may be more easily made outside the universities rather than within them.

This introductory chapter opened with the claim that we need to provide children and teachers with increased opportunities for personal growth. Renshaw, in Chapter 12, provides a detailed discussion of this viewpoint. He argues that if we seek to satisfy the growing needs of future generations, we must increase the quality of the professional education of teachers. He believes that this might be done by developing a viable body of professional knowledge. If this were achieved the status of the teaching profession would be enhanced, and the teacher training institutions would be changed. If teacher training were free to develop within the broader perspective of higher education, then colleges could become multi-purpose institutions with a flexible curriculum designed to meet the requirements of students with a wide range of personal objectives. Vocational choices could be left open at the age of eighteen, and the current academic, professional and social isolation of students could be ended.

As Renshaw points out, at the centre of these discussions of the future of teacher education is the evaluation of the contribution which has been made, and may still be made, by the universities. The universities have been concerned with academic standards and with the planning of the curriculum. He believes that the links between colleges and universities have grown during this century and should continue, to enable academic standards to be maintained and advanced. However, it is right to question whether this determination to raise the level of academic standards has necessarily increased the quality of professional education. Is it not possible that the prevailing scholastic attitudes, which are found in some departments, may have militated against the establishment of a valid professional degree?

Renshaw does not claim that his suggestions for a flexible curriculum for teacher education are revolutionary, but he believes them to be innovatory in the sense that they question many of the assumptions underlying existing teacher education programmes. He believes that it is impossible for

student teachers to master the specialized theoretical and practical knowledge which is fundamental to teaching. Universities and colleges need to
establish their curricular priorities, not only for initial training but also for
in-service education. We must face changing social and educational demands
which force us to redefine the roles of teachers. If teachers are to be
involved in the processes of redefinition then continued professional study
is essential. As Aspin points out in Chapter 11, however, we may expect
to see reflected in our universities, colleges and schools the tensions and
conflicts of those differing value systems which may be observed in our
society. To a certain degree these institutions may usefully be regarded as
agencies of stabilization, being responsible not only for innovation in
changing value commitments, but also for the reassertion and promotion of
traditional cultural values.

In his insightful analysis of the problem of values in teacher education
and training, Aspin notes that in many recent discussions there has been
little rigorous consideration given to 'aims' and 'objectives'. He finds that
all too frequently the principal areas of controversy concern the problems
of organization, course construction and relationships within or between
institutions. Yet he finds that close examination of the curricula and
organization of teacher training institutions reveals that they are permeated
by 'aims' and 'objectives'. It would seem that adherence to these 'aims' and
'objectives' is based on considerations of value. He concludes that consideration of the problem of values should be first in order of treatment in
any reflections on the construction of an optimum model for the education
of teachers.

The over-riding questions of defining objectives and evaluating courses,
as Collier says in Chapter 14, raise in an acute form the general problem of
innovation. How may a college of education recreate itself as a consciously
self-evolving academic community? In his earlier chapter dealing with
college administration, he details the fundamental changes in structure
which have occurred during the last ten years. He describes an organic
structure in the academic sphere in which communication is effective
upwards, downwards and laterally. In this model much depends on certain
shared attitudes and values permeating the organization. It is not easy,
however, to create a satisfactory climate of opinion. Although much
depends on the customary relationships established in the institution in the
past, even more depends upon the college principal's success in maintaining a just and dependable structure of authority. It is too optimistic, however, to assume that a highly innovatory institution will automatically evolve
from the organic pattern of organization which Collier describes, although
it will obviously assist change and development. He believes that there are
two areas in which most colleges fail to facilitate innovation. These are in
the formulation of objectives and in the evaluation of experiments. It is

clearly essential to create procedures for investigating and making explicit the assumptions which underlie college work.

One example of an area of the training course within which both colleges and departments of education are increasingly questioning underlying assumptions is practice teaching in schools. In her rigorous study of this area Edith Cope, in Chapter 13, points out that practical experience in schools has always been considered an essential element of teacher training courses. Earlier in the present chapter reference was made to the pupil-apprenticeship scheme which was the main route into the profession in the nineteenth century. Conventions established in these early days have proved exceedingly resistant to change. Even the warmly welcomed extension of the college course from two to three years left most of the assumptions which underlie teaching practice largely unchallenged. In 1966 Tibble drew attention to the fact that there had been little serious evaluation of the aims and methods used in this section of the course. It was fair to say, he claimed, that in the teaching practice area, a set of procedures had been taken over from the Board of Education which had remained virtually unchanged up to the present time. Cope surveys recent researches which have served to make limited changes in this curiously static situation. But the experiments she describes are small-scale innovations, and still the overall national pattern is the traditional one of the student visiting the school to simulate the conventional role of the teacher. As Cope points out, the primary aim of the college or department of education is to facilitate student learning, whereas the school's primary aim is the facilitation of children's learning. These aims are obviously sometimes incompatible. In her own research she finds ample evidence of the teachers' uncertainty concerning their school practice responsibilities and indications of the existence of mistrust between college staff and school teachers. It would appear from the results of the Bristol research that, even within colleges, there are dichotomies which remain unfortunately unresolved. For example, some tutors see their role to be that of fostering student academic under-standing while others conceive their role to be essentially concerned with the development of professional skills. The raising of academic standards in colleges has only served to intensify these differences. It is usual of course for students to claim that teaching practice is a valuable experience, although some certainly find the exposure to the school environment traumatic. A reasonably representative picture of the students' viewpoint was provided recently by Lomax (1971) in a description of students at a large college of education:

> Faced by much in their studies that seemed to be irrelevant to their career prospects, the young teachers approached teaching practice with added enthusiasm. Even though the experience in schools had some-

times been difficult, students as a whole rated it as very valuable. Though it was not unknown for some to find periods of practice 'irksome', 'ill-planned' and 'badly directed', it seemed that this work was at least relevant to the job waiting to be done in the real world. No other area of college work was considered to be of equal value. Perhaps in an ideal college course, teaching practice would be one of a number of equally exciting experiences, but with courses being what they were, the memories of a few weeks spent in the town primary school were still vividly retained when a hundred lectures had been lost beyond all recall.

In summarizing her findings from a comprehensive study of work in this field, Cope suggests that if professional learning in the practical teaching situation is to be increased we must help students to accept the necessity for sophisticated analysis, diagnosis and evaluation. It will also be necessary to create differentiated forms of practice to meet a variety of objectives. It is interesting to note that Collier (Chapter 10), in providing a principal's view of college administration, believed that the three aspects of college life which have major significance for effective innovation are, the specification of aims and objectives, the establishment of an organic type of organization, and the creation of machinery for evaluation. The stress which these educationalists both place upon the importance of the rigorous definition of aims and objectives, upon sophisticated evaluation and upon forms of institutional organization is echoed many times by other contributors to this volume.

Earlier in the present chapter attention was drawn to the need for university departments and colleges of education to establish curricular priorities, not only for initial training but also for in-service education. In their review of their research into the first year of teaching, Taylor and Dale (Chapter 15) claim that it is vital for all who are concerned with the organization of the probationary year to meet regularly in an attempt to formulate precise aims, and to assist in the development of a body of knowledge and a range of materials. They argue that the experiences encountered during the first year in full-time service are crucial in their influence on the young teacher's career. As teachers tend to a large extent to work in isolation from one another, they may be less conscious of any association with an organized body of professional knowledge. If professional standards are to improve, the probationary year must be regarded as a bridging period between initial training and a comprehensive in-service programme. In support of this claim, Hollins (Chapter 16) stresses that initial training is now widely recognized as being an inefficient method of preparing students for the classroom. He believes that there is now wide acceptance of the view that in-service training may provide the answer to our problem, for education and vocational training are now recognized as being lifelong processes.

The purpose of this chapter has been to provide a brief introduction to some aspects of teacher education which have merited the attention of educationalists. In the chapters which follow, these and other issues will be discussed in greater detail.

# CHAPTER 2

## Teacher Education in England and Wales: a Comparative View

### BRIAN HOLMES

The Committee of Enquiry into teacher education and training in England and Wales was asked to recommend on the content of teacher education, the kinds of institution in which it should be provided, and relationships between colleges of education, institutions of further education and the universities. In fact the James Report (1972) provided a framework for the expansion of higher education in England and Wales and made proposals for the training of teachers for an emerging system of universal secondary education. It offered possible solutions to world-wide problems which have resulted from the recent rapid growth in education and the democratization of secondary education. Many of these problems stem from the present dominance of the universities and their unwillingness to change. The James Report assumed that they will not change much. The Report was broadly accepted by the Government (White Paper, Dec. 6th, 1972) and its proposals will open up higher education and make it possible to restructure teacher education while retaining the benefits of their university origins.

### The Expansion of Higher Education

The 1960s – and particularly the period 1960 to 1965 – was a decade of unprecedented world-wide university expansion. By the end of the 1950s the postwar baby boom was making itself felt at the point of entry to higher education. Expansionist secondary school policies increased upper secondary school enrolment rates (OECD, 1969) and the overall numbers of pupils qualified to enter universities. Demand far exceeded the supply of places at prestige universities (Bowles, 1965). Old universities expanded and new ones were established. Towards the end of the decade the pressure eased but these institutions in Britain, and United States, the Soviet Union, Japan and elsewhere are still able to select rigorously from a large number of applicants. In countries such as France and the Federal German Republic, where final school-leaving examinations formally conferred on successful candidates the right to enter a university, the problems of containing the demand for places were severe.

In many OECD countries, enrolments in post-secondary education almost doubled between 1960 and 1965; in Sweden by ninety-four per cent., in France by eighty-four per cent. and in Canada by eighty-six per cent. (OECD 1971 a). In another group of countries, including the United Kingdom, Japan and the United States, growth over the same period was around fifty per cent. It was much lower in the German Federal Republic (twenty-six per cent.), where more rapid expansion than elsewhere had taken place earlier. During the early years of the decade, with some exceptions, the universities grew more rapidly than other types of higher education (OECD 1971 b). Swedish universities grew at an annual rate of 14·7 per cent., the rate for non-university post-secondary education was 9·5 per cent. Comparable percentages in France were 13·8 and 10·6; in Canada 14 and 8·9. By this time, university growth in the United States and Japan had eased off and was exceeded by the rate of growth of non-university higher education. Figures for the United States were 13·3 per cent. each year in the non-university and 8·4 in the university sector. In Japan, the percentages were 12·3 and 8·4. In the United Kingdom, growth was more evenly balanced. During the period 1960–5, non-university enrolments increased at an annual rate of 9·4 per cent., university enrolments at a rate of 7·6 per cent. There appears to be an optimum expansion for universities the size depending on a number of national factors.

By 1965, certain trends of expansion were clear. When enrolments in higher education reach a certain level (in the United States there were four and three-quarter million university students) demand is absorbed by the non-university sector. It should be noted that the optimum level varies. In 1970, some twenty per cent of the age group in the United States were in receipt of a university degree, while in the most advanced western European countries, in spite of expansion, less than five per cent. of the age group were receiving university degrees. In Europe, while the potential exists for further expansion in the 1970s, it is not likely to take place in the universities. In the first place university per capita costs are high, and secondly, few governments are any longer willing to allow expansion patterns to be dominated by university politics.

Expansion in the 1960s rarely fulfilled government hopes. The arts faculties in France more than trebled, the natural science faculties barely doubled. In Britain, the increase in natural science students was 30,000, but social scientist enrolments increased by 35,000. More alarming was the lack of demand for courses with a high professional or vocational bias.

By the mid-1960s few university systems were expanding in response to specific manpower needs and new institutions were created. University institutes of technology were set up in France in 1966 at about the time polytechnics were established in Britain and district colleges in Norway began to absorb the flood of entrants to higher education. Annual university growth rates dropped, in France from 13·8 per cent. (1960–5) to 9·7 per cent. (1965–70); in the Federal German Republic from 4·2 per cent. (1960–5) to 3·6 per cent. (1965–70); in Japan from over 8 per cent. to less than 5 per cent. (1969); and in the United States from 8·4 per cent. (1960–5) to 4·9 per cent. (1965–70). In the United Kingdom a comparable decline took place from 7·6 per cent. (1960–5) to 4·8 per cent. (1965–70). Growth rates in post-secondary education as a whole were maintained, with some exceptions, above an annual rate of ten per cent. The exceptions included the United Kingdom and the United States. Sweden, almost alone, maintained exceptionally high rates of university growth (OECD 1971*). But by 1970, in general, the period of massive long-cycle university expansion was over. Demand was still high and two policies began to emerge.

One of these was to introduce short-cycle higher education lasting two years. At an OECD conference* in Grenoble (November 1971) delegates from seventeen countries grappled with the problems of devising systems which would 1. provide vocationally oriented post-secondary education, leading to terminal awards acceptable to employers; 2. offer remedial education to students with an incomplete secondary education; 3. extend the general education of large numbers of young adults as part of their 'life-long' education. Employment opportunites for short-cycle graduates were discussed. So were problems of transfer from short- to long-cycle education. A third issue was the provision of courses common to short- and long-cycle education. Continental European attitudes favoured a short-cycle higher education geared to vocational preparation. In the United States, two-year junior colleges offer terminal courses to a large number of students and to others the first two years of a four-year liberal arts college degree course. Their position today is somewhere between the high school and college. The James Report suggested, in accordance with English tradition, a continuation of general rather than vocational education in the first cycle. It allowed for concurrent educational studies in colleges of education and universities. This policy is one which divides higher education into two stages, i.e. it represents horizontal differentiation.

The second policy represents vertical differentiation. Massive expansion under a university umbrella is over. Binary, or tripartite systems are bound to develop because in many countries the universities are unlikely to change. Many observers want a 'comprehensive' pattern of higher education and oppose differentiation. They point to its divisive consequences at the secondary stage and argue that these should not be reinforced by policies at the

* OECD Working Papers, restricted circulation.

stage of higher education. Parenthetically the case for greatly enlarged comprehensive universities is not proven. It may not be possible to retain in a mass system of higher education university traditions of autonomy and academic freedom. Against the social divisiveness of a binary or tripartite system should be weighed the advantages of retaining elitist institutions where scholars can pursue without interference the disinterested search for new knowledge and disseminate it freely to students and an international community of scholars (Holmes and Scanlon, 1971). These traditions are threatened when governments expect the universities to undertake secret applied research. Classified findings have little place in the university community. The latter should also be free, unfettered as it is by party political allegiances, to stand back and criticize society and politics. The price it pays is that it should not involve itself in partisan political action. Unless the university community can perform this vital, critical role in a democratic society, who can? But can any society encourage a sizeable minority of its young citizens to be highly critical? In the United States thirty-five per cent. of the age group is enrolled in universities. The situation there suggests, as the late Senator Joseph McCarthy amply demonstrated, that when universities grow massively attempts may be made to suppress the social criticism of students and faculty. If the university community then chooses to take political action we may well see an extension of the violence associated with student protests during the 1960s in Japan, Berlin, Paris and in the United States at Berkeley, Columbia and Kent State. Freedom in society may well depend upon a restriction rather than an increase in the growth of universities.

In summary, short-cycle higher education will absorb much of the future demand. Institutional differentiation will break down at this stage first. For the time being, long-cycle institutions will remain selective on the basis of academic achievements. They may serve different functions, i.e. professional or non-professional, but are certain to be dominated by the universities. Short-cycle institutions on the other hand may well be able to establish distinctive curricula and a multiplicity of purposes unless greatly expanded systems of higher education are dominated in future, as secondary education was in the past, by university interests. The issue is relevant to the future of teacher education in England and Wales when, as the achievement of 'secondary education for all' draws near, there is need to set up a new and appropriate system in which to train teachers for universal second-stage schools. Many present problems stem from the university origins of teacher education for a grammar school elite and from the fact that attempts have been made to bridge the gap between this pattern and the one which emerged during the nineteenth century for elementary school teachers by bringing the latter under the influence of the universities.

## Teacher Education in Europe

Everywhere in Europe the origins of two distinct systems of teacher education are similar*. When a small number of grammar schools prepared pupils for entry to the universities, teachers were recruited from among university graduates. A master's degree admitted a student to the community of scholars and allowed him to enter the church, medicine, the law or teaching. In European countries an academic university degree was a licence to teach, it remained so until recently in England and Wales. Graduate teachers either stayed in the university or returned to an academic secondary school. This closed system was strengthened by the fact that many graduates taught in a school and lectured at a university. Clustered around the Sorbonne are several of France's most famous lycées whose professors may well teach regularly at the university. The Société des Agrégés consists of lycée and university teachers. It is a powerful body. Again, most lawyers in continental Europe have university degrees and a degree in law is often a prerequisite for entry into the bureaucracy. Traditionally, a university education trained carefully selected students for one of the four professions.

Parallel systems of teacher training developed in the nineteenth century to supply teachers for expanding elementary education. By the 1840s normal schools were being set up in many countries. They drew inspiration from Prussian legislation which stated clearly what these schools for teachers should do. Students should be brought to love teaching, to accept religious sentiments, to treat pupils humanely, to acquire basic knowledge and to learn how to teach through practical experience. Normal schools became secondary schools for teachers. Students were recruited from elementary schools, completed a secondary education, received instruction and practice in methods of teaching and returned as teachers to the elementary schools. Another closed system was established.

The two systems were connected by examinations which were originally initial university qualifications, then prerequisites for university entry and finally became school leaving awards. Success in the French baccalauréat, the German Abitur, the Scandinavian studentereksam and English 'A' levels gives entry to a university and is accepted by employers as a measure of educational background and attainment. In England, a general certificate of education may exempt a candidate from the first examinations of some para-professional bodies. In most European countries today all intending teachers are expected to possess these school leaving certificates before they

---

* OECD, Study on Teachers Series gives information on teacher education in various countries, e.g. Austria, Greece, Sweden (1968), Germany, Belgium, UK, (1969). All published in Paris by OECD.

enter college or to obtain them during their period of training (Lauwerys and Bereday, 1963). But the baccalauréat, the Abitur, the studentereksam and 'A' levels still reflect the interest of universities in the selection of students who aspire to be research scholars. It has been argued that they unreasonably dominate secondary education. Could it be that they should no longer determine concepts of general education for all teachers?

Again, should university interests dominate the special knowledge of teachers? In most countries – the United States is an exception – university study emphasizes pure rather than applied or professional knowledge. An esoteric knowledge of one subject or perhaps two related subjects is the academic purpose. Professional studies as such play a small part. On the continent, to be sure, undergraduate lectures in education are offered as part of a broad, loosely organized spectrum of studies. In the Soviet Union all undergraduates receive instruction in how to teach their main subject. A fierce debate has been waged in the United States involving university academics who claim a more powerful voice in the determination of the content of teacher education (Conant, 1963). They want students to study traditional subjects in greater depth and to pay less attention to education courses. The influence of the university over the content of graduate teacher education persists. In England academic professors determine the content of highly specialized undergraduate courses. Postgraduate professional studies are devised by members of university departments of education with an eye on university standards of scholarship. Present B.Ed schemes may represent an uneasy compromise between professional and academic forces. It is by no means certain that an academic content suited to teachers in selective academic secondary schools is appropriate for teachers in primary and middle schools.

National policies reinforce university domination by preparing teachers in training for the school leaving examinations. Pupils may enter French écoles normales primaires at the age of fifteen. They then prepare for the baccalauréat over a three-year period. Older pupils take two years. Danish teacher training college students who have not completed a full general secondary education take an extra year to bring themselves up to the level of the studentereksam. Primary school teachers in Sweden follow a two or four-year course depending on whether or not they possess the gymnasium (upper secondary school) leaving examination. Up to 1967 primary school teachers in Belgium were trained in secondary schools after having had a middle school general education. After that date the normal school course was prolonged by one year to ensure that intending teachers have the same level of general education as students qualified to enter the university. In the United States all future teachers will have graduated from high school. In the Federal German Republic they must possess the school leaving university entrance examination (Reifezengnis or Abitur). In England and

Wales most entrants to colleges of education are recruited from the sixth forms and may have minimum university entrance qualifications. The James Report, with some hesitation, recommended that the majority of future teachers should have two 'A' levels before entering a college of education. Undoubtedly such a requirement would make it easier to place all institutions of teacher education unequivocally in higher education. But such an achievement does not automatically confer on them university status.

The status of teacher training institutions varies greatly. In France the Ecoles Normales Supérieures have a higher status than the universities. Students are recruited from the best lycées on the basis of highly competitive concours. They then prepare for a degree and for the highly competitive agrégation, success in which depends on the number of available teaching posts throughout France. Agrégés occupy top positions in all walks of French life. Graduates from the Ecoles Normales Supérieures are among the elite. The reputation of these institutions depends on the academic excellence of faculty and students and not on pedagogical expertise. The same may be said of the Russian pedagogical institutes where academic research is stressed. At the Maurice Thorez Pedagogical Institute for Foreign Languages in Moscow, for example, there are five specialist Chairs in English. The Lenin Pedagogical Institute in Moscow and the Herzen Pedagogical Institute in Leningrad are virtually multi-universities with many famous academics on their staff engaged in fundamental research. The Paedagogische Hochschulen in the Federal German Republic lay claim to university status. But alongside these institutions are some, the Paedagogische Academie, which rank somewhere between the academic secondary school and the university. Few training institutions for elementary school (Volkschule) teachers have acquired even this status. And at this end of the scale secondary schools for teachers still exist in the Soviet Union, and the smaller departmental écoles normales in France are little more than secondary boarding schools for teachers. Status, where it has been acquired, has depended on successful competition in academic terms, with the universities or at another level with the academic secondary schools.

Problems of status are endemic in Europe. Except in Britain European universities did not respond in the nineteenth century to specific manpower demands and excluded the new professions and para-professions whose members had to be trained in commercial academies and technological institutes. A binary system, for example, developed in Germany, pure knowledge was offered in the universities, applied studies, e.g. engineering, were left to the Technische Hochschulen which, to be sure, over the century acquired a status in many respects equal to that of the universities. Similar developments took place in the Netherlands and the Soviet Union. In England engineering departments were constituents of the new civic universities, but they did not dominate them. In some respects English universities are in a better position than most to absorb new forms of professional training.

## Higher Education Developments in the United States

American universities have been transformed by these. The professionalization of American higher education gained impetus when in 1862 the first of the Morrell Acts set aside public lands to support state colleges of agriculture and mechanical arts. A comprehensive system of higher education then became possible in the United States. These Land Grant colleges grew into huge modern universities which in many respects lead rather than follow the Ivy League universities like Harvard, Yale, Princeton, Columbia and William and Mary. Later in the nineteenth century purely postgraduate universities such as Johns Hopkins and Chicago were established. Since 1900, the balance of undergraduate studies in American universities has swung heavily towards professional degrees. Short-cycle higher education developed after 1900 when the two-year junior college movement started. Now they enroll a high proportion of students following first- and second-year undergraduate programmes. Finally, around 1920, the normal schools in the United States began to evolve as teachers' colleges and award professional degrees. They were committed to the training of large numbers of teachers for a high school system which had expanded phenomenally after the Kalamazoo case in Michigan (1874) had allowed public funds to support high schools. During the 1930s, many teachers' colleges became liberal arts colleges granting a range of first degrees, although their main commitment was the professional training of teachers. Later they absorbed much of the demand for higher education and became huge universities as part of state systems.

For example, Kent State University started life in 1910 as a normal school, and by 1915 it was offering four-year degree courses in education. In 1929 its name was changed to Kent State College and it was able to grant bachelor's degrees in arts and science. In 1935 it became Kent State University and awarded a master of arts degree. In 1959 this rapidly expanding institution was authorized to award doctorate degrees. Enrolments numbered 600 in 1929; they had grown to over 8,000 full-time students by 1960, and by 1970 the student population was over 30,000. Kent State typifies the movement from normal school to university in half a century and illustrates how teachers' colleges in absorbing demand transformed themselves and in so doing set a stamp on the character of comprehensive university education in the United States.

There is, of course, diversity in this system. Teacher education is provided in various institutions, all of which clearly belong to higher education. The main types are teachers' colleges (of which relatively few remain), liberal arts colleges and universities. Only a small number of students train in institutions exclusively for teachers. First and second-year education courses may be offered in junior colleges. Some university schools or colleges of education provide only third and fourth-year education courses, while institutions like Teachers' College, Columbia, and the Department of Education, Chicago University, cater only for postgraduate students. Students 'find their own level' by moving from one institution to another as they take first a bachelor's degree, then a master's, possibly a professional certificate, and finally a doctor's degree. In this way an older German tradition which encouraged the movement of students between universities has been recaptured in the United States.

Admission requirements to teacher education programmes are the same as for any other college or university department. In some states legislation decrees that any pupil graduating from a recognized (accredited) high school has the right to higher education. Standards vary from school to school and from college to college. The latter may have to undertake remedial instruction and can usually compel a student to leave if he has not reached sufficiently high standards of achievement. Many students leave for colleges where expectations are less high. Even so, perhaps, no more than forty per cent. of pupils entering college complete their degree in the minimum four-year period. Undoubtedly movements within a college or university and between institutions are greater in the United States than in Britain.

A major influence of teacher education in the United States has been on the content of education. Progressive educationalists in colleges and university departments of education have given meaning and practical expression to pragmatic curriculum theories. These broke new ground compared with prevailing European essentialist and encyclopedic concepts. The former, stemming from Aristotelianism, justifies in England specialization based upon the inclusion of a few subjects chosen on the grounds of their distinctive internal logic. It is in sharp contrast to the broad curriculum of French schools where a pupil from the 'modern' stream of a lycée (there are classical, scientific and technological streams as well), takes French, two modern foreign languages, physical science, mathematics, history and geography and several oral examinations in his baccalauréat. Such a range of subjects is typical of the Low Countries, Scandinavia, the German Federal Republic and eastern Europe. Such an encyclopedic curriculum is followed by teachers in training. It contrasts sharply with the view held in England that a sound general education can best be acquired through depth studies of a very few subjects.

American curriculum theory* (following Herbert Spencer) suggests that

* See *The Seven Cardinal Principles of Curriculum Development* published by an NEA Committee in 1918.

the content of general education should consist of the knowledge, attitudes and skills young people need to solve problems of healthy living, family life, earning a livelihood, participating in civic affairs, using leisure time, and making moral decisions. In practice at all levels the constituents of general education are drawn from the social sciences, the natural sciences and languages and fine arts. Hence to graduate from high school a student must have successfully completed courses in these three areas and, in addition, must have taken some optional subjects (electives). The basis of general education in colleges and universities is the same. It provides a framework within which very conservative or quite radical programmes can be offered. This curriculum theory probably finds its best expression when activity, problem-solving, methods of teaching are used.

One challenge offered by James if colleges of education expand by accepting large numbers of students who do not intend to teach is to devise courses for the first cycle of higher education which will extend general education in ways which seem relevant to young adults in the final decades of the twentieth century. To perform this task, colleges in England and Wales may well have to break away from an accepted essentialist theory and propose less specialized programmes of study. They may well analyse continental and American curriculum theories and practices prior to developing appropriate English models. There is no doubt, of course, that over the years there has been considerable interaction between American and English educationalists. Much that is going on in English colleges of education reflects 'progressive' traditions, but attitudes towards specialization, though ambivalent, are for the most part favourable, particularly at the university level.

## The Organization of Courses

Another point of comparison is the way university courses are organized. A European tradition strongly exemplified in the German universities is for professors to lecture on topics of interest to them and for students to choose rather freely which lectures to attend. Departmental structures are virtually non-existent and some students have complained about the absence of coherent planned courses of lectures and about the lack of relevance to modern life of many lectures which are delivered. A lack of flexibility is the price the departmentalized English systems pay for the efficient way students complete a degree in one or two well-organized course sequences. On the other hand colleges of education achieve coherence through a tutorial system which permits flexibility, but militates against expertise. The introduction of course units as a way of organizing London undergraduate science programmes holds promise for greater flexibility while retaining expert tutorial help. It operates rather as the American credit system where each course is examined separately by the professor in charge who 'grades' each student in the class. Students come into contact with many teachers and carry with them a transcript of courses taken and marks obtained. Emerging structures and methods of teaching in England and Wales may well move in the direction of the organization of academic degrees in America.

In a typical four-year programme 120 semester hours or 180 quarter hours of credit have to be obtained. One college credit hour represents one class hour each week throughout a semester (sixteen weeks) or a quarter (about twelve weeks). This means that throughout his four-year course a student attends fifteen class hours per week, often three hours in each of five subjects. To graduate a certain standard must be achieved. An 'A' represents 4 marks, a 'B' is 3 marks, a 'C' is 2 marks and a 'D' is 1 mark. A point average of 2 (or 'C') is required, but a higher average of 2·25 must usually be obtained in a student's main (major) and subsidiary (minor) subjects. The components of a first degree in arts (A.B.) include courses from the humanities (e.g. English literature, a modern foreign language, philosophy) amounting to about fourteen per cent. of the whole programme; from the social sciences (e.g. economics, history, sociology, political science, psychology) adding up to around twelve per cent. and from the natural sciences (e.g. biology, chemistry, physics, geology, mathematics) occupying just over ten per cent. of the whole programme. In his major field, a student must follow a coherent sequence of courses in the subject which may total between twenty-three and thirty per cent of his work. A minor or subsidiary subject takes up between twelve and seventeen per cent. In general, therefore, about thirty-six per cent. of a four-year programme is devoted to general education, a further forty per cent. of the time will be taken up by the major and minor subjects. For the rest (about twenty-four per cent.) it will consist of freely chosen options. The general education component in a science degree is very similar, but a student may be expected to spend over seventy per cent. of his time in a chosen field of concentration but not more than three-quarters of this specialized work can be in one department. Obviously, science degrees are more specialized than arts degrees in the United States but what really distinguishes American from English first degrees is the general education component which in the former give breadth while major/minor sequences give some depth.

Professional courses can fit into this kind of organization in various ways. It should be noted that, while students may attend education lectures throughout their degree course, in continental Europe practice teaching is usually postponed until the last year. A student completes his general education in a training college before taking education and professional courses. Concurrent sequences in England and Wales are based on the assumption that a student has completed his general education in the sixth form. A graduate in England completes his special subject study prior to taking postgraduate professional courses. Lawyers and medical doctors in America complete a liberal arts bachelor's degree before entering a law school or medical school for professional studies. Intending teachers may take education courses throughout the four years though, in fact, they are usually concentrated in the third and fourth years. As in England and Wales intending primary school teachers tend to choose concurrent sequences, future high school teachers concentrate in the first instance on their major teaching subject and take education courses in the third and particularly the fourth year (Holmes, 1971).

An emerging pattern of teacher education is the master of arts in teaching (MAT) programmes Students complete a four-year liberal arts or science degree before taking professional courses. They usually enrol during the summer for a theoretical introduction to education and then go into a neighbouring collaborating school where they teach as internees on a half-time basis from September to the following June on half salary. During this period they attend lectures at the university and collect education 'credits'. The following summer they make these up to the number prescribed by the state to obtain a certificate to teach. Examples of such programmes are at Johns Hopkins, Teachers' College, Columbia, the University of Pennsylvania and the Liberal Arts College at Oberlin. They represent a move towards legal and medical forms of education and training, but the postgraduate course lasts one year, instead of three or five.

Advocates of MAT training schemes claim that they appeal to students who wish to acquire a depth knowledge of their teaching subject. They maintain that such knowledge should be an essential and dominant ingredient of all teacher training. Postponement of professional courses and practice teaching means, of course, that vocational choice can be delayed. In the comprehensive university it brings future teachers into contact with future doctors and lawyers in general education classes. On the other hand a student committed to teaching sees nothing of practice until his fifth year. Such a postponement of teaching practice, it is argued, makes it more difficult to relate theory with practice. The debates over the respective merits of concurrent and consecutive sequences tend to involve as principal protagonists professors of education and professors of the older so-called academic 'disciplines'. Each group has its allies. In the United States big business representatives have tended to side with the academics – school administration and social workers with the professors of education. The controversy was not about course sequences, but about the balance of studies in a professional degree. A debate which smouldered in the early 1950s burst into flames after sputnik. Education courses and professors of education were vilified as sloppy, repetitious and lacking in content. The solution offered by men such as A. E. Bestor, R. M. Hutchins, T. D.

Koerner and H. Rickover (Holmes, 1956) was a return in teacher education to an emphasis on academic knowledge typical of the university system of teacher education in Europe.

In this tradition university academics controlled the general educational content, the specialized subject matter and indeed the content of education courses. They also controlled access to the profession at the point of entry to the universities and by running final examinations. While systems of teacher training for elementary school teachers remained separate conflict could be avoided. It became acute in America when departments of education responsible for the training of all (and not a chosen few) became integral parts of the universities. This kind of conflict may arise in Europe as teacher education moves more fully into higher education. The introduction of bachelor of education degrees in England and Wales has brought some issues to the forefront of debate. They include the balance of studies in teacher education and the validation of course work and awards.

## The Content of Teacher Education in the United States

The distinction drawn in the United States between academic and educational courses and between non-professional and professional degrees are useful. To obtain a certificate to teach, an American student must take a number of education courses. The number and some general characteristics of these courses are laid down by State Boards of Education who issue certificates to teach. In many cases university degree requirements exceed the minimum requirements for certification. Three ingredients are found in professional degrees which are approved for certification purposes – general education, specialized subject matter and professional courses. The components are mixed in various proportions.

It is within this context that teacher education in the United States should be viewed. To the general educational and main subject components of the arts or science degree are added professional courses. The way the three ingredients are mixed depends on the level at which the student intends subsequently to teach. Broadly speaking distinctions can be drawn between primary and junior high school teachers and those in the senior high school. State Boards in consultation with accredited teacher education institutions establish course requirements which differ with the kind of certificate aimed at. Certificates vary according to their permanence (e.g. temporary, provisional, permanent) and the level of teaching (e.g. primary, junior secondary, special education, high school). A high school certificate qualifies a teacher to teach a named subject in which he has 'majored' as an undergraduate. State Boards of Education lay down the number of credits in education, these vary in a semester system from about eighteen credit hours to over thirty or from fifteen per cent. of the programme to over twenty-five per cent. Critics of teacher education in America have argued that the amount of time devoted to professional courses is often too high.

The fact that State Boards lay down education course requirements does not mean that the freedom of professors of education is restricted. They select and organize their material in the light of professional opinion, they are free to teach as they think fit and grade students at the end of the course. Education courses are provided in ways quite compatible with university traditions. State Boards are, however, guardians of the public interest and work in close co-operation with local education officials, advisers and professors of education.

All college (department) of education students, future primary, junior high or senior high school teachers follow similar general education requirements as undergraduates in arts and science. They will include courses from the humanities, the social sciences, and from the natural sciences and mathematics. About thirty per cent. of the whole programme will be occupied by this component. Intending high school teachers follow a coherent major and a coherent minor sequence, often chosen by the student on advice towards the end of his or her freshman (first) year. A future primary school teacher may 'major' in education and take a 'minor' in another subject. The proportion of education is consequently geared to particular student needs. Course sequences and balance will differ for future high school and future primary school teachers.

This system has evolved from origins which for elementary school teachers were as humble in America as in most countries. Now it places all teacher education in the stage of higher education and its admission requirements are the same as for other departments or colleges of the university. Personal choice may, and frequently does, direct very able students towards non-professional first degrees. The law and medicine draw on wealthy students. Education attracts a large number of women who want to be primary school teachers. Teachers are educated alongside students with different or no professional intentions. And while many schools of education have an elementary school department and a high school department future primary and high school teachers are likely to attend common courses. Teacher education programmes are not dominated by university research interests, but rather by representative educationists. Special subject sequences are determined by appropriate non-professional professors, i.e. academics. The ingredients of the general component reflect consensus among educationalists, academics and school teachers generally.

Many of the dichotomies which occur in European models have been reduced in the United States. Today virtually all high school teachers are graduates and about eighty per cent. of primary and middle school teachers have degrees. Advanced studies in education are widespread at the master's and doctoral levels. In-service training is extensive and salary scales are linked with advanced study and higher degrees. The fund of research information available to the profession is extensive. The National Education Association – a federation of autonomous departments representing special interests – offers professional leadership at the national and state levels. Certification procedures are largely in the hands of professional educationalists. The content of professional courses for teachers at all levels is determined by members of the profession. Specialized subject courses remain under the control of the professors of non-professional subjects. A measure of professional unity has been achieved.

What can be learned from this evolution? Can desirable aspects of American teacher education be incorporated into colleges of education in England and Wales? Did the James Report facilitate this while making it possible to avoid some of the undesirable features of the situation in the United States? I think so, particularly if colleges accept the challenge of offering a general education to large numbers of students who do not intend to teach, and if they are prepared to accept a course-unit system of curriculum organization and teaching and the postponement of supervised teaching practice. They will also, perhaps, have to forego the coherence at present achieved by the English college tutorial system in order to increase flexibility. Coherence will then be the result of careful curriculum planning.

## Possibilities Under James

It is evident, even at the risk of oversimplification, that the James Report offered several possibilities. The first was that teacher education should clearly become part of higher education and entrance requirements should be the same as for polytechnics and universities. Secondly, it suggested that the general education of all teachers should be broadened and extended. Thirdly, that the present three-year certificate programme should become a four-year programme of education and training leading to a degree. The present four-year course – degree plus graduate certificate – should become a five-year course. In each pattern an internship year (the fourth or fifth) should be an integral part. Present in-service advanced diploma and degree work should increase on a voluntary basis.

First-cycle courses will provide a general education for students who will remain in higher education for only two years. Any terminal award will have to satisfy employers. College of education awards at the end of this cycle are likely to appeal to a range of employers different from those who look to the polytechnics for trained personnel. The first cycle will also offer a general education component for intending teachers. It must be hoped that this will be more broadly based than most present university courses.

Critics of undue specialization in sixth forms and universities should welcome the opportunities the first cycle offers to create novel short-cycle curricula. One theory on which they may rest derives from Herbert Spencer's claim that knowledge should be related to the problems that young adults are likely to meet. They include the problems of mental and physical health, earning a living, participating in civic life, preparing for marriage and family life, using leisure profitably and making moral decisions. In practice American curricula illustrate how this theory can work. As a basis of general education today, it seems preferable to English essentialism and continental European encyclopedism. Colleges of education could make a real contribution to the evolution of up-dated curricula by devising sound first-cycle courses.

Seen together as a four-year period of education and training for intending teachers, first- and second-cycle courses could be arranged as in America to meet individual needs. Concurrent sequences are possible by introducing in the first cycle, as part of the general component, subjects of direct relevance to the future teacher, e.g. psychology, sociology, and educational studies. Moreover, some special subject courses could deal with material in a manner useful to a future teacher. Literature courses might rigorously examine children's stories, poems and plays. Much modern science which excites young children can be presented at a level appropriate to students in higher education. Of course, future middle and upper secondary school teachers may wish to increase their depth knowledge of one or two subjects. First-cycle courses for them would consist almost exclusively of general education and special subject courses. Education courses would be postponed to the second cycle. Course profiles and sequences would vary and a course-unit system of teaching would allow for mistaken choices. Nevertheless, clearly defined patterns of first- and second-cycle work would be the norm.

A student wishing to become a primary school teacher may be advised to follow this kind of programme:

Year I    English language study
          Speech
          Art
          Sociology
          Political science
          European history
          Mathematics – basic set theory
          Science – human biology or elementary electricity
          Physical education
Year II   History of the development of English grammar
          Music

Twentieth-century history of the USA
General psychology
Science – general biology and laboratory work or
    introduction to modern physics
Mathematical topics of relevance to primary school
    lectures
Music for the classroom teacher
Introduction to child study
English literature

Year III  Learning and teaching
Social studies in the primary school
Communication into the primary school
Mathematics for primary school teachers
Introduction to educational technology
Industrial materials suitable for use in primary
    schools
Music
Speech
Art

Year IV  Practice teaching as a licensed teacher
Student teaching seminar – problems encountered in
    practice
Evaluation techniques
Teaching science to children*
Reading – trends – diagnosis*
History and philosophy of education*

A student preparing for work in a middle or upper school might choose not to study any courses of direct professional relevance in the first or second years. These could well be devoted to general requirements drawn from English, the natural sciences (physics, chemistry, biology), history, psychology, philosophy plus either art, economics, music or speech and drama. Third-year courses could include history of education, philosophy, of education, educational psychology, sociology, methods of teaching a secondary school subject and an educational option of the student's choice. The fourth year would be spent in a school as a licensed teacher with college-based education options and/or main subject courses.

A course-unit system in which each selected section of study is separately examined and graded facilitates transfers from one course profile to another, and from first-cycle to second-cycle work. It also makes it possible to draw a distinction between professional and non-professional units. A

* Electives or options chosen from a list of courses geared to the needs of primary school teachers and their special interests.

minimum number of units in each of the components can be prescribed by appropriate authorities. University or CNAA authorities could lay down the balance of general education and special subject units expected of a student whose aim is to obtain a non-professional degree. The number and kind of education units expected of a student who wants a professional degree in order to become a licensed teacher could be laid down by an appropriate professional body – the non-professional component by the universities or CNAA. This would leave colleges free to devise their own courses, teach as they think fit and examine students appropriately. Course-unit syllabuses could be scrutinized either by a council for academic awards or by a council for professional awards.

## Control Procedures

Such procedures would undoubtedly leave room for a restructuring of control over teacher education. The McNair system of Area Training Organizations leaves the validation of professional certificates in the hands of university and college examiners. The Department of Education formally accords 'qualified' status on the basis of certificate results. Local education authorities have no say in who should become qualified teachers. Neither the central nor the local public authorities can do much to influence the content of teacher education. How then is the public interest safeguarded? The assumption is that now for all teachers, as in the past for a small elite, the universities are suitable guardians. In reality ATO Committees serve this function for college of education awards. It does not seem un-reasonable to suppose that a professional council should pass judgement on professional competence. A partnership of colleges, universities, poly-technics and local education authorities in a Regional Council as proposed by James would bring together members of the profession. A proper balance of interests would be important and the role of special certification (or licensing) boards would correspond to that of the State Boards in America. In effect, they would require a minimum number of specified education course-units in a B.A.(Ed.) profile and postgraduate professional degrees such as the B.Ed., M.Ed. and Ed.D. Such a scheme would, of course, shift the administrative structure of teacher education control from its present university locus to an administrative region. What constitutes a proper balance of power on a Regional Council is open to debate, but clearly university representation would be strong although not overwhelming. The same may be said of college representation. The proposal offers a way of bringing the two distinct patterns of teacher education under a broader spectrum of professional control.

It also seems desirable to create for education a national body representative of professional interests which could perform a number of tasks. First there is need for a register of teachers. At the moment the Department of Education and Science is alone responsible for the award of qualified status. Professional educators should constitute a council which would safeguard the public interest by satisfying itself that persons placed on the register meet criteria of professional competence. It would have to ensure that the general education and esoteric knowledge of licensed teachers were adequate in breadth and depth. It would establish codes of professional behaviour and sit in judgement on teachers alleged to have deviated from them. It would review supply and demand policies. In short, a national council of members of the profession should be responsible for the ethical code, for teachers' skill and knowledge requirements, and for control of entry to the profession. The proper balance of interest and power on such a council is debatable, but it should be overwhelmingly professional.

The framework provided by James seems well devised to place teacher education within a professional framework. It would be foolish to imagine that divisions in teacher education which are of long standing can be removed immediately. But the scheme would make it possible for all types of teacher to be educated in colleges and professional centres. The majority of primary and secondary school teachers would receive their general professional education in the same institution. Special centres of excellence would prepare selected students in effect to participate in operational research into new methods of teaching and to initiate practical reforms. The general education of all teachers would be strengthened perhaps at the expense of professional studies. A national system would be created through the regional and national councils. Control of the professional aspects of training would more clearly be in the hands of members of the profession.

## Some Open Questions

This analysis has been based upon some assumptions which are very debatable and others that would seem to command general support. Informed opinion, for example, agrees that teacher education should become fully part of higher education. There is a general desire to bring together the two historical systems of teacher education, namely that for academic secondary school teachers and that for 'elementary' school teachers. It is generally agreed that links between the universities and teacher education should be maintained. And finally educationalists hope that they may acquire full professional status.

Alternative solutions are possible. A major issue is whether universities as such will expand greatly and if so how they will change to accommodate large increases in the number of students. Will they become, as in the United States, comprehensive institutions in which professional studies and degrees are emphasized? Or will they remain exclusive institutions, expanding slowly, in which faculty members pursue knowledge for its own sake through research and teaching? The James Report implied that English universities ought not to and will not change very much.

If this is so, can the expansion of teacher education take place within the traditional university structure informed as it is by concepts of academic freedom and autonomy? It seems likely that government agencies will wish to influence more aspects of teacher education policy in future than has been possible in the past. The stage is set to refashion the balance of power between the Department of Education and Science, the local education authorities and the universities. The White Paper suggests that Area Training Organizations will disappear. The outcome of this struggle is uncertain.

If the universities do not change, then the expansion of higher education in the immediate future will be in parallel institutions. The polytechnics have accepted expansion, at the moment as institutions in a second sector. Colleges of education face a choice between expanding within the polytechnic sector of higher education or as a third sector. It seems doubtful that they will be able to expand greatly as full members of the university community.

The next question, therefore, is whether colleges of education should expand as single purpose professional institutions or as multi-purpose institutions willing to absorb some of the pressure to expand higher education generally. I think their most exciting opportunities lie in the direction of expansion as multi-purpose institutions in which non-professional as well as a range of professional courses are offered. In this way colleges of education will be able to give direction to the quality of higher education and will not be isolated as the only single-purpose professional institutions in higher education.

If they are to participate in the general expansion of higher education, colleges of education will necessarily have to revise the content of courses offered and the sequences in which they are offered. Comparative evidence suggests that in most countries a first short-cycle system of higher education will develop. Should colleges direct their attention to developing courses for short-cycle higher education? And are they prepared to move in the direction of consecutive rather than concurrent courses? Where does the balance of evidence lie? Conventional wisdom suggests that primary school teachers benefit most from concurrent courses while secondary school teachers are best prepared when professional courses follow the completion of general and specialized subject courses. Thus the content of education in colleges of education should be viewed in the light of the need to extend the general education of large numbers of young adults and the need to train an increasing number of teachers for all types of school.

If a distinction is drawn between academic and professional courses then the question arises: Should both types of course be validated by the same agencies? Another question is: Should professional requirements and academic requirements in teacher education be laid down by the same agencies? Spokesmen who wish in the present climate of opinion to retain close links between colleges of education and the universities seem to imply that the universities should lay down curricula and syllabuses in both professional and non-professional areas. In my opinion there is a need to reconsider this assumption and to ask which courses should rightly be controlled by the universities and which courses should be controlled by members of the teaching profession. Can it be disputed that classroom teachers, LEA and HM Inspectors, college and university department lecturers are important members of the teaching profession? Should not all of them be involved in the control of some aspects of teacher education? Namely, over entry to training, over the professional aspects of training courses and over admission through examinations and other forms of assessment to full membership of the profession? Given this assumption what agencies may best discharge these tasks? The existing Area Training Organizations or the proposed Regional and National Councils?

The James proposals offered one pattern of alternatives, namely a tripartite expansion of higher education, the growth of multi-purpose general and professional colleges of education, the validation of some courses by universities or the CNAA and the validation of professional courses by organizations representative of professional opinion. Such developments would release teacher education from domination by the universities. It would leave the universities free in an expanded system of higher education to perform tasks for which they alone by tradition and sustained endeavour are uniquely capable of undertaking. It is doubtful whether large comprehensive universities could retain the independence necessary to perform these tasks. It is doubtful whether they are able or whether they should attempt to provide an education for the traditional and for the new professions and para-professions. Teaching, by virtue of its history, falls between the old and new professions. All these groups, however, have a public service to perform. They have to be responsive to public pressure and demands. The university, if it is to perform its historic social function, cannot afford to lose its freedom and independence. The implication is clear, new configurations of forces have to be created to ensure professional autonomy and responsibility. For this reason, I welcome the James Report. It makes it possible to create in England and Wales a system of teacher education which bridges the dichotomies inherent in European patterns and which yet avoids some of the problems created by the rapid evolution of education in the United States.

# CHAPTER 3

## Teacher Education in Scotland

JAMES SCOTLAND

When a country has an independent history of systematic education stretching back, as far as its national church is concerned, over a thousand years, and in public statutes almost half that time, it may be expected to have its own educational tradition. The Scottish system has always been distinctly, sometimes resolutely, different from the English, and although the two structures have tended to move together in the last century (Osborne, 1966), they still diverge sufficiently to be supervised by separate government departments through separate statutes and regulations. What this means in practice is that, while fundamental parliamentary decisions are effective on both sides of the border – it is, for instance, virtually inconceivable (though some people have conceived it) that the leaving age should be different in the two countries – the methods and machinery for operating the system vary widely. Thus, for example, the independent sector is much smaller and much less influential in Scotland; the normal pattern of individual education, as shown both in school certificates and in the famous 'ordinary' degree, is broader and less specialized; teacher training is the work, not of the universities, but of the colleges of education, which are larger than in England, fewer in number, and independent of local authority control. These differences, however, should not be overstated, nor too naïvely regarded. The road to comprehensive education, for instance, has been no smoother in Scotland although 'neighbourhood' schools have existed there for centuries; within them academic segregation by streaming has been, if anything, even more decided than in England.

Elsewhere (Scotland, 1969) I have discussed at some length the 'Scottish tradition in education'. It has several striking features. Unlike her southern neighbour, Scotland has been consistently proud of her educational system, and indeed of being educated; there has been no 'good form' in concealing the fact. Her chronic poverty, at least until the Industrial Revolution, and for many parts of the country thereafter as well, has compelled her to regard education, not as an instrument of gracious living, but as a weapon; it has also led her towards continual economy, even parsimony, and the inevitable conservatism which these entail. Scotland has had no brilliant record of educational experiment, largely because she has not had the resources to redeem failure. A strongly authoritarian strain may have owed something also to this need to economize, but its roots are probably deeper in the Scottish character, which has usually been prepared to work long and hard for preferment, and having achieved this, wants to exercise power. Whatever the reasons, Scottish schools and universities have always been full of older people laying down the law for the young. There has also been a powerful academic bias: if the only weapon a man has to help him get on is his brain, he is not likely to undervalue intellectual agility. The respect shown in all generations to the 'lad of parts' is famous, but there has been a persistent tendency to interpret 'parts' narrowly in terms of first-class degrees: physical and aesthetic prowess have not been highly regarded in Scotland. On the other hand, the classics have, especially Plato, whose educational theories have been vastly influential, from the Reformation to the present century.

They might have had even more influence if it had not been for the militant democracy which characterized Scottish educational thinking, the conviction that every child should have the right to higher teaching, that there should be no helots. This was largely the work of Scottish presbyterianism: the national church played a leading part for centuries in providing schooling and teacher training, and its doctrine of salvation through labour was widely accepted by the Scottish people.

The 'Scottish tradition', then, may be summarized as follows:

1. That education is, and always has been, of paramount importance in any community;
2. That every child should have the right to all the education of which he is capable;
3. That such education should be provided as economically and systematically as possible;
4. That the training of the intellect should take priority over all other facets of the pupil's personality;
5. That experiment is to be attempted only with the greatest of caution; and
6. That the most important person in the school, no matter what theorists say, is not the pupil but the (inadequately rewarded) teacher.

In Scotland, as elsewhere today, we live in a time of the 'shaking of the foundations'; few of these traditions are as solid as they were even one generation ago, and some have decayed very rapidly indeed – temporarily or not, of course, no one knows. The national church occupies a much less prominent place in the community than it did; membership has declined from 1,292,617 in December 1961 to 1,154,211 in December 1970, a drop of almost eleven per cent. in less than a decade. In the same period the total population of Scotland remained almost exactly steady at a little over five million.* Although there have been vigorous efforts to reverse the trend – a stewardship campaign, missions in poor districts and at the seaside in summer – these have not been enough to silence the facile generalization that the Church is out of touch in the world of the late twentieth century. Even the Roman Catholic Church, whose hold on its adherents has been traditionally firmer, has been concerned over its waning influence. The decline is noticeable in education as in other fields: ministers remain on many committees, but some people suggest that this is not so much because of the expertise that they can contribute as because they are among the few highly educated people who can spare the time. There are indeed plenty of critics to suggest that clerical influence is too strong in the educational system of an essentially irreligious community, but it is doubtful how much effective power church members wield: in the main national and regional committees it is certainly substantially less than fifty, or even thirty years ago, when the Rev So-and-So might virtually run a training college or an education committee in his spare time.

Another obvious change in the spirit of the time is the strong revulsion against any form of authoritarianism – indeed, some suggest, against authority. There is much more talk of rights and much less of duties; discipline is to be agreed, not imposed; democracy is rampant in the universites and even increasingly in the schools, with movements, admittedly much less violent than outside Britain, towards 'student power' and towards removing the headmaster from his absolute position at the nerve-centre of the school. Inevitably such a trend has attacked the favourite Scottish educational philosophy of idealism. Plato and his philosopher-kings are out of fashion; Dewey, half a century after his main period of writing, has come into his own.

In short, for Scotland in the early 1970s, the statement of educational tradition set out above must be substantially altered. True, education is still regarded as important, perhaps more than ever. It is now so important indeed in people's minds that it has been made a political bargaining counter; compare the place given to it in the 1970 party programmes with that in earlier manifestos. Much of the public desire for it is uninformed, but the desire does exist, and presumably weighs when voting decisions are taken.

The aggressive democracy of John Knox and his reformers, as set down in their *First Book of Discipline* of 1560† might be a watchword for comprehensive education:

* *Report to the General Assembly of the Church of Scotland*, 1971, p. 17.
† *The First Book of Discipline, or the Policy and Discipline of the Church...* *presented to the Nobility, anno 1560, and afterwards subscribed by the Kirk and Lords.* Appendix to Knox's *History of the Reformation of Religion in Scotland*, Blackie, Glasgow, 1832.

The rich and potent may not be permitted to suffer their children to spend their youth in vain idleness, as heretofore they have done, but they must be exhorted and ... compelled to dedicate their sons ... to the profit of the kirk and the commonwealth, and that they must do of their own expenses, because they are able. The children of the poor must be supported and sustained ....

The next phrase, however, might command less approval: 'trial being taken whether the spirit of docility be in them found or not.' Indeed it might be fairly claimed that the present generation is the first in which a genuine effort has been made to pay more than lip service to universal democracy, to make it work for every child. The danger, of course, is of slithering into a suspicious egalitarianism, as if there was only just enough education to go round, and anything extra my neighbour's boy gets will have to be subtracted from mine.

The direst educational poverty has gone. The schools, colleges and universities command a higher proportion of national expenditure than ever before – more than most of us would have believed possible in 1945, though by no means enough to satisfy all. Experiment breeds experiment. Generosity sets a higher level of expectation. There are so many new projects in the queue for funds that economy and systematic organization are as essential as they ever were.

There are at least three areas, however, in which the old traditions are under serious assault. At least in theory intellectual education has been dislodged from its central position in the Scottish system; it is still of course important, but no longer self-sufficient. The influential SED memorandum, *Primary Education in Scotland* (1965) summarizes current thinking:*

In addition to those (able pupils) who have obvious intellectual gifts which reveal themselves generally over the whole curriculum, there are those whose ability expresses itself in only one branch – for example art, or music, or drama. ... The teacher must recognize the various ways in which ability manifests itself.

With the opening of high promotion to ordinary graduates, the unique position of the honours graduate in Scotland appears to have been lost; members of the Honours Graduates' Association certainly think it has. A whole new promotion structure in guidance for pupils is being set up by many authorities, and qualifications here are not related to intellectual powers. For all this, however, with so many of today's Scottish teachers having been brought up in an academic atmosphere, there is still wide respect for the gifted pupil, and one of the main criticisms of the colleges of education is of the undemanding intellectual content of their courses.

* See pp. 57–8.

There is a marked change also in attitudes to educational experiment. Although prudence is still extolled, conservatism appears to have gone by the board, and experiment, once frowned upon unless undertaken with enormous care, has become downright respectable. The most useful function of specialist organizers in the present era, according to *Primary Education in Scotland,** is to initiate and guide development and experimentation', and the same document mentions 'quite drastic revision of the curriculum', and schemes of work giving 'freedom to individual teachers to experiment'. But such exhortations can be found in any period; what is more significant today is the amount of general acceptance they receive. At conferences and in-service courses and when visitors reach the schools, teachers often feel called upon to apologise – or launch a counter-attack – because their programme this session is not sufficiently different from last year's. It is very difficult to establish what proportion of Scottish teachers are actually 'trying something out', but there has been for some years now general agreement that as true professionals they ought to be. There has also been a reaction, with many to suggest that the swing has gone too far, so that the stage of experiment is being omitted altogether. This has been the main contention against comprehensivization – too much too soon, with the heart ruling the head. In the field of teacher training the problem for many educationalists is not whether to reform the process, nor even perhaps how, but how to prevent sweeping changes without controlled experiment.

There is a very serious difficulty in all this. The changes advocated for Scottish education today are fundamental. They reflect a change in attitudes to life, and the more radical they are, the less scope exists for controlled experiment. Comprehensive education is comprehensive or it is nothing; what valid lessons can be drawn from an experiment with one group or in one area or in one system?

Finally, the traditional role and status of the Scottish teacher has changed. Within the educational system his importance has actually grown: no major educational decisions are now made, as once they were, without consulting teachers. The General Teaching Council has a majority of 'practising teachers' from schools and colleges, and there are no important educational bodies (except certain local education committees) without teacher members. In the board of governors of each college of education they form probably the most influential, certainly the best organized bloc. Outside the system at a wider level, however, the Scottish teacher is probably less influential than he was before 1939. If status is to be measured by remuneration, a teacher, even a well-promoted one, is now worse off in comparison with many other professionals, and all professionals have lost ground to the non-professionals. Within his classroom, moreover, the

* See pp. 31, 35, 39.

Scottish teacher has generally ceased to be an absolute monarch, and has had to learn (when he can) the techniques of democratic leadership.

Recent developments in Scottish teacher education have reflected many of these changes in tradition. Before considering this thesis, however, it will be useful, in a book of which this is only one chapter, to summarize the present Scottish system and mark its differences from the English. In the first place, under the Regulations,* the training of virtually all Scottish teachers before they enter on service is conducted by the ten colleges of education in the country. In contrast to the situation in England, the universities and specialist colleges take no part in basic training; the only true exception to this as a general rule is the University of Stirling, which, by special permission of the General Teaching Council, trains its own students. The older universities offer a diploma in education, but this forms the first stage towards a master's degree; it is not a teaching qualification.

The Scottish colleges of education, therefore, are national institutions, regionally organized. They have their independent boards of governors and are financed, on estimates, by the Scottish Education Department; they are not under the jurisdiction of the local education authorities. Aberdeen, Dundee, Jordanhill (Glasgow) and Moray House (Edinburgh) are multi-purpose institutions. Dunfermline College (now located at Cramond, near Edinburgh, but retaining the old name) confines itself to physical education for women. Hamilton, Craigie (Ayr) and Callendar Park (Falkirk) take only primary students, hardly any of them university graduates. Notre Dame (Glasgow) and Craiglockhart (Edinburgh) are Roman Catholic institutions; both offer postgraduate courses, but well over ninety per cent. of their students are working for the three-year primary diploma.

Because of their multi-lateral tradition, the older colleges have generally been much larger than comparable English institutions. In 1972–3 Jordanhill had about 3,700 pre-service students, Moray House 3,000, Aberdeen 2,000, Dundee 1,200. The others were generally smaller: Hamilton had 900, Craigie 700, Callendar Park 700, Dunfermline and Craiglockhart about 450. Notre Dame, largely because of the huge Roman Catholic population in the Glasgow area, had over 1,500.

The responsibility for supervising standards of entry to the profession rests with the General Teaching Council, and its Visitation Committee keeps itself informed on training courses, though it may not lay them down. There is some parallel with the General Medical Council and the university medical schools.

The four large colleges offer many courses. Those for postgraduate and postdiploma students extend over one session. The primary diploma course has run to three years since 1931, though apart from a postwar emergency

* Teachers (Education, Training and Registration) (Scotland) Regulations 1967; Teachers (Colleges of Education) (Scotland) Regulations 1967.

arrangement, men have been admitted only since 1967. There are specialist secondary diplomas in music (three years), physical education (three years), technical subjects (four years), speech and drama (four years). There are courses leading to non-teaching qualifications – youth, community and social work – in Jordanhill and Moray House, Aberdeen and Dundee. And there are the four-year bachelor of education courses, offered in partnership with nearby universities or CNAA. The relationship differs from that in England, since the Scottish universities, as we have seen, have no basic training function.

So much for pre-service training. For many years the colleges have also been the Secretary of State's main instruments for in-service training; the SED, unlike the Department of Education and Science, mounts no courses of its own.

These are the main features of the Scottish training system, and the ways in which it differs from the English. Here, as elsewhere in the educational system, there have been important changes in the tradition.

Poverty and the need to husband scarce resources developed a strongly utilitarian element in Scottish teacher training: there was generally much more of methods than of academics in the course, and the universities, apart from a brief flirtation about 1900, were not involved. This is no longer true. Since 1945 the balance of academic and professional in a student's course, particularly a student trained entirely in the colleges, has shifted towards the former – not very far, and not without strenuous opposition, but appreciably. In the early 1950s a girl in the three years of her primary diploma course devoted little time to her own higher education; her English and mathematics were primary English and mathematics (in fact, arithmetic), biology was 'nature study', and there was no place for modern languages or physical science. The next few years saw the introduction of 'special subjects', and by the mid-1960s one or more 'main studies' formed an important part of the course; a student might spend as much as 400 hours, a seventh of her total time, on French or art or 'classical studies', with benefit largely to her own wider culture. Even then however, the relevance of this to primary training was questioned. In particular, it took a Board of Studies with firm convictions to recommend termination for any student purely because of failure in a main study. The attitude of today's students is ambivalent: they complain when college courses do not 'stretch' them, but protest when they are failed on any but narrowly professional grounds, usually classroom practice.

There have been similar developments – and similar attitudes – in the postgraduate courses. Ten years ago the simple principle was still accepted: the universities and specialist colleges – of art, of music, of domestic science – provided higher education, the colleges of education strictly professional training. This is still of course broadly true, but the armoury of a modern secondary teacher can seldom be provided entirely in a first degree. Evident in science and modern studies, this is increasingly visible also in English, history and even mathematics. Precisely at a time when specialization is growing in university departments and art colleges, the secondary schools are calling for more Admirable Crichtons.

Nevertheless, within the last decade the Scottish universities have, somewhat tentatively, entered more into the training picture than at any time since the abolition of the 'concurrent course'* in which, with an extra year, a student was able to complete his degree and his training at the same time. One of the newest, Stirling, departs farthest from the Scottish pattern by training its students concurrently with their academic course, so that one may qualify in 'English and education' at either ordinary or honours level, and be awarded both a B.A and a Dip.Ed., the latter as a teaching qualification.† The course has proved to be a demanding and expensive one, but shows promise of success, especially in the use of micro-teaching techniques. Bachelor of education courses have fostered partnerships between the large colleges and the older universities. The first B.Ed. teaching began in Aberdeen in 1965 and its first three graduates emerged in 1968.‡ Courses at Jordanhill and Moray House followed in 1966, at Dundee in 1967. Notre Dame, by arrangement with CNAA, began in 1971, and so did Craigie and Hamilton, in partnership with Strathclyde. Callendar Park reached an agreement with Stirling. Dunfermline began negotiations with CNAA. Two patterns have emerged so far. Colleges working with the older universities – Aberdeen, Jordanhill and Moray House – have something very like the Scottish ordinary degree, with students accumulating credits for seven or eight one-year units, and one or two subjects studied for more than one year. There was no provision at first for an honours course, and this was a grave weakness, preventing gifted students from enrolling. Aberdeen, however, introduced honours courses in 1972, with the last two years taught in the university, and Gasgow and Edinburgh began negotiations shortly afterwards. The problem is twofold – first, that Scottish honours and ordinary programmes are distinct from an early stage; secondly, that in all three cities the university awards the degree, but the college does most of the teaching (in Aberdeen, all). A college strong enough to teach Scottish honours courses in a dozen subjects would cease to be a truly professional institution. What gives the B.Ed. its distinctive pattern are the compulsory professional and aesthetic subjects such as art, drama, music and physical education,§ and above all the concurrent course, including teaching practice, leading to a college certificate. Students in

---

* 1873 to 1955, but never popular after 1918.
† This last point has caused some trouble, since the Dip. Ed. in the older Scottish universities is an *additional* diploma, purely theoretical and generally regarded as more taxing intellectually than the teaching qualification.
‡ Normally it is a four-year course.
§ In Aberdeen a pass in one of these is compulsory.

Aberdeen, Jordanhill and Moray House must enter on the course from the beginning; there is no element in common with the primary diploma or other courses.

Dundee's pattern is much nearer the Robbins (1963) blueprint, with a common first, and even second year for B.Ed. and primary diploma students, and a process of rigorous selection. It makes no provision for any single academic subject to be studied for longer than one session, and this has drawn criticism, especially from students in the more traditional programmes. Notre Dame's proposals, approved by CNAA, are for a first year common with the diploma. The Strathclyde plans include the first two years along with the diploma, the third year in college and the fourth in university, with a good deal of staff exchange. The pattern of Dundee and the new colleges is therefore closer to the English B.Ed., and has the advantage of drawing on diploma students who prove their ability in the first or second year of their original course. It remains to be proved, however, whether enough time remains in the last two years for an adequate amount of 'university standard' work.

Almost all the Scottish universities, therefore, are now collaborating in teacher training, generally by setting academic standards for the colleges. To this there is no lack of opposition by the 'pure professionalists', who consider academic teaching to be none of the business of a college, and by the (much less numerous) 'college academics', who cannot envisage a truly integrated training course until all the teaching, academic and professional, is done in college. The picture is different in each partnership; the present problem is to foster mutual faith and security, so that a flexible pattern can emerge.

A shift has also occurred in traditional Scottish attitudes to conservatism and experiment. Her training colleges have not been on the whole conservative institutions. When the national predilection was against change, they were often severely criticized for advocating theories conceived in the study and never tested in the battles of the classroom. Generations of students were welcomed to their teaching practice or their first posts with 'now you can forget all that airy-fairy stuff they told you in college and get down to the hard graft of the three Rs'. In many schools they still are, though this is more of a windy generalization than a real knowledge of the situation. More interesting at the present time, however, is the complaint, often voiced by professional educationalists, that, in a system now dedicated to experiment, the colleges are not playing a sufficiently dynamic part.

How true is this? General estimates are naturally difficult, even with only ten colleges to examine, but a few points can be made. In the kind of research which is strictly planned and written up in professional journals the college's record is poor, falling far behind that of the university departments of education. What has been done has usually originated with a handful of lecturers working for higher degrees. The majority of the staff have no time, no inclination, and in many cases no proficiency in 'pure research'. In 'applied' work it is a different story, but here also it could be better. The report of the Secretary of State on *Education in Scotland in 1971* lists fifty projects in receipt of specific governmental financial aid: only three of these are college-based, two in Dundee and one in Moray House. There are, however, several others not listed in the report, including an ambitious reading enquiry at Craigie and projects in Aberdeen on comprehensivization and on school hostels. There is also what has been called 'development work' rather than research, and there is no doubt that much of this goes on everywhere.

As an example, the work of one college* included the publication of its own annual journal and of newsletters in two subject areas; contributions by staff to various periodicals; text-books published by nine lecturers and substantial books by the principal and vice-principal. 'Formal' research was undertaken into the development of originality, spatial ability and number concepts and a test of school anxiety. There were two substantial projects, one on the effects of comprehensive reorganization on pupils' personal aspirations, the other on the role of hostel warden and the effects on pupils living in hostels. Several enquiries were conducted in co-operation with, and at the invitation of local authorities. Three lecturers had plays produced professionally; one published music; seven had works exhibited at national academies of art. The college also housed a national curriculum centre in modern languages; each of the four older colleges was the centre for one subject in this way.

This is a fair record. Some of it is no doubt desultory and unproductive for all but the lecturer concerned, but a good deal is of real value, and more could be done with more generous staffing. Teacher training in Scotland has always used fewer lecturers and more class-contact hours than south of the border. Given more free time, lecturers could tackle more research. Given a better college record of research, the SED might provide more staff (though this, when schools are starving in some departments, is not certain). In short, the criticism of colleges by experimental educationalists, though substantially overstated, is not unreasonable.

This, however, refers to experiment in the field of education generally. In the narrower area of teacher education the colleges have done rather well. In the 1960s alone substantial new courses have been established in music (three years) and speech and drama (four years). The course in technical education has been extensively revised and lengthened to four years. New courses have appeared in youth, community and social work, and for teachers of handicapped children. Three new primary colleges have been planned, built and opened and have already made a notable impact

* Aberdeen College of Education, Quadriennial Report 1967–71.

on the educational life of their neighbourhoods. Seven colleges are now teaching courses of university standard for the B.Ed. degree, and the others are planning to join them. The older courses have been under constant review, and there have been interesting experiments in teaching practice, notably Aberdeen's 'area survey' for art students, Craigie's exchange scheme for teachers and final-year students and Jordanhill's 'staff tutors'. Field work now takes hundreds of students every year to specialist weeks or fortnights in many parts of Scotland, England and the continent. In-service work has expanded many times, and its pattern has been transformed with the reduction of the 'conference-talk' and the vast increase in the number of workshops and working parties. The record of the last decade is far from conservative – as good certainly as the record in most other quarters of Scottish education in the period. Where have new ideas originated in that time? Mostly, as in science and mathematics, from abroad; occasionally, as in modern studies, with some gifted teachers. Just as important as the idea, however, is the second stage – recognizing its potential, systematizing, disseminating. Here the best work has been done by the Scottish Inspectorate – by the late Donald McGill for instance in physics – but the colleges have not been far behind.

Whatever their achievement, it has not excused the colleges from attack: one practice has existed so strongly and for so long as to become a tradition – continual criticism of the training system. Individual teachers often say nowadays that things are better than they were, but their pronouncements en bloc, at conferences and through their professional associations, still hit the colleges hard. This is not perhaps cause for wonder. Call a conference on teacher training, and you must expect delegates to seek out points for improvement. Consult a professional manifesto, and you are unlikely to read that no reform is necessary. But criticism comes from more than teachers; there are constant calls by students, college and university, for enquiries and investigations. Within the last year or two there have been demands from several student representative councils, from the Scottish Union of Students and, when that body fell upon evil days, from the National Union of Students.* The most obvious cause among post-graduate students – the most virulent critics – is the long period of waiting between graduation and the first pay cheque; some defenders of the colleges have gone so far as to suggest (wrongly, I think) that salaries for students would put an end to virtually all the complaints. A second cause of unrest is more securely based in psychology – unwillingness in new holders of a degree to be told that they still have a lot to learn; even moderate students who recognize the symptoms in themselves cannot easily escape the disease. And there is a third explanation which applies to students and teachers

---

* This attitude differs, in Scotland at least, from student attitudes to the universities; these institutions are often objects of attack, never of contempt.

alike – the need, in a disgruntled profession, for whipping-boys. The colleges, working continually in an artificial, regulatory situation, are prime candidates for that role.

There is undoubtedly some truth in each of these explanations, and many explicit accusations can be easily rebutted – for instance, lack of academic ability in the lecturing staff; at one college in 1971 the staff of 78 in academic and professional subjects included twenty-one with first class honours and twenty-eight with more than one degree, including ten with doctorates. Anyone with experience of selection techniques for college posts also knows that no candidate is appointed without good references for his teaching ability. As for the commonest complaint – that lecturers' classroom experience dates from another, more leisurely day, the position in 1971 in two of the largest colleges was that well over sixty per cent. of the staff had actually taught in a school within the previous five years.

The force of many students' attacks is diminished moreover by the immoderate language in which they are expressed: words like 'appalling', 'disgraceful' and 'national collapse' carry little weight nowadays. But when all this has been said, there remains overwhelming evidence of dissatisfaction among students, teachers and the community at large, which has forced enquiries like those of the Parliamentary Select Committee, abruptly halted in 1970 with the change of government, and the General Teaching Council's Working Party on Postgraduate Training, which reported in 1972.

The problem is whether the colleges are trying to do the wrong things, or trying to do the right things but doing them badly, or in the wrong way. The weight of evidence so far available tilts towards the last of these possibilities. There seems no doubt, especially in postgraduate training, that the student persona remains too long in existence; trainees never cease to complain that they are 'treated like children', and it is one of the main reasons for their proposal that postgraduate and undergraduate students should be trained in separate establishments. Since there is also a frequently expressed desire among teachers that they should take a larger part in the training processes, the most likely development is towards the 'apprentice teacher'. Widely canvassed currently is some form of 'sandwich' training, in which candidates will spend an introductory period in college, then enter on their first post, but return one or two years later for a further term in college. This is the scheme proposed by the GTC working party, and its educational advantages are substantial, with opportunities to relate principle and practice beyond any so far enjoyed. The difficulties, however, are formidable. How long, for instance, should the first stage be? As a pure introduction, one term is enough, some would claim too long: after all, what do the colleges have to do except mention what to look for? But there is another task – to eliminate or delay the comparatively small number of students who ought never to be teachers at all. Opinions vary on how many of these there are; experience suggests well under ten per cent., but in the present national economic situation, with more graduates attracted to teaching not for interest but security, the proportion is likely to grow. The consequence is a longer introductory period, with spells of teaching practice. The notion that the schools themselves could be left to eliminate poor teachers is, even with more generous staffing, unrealistic.

But this is on the whole a minor difficulty, a problem of detail. The scheme has several major drawbacks. It departs from the normal scholastic year, and therefore raises educational and financial complications. A flood of new teachers would pour into the schools in November, or January, or March or April, depending on the length of the first phase; and unless phase three could be arranged during holidays, a fair proportion of a school's staff – in some cases, by current standards, almost half the ordinary teachers – would vanish into the colleges again during the summer term. Even arranging phase one to end as phase three begins does not solve all the problems: teachers cannot be manoeuvred here and there like chess pieces.

On this ground alone one or two directors of education, especially in the 'starvation' areas, have expressed grave doubts as to whether the scheme is workable. There is also the problem of establishing a fruitful and efficient partnership in phase two between schools and colleges. As teachers already but students still, the candidates would be the business of both institutions, and that kind of relationship is far from easy to maintain.

Further, how are candidates to be induced to return to college for phase three, especially if they have met, as many will, with considerable success in their posts? The final term in college would be, more than anything else, a time for generalization, for discussing principles as they have been illustrated in practice, and there is not a lot of evidence that modern Scottish teachers have much time for educational philosophizing, or for any but the most practical psychology. Sanctions would be needed – a salary and possibly a promotion bar are the most likely – and sanctions are not in favour in modern democracy.

The difficulties of the sandwich system, then, are many. My own view is that they are not insoluble, but there are plenty of critics, especially in the colleges, who believe they are. A more immediately profitable form of immediate action is to increase the contribution made by 'practising teachers' to training, and improve collaboration between schools and colleges. This is the policy of all the Scottish professional institutions, and a recent inquiry suggests that almost ninety per cent. of head teachers and heads of departments are in favour. What is proposed is systematization, with a 'teacher tutor' or 'teacher regent' appointed in each school to supervise student matters, and appropriate arrangements made for finance and accommodation. There would, of course, be substantial problems in assigning fields of responsibility between schools and colleges, but these could be worked out. The crucial problem remains the status of the student teacher, expressed financially; there must, in some way, be a shortening of the period of tutelage.

Traditionally the Scottish teacher, at the end of his college course, has regarded himself as trained for life. Until comparatively recently, therefore, there was not a great deal of in-service training. What there was, unlike the English provision, was run to a very great extent by the colleges, using predominantly their own staff. Some local authorities provided training for their teachers, and an occasional university department, generally by arrangement with the nearest college, offered a 'refresher' course; the chemistry department in Aberdeen and the mathematics in Dundee were good examples. The major part of the colleges' effort was concentrated in three weeks in July, immediately after the schools closed; there were also a few courses meeting every Saturday morning from October to March, with a break for Christmas. The longer of these courses, summer and winter, led to an additional teaching qualification, secondary, primary or infant, but by far the larger proportion consisted of conferences and short courses, lasting from a day to a week, and offering no 'paper qualification' to students. In Aberdeen in 1959, for example, eight summer courses were held, three leading to additional qualifications, and there were two conferences at week-ends during the session.

In the last five years there has been wide acceptance of the need for a much more ambitious system. The National Committee for In-Service Training was established in 1967. An essentially advisory and planning body, it runs no courses of its own, but may, when it sees the need, invite the colleges or some other providers to mount them. Its original remit was:

> To keep under review the general arrangements for the in-service training of teachers, including needs and the pattern of provision, and to advise as regards appropriate co-ordination, including co-ordination at regional level, among education authorities, colleges of education and other agencies.

In its first report, in August 1969, the Committee gave its own interpretation of its duties:

1. To identify training needs and priorities within them;
2. To guide the general organization of facilities and remove financial inhibitions;
3. To devise and set up adequate administrative machinery at all levels.

The most important practical duty it has undertaken so far has been to advise the Secretary of State on which courses are 'eligible for pooling', that is for special treatment in local finance. By using this device the Committee has been able to encourage local authorities to release their teachers for additional training in term-time. Further, by removing short college courses from the eligible list, it is trying, with some success, to change the balance of in-service effort, so that local authorities take over the running of short courses and conferences, and the colleges concentrate on substantial efforts of a month or more. Four Regional Committees were set up in 1969, intended similarly to bring together local interests, to estimate requirements, and to co-ordinate effort. In some regions, where competition among providers took the place of co-operation, their work proved more necessary than in others.

The National Committee has met some criticism, largely to the effect that it has been slow to produce any clear improvement in the system. But four years is a short period in which to look for results – long enough only in the modern mania for instant living. There are signs that a system will indeed appear where none previously existed. Courses will increasingly take place in winter, spring and summer terms, less during vacations: the figures for the northern region given in Table 3·1* show the change in balance:

Table 3.1

| Period | Sessional courses with attendance | Vacation courses with attendance |
| --- | --- | --- |
| May – Sept. 1967 | 4 (83) | 35 (1,141) |
| Oct. 1967 – Sept. 1968 | 23 (941) | 37 (724) |
| Oct. 1968 – Sept. 1969 | 43 (1,730) | 41 (1,107) |
| Oct. 1969 – Sept. 1970 | 59 (2,319) | 38 (647) |

And there are more courses to extend a teacher's armament – for instance for head teachers, primary and secondary. The National Committee has issued a programme of priorities for longer full-time courses. The Committee can take some credit for progress made, and will probably acquire more, if for no other reason than 'because it is there'.

The most hopeful proposal in this field is the institution of a 'modular', or 'credit' system through which, as in North America and elsewhere, entitlement to additional qualifications can be built up. This will come: the only question is when?

The future of teacher education in Scotland is bound to be far from placid, with inevitable changes in balance. The universities, especially the newer ones, may take a larger part in the process, both before and during service; if they do, there will be a number of observers to acclaim them, though not necessarily for professional or even for very logical reasons.

* Aberdeen College of Education, *Quadriennial Report 1967–71.*

The colleges, especially the smaller ones, will continue to diversify their work. They will all, probably, be offering a B.Ed. programme within the next three or four years, and the next step is for all to train secondary graduates. The staff does not exist to do all these things really well in ten separate colleges unless the schools are plundered even more than at present. Or, of course, unless the basic methods of training change, and the schools extend their contribution greatly. Certainly teachers will play a much more important role in training their successors than they do now, though not with such instant expertise as some imagine. Meanwhile the larger colleges seem destined to continue in growth. By the end of the century, possibly a good deal sooner, Jordanhill and Moray House may be universities.

But the most significant factors in the immediate situation are, first, the move from local to regional units in education, and, secondly the staffing position in the schools. The government's proposals, based on the report of the Wheatley Committee, allow for eight regions, and the committees which will administer education there will be much more powerful and efficient than most of the present local bodies. The effect on teacher training remains to be seen. There may even be takeover bids, and none of the colleges is likely to view such a development with pleasure. On the other hand the impact on in-service training could well be beneficial. The staffing position in the schools is likely to improve dramatically in the 1970s, particularly with graduates taking the place of diploma holders in the primary sector. If this happens, and if the schools take a bigger part in training, the college commitment in pre-service work will be reduced, leaving room for a substantial expansion in long-term in-service courses. This, indeed, is the change in balance forecast by the Government White Paper of 1972.

So much for the administration of training. The courses themselves will certainly change and probably lengthen. A decade from now it will very probably be impossible to train for any diploma in less than four years. The issue between the pure professionals and the proponents of more higher education will soon be resolved. The James Report does not apply to Scotland, but the Thatcher pattern is bound to exert some influence north of the border, and although the Scottish colleges do not want to develop non-professional courses, they may be forced to do so. Whether the result of all this change and proposed change will be a system attracting less criticism from teachers in service and training is at least doubtful. There is a fair chance, however, that it will produce better teachers, by which is meant an improvement in the average performer and fewer who just scrape through. Really, of course, good teachers take what they need out of any system: as the Talmud says, a good teacher is an angel of the Lord of Hosts, and there are no training courses for angels.

# CHAPTER 4

# *The Teaching Profession*

### SIR RONALD GOULD

Is teaching a profession? The answer depends on what is meant by the somewhat nebulous word 'profession', which is used in many different senses. 'When I use a word,' said Humpty Dumpty, 'it means exactly what I want it to mean, neither more nor less.' The word 'profession' is often used to mean what people want it to mean, and this makes communication confusing. Dickens used it for any paid employment, and Shaw to describe prostitutes. The notice 'Rooms for the Profession' appears in the windows of theatrical lodging houses. Footballers, cricketers and tennis players are divided into professionals and amateurs, the former being paid for playing. Divinity, law and medicine have been regarded as professions for many years, and in more recent years so too have architecture and dentistry. Teachers, estate agents, practitioners in advertising and public relations, journalists and many other groups also describe themselves as belonging to professions. Yet despite the many meanings carried by this pantechnicon of a word, most people, in speaking of teachers, link them with the learned professions, the clergy, lawyers and doctors, and not with any paid occupation, prostitution, the theatre or sport, and not even with estate agents, practitioners in advertising and public relations or journalists.

Thus the principal of the Singapore Teachers' College assumed teachers belonged or should belong to a learned profession when, in welcoming diploma students in 1969, he said,

> There is today a growing sense of professionalism which you should pay attention to. Briefly, a true professional takes his intellectual and practical training seriously, keeps abreast of his studies, practises his profession to his utmost ability and integrity, infuses idealism and altruism in the practice of his profession and collectively safeguards the standards, status and good name of his profession. The teaching profession needs a high sense of loyalty to the highest ideals of professionalism.

Perhaps, then, I could demonstrate whether or not teachers are a learned

3—EOT * *

profession by analysing professionalism, breaking it down into its component elements, and then examining how far teachers have advanced towards incorporating these elements into their convictions, beliefs and practices, individually and collectively.

## A Learned Profession: a High-Grade Non-manual Occupation

The first and most obvious sign of a learned profession, like that of the clergy, lawyers and doctors, is that its work is high grade and non-manual, or if manual work is done, it is based on considerable theoretical knowledge. I have never heard anyone suggest that most teaching was anything other than non-manual. Of course domestic science, handicrafts and practical work have been introduced into the curriculum, but their purpose is educational and their basis intellectual.

That teaching is a high-grade occupation, however, has been disputed again and again. The Society for Promoting Christian Knowledge, for example, unlike many others in the nineteenth century, tried to establish some standards for the teachers they employed. The standards, however, were hardly high grade. Masters, they claimed, should have 'a good genius for teaching' and should 'write a good hand and understand the grounds of arithmetic'. Mistresses, however, though expected to possess the 'genius for teaching' were not required to be able to write or count. Clearly this Society did not regard teaching as a high-grade occupation. Others, too, at about the same time, held similar views. Speaking in the House of Commons in 1847, Macaulay said,

> The masters, the refuse of all other callings, discarded footmen, ruined pedlars, men who cannot work a sum in the rule of three, men who cannot write a letter without blunders, men who do not know whether Jerusalem is in Asia or America . . . to such men, men to whom none of us would trust the key of his cellar, we have entrusted the mind of the rising generation, and with the mind of the rising generation, the freedom, the happiness and the glory of our country.

Even if one allows for rhetorical exaggeration, there is little doubt teachers were often recruited without further training from unskilled jobs, that many could not write or count accurately, that they possessed little or no knowledge of geography, and that some were dishonest. Their employers, or the parents of the children they taught, must have regarded teaching as a low-grade job or they would have insisted on teachers of better quality. Lancaster, who sponsored the monitorial system, did not rate teaching highly, for he declared, 'Anyone who can read or write can become a teacher'.

Nor must it be assumed that the twentieth century is so vastly superior.

Clearly the Board of Education in prewar days must have thought of teaching as requiring little skill, for they permitted the employment of supplementary teachers, whose only qualifications were that they were over the age of eighteen and vaccinated. When in postwar years there was a serious shortage of teachers, attempts were made by the Ministry of Education to allow untrained people to be employed as teachers, but this was prevented by the teachers' organizations. Indeed, it is a universal experience that shortage of teachers and economic pressures induce governments to regard teaching as a low-grade job, or at least, to treat it as such.

Nor are the trained teachers of today invariably regarded as skilled practitioners whose skills should be used to the greatest possible effect and not be wasted on lower-grade tasks. Teachers are often overburdened with clerical work, keeping school meal accounts, issuing meal tickets, organizing medical and dental inspections, dressing and undressing children and performing many tasks that could easily be undertaken by others with less skill. This is economic folly as well as being demeaning to teachers. Here again, some local authorities, though a decreasing number, excuse themselves on the ground that financial stringency compels them to ask teachers to undertake unskilled work, even at the expense of skilled work.

So, is teaching a high-grade non-manual occupation? Teachers affirm that it is. More and more outside teaching agree, but the conviction, at least in governments and employers, weakens under stress.

## A Social Service

It is generally accepted that a learned profession provides a definite social service. Unlike those working in most industries, whose end-products are material and quantifiable, learned professions provide public services whose end-products are largely intangible and unquantifiable. In the debates preceding the Education Act of 1870, it was vigorously argued that teaching was a social service, and an essential one, too. Teaching ensured moral standards, provided better-equipped recruits for industry and the armed forces, and enabled democracy to function more efficiently. It must be admitted, however, that the results could not be expressed with statistical accuracy. Anyone in these days who has listened to an education debate in the House of Commons, or who has attended a school speech day, or a teachers' or an education committee's meeting or conference, could not seriously dispute that most people today think teachers are engaged in a very important social service. If this is a criterion of professionalism, there can be no doubt that in this respect teaching is a profession.

## Service as well as Remuneration

A mark of a learned profession is that it emphasizes duties more than rights. Doctors, whether they actually take the Hippocratic oath or not, are bound by it. This makes the well-being of the patient their prime consideration. The clergy generally think more of their work than their pay. Indeed, the pay is so meagre that it could not of itself attract sufficient recruits. Lawyers claim, and generally act on the principle, that the establishment of justice is their prime concern, and is more important than personal advantage. Thus to do right rather than what is profitable is an essential element in the concept of a learned profession.

For centuries these high standards have been expected of the clergy. Lawyers and doctors organized themselves on this basis in the nineteenth century. Their professional organizations guaranteed technical efficiency. They protected the public from the unqualified. They imposed ethical codes. They offered their services whenever and wherever they were needed and promised to give of their best at all times. They rejected the practices of the market place. They neither haggled over their remuneration nor engaged in advertising. They respected the confidences of clients. In these ways duties loomed larger than rights.

In the early days of professionalism, entrants had to show evidence of being a 'gentleman' as well as a 'scholar'. No doubt this was somewhat snobbish, for those who could not claim gentle birth were excluded. But gentle birth in itself was not enough: the entrants were also expected to be of good moral character so that they could later become truly professional in stressing duties. Less is said about these questions today, but morality and character are still demanded by the professional organizations from all their members. Human nature being what it is, however, few would expect each and every lawyer or doctor to observe these high standards at all times. Shaw, it would appear, had very low expectations, for he declared that when members of a profession met together, the meeting quickly degenerated into a 'conspiracy against the laity'. It is easy to accuse doctors or lawyers, individually or collectively, of self-seeking, but, even in these materialistic days, there are very many who still emphasize service rather than self. Tawney's definition of a profession is near the truth, so far as clergy, doctors and lawyers are concerned: 'a body organized, imperfectly indeed but genuinely, for the performance of essential duties'.

Of course, members of learned professions, like other people, think the labourer worthy of his hire. Individually and collectively they try to ensure that their financial rewards are adequate. Fortunately, for them, they seldom reach a deadlock with governments over remuneration. The political pressure they can exert is usually sufficient to secure a reasonable settlement, and so strikes are virtually unknown. The doctors' failure to reach agreements with the governments of Alberta and Belgium were rather exceptional. So nobody, certainly not I, would argue that doctors and lawyers ignore questions of material gain. Yet Tawney was right. There is still plenty of evidence that the learned professions are deeply concerned with the services they should render. But how do teachers feel about this moral element in professionalism? Do they, like doctors and lawyers, have a written professional code of ethics? Most teachers' organizations do, but the codes are not always rigidly enforced, and codes without supervision or sanctions are of very little value. Generally, the codes confine themselves overmuch to what teachers should not do. Usually they condemn certain acts which have a bad effect on other teachers. But the biggest weakness is that all the codes apply only to members of the organizations, and not to teachers generally. This is a great weakness.

Do teachers as a rule do what is right rather than what is profitable? In the main, just as with clergy, doctors and lawyers, the answer must be yes. The prospect of more money, rapid advancement or smiles of approval from those in authority do not persuade teachers in general to deviate from what they believe to be best in the interests of the child. Are teachers prepared to do more than their contracts prescribe? Are they willing to go the second mile? Of course, all must travel the first compulsory mile, being present and on duty during the prescribed hours and conforming to the regulations laid down. But many go beyond this and travel voluntarily the second mile. They strive in their own time to improve their expertise: they seek excellence in themselves and their pupils: they render exceptional service to those in special need, often in their own time and with no thought of recognition or reward. Do teachers recognize their obligations to their colleagues not only in their own school but everywhere? In the main they do, and more today than at any time in the past. Where their own theory or practice is in any way exceptional they feel under an obligation (and as professionals they should) to share their expertise with others, by writing in professional journals, lecturing, or having discussions with their colleagues in teachers' centres and inviting other teachers to their schools.

Francis Bacon, in his introduction to *Law Tracts* wrote, 'I hold every man a debtor to his profession, from the which as men do of course seek to receive countenance and profit so ought they of duty to endeavour themselves, by way of amends, to be a help and ornament thereto'. The attitude here described is that of many teachers. I freely but sadly admit it is not found in all. Yet it is an essential element in professionalism as I understand it. Many teachers must share my view, for were they not dedicated people, is it likely that the government, the local education authorities, and the public would allow them so much freedom of action in the classroom?

For years I have read teachers' magazines from all parts of the world. In no country have I discovered teachers enjoying so much academic freedom as they do in England and Wales. Her Majesty's Inspectors are more advisers than inspectors, wielding influence rather than power. The relationship between teachers and their employers is seldom the normal employer/employee relationship. Of course at times their interests do clash, but for most of the time teachers and LEAs form a real partnership in the interests of the children. So teachers are consulted on matters of policy and a real comradeship develops. Underlying this relationship is trust and a belief that teachers and authorities have a common interest in serving the child. Such a relationship could not exist unless teachers had a high regard for their duties. In this respect, teaching can be regarded as one of the great professions and in no way inferior to law and medicine.

## Advanced Education and Training

Another mark of a profession is that it demands a rigorous study of the theory and practice of the service concerned. No man or woman is admitted to the medical register unless he or she has followed a lengthy course of study in the theory and practice of medicine, surgery and obstetrics, and has obtained one of a number of prescribed qualifications. No man or woman is admitted to the register of barristers or solicitors unless he or she has followed a theoretical and practical course in the various branches of the law and has passed the prescribed bar or law society examination.

Teachers, however, until recently have been allowed to practise even when they had not followed a course in the theory and practice of education and had no professional qualifications. But when Mr Edward Short was Secretary of State in 1969 he decided that in future no man or woman would be permitted to teach in a publicly provided or aided primary or secondary school unless he or she had successfully completed a three-year course of study, including the theory and practice of education, or alternatively had successfully completed, after graduation, a one-year course on the theory and practice of education. Thus, in a short time the door to teaching will be barred to the untrained and the uneducated: it will be open only to the educated and trained. For more than a hundred years teachers have struggled to achieve this, and it had been a tough struggle, as a few illustrations will show.

In 1861 the Rev James Fisher, who later became Bishop of Manchester, told the Newcastle Commission,

Even if it were possible, I doubt whether it would be desirable, with a view to the real interests of the peasant boy, to keep him at school till he was fourteen or fifteen. . . . We must make up our minds to see the last of him, so far as the day school is concerned, at ten or eleven. ... I venture to maintain that it is possible to teach a child soundly and thoroughly ... all that is necessary for him to possess in the shape of intellectual attainment by the time he is ten years old.

The Commission adopted these sentiments and incorporated them in their report to the government, and the government's subsequent policies were based on them. Not unnaturally it followed that if a working-class child was to be denied a worthwhile education, the teachers of the working-class children had no real need of a worthwhile education themselves. So in the main training colleges accepted low standards. When Derwent Coleridge, the Principal of St Mark's Training College, broke with tradition and introduced a rather ambitious programme of academic studies in the two-year course, he was bitterly attacked for educating his teachers above their station. Indeed, in the nineteenth century the critics of the education service constantly complained that working-class children were being educated above the station in life to which they had been accustomed, or, as some said, which God had intended. Whenever teachers sought an improvement in their education, salary or conditions of service, they too were reminded they taught working-class children, came themselves from the working class and should not seek to rise above it. Thus, a lowly view of the function of the elementary education service, and a lowly view of what should be provided for children, inhibited the development of a sound education for all teachers.

Money was the other main cause of slow development. Education cannot be anything other than 'labour intensive', for it is a human service provided by people for people. Thus the cost of teachers' salaries must always loom large in educational expenditure. 'We have no choice but to employ teachers and highly qualified teachers would be expensive,' ran the argument, 'so let us make do with a few qualified teachers and make up the deficiency with the partially qualified and the unqualified'. So, even as late as 1911, 60,000 teachers with partial qualifications were employed and in many rural districts many were employed who had no qualifications at all. When I began teaching in Somerset in 1924, some of my colleagues were qualified, having attended a training college for two years; some were qualified, having passed an external examination whilst still employed as teachers, but having received no full-time training; some were uncertificated teachers, that is, they had never studied the theory and practice of teaching, but had merely obtained a school certificate; and some had no educational qualification and had followed no educational courses at all at secondary school or college level. In my first school the headmaster and I were the only trained and qualified teachers on the staff.

At the end of the Second World War, after a struggle between teachers and local authorities which provoked much bitterness, the Minister of Education decreed that no more uncertificated or supplementary teachers should be appointed or in other words, people whose only qualifications were a school certificate or something less, could no longer be admitted to schools as teachers. This was a great step forward. But unfortunately, both the government and local authorities feared that this decision would limit the flow of entrants into teaching, and would aggravate the already acute problem of the shortage of teachers. So the Minister decided that any man or woman who had the necessary qualifications (the school certificate or five GCE 'O' level passes) and who intended to train as a teacher but could not obtain a training college place, could be allowed to teach for a few years, whilst awaiting entrance to college. As these people were only to be recognized as teachers for a prescribed period, which varied from time to time, they were designated 'temporary'. In education, however, the word 'temporary' has a peculiar meaning. 'Temporary buildings' have remained in use for twenty or thirty years or even longer. 'Temporary teachers' were not always dismissed or required to train even when their period of temporary service was technically over. This led to much discontent amongst teachers generally, who thought the category of uncertificated teachers which had been abolished was reappearing under another name. Above all they wanted a trained qualified profession, with its concomitant, the rapid elimination of the unqualified.

One advance, however, was made in 1961. This was for a variety of reasons, one of which, to say the least, was dubious. For more than a hundred years the training college course had been limited to two years. It was a two-year course when children were leaving school at the age of ten, when all they were legally expected to learn was reading, writing and arithmetic, and when there was little or no knowledge of the psychological or sociological aspects of education or of child development. Thus, some of us argued, the course needed to be extended to enable teachers to gain mastery of some of the relevant modern knowledge and to apply it to the tasks of teaching. This was the soundest argument for the three-year course. But there was another dubious argument which, although supported by practical, economic and political reasons, was based on an assumption which was later proved to be false. The demographers had warned us that the birth rate would fall, that in the early 1960s the number of children in school would decline annually, and would then stabilize at a lower level. Obviously when the number of children in school falls, adminstrators have, broadly speaking, two choices. They can either improve the quality of the education provided by maintaining the output of trained teachers, reducing the size of the groups taught and increasing individual tuition, or alternatively, they can maintain the quality of education provided by reducing the supply of teachers and employing only as many as are needed to maintain teaching groups at their existing size.

The leaders of the authorities in the late 1950s, however, feared that local authorities generally would not seize the opportunity of reducing class sizes by welcoming every possible teacher recruit because of the heavy cost involved. So they argued that if the number of places in training colleges remained constant, an increase in the length of the course from two to three years would have the effect of substantially reducing the number of teachers produced and this would avoid the possibility of unemployment amongst teachers, which, to say the least would be politically embarrassing. Which of these arguments weighed most with the Minister only he could say, but he decided to increase the length of the course.

In a few years, however, it became obvious that the demographers had been very bad prophets. The birth rate refused to go down: it increased. So there was no alternative to the rapid expansion of colleges of education to meet the pressing needs of the schools. The colleges of education really deserve our sympathy. While they were still wrestling with the problems of the three-year course, the new problems of expansion were added. That they succeeded so well says much for the ability, devotion and patience of the principals and staffs. I have said before and I repeat, that the establishment of the three-year course was the most significant professional event in the whole of my career. It made training more meaningful and efficient. It necessitated bigger colleges with bigger staffs, which provided a wider range of expertise. It enabled the B.Ed. degree course to be developed.

I have already described how in 1969 Mr Edward Short, then Secretary of State for Education and Science (who, more than any other postwar minister, appreciated the teachers' professional aspirations) took the next logical step. He decided graduates must train and abolished the category of temporary teacher. The hopes of more than a hundred years have now been realized. In future all teachers will have received higher education and professional training. The unqualified will have been eliminated. No doubt it will be said that in length of training and in standards demanded the teacher's preparation does not equal that of a doctor, barrister or solicitor. I agree, but the preparation of the doctor is not equal to that of the barrister, nor that of the barrister equal to that of the solicitor. What is important is that all teachers will now have more higher education and knowledge of the theory and practice of teaching and that the unqualified will be fairly quickly eliminated. The fourth criterion of professionalism is thus met.

## Professional Freedom

Another mark of a learned profession is that the individual practitioner is free to act on his own within very wide limits, and without reference to others. Thus the doctor or the lawyer advises his patient or client and the layman plays no part. In the nineteenth century doctors and lawyers did not find this very difficult to achieve. Both enjoyed independent status. They were not employed by governments or local authorities. Indeed, they claimed to be self-employed. Their clients or patients sought their help and advice unasked, and their expertise was respected and usually accepted. They were the experts and were accepted as such. Teachers, however, are public servants and do not enjoy a relationship analogous to the pure doctor/patient or lawyer/client relationship. There is a teacher/pupil relationship, but parents, inspectors, managers and governors modify the relationship in ways unknown in medicine or law. That the relationships are different is obvious. The reasons are somewhat complex, but two are important. Teachers are public employees: lawyers and doctors (despite the development of the National Health Service) are still in the main self-employed persons, remunerated not on the basis of salaries but fees. Teachers, too, have an art which is less of a 'mystery' than medicine or law. All parents think they know something of education in a way they never claim of medicine or law. Yet there is an educational 'mystery' or expertise which is slowly being recognized. In time teachers may be able to persuade the public that their skill demands greater appreciation and this will dissuade amateurs from involving themselves in decision-making on those educational questions they do not fully understand and which really require professional expertise. For good or ill, however, it must be accepted that teachers are public servants, that they will remain public servants, and that this very fact creates problems unknown to the self-employed lawyers and doctors.

'Security of tenure', for example, has no meaning for a self-employed man, for his security does not depend upon tenure, but upon a constant demand from many people for services which only he can render satisfactorily. A teacher is in a different position. He has an employer. Under the Education Act of 1870, the teacher held office 'during the pleasure of the board'. It followed that when pleasure turned to displeasure, the teacher was reprimanded or dismissed, and sometimes for the most trivial reasons.

In 1871, in the first year of its existence, the National Union of Teachers fought a legal case against a vicar who had dismissed a teacher for no valid educational or professional reason. The case was by no means exceptional. It was not uncommon for teachers to be dismissed for failing to show due respect to their employers, for unwillingness to undertake duties which had no real connection with those of a teacher, for attempting to secure the regular attendance of children at school, or for buying provisions at shops other than those owned by managers. Against these unfair dismissals teachers collectively waged continuous war using every available weapon, reasoning with managers, publicity in the local press and, when it seemed appropriate, legal action.

The risk of unfair dismissal remained real until after the Second World War by which time local authorities and teachers, having resolved salary problems by negotiation during more than two decades, thought that tenure was also a subject for national negotiation. As a result a national tenure agreement emerged, which determined the dates on which notice should be given, the length of notice required and (most important of all) established machinery giving teachers the right of a hearing before dismissal. Only very rarely indeed today is there any complaint of the employers' abuse of power, and English and Welsh teachers enjoy a security of tenure few other countries can match.

Similarly, the right to take part in party-political activity outside his professional duties is peculiarly a teachers' problem, never shared by doctors and lawyers. For if doctors and lawyers wish to take part in politics, who can say them nay? Their patients and clients might not all agree with them, but it was seldom or never thought that professional practice and political action were incompatible. Many parents and managers, however, believed, and still do, that teachers should refrain from taking part in politics and some went further, demanding that they should be restrained from doing so. Even as late as 1926, during the General Strike, a teacher was imprisoned for publishing something alleged to be seditious. She was punished a second time for the same offence by the Board of Education, who withdrew her certificate and thus prevented her from being employed as a teacher in a publicly provided or supported school. During and after the Second World War, some local authorities, such as Bury and Southend, refused to employ conscientious objectors. In 1949 Middlesex decided it would not appoint a communist as a head teacher. The teachers' organizations fought as best they could against these decisions, but it is never easy for a professional organization to battle on behalf of an unpopular minority. Destroying prejudice takes time, so it was not surprising that in each case it took years to establish the right of a teacher to take part in politics should he so wish and without paying a professional penalty.

Yet in one respect, teachers' rights are not dissimilar to those of doctors or lawyers. Within the sphere of their own expertise in the classroom, surgery or office, they can all decide and advise. In the case of teachers, however, it should be added that their colleagues in the same school expect some co-ordination, as no doubt doctors do in hospitals. This right was not easily conferred: it emerged after a long and bitter struggle. In 1861

Robert Lowe issued what was known as the Revised Code, which determined that all existing monetary grants to schools should be abolished and a new one substituted – so much per child according to age and paid to the managers. No grant was payable for children over the age of twelve and (most important of all) a deduction was made for unsatisfactory attendance and for unsatisfactory performance in the annual examination in reading, writing and arithmetic set and marked by HMIs. This system was popularly described as 'payment by results'. Sir Robert Lowe claimed that the system ensured that if education were not efficient it would be cheap, and if not cheap it would be efficient. Teachers disputed his view of efficiency. They did not and could not dispute that the system would save money. In three years the amount spent on grants fell by twenty per cent.

Why were teachers so bitterly opposed to this system? Because they thought it unfair to themselves and the children. If the grant to their school fell, their salaries were adversely affected. They felt this unjust, and they argued that the results of an annual examination were not a fair assessment of the quality of their work. They felt it unfair to children too. 'Was it not unjust to children,' asked Mr J. J. Graves, a Northamptonshire village school master who subsequently became the first President of the NUT, 'to try to make all children equal in point of achievement?'

Of course, when a teachers' standard of living depended on examination results, he read the rules carefully and used every ruse to get good results. First, he ceased to take any interest in training pupil teachers. No grants were paid for them, so why bother? Secondly, he tried to eliminate absenteeism by sweet reason, cajolery, threats, or even punishment. Thirdly, he prepared lists (as he was required to do) of all those who by reason of some infirmity should not sit the examination, but he sometimes added some who should have sat, but whose results might have reduced the grant. In such cases carefully concocted reasons were added. Here the teacher's skill was surely tested, for if HMI accepted the reasoning, 'E' (exempted) was writtten beside the child's name and he did not sit the examination, but if the reasoning in any case were rejected 'NE' (not exempted) was written against the name, and then every child on the list sat the examination. Obviously, skill in advocacy paid dividends. Fourthly, and most important of all, he geared the work of the school to achieve examination results, regardless of the narrow nature of the instruction and the boredom and cruelty suffered by the children.

Matthew Arnold, HMI, unlike most of his HMI Education Department officials and School Boards, deplored this kind of education. In his Annual Report in 1869, he wrote:

I have repeatedly said that it seems to me the great fault of the Revised Code, and of the famous plan of *payment by results*, that it fosters teaching by rote: I am sure of that opinion still. I think the great task for friends of education is, not to praise *payment by results*, which is just the sort of notion to catch itself popular favour, but to devise remedies for the evils which are found to follow the applications of this popular notion.

Matthew Arnold saw clearly that it was possible to get children through the examination in reading, writing and ciphering without their really knowing how to read, write and cipher. He realized, too, how this was achieved. The reading test was conducted by asking each child to read 'a paragraph from a reading book used in the school'. What was easier than to make the children read and reread the same book throughout the year, until they virtually knew it by heart? Most of them would then be able to read a paragraph from that book, but possibly from no other. To conduct the writing test a sentence from a book in common use had to be slowly dictated to the child, who then had to reproduce the sentence with as few errors as possible. Here again, the same reading book was used to ensure a minimum of errors, but there was no guarantee that dictation from another source could be successfully done. Two sums out of the three set had to be worked correctly. What could be easier than to drill the children in the various operations just to get accurate results, without their understanding anything of arithmetical principles?

Thus, payment by results led to teaching for results, and for results only. The narrowness and sterility of such an education was vigorously condemned by teachers for more than thirty years. At last, others joined the teachers. In 1887 Mr Mundella, Vice-President of the Committee of Council (that is, roughly, Minister of Education) supported the teachers and in 1895 the system which had lasted thirty-four years was abolished by the enlightened Sir George Kekewich.

Only a few years later, in 1902, School Boards were abolished and their functions, including control of the curriculum, were handed over to county councils, county boroughs and the larger non-county boroughs and urban districts. All these authorities were new to educational administration. The county councils and county boroughs were busily engaged on secondary school development. Perhaps all the authorities felt themselves ill-equipped to deal with curricular matters, as indeed at that time they were. At all events, authorities generally, by accident or design, took little interest in the curricula and the responsibility had to be accepted by the teachers. This situation remained unchanged for more than half a century, until Sir David Eccles was Minister of Education. He saw clearly that the world was changing so rapidly that teachers needed some guidance on curricula and methods. When he decided that a curriculum study group should be established within his department fears of a centralized control of the curriculum were aroused. The local authorities saw in the proposal a diminution of their power. The teachers feared their liberty of action would be curtailed. So local authorities and teachers joined forces in attacking the proposal. The idea was then modified. All agreed some central body was needed to give advice. All ultimately agreed that the central body should be representative of the government, local authorities and teachers. Then under the wise guidance of Sir Edward Boyle, who had succeeded Sir David Eccles, a purely advisory body called the Schools Council was established, the teachers being in a majority in committees where curricula was discussed, and the local authorities being in a majority when finances were discussed. Though the Council is now taken for granted, it is a remarkable, indeed a unique institution. No other country has trusted its teachers sufficiently to establish such an advisory service. It is the envy of teachers elsewhere.

Thus it can be seen that because they are employed on different bases, the freedoms of the teacher are not and cannot be precisely the same as the freedoms of doctors and lawyers. Yet teachers have achieved freedom from fear of arbitrary dismissal, freedom to take part in politics, and freedom to choose text books and determine curricula, all of which are marks of a true profession.

### Largely and Wholly Self-Governing

The most distinctive mark of the great professions is that they are largely or wholly self-governing. The Law Society determines the standards expected of entrants to the solicitors' profession, the Bar Council to the barristers', the General Medical Council to the doctors'. The first two are responsible for the entrance examinations set: the last named decides what external examinations will be acceptable for registration. All are responsible for the discipline of their professions, being able to reprimand offenders or even prevent their practising. Here teachers fall short. They cannot set their own standards: they cannot prescribe courses of study or examine candidates for their profession: they cannot discipline their members nor banish transgressors. This is not really surprising. For (as has been shown earlier) little was expected from teachers of a truly professional nature in the past. Further, governments have traditionally determined who should be allowed to teach, and for a variety of reasons. One in particular is difficult to rebut. The government enforces attendance at school. It is therefore responsible for the quality of the education provided, so it determines who should teach and who should be refused that right. Doctors and lawyers have a different relationship to patients and clients, who voluntarily seek the aid of the professional. Thus, the learned professions, when establishing self-government, did not have to contend with a government which felt it was primarily responsible for the quality of service provided, and so was unwilling to take the risk of trusting completely the professionals.

Thus, to date, every attempt at teachers' self-government has always been baulked. In the nineteenth century teachers felt that a register of teachers should be established, as a sort of symbol of professionalism. I see little value in a register unless the government is prepared to employ registered teachers only, though I would agree that it is a small step to professionalism. Alas, not only were governments indifferent, they were often prejudiced against elementary teachers. Worse still, the teachers themselves were divided. In 1898 the Conference of Headmasters declared that in the register of teachers a distinction should be drawn between teachers and persons qualified to teach in elementary schools. Elementary teachers, for their part, insisted on one list for all teachers. At times legislation favouring a register for secondary teachers seemed imminent but the resistance of elementary teachers prevented action.

At long last in 1902, controversy between elementary and secondary schools subsided and the government allowed a register of all teachers with certain qualifications to be compiled. Subsequently the Royal Society of Teachers was established as the body in charge. In a short time, teachers became disillusioned with the Society, because registration had no effect upon employment, and hence had little meaning. Both registered and unregistered teachers continued to work side by side. The Society proposed that only registered teachers should be promoted, but the government and local authorities refused to allow even that small step towards professional self-government to be taken. At the end of the Second World War the funds of the Royal Society were virtually exhausted. The register still had no effect on employment; and when the Ministry of Education redefined qualified status, it was discovered that some registered teachers were not even qualified under the new conditions. So the activities of the Society ceased, while the existing rights of members were preserved. These included the right to wear a gown and to append the letters MRST to their names.

Teachers generally now turned their attention to achieving self-government, but every Minister approached rejected the request, until the arrival of Mr Edward Short. He set up a working party, chaired by an official from his Department and a representative of local authorities and teachers, to report on suitable machinery. There was no problem in handing over the power to eject members from the profession to teachers. This function is relatively unimportant and not very popular. But for reasons mentioned earlier, control over entrants proved the stumbling block. A compromise gave the proposed teachers' council some powers, but in the final analysis the power of entrants still lay with the Minister.

Obviously, teachers' self-government, irresponsibly used, could create a shortage of teachers and the shortage could affect adversely the quality of education provided and could also be used as an argument for higher salaries. So the government and local authorities were not prepared to trust the teachers with complete control over entry. Whether a general teachers' council will be established remains a matter of conjecture. I have seen no evidence that the present government has any enthusiasm for the idea. Local authorities at best are luke-warm, and teachers' organizations are, in some cases, very critical of the working party's report. So it is likely that hopes will again be deferred. Personally, I think it most unlikely that in the near future complete self-government for teachers will be revived as a real issue, and when it is I doubt whether any teachers' council will be given controls equal to those enjoyed by doctors and lawyers, at least at first. Teachers have advanced to the exclusion of unqualified entrants. But, in addition to the difficulty of handing complete control of the quality of education to teachers, internal conflict between teachers' organizations must make governments and local authorities wonder whether teachers can be trusted to work a general council in a socially acceptable way. The official statement issued by the Registration Council of the Royal Society of Teachers declared that 'unity is the first condition of progress towards a larger measure of self-government for teachers'. The lesson has not yet been learned. Thus self-government, the essential element in the concept of a learned profession, still eludes teachers, and teaching, judged by this criterion, is not a profession.

### Is Teaching a Profession?

Is then teaching a profession? Is it a high-grade non-manual job? It is now generally accepted as such. Does it perform a definite social service? It does. Does it emphasize duties as well as rights? Generally speaking, it does. Does it demand rigorous study of the theory and practice of education? From now on, it will. Does it allow the individual practitioner a substantial degree of freedom in his work? Yes, it does, but it needs other freedoms irrelevant to doctors and lawyers. And does it enjoy self-government? No, it does not, nor is anything approximating to it likely in the near future. So, granted the criteria I have established, teaching is a learned profession in most senses, but (alas) not in all.

# *Part 2*

## TEACHER EDUCATION IN THE UNIVERSITIES AND POLYTECHNICS

# CHAPTER 5

## From Day Training College to University Department of Education

JOHN TUCK

It is commonly supposed that the English and Welsh university departments of education have been mainly concerned with the training of teachers for secondary schools, but in fact they were founded as the second phase of the public provision of institutions for the training of teachers for elementary schools. The first phase, from the 1840s onwards, was the establishment of voluntary residential colleges, of which forty-three existed by 1890. The third phase, from 1903 onwards, was the establishment of local education authority colleges, both residential and day. Shortly before 1890 the newly founded university colleges, some of which had already provided part-time classes for serving teachers who were preparing for the certificate examination, let it be known that they were interested in the training of teachers. At the same time both Oxford and Cambridge expressed willingness to be associated with the new development, and by the end of the century all the universities and university colleges, eighteen in number, had established departments for the training of teachers for elementary schools.

The detail of how this came about is a fascinating story. The training of teachers before 1890 was based on the pupil teacher system, the final examination for pupil teachers being at the same time a competitive entrance examination to the residential colleges, the successful candidates being known as Queen's Scholars. Only about half the pupil teachers who completed their apprenticeship were admitted to the two-year courses at the residential colleges: the remainder entered the schools and while 'acting teachers' took their certificate examination, which was conducted by the Inspectors under arrangements made by the Education Department, as external candidates. Since, however, nearly all the colleges were religious foundations, mainly Church of England, the pupil teachers who sought entry to the colleges were mainly those who had been apprenticed in Church elementary schools. Those who had served in Board Schools, and who were used to undenominational religious teaching, had little opportunity of college training, except in the very small number of un-denominational colleges.

It was natural that the School Boards should be dissatisfied with this situation, and during the 1880s they proposed two new ideas, the first to concentrate pupil teachers for what amounted to secondary education in pupil teacher centres, and the second to establish their own colleges, which under the Elementary Education Acts they had no authority to do. The Birmingham School Board presented a memorandum to the Education Department in 1885 outlining a scheme for opening ten undenominational day training colleges, under School Board management, two in London and eight in other major urban centres, all to have some relationship with neighbouring university colleges. The scheme involved admitting students at the age of sixteen, after two years of grant-aided secondary education, for a two-year course followed by a year split between college and school and two years of probationary service. In 1887 a deputation including representatives from Nottingham and Newcastle upon Tyne attended the Department to urge a scheme in the local university colleges, while the Victoria University with colleges at Liverpool, Manchester and Leeds expressed willingness to embark on schemes in all three colleges.

The Committee of Council took no action until the Royal Commission on the working of the Elementary Education Acts (the Cross Commission) had reported.* The Commission was established in 1886, and was specifically empowered to enquire, among other things, into the pupil teacher system and the efficiency of the training colleges. The evidence of witnesses called before the Cross Commission provides a valuable cross-section of educational opinion at the time. The Commission did its work very thoroughly, interviewing the Secretary of the Department, senior Inspectors, representatives of university colleges, principals of training colleges, representatives of the Churches and of the National and the British and Foreign School Societies, and chairmen and secretaries of School Boards. The evidence given by the Inspectors was cautiously critical of both the pupil teacher system and the colleges: the Rev T. W. Sharpe pointed out that college places would have to be doubled if all students were to be trained; Matthew Arnold expressed a liking for the pupil teacher system, but wished to see the college course lengthened to three years and the colleges taken over by reconstituted local education authorities, while he was sceptical of the value of any contribution by the universities; both Joshua Fitch and H. E. Oakeley, who were the Inspectors of training colleges, favoured equally the scheme put forward by the Victoria University and one drafted by the Leeds School Board, both of which proposed the establishment of day training colleges in connection with university colleges, though the

* Final Report and three volumes of evidence of the Royal Commission on the working of the Elementary Education Acts, 1886–8.

Leeds scheme advocated maintenance by the School Board. Fitch was very doubtful about the value of any contribution which might be made by Oxford and Cambridge.

Professor Nathan Bodington, Principal of Yorkshire College, Leeds, and later Vice-Chancellor of the University of Leeds, stated that the college was willing to establish a teacher training department, with professional and some elementary teaching by a Master of Method, and with the opportunity for some students to take a three-year degree course. He pointed out that the college was already teaching a large number of acting teachers in part-time classes (as was also the case at Liverpool) and emphasized the quality of the courses which could be provided in a university institution. He also mentioned that ten or twelve other similar colleges were equally willing, thus revealing that a concerted plan had been worked out between the interested institutions. Professor Henry Jones, Professor of Political Economy at the University College of North Wales at Bangor, expressed himself in favour of two different schemes: that the university colleges should teach the more advanced subjects to students from neighbouring training colleges, as in Scotland, but that where no training colleges existed in the area of the university college, the university college itself should establish a day training department.

The principals of training colleges were unanimous in praising the religious, moral and practical discipline resulting from residence in a single-minded denominational community. Some of them (but by no means all) recognized the value of a three-year course for a minority of students (an experiment having been tried in the 1860s and abandoned because of the cost), while most of them were critical of the quality of the pupil teachers who were admitted and of the instruction they had received in the elementary schools. Few had anything good to say about the idea of setting up day training colleges in the universities, and the Rev Canon Daniel, Principal of St John's College, was unwilling to admit either the value or the possibility of establishing Chairs of Education in the universities. The Rev Canon Cromwell, Principal of St Mark's College, felt that a scheme to affiliate colleges to the universities would be valuable, and revealed that he had begun to negotiate an arrangement with the University of Cambridge, presumably to allow good students to migrate and obtain degrees.

The views of the representatives of the Churches varied. Canon W. P. Warburton of Winchester wished to see students from women's colleges attending lectures at Oxford from a boarding house to be established there, but was half-hearted about the idea of the universities undertaking training. The Ven J. P. Morris, Archdeacon of Bristol, was hostile to the idea of day colleges of any kind, while several non-conformist witnesses were strongly in favour of undenominational training and of the introduction of a conscience clause for students in the colleges: indeed one of them wished all the colleges to be taken over by the state. Most of the witnesses from the Churches and the religious societies wished the training system to develop and some even of the Church of England witnesses agreed that the number of undenominational colleges should be increased, but they all tended to feel that the lack of communal discipline would constitute a moral danger if day colleges were established.

The most uncompromising witnesses were the chairmen or secretaries of School Boards. Mr Lewis Williams, Chairman of Cardiff School Board, wished to see Queen's Scholarships made tenable at the three Welsh university colleges; Mr W. Lee, Clerk to the Leeds School Board, spoke in favour of the Leeds scheme already mentioned, while Mr Mark Wilks, a member of the London School Board, spoke in favour of undenominational day colleges attached to universities and stressed the value of educating teachers side by side with students going into other walks of life. Finally, the Rev E. F. M. MacCarthy, on behalf of the Birmingham School Board, introduced the ambitious scheme mentioned above (p. 72), which he had worked out in great detail and had costed very carefully. This scheme had the merit that it was aimed at running down the pupil teacher system, but had the disadvantage that it excluded the possibility of degree courses.

A number of other witnesses added points of great interest: a Scottish witness, Dr Thomas Morrison, Rector of the Free Church Training College in Glasgow, stated that sixty-four per cent. of his students attended classes at Glasgow University and that similar arrangements existed elsewhere in Scotland, though he was unable to say whether training college students attended Professor S. S. Laurie's lectures on Education in Edinburgh; Mr E. B. Sargent, Warden of Toynbee Hall, spoke strongly in favour of establishing training departments at Oxford and Cambridge; while Sir H. E. Roscoe, MP, FRS, spoke in favour of both the Birmingham and the Victoria University schemes, especially from the point of view of the value of the university classes in science.

Mr Patrick Cumin, Secretary of the Education Department, had been interviewed continuously for seven days in the early hearings and had written to the Commission protesting that they appeared to hold him responsible for policy decisions which had been taken by his predecessors in office. Why, he asked, had they not called his predecessors as witnesses since some of them were still available? Towards the end of the hearings he asked permission to be interviewed again on the subject of teacher training. He proceeded to produce a well-worked-out and fully-costed blueprint for the establishment of day training colleges in the universities and university colleges: this had evidently become Department policy while the Commission was in session.

It might be thought that the evidence in favour of substantial changes in the arrangements for teacher training was overwhelming, but the majority report of the Commission was cautious on this subject. They endorsed the view that residential colleges were the best, and that the pupil teacher system should be retained. On the subject of day colleges they concluded as follows:

> Considering the demand that already exists for more ample or generally available opportunities of training, and the importance of giving every facility for training to those who now obtain certificates without it; considering further, that such schemes as those submitted to us would, in their nature be tentative, that they would not involve a large outlay of capital, and would only be adopted when local circumstances seemed to invite the adaptation of some existing educational machinery to this purpose, we think it might be well that some such experiment should be made, subject to the condition, that only a limited number of students should receive government assistance towards their training.

It is clear from the context of the passage that Mr Patrick Cumin's scheme had carried the day, since it was specifically stated that no expenditure from the rates was envisaged. The School Boards were no doubt disappointed, and the universities gratified, but the decision seems to have been made on the grounds of cheapness rather than because the administration of the new day colleges would be more appropriately placed in the hands of academic institutions. The Commission added a number of conditions, that there should be some security for the moral and religious instruction of students; that there should be a separate governing body for the training department which would be responsible for the professional education of the students; that model practising schools should be made available; that the students should give some undertaking to serve as elementary school teachers, and that the supply from this new source should not exceed the demand.

A minority of eight members of the Commission, led by the Hon E. Lyulph Stanley, produced a dissenting report, advocating the generous introduction of three-year training, the introduction of conscience clauses in residential colleges, and the rapid expansion of the training system by instituting both training departments in the universities and training colleges established and maintained by School Boards. Five of this minority group in addition produced a minor report of their own, outlining their arguments in greater detail and criticizing the Commission's interpretation of the evidence before them. It should be added that the training of teachers was only one relatively small though important part of the Cross Commission's enquiry. Their Final Report advocated not only cautious experiment with university day training colleges, but also the extension of the pupil teacher centre system and the admission of day students, subject to a religious conscience clause, to the residential colleges, while they also expressed by implication the hope that more undenominational residential colleges would be established by voluntary bodies.

It could well be that an objection to recommending the establishment of training institutions by the School Boards was the feeling on the Commission that the School Boards might soon be superseded. The Local Government Bill of 1888 had been published before the Cross Commission's final report was drafted, and one member of the Commission (Sir Francis Sandford) drew up a memorandum which was published by the Commission indicating how the Local Government Bill might be amended in order that the new councils of the counties and the larger boroughs might take over the function of the School Boards. Thus the establishment of teacher training in the universities at the time when it took place could be attributed not only to cheapness, but also to the chance that the local government of education was in an uncertain state at the critical moment when the opportunity arose. Some importance must no doubt also be attributed to the influence of the Scottish example, though the Commission's recommendation went further than that by proposing actually to place the responsibility for the training of teachers in the universities. One must bear in mind that most of the Inspectors, administrators and clergy were themselves university men and felt that the time had come when the raising of academic standards in the schools required a new approach to the training of teachers: some of the Commissioners, to judge from their references to the training of secondary teachers, envisaged that if universities established elementary school training as a first step, the development of secondary school training would follow in due course; indeed the universities of Cambridge and London had already interested themselves in this matter by establishing certificate and diploma examinations for secondary teachers in 1879 and 1883 respectively.

Soon after the publication in 1888 of the Report of the Cross Commission it became known that the Committee of Council had accepted the recommendation that day training colleges should be provided in university institutions, and some university colleges sent preliminary proposals to the Department. The regulations for the training of teachers at this time formed part of the Elementary School Code, and the Code for 1890, issued in 1889, contained important, if brief, modifications to incorporate the new institutions in the system. The definition of a training college, hitherto a residential institution, was altered to permit day colleges, which 'must be attached to some University or College of University rank', to be recognized. The authorities of the day college must be 'a local committee who will be responsible for the discipline and moral supervision of the students and for their regular attendance at professional and other lectures', and a limit of

200 was placed on the number of day students who could be recognized as Queen's Scholars. (This was removed a year later.) Colleges were to propose to the Department the number they would admit, and maintenance grants of £25 for men and £20 for women, with tuition grants of £10 were authorized. The length of the course remained at two years, the syllabuses and regulations for the certificate examination remained unaltered, and the requirements of a medical certificate of fitness and a declaration of intention to teach in an elementary school were unchanged.

In May 1890, however, the Department issued Circular 287, which contained special instructions for the day training colleges, in considerable detail, and it was on the basis of applications framed in reply to this Circular that the university colleges' final proposals were considered. The Circular laid down that students must be full-time, and resident either at home or in a house kept or lodgings approved by the local committee, that the private study of the students must be supervised, that a 'normal master or mistress' must be appointed to lecture on the history and theory of education, to supervise teaching and to give a course of model lessons and preside at criticism lessons, that a practising school or schools must be approved by the Department, and a time-table similarly approved, while a register of attendance at lectures must be kept and made available for the Inspector.

It might appear that the Department intended to control and organize the work of the new day colleges as closely as it controlled the residential colleges; but there was an important difference, for on the academic side the day colleges were free not to follow the Department's syllabuses or to take the Department's examinations, provided that copies of the syllabuses and the worked papers were sent to the Department. This was the germ of an academic independence which the residential colleges also were eventually to enjoy. The subjects to be taken differed little from those laid down for the residential colleges. All students had to take and pass examinations in arithmetic and mathematics, English, geography and history; tests were set by Inspectors in reading and recitation, practical teaching and (for women) needlework and domestic economy, with music as an optional subject. Examinations in drawing and science subjects could be taken in connection with the Department of Science and Art and extra grants earned in this way. The regulations listed political economy, languages and sciences as optional, but in practice no doubt it was assumed that, as in the residential colleges, most students would take two science subjects or two languages or one of each, unless they took political economy.

It will readily be seen that in a university college opportunities existed for the day training college students to attend degree classes in mathematics, the sciences and sometimes in classics, history and one or more modern languages: but there were some colleges in which English and geography had not yet been established and many in which music and art were not taught. The addition of a day training department in a university college therefore provided it with a strong incentive to improve its staffing to cover as wide a range as possible of the subjects required by student teachers, and in some colleges with a bias towards scientific and technical subjects this amounted to a substantial development of the arts faculty. But where the existing resources of the university college were inadequate, or where the teacher training students required more elementary instruction, the staff of the training department undertook it, so that in addition to the professional subjects of school management and teaching method, Masters and Mistresses of Method were found teaching arithmetic, needlework, drawing, music, English and geography, and visiting teachers of domestic economy were employed.

The Inspectors watched the new departments very closely, as indeed they had to since they were responsible for part of the examinations, and throughout the thirteen years from 1890 to 1902 they issued detailed printed reports on the work of the departments. The fact that the students were taking courses leading to university examinations in some subjects and that a few were aiming at graduating, led to a change in the Code for 1891, whereby a third year of training was reintroduced for selected students, and this applied to both residential and day colleges. In addition the syllabus was divided into Part I, the professional subjects, which included practical teaching, the art, theory and history of teaching, singing, drawing, needlework for women, and elementary English and arithmetic, and Part II, which included mathematics, the sciences, English, elementary geography and history, languages, political economy and domestic economy for women. University examinations were recognized in Part II subjects, but the Department's examinations were required in Part I subjects. A one-year course had previously been available in the residential colleges only for teachers who had taken the certificate externally, but in 1891 a one-year course was permitted also for graduates and students holding advanced university qualifications, and this became one of the two prototypes of the present training year, though the students at first had to take all the subjects of Part I. This course was intended for elementary school teachers, but there was nothing to stop the day colleges from accepting similar students for one-year courses of training for the secondary schools, as some of them soon did, though in very small numbers. The secondary students took the Cambridge certificate or London diploma externally, until other universities established their own diplomas. Students taking these secondary courses would not at this date qualify for grants, but the courses represent the other prototype of the present training year.

The Inspectors were dissatisfied with the examinations in some Part II subjects in the very first year of the new scheme. They complained that students were taking college examinations specially devised for them by the training department, whereas the intention had been to recognize only the formal university examinations set by the academic departments as part of the degree course. The Department therefore instituted a special general paper in English, geography and history, for students whose college did not provide a genuine university examination in these subjects. The syllabus for the third year allowed students to take two groups from English, mathematics, a group of languages and a group of sciences, so that they could graduate either in arts or in science or take a combined course if one was available.

This system has been described in some detail, because it obtained without substantial change until 1904, five years after the Committee of Council was replaced by the Board of Education, and traces of it lingered even until 1926. The comments of the Inspectors show a general appreciation of the academic opportunities offered in the university classes, of the value of the liberal education provided, and of the opportunity of mixing with other students which the new departments offered. They looked forward to the possibility of adding secondary to elementary training in the universities, and hoped that the residential colleges where possible would develop connections 'with neighbouring institutions of higher academic rank'. Three difficulties arose quite early. One was the unsatisfactory arrangements for the residence of students. This difficulty led to the movement to establish halls of residence in university colleges which had originally been established as entirely day institutions. The second difficulty was connected with practising schools. The university colleges could not be expected to set up model grant-earning elementary schools on the lines of those established as 'demonstration schools' by most of the residential colleges, since the university colleges, unlike the training colleges, were not maintained by bodies which also provided schools. In practice, however, it was found that the School Boards were very willing to co-operate by providing practising places in appropriate neighbouring schools. The third difficulty was connected with the conflict which arose quite early between the academic and the professional studies of the students. They were taught in two different atmospheres concurrently and in some institutions the degree work led to a neglect of professional studies, while in others students who were scarcely capable of it were encouraged to take degree courses when a more elementary course would have been more suitable. On the other hand the Inspectors were impressed by the development of educational studies, expressing their appreciation of the courses in logic, ethics, mental philosophy, and the history of education which were provided in the new institutions, some of which established Chairs of Education in the early years. An interesting detail is that many university colleges allowed the day training college students to enter degree courses at reduced fees, it being assumed no doubt correctly that former pupil teachers would be poorer than the other students.

The first colleges which applied for recognition as day training centres were obviously very well prepared, for between May and September 1890 Mason Science College, Birmingham (established in 1880), University College, Nottingham (1881), University College, Cardiff (1883), Owens College, Manchester (1851), King's College, London (1829), The Durham College of Science, Newcastle upon Tyne (1871) and Firth College, Sheffield (1879) all applied and were accepted, though Sheffield had no students in the first year. How the other colleges obtained Queen's Scholars at such short notice is something of a mystery, although it is possible that some of them withdrew from places at residential colleges or from teaching posts. Birmingham accepted only women until 1896, Manchester only men until 1891, and King's, London, only men until as late as 1925: the other colleges accepted both men and women. In 1891 the Sheffield course started and day training colleges were also recognized in 1891 at Cambridge, University College, Liverpool (1881), and Yorkshire College, Leeds (1874). Cambridge accepted only men, a secondary school course for women being already available at the Cambridge Training College, established in 1885. It was not until 1949 that the two institutions were combined. Liverpool and Leeds accepted only men, women being admitted for the first time in 1896 at Leeds and in 1900 at Liverpool.

In 1892 day training colleges for men were opened at Oxford and at University College, London (1826) and for women at University College, Bristol (1876) and Bedford College, London (1849). A secondary department for men and women was opened at Oxford in 1897 and the two institutions were combined in 1919. The day training college at University College, London was closed in 1896 and the remaining students transferred to King's College; men were admitted to a separate training college at Bristol in 1905, and the two institutions were finally combined, together with a secondary training department which had come into existence in 1902, in 1920. The department at Bedford College, London, appears to have confined itself shortly after its establishment to secondary school training, and was finally closed in 1922. Also in 1892 a mixed day training college was established at the University College of Wales at Aberystwyth (1872).

Finally, the first phase of foundations was completed by the establishment of mixed day colleges at the University College of North Wales at Bangor (1884) in 1894, at Reading College (formerly the University Extension College) (1892) in 1899, at Hartley Institution, Southampton (1862) also in 1899, at the Royal Albert Memorial College, Exeter (1893) in 1901, and by the establishment by the London County Council of the London Day Training College in association with the University of London in 1902.

Thus within twelve years twenty new institutions had been established, of which eighteen are still in existence.

The scale of operation of the day training colleges was modest in the early years, as the figures in Table 5.1, compiled from the Annual Reports of the Committee of Council, show.*

Table 5.1

| Year | Student Numbers | | |
| | First Year | Second Year | Third year |
| --- | --- | --- | --- |
| 1891–2 | 233 | 164 | — |
| 1892–3 | 322 | 128 | 14 |
| 1893–4 | 359 | 343 | 59 |
| 1894–5 | 384 | 367 | 55 |
| 1895–6 | 355 | 397 | 62 |
| 1896–7 | 413 | 374 | 54 |
| 1897–8 | 465 | 428 | 63 |
| 1898–9 | 495 | 457 | 98 |
| 1899–1900 | 593 | 505 | 98 |
| 1900–01 | 635 | 596 | 124 |

One needs to bear in mind, however, that during these years there were only from 3,400 to 3,700 students in the residential colleges, and that the day training colleges were already, after ten years of work, providing nearly twenty-five per cent. of the training places. The small numbers of third-year students reveal the comparatively low percentage who graduated, though it is possible that some few able students graduated at the end of the second year, and a few others may have done so after attending part-time courses during the early years of teaching.

When the regulations were altered in 1891 to permit students in training colleges to take university examinations as approved alternative examinations for Part II of the certificate, students at the residential colleges as well as the day colleges were permitted to do so, provided an arrangement could be made with an appropriate neighbouring university. Arrangements were in fact made by a considerable number of colleges with the University of London and by a few with the Victoria University and the University of Durham. By 1900 467 students in the residential colleges and 252 students in the day colleges entered for the university examinations, 223 of the residential college and 217 of the day college students being successful. It must be remembered, however, that they were not all

* Source: *Annual Reports and Appendices of the Committee of Council on Education 1889–98. Annual Reports. Appendices and Statistics of Public Education.* Board of Education, 1899–1901.

candidates for final degree examinations. The matriculation examination was commonly taken by first-year students, the intermediate examination (first year of the degree course) by second-year students, but those who were candidates for degrees would need to be a year ahead of the others, since they would take their final degree examination in the third year. The figures given above are quoted by Asher Tropp in *The School Teachers* (Heinemann, 1957, page 169) as if all the students were candidates for final degree examinations. Of those in the residential colleges 267 were first-year students and 180 second-year students. The number of third-year candidates was twenty, of whom twelve were successful and these are probably the only ones who graduated. Similarly in the day colleges, there were only ninety-eight third-year students so that it is unlikely that more than sixty or seventy graduated. A pass in the certificate could be granted to those who failed university examinations, while some third-year students no doubt took the Department's examination.

An important aspect of the development of the training of teachers in the universities is the extent to which the study of education became a university discipline, and the rate at which Chairs of Education were established. Scotland had established two Bell Chairs at Edinburgh and St Andrews in 1876, held by S. S. Laurie and J. M. D. Meiklejohn. Interestingly enough the first Chair in England and Wales was established in Wales in 1895 at Aberystwyth and was held for a year by Henry Holman, who then joined the Inspectorate. He was succeeded by Foster Watson, who was at first appointed as a lecturer, but was promoted to the Chair in 1896. Foster Watson's work in the history of education was outstanding and his remains one of the great names in educational studies (Armytage, 1961). The second Chair to be established was also in Wales, at Bangor in 1894, and was held for twelve years by J. A. Green, a Sheffield graduate who returned to be the first holder of the Chair at Sheffield in 1906. Green is well known as the author of standard works on Pestalozzi. The third Chair of Education, and the first in England, was established by the University of Durham at the Durham College of Science in Newcastle upon Tyne in 1895, and the first holder was Mark R. Wright, whose outstanding contribution was in the practical work of running a good department, though he published a few science text-books and was first Chairman of the Training Colleges Association (now the ATCDE) and Editor of the *Training College Record* (now the *British Journal of Educational Psychology*).

In 1899 both Manchester and Liverpool established Chairs of Education. That at Manchester was held for three years by H. L. Withers, a historian whose untimely death was a great loss to educational studies. He was succeeded in 1903 by J. J. Findlay whose publications on education were authoritative and monumental. In 1903 Manchester also established a second Chair, held part-time for eight years by Michael Sadler, later Vice-

Chancellor of Leeds, who was one of the greatest educationalists of a great era, and whose work as head of the Department of Special Reports at the Board of Education has left a documentary record of comparative studies in education at the turn of the century which is of inestimable value. The Chair at Liverpool was held by W. H. Woodward whose pioneer works on the educators of the Renaissance are still a delight to the scholar.

In 1902 a Chair of Education was established at the London Day Training College, where John Adams produced an outstanding series of works on educational theory (Rusk, 1961); while in 1903 Chairs were also established at King's College, London, held by J. W. Adamson, probably the most distinguished English historian of education (Barnard, 1961), at Birmingham, held by Alfred Hughes, and at Exeter, held by A. W. Parry.

There were of course contributors to educational studies in other universities which did not establish Chairs, for instance Oscar Browning and R. H. Quick at Cambridge, and a great deal of patient and perhaps now forgotten teaching was provided by lecturers and tutors with school experience who were also scholars and built up the traditions of their departments by sacrificing the fame of publication to the versatile teaching demanded by their students. It is significant that the most outstanding work was done in the history of education, where the discipline and the material lay to hand: for a great deal of experimental work and analysis of concepts was necessary before a similar achievement either in psychology or in philosophy would prove possible.

The Board of Education* lost no time in the years between 1899 and 1904 in tidying up and reforming the administration of education, and in 1904 the arrangements for the training of teachers were clarified and considerably altered. The Report of the Royal Commission on Secondary Education (the Bryce Commission) in 1895 had emphasized the need to extend the training of secondary school teachers, a view echoed in the Inspectors' reports before 1900, and from 1903 onwards the Board interested itself in secondary training. The expansion of secondary education which was envisaged in the 1902 Act, and the tendency to raise the school leaving age, meant that many of the problems which the Cross Commission had faced in the elementary schools still awaited solution in both the elementary and secondary systems. The remedy was obviously to encourage the new local education authorities to establish training colleges, while at the same time trying to induce them to supersede their pupil teacher centres by providing a satisfactory secondary education; and to encourage the university departments of education to expand secondary training. In 1899 the Code was altered to permit students who had passed the higher or senior local examinations or university matriculation examinations to enter both the residential and the day colleges. The monopoly of the former pupil

* Board of Education, Parliamentary Papers containing Regulations, 1903–1918.

teachers was thus at last broken. In 1901 Circular 454 asked the colleges to draw up their own courses of study to operate from 1903 onwards, although since the certificate examination was still open to acting teachers the Board continued to publish its own syllabuses.

The relationship between elementary and secondary training is one of the most confusing aspects of the history of the training of teachers in the universities. The movement to introduce training for secondary school teachers began, as has already been mentioned, by the institution of examinations for their benefit, though the College of Preceptors was in fact in the field ahead of the universities. The first colleges established for the purpose of training secondary teachers, Maria Grey and the Cambridge Training College, were for women, and both institutions took the Cambridge certificate. One college established in London for men lasted only three years. But the training institutions for women were soon supplemented by two more, attached to girls' schools, namely Cheltenham Ladies' College and Mary Datchelor School.

When, therefore, the universities had established their own training institutions for elementary school teachers, it was a natural development for them to provide courses also for secondary teachers. But the early provision which was made was piecemeal, the number of students was small, and the secondary school students were either trained in separate departments, sometimes under only one tutor, or in separate groups in the same department. It is important to realize, too, that secondary students were not all graduates, nor were their courses always of one year's duration, though a year was the normal period required for the professional part of the course and the teaching practice. Many of the secondary students had, like the elementary students, further studies to make in the subjects which they were preparing to teach, and like the elementary students they took these subjects in the university under the guidance of the education department, although by no means all of them reached final degree standard.

In 1903 the Board issued a list of departments recognized for secondary training, which included Oxford, Cambridge, Durham (i.e. Newcastle upon Tyne), Birmingham, Manchester, Liverpool, Leeds, Bangor, Cardiff, Aberystwyth, Bristol, and Bedford College, London, among university institutions, together with the celebrated women's institutions already mentioned, the Cambridge Training College, Maria Grey College, Cheltenham Ladies' College and Mary Datchelor School, and three Roman Catholic Colleges. No grants, however, were yet made available for secondary students, but the universities of Oxford, Birmingham, Durham, and the Victoria University all established diplomas for secondary teachers by 1903. The Durham qualification was first instituted as a certificate as early as 1895.

The slow growth of secondary training can be attributed partly to the absence of grants for students, and partly to the reluctance of the authorities of secondary schools to accept the principle of training. It must be remembered that few secondary schools were provided and financed from public funds until after 1902. Over the years, as the university colleges developed and most of them became full university institutions, and as standards rose, it became possible to require all students accepted for secondary training to have obtained university degrees. As has been pointed out already, since the regulations from 1891 onwards allowed elementary students to take one-year courses if they entered the training department after passing certain university examinations (not all final degree examinations), there were two different kinds of one-year course, the secondary course for university certificates or diplomas, and the elementary course for the Board's examination, which included curriculum as well as professional subjects. The one-year professional courses could not supersede the concurrent course, however, until the majority of the elementary students were capable of passing university examinations, since it had always been assumed that the possession of either a teachers' certificate or a university qualification was a necessary requirement for admission to so short a professional course: and it was only after some years of development that the one-year courses became truly postgraduate.

In the early years of the century, with rising standards, the universities saw the opportunity gradually to move out of two-year training, though the change was to take years to complete. In 1901 the Welsh colleges and the colleges of the Victoria University (Manchester, Liverpool and Leeds) decided that all students admitted to their day training colleges should be of degree calibre. In the same year, in order to reduce the pressure of the three-year concurrent course, Birmingham, the Victoria University, and the Welsh colleges introduced education as a subject which could be taken in degree courses, and Durham followed later (for Newcastle students). No doubt this move was aimed also at improving both the prestige and the standard of educational studies.

Changes in the preliminary education of teachers introduced in 1903 deferred the age of entry to pupil teachership until sixteen (although it was later relaxed to fifteen) in order to encourage intending teachers to complete at least a two-year period of secondary education. In 1907 the bursary system was introduced, to encourage intending teachers to stay on at secondary schools until the age of eighteen, though much of the final year could be spent as a student teacher in elementary schools. In other words an attempt was made to divert at least the supervised studies of pupil teachers from elementary to secondary schools, although it was a long time before the change was fully effective. The result, however, was that the universities could draw more and more on applicants for teacher training who had at least matriculated and many of whom had stayed on at

4—EOT * *

school until seventeen or eighteen. This made it easier to select only potential graduates, and indeed the regulations as early as 1905 had encouraged the day training colleges to do this.

The Regulations for the Training of Teachers, which had been removed from the Code and issued separately in 1903, were redrafted, co-ordinated and substantially changed in 1904, and provided with a brilliantly clear introduction by R. L. Morant. The distinction between residential and day colleges was abolished, and at the same time the requirement that a day college must be attached to a university institution was dropped. This removed the anomaly that some of the so-called day training colleges were in fact residential, at least for some of their students, since they had, under encouragement from the Education Department, established their own hostels; and it also allowed local education authorities to establish day colleges. It was also made possible for a training college to be 'a department of a higher education institution', i.e. of a secondary school or even (though no cases arose immediately) of a technical college. The distinction between Part I and Part II subjects was removed, making the regulations consistent with the examination of education as a degree subject, and making it possible at last for approved alternative examinations in the professional subjects to be recognized. Training colleges not attached to universities were encouraged to set up in association with the Inspectors and independent examiners their own Joint Boards of Examiners, and the role of the Inspectors as examiners was much reduced. The Board evidently did not expect all colleges to abandon the government syllabuses, for the regulations print five alternative syllabuses in education, graded in difficulty, the best of which would stand comparison with many present-day syllabuses. Hygiene was included for the first time in four of these syllabuses. A distinction was made in the regulations between a three-year student and a third-year student, the former attending a university department and taking a degree course, the latter taking what became known later as a supplementary course, and between a certificated and a one-year student, the latter being either a graduate or a student who had passed certain university higher or senior local examinations.

One-year elementary students were henceforward expected to devote themselves mainly to professional training, with a reduced number of subjects; while three-year students were still required to take courses in some of the former professional subjects, such as reading, drawing, music and needlework, but in others, such as history, geography, elementary English, mathematics and science, proof of adequate instruction on entry, i.e. matriculation or its equivalent, was accepted.

In the Regulations of 1905 all applicants for degree courses were required to have passed a school leaving examination or to have obtained a distinction in the preliminary examination for the certificate (which had replaced the former Queen's and subsequently King's Scholarship examination). At the same time notice was given that all applicants for one-year courses from 1908 onwards would have to hold degrees or equivalent qualifications. In 1907 the conscience clause was extended to all colleges, emphasis was given in the regulations to the importance of manual training and hygiene, and physical training was made a compulsory subject. In the following year a compulsory test in physical training was introduced, hygiene became a compulsory subject, and day colleges were required to provide hostels for women students.

The first Regulations for the Training of Teachers in Secondary Schools appeared in 1908, offering grants of £20 per student for any number of students between five and thirty. The Regulations stated that secondary departments must be separately provided but could be part of another institution, that all the work must be professional, that the teaching of one branch of the curriculum must be specially studied, that the course should be of one year's duration, should include sixty days of teaching, and that only graduates or holders of equivalent qualifications should be accepted.

A curious episode happened in 1909. The Board made religious instruction a compulsory subject in all training colleges, only to withdraw the regulation (no doubt under a storm of protest) in the following year. It is difficult to imagine what the university departments of education, which have never, with the possible exception of King's College, London, had any denominational attachment, would have made of this regulation, although many of their students have studied divinity, and some of them have followed Method courses in religious knowledge. But the fact that it remained possible to introduce new compulsory subjects by regulation is significant. Although the Board claimed to have given the colleges and the university departments (as most of them were now called) more freedom, the regulations were still used to enforce a curriculum which made unreasonable demands on students taking the three-year concurrent elementary school course. The addition of hygiene and physical training required special staff and the glaring contrast between the professional courses of the secondary students and those of students preparing for elementary schools was clearly a source of future trouble.

The Board had its remedy. In 1911, instead of adding another chapter to the Teacher Training Regulations, it added as if by stealth to the annual *Statement of Grants available from the Board of Education in aid of Technological and Professional Work in Universities in England and Wales* a completely separate set of regulations for four-year courses of teacher training. It is possible that the regulations were included in this document in order to prevent their being automatically available to the university colleges and the non-university training colleges, although this could have been achieved in the ordinary regulations, which in any case referred to the four-year arrangement. The four-year regulations laid down that the first three years were to be devoted to degree studies and the final year to professional studies. The professional course remained the same as for three-year students, including the principles and practice of teaching, hygiene, physical training, reading and repetition, and singing; drawing and needlework could be omitted if candidates were good enough in these subjects, and music could be omitted if candidates were 'incapable'. The final year's examination was to include tests in most of these subjects. The major departure from the three-year regulations was that extra courses in English, history, geography and elementary mathematics were abandoned, but a course in elementary science remained.

Obviously these arrangements were a great improvement on the three-year concurrent course, although many departments used the undergraduate years and the vacations to cover introductory teaching practice and some of the professional subjects. A relaxation of the arrangements occurred in 1913 when training college subjects were classified into professional, general and additional, two standards, ordinary and advanced were introduced, and it was conceded that it was no longer necessary for all students to continue the study of all subjects. In the same year the four-year regulations were published as an appendix to the normal Teacher Training Regulations and from then on formed a separate chapter; the three-year concurrent course, however, was not formally abandoned until 1926.

A re-issue of the Secondary School Training Regulations, also in 1913, removed the limits on numbers of students and formally recognized secondary schools as training institutions, while in 1915 provision was made for the colleges (including of course university departments), if they wished, to delegate all responsibility for teaching practice to a secondary school or schools. It may well be that this was a result of wartime staff shortages, but it is also possible that it recognized the strong feeling on the part of secondary school staffs that they had a valuable contribution to make to training. The fact that payment was involved, at the discretion of the college or department, no doubt made the arrangement popular.

The period from 1902 to 1914 was one of rapid expansion of numbers, but the only new college to be established which ranked as a university institution was Goldsmiths' College, London (1905), which was originally a two-year college. The figures shown in Table 5.2 give some idea of the rate of expansion of student numbers, and draw attention to the very small numbers taking secondary courses.*

* Source: *Annual Reports, Appendices and Statistics of Public Education*, Board of Education, 1901–1914.

Table 5.2

| | Student Numbers | |
| | Elementary | Secondary |
| --- | --- | --- |
| 1901–2 | 1,426 | — |
| 1902–3 | 1,607 | — |
| 1903–4 | 2,196 | — |
| 1904–5 | 2,292 | — |
| 1905–6 | 2,811 | — |
| 1906–7 | 2,050 | — |
| 1907–8 | 2,132 | 168[1] |
| 1908–9 | 2,648 | 188 |
| 1909–10 | 2,762 | 199 |
| 1910–11 | 2,954 | 163 |
| 1911–12 | 3,196 | 199 |
| 1912–13 | 3,015 | 216 |
| 1913–14 | 2,944 | 180 |

[1] Figures were not collected for earlier years.

During the same period, the numbers in the non-university colleges rose from 4,000 to 9,000 and so the universities' contribution, having risen to about thirty per cent., fell off again to twenty-five per cent., and to a slightly lower proportion in terms of output as the proportion of three-year students increased.

Although the number of institutions remained relatively static, staff numbers increased; yet the records of a few sample departments suggest that all the departments remained desperately poorly staffed, one or two senior people carrying an enormous burden of teaching and administration. The only new Chairs established during this period were at Leeds, where J. Welton, author of an interesting attempt to relate logic to educational studies, became Professor in 1904, at Nottingham, where A. Henderson was appointed in 1905, and at Cardiff, where two Chairs were established in the same year, T. Raymont, who was shortly succeeded by R. L. Archer, being appointed to one, and Miss H. M. Mackenzie, the first woman to hold a Chair of Education, to the other. Cardiff had two further women as Professors, Barbara Foxley who moved from Manchester in 1915, and served for ten years, and Olive Wheeler, who united the men's and women's departments at Cardiff in 1925, as Miss H. M. Wodehouse had already done as the first Professor at Bristol in 1920. Sheffield established a Chair in 1906, to which J. A. Green, already mentioned, moved from Bangor: and Sheffield also solved the problem of the two-year course by the drastic operation of handing it over, together with the Mistress of Method, Mrs Henry, to the city local education authority college in 1905.

The period between the First and Second World Wars saw the establishment of four more university departments of education, at Swansea in 1921, Durham (the Durham Colleges) in 1922, Leicester in 1929, and Hull in 1930. A Chair was established at Swansea immediately and was held by F. A. Cavenagh, who later moved to Reading as first Professor in 1934, and then to King's College, London, two years later. At Durham also Arthur Robinson was appointed immediately to a Chair.

The period saw the appointment of a number of men, many as second holders of Chairs, who were to achieve eminence as educational scholars: C. W. Valentine at Birmingham in 1919, Godfrey Thomson at Newcastle upon Tyne in 1920 (Vernon, 1962; Duff, 1969); T. Percy Nunn at the London Day College in 1922 (Tibble, 1961), G. H. Turnbull at Sheffield in 1922, John Dover Wilson at King's College, London in 1924 (Wilson, 1969), Cyril Burt at the London Day College in 1924, Frank Smith at Newcastle upon Tyne in 1925, James Duff at Manchester in 1935, Fred Clarke at the London Day College in 1936, while Charles Fox at Cambridge and M. W. Keatinge at Oxford did distinguished work, though neither university had established a Chair of Education. Although historians and literary scholars still figured amongst professors of education, the second generation produced psychologists who developed a new discipline in educational studies, and whose new techniques made an immediate contribution towards solving some of the problems of selection and assessment.

The four-year course in the departments of education was well established in the years from 1918 onwards, and the three-year concurrent course gradually died out. An important change in 1918 allowed students taking the four-year elementary training course to transfer, if they obtained honours degrees, to the secondary postgraduate course in their final year, and from then on there was a tendency to bring the two courses for the final year together, although the distinction between them in the regulations was not finally abandoned until 1926. It did not of course follow that no departments continued to make different provision for the two groups of students. In 1920 four-year courses were permitted at the residential training colleges and in a number of cases, at Birmingham, Leeds, London and Durham, arrangements were made for college four-year students to take degrees at neighbouring universities. It should be mentioned, too, that four departments of education, those at Exeter, Nottingham, Southampton and Reading continued to provide only two- and three-year courses for some years after most departments had completely changed over to the four-year system. These were the only remaining university colleges, their students taking

London degrees, and they were not recognized for four-year courses until 1926, in which year the University of Reading was established, thus automatically entitling its department to offer four-year courses, while in the same year the Board of Education decided to permit four-year courses in university colleges, thus bringing Exeter, Nottingham and Southampton within the four-year arrangements. They continued to provide two-year courses, however, until 1933, and no doubt some of the two-year students took a third year in order to complete their degrees. The University of Birmingham, also, appears to have prolonged its two-year training much longer than other universities.

In 1925 the training colleges throughout the country were warned that the Board's examination would cease after 1927 (though in fact it went on until 1930), and between 1927 and 1929 nine area Joint Boards based on the universities, in which the departments of education played a prominent part, were established to conduct training college examinations. The Joint Boards set up subject committees to draw up syllabuses, and ultimately drew up their own general regulations. For some colleges, which had individual or smaller group Joint Boards under earlier arrangements, this new system meant a loss of independence, but for those who still took the Board's examination it was a welcome change. The Regulations of 1922,* which continued in force until 1926, still gave minute guidance as to the subjects to be studied in courses of all kinds. The Board, however, by this time had already made arrangements whereby the university departments did their own examining in the professional subjects, with the single exception of the final assessment of a sample of students on teaching practice. It was an easy change therefore in 1926 to abandon the whole complex apparatus of regulations and required subjects, leaving the initiative and responsibility for the design and examination of courses from then on in the hands of the university departments and the Joint Boards. The simple formula in the Regulations reads: 'Courses must be in accordance with a suitable curriculum and must include the principles and practice of teaching and satisfactory arrangements for examining.' Down to 1926 the Regulations have the 1904 pattern: from then onwards they assume the general and brief pattern which still applies today. The training of teachers did not escape the consequences of the economic crisis which beset the country in the early 1930s: in 1932 tuition grants were reduced by £3 per student as part of a national economy drive, and in the following year, since student numbers had increased rapidly, it was decided to cut the admission of students to the university departments by ten per cent. After protests it was decided to spread the cut over two years.

The figures shown in Table 5.3 illustrate the growth in numbers between

* Board of Education, Statutory Rules and Orders containing Regulations, 1919–39.

Table 5.3

| | Elementary Students | Secondary Students | | Four-Year Students | One-Year Students |
|---|---|---|---|---|---|
| 1914–15 | 2,716 | 237 | 1926–7 | 4,907 | 499 |
| 1915–16 | 2,356 | 214 | 1927–8 | 4,981 | 498 |
| 1916–17 | 1,946 | 126 | 1928–9 | 5,164 | 632 |
| 1917–18 | 1,991 | 115 | 1929–30 | 5,406 | 695 |
| 1918–19 | 2,614 | 144 | 1930–1 | 5,663 | 834 |
| 1919–20 | 4,348 | 225 | 1931–2 | 6,462 | 861 |
| 1920–1 | 5,128 | 258 | 1932–3 | 5,526 | 882 |
| 1921–2 | 4,743 | 485 | 1933–4 | 5,243 | 696 |
| 1922–3 | 4,877 | 670 | 1934–5 | 4,949 | 679 |
| 1923–4 | 4,593 | 636 | 1935–6 | 4,608 | 703 |
| 1924–5 | 4,531 | 811 | 1936–7 | 4,622 | 730 |
| 1925–6 | 4,602 | 917 | 1937–8 | 4,577 | 720 |
| | | | 1938–9 | 4,558 | 670 |

1914 and 1939, and reveal the effect of the ten per cent. cut.* Beside these figures should be set the fact that numbers in the non-university colleges rose from 9,000 to 12,000 between 1914 and 1920 dropping to just under 10,000 in 1939. In terms of numbers of students in training, therefore, the universities' contribution rose from twenty-five per cent. to about thirty-three per cent., which, allowing for the fact that the four-year course was well established in the 1920s, would mean that in terms of output they were still providing about one-quarter of the nation's trained teachers; and a high proportion were employed in the elementary rather than the secondary schools.

It must be borne in mind that the four-year course was, like the three-year concurrent degree and training course before it, grant-aided on condition that the student became a teacher though no longer specifically in an elementary school – and that the Board of Education preserved the right to control the number of students admitted. This of course indirectly affected the size of the undergraduate population, since even taking into account the growing number of local education authority grants for highly qualified candidates for university admission, the students accepted for teacher training probably formed the largest single group of students at the universities.

In the years before the Second World War the four-year system itself

* Source: *Annual Reports and Statistics of Public Education*, Board of Education 1914–1939.

in turn produced its own tensions, because of the contrast between the freedom of the student with a local authority award to choose his own occupation, and the obligation of the four-year student to complete his training and become a teacher. The final-year group in an education department consisted of two types of student: those who were there by free choice, and those who had made a declaration of intention to teach mainly in order to obtain a university course and so were under an obligation to complete their training; some of these no doubt did not regret their original commitment but others were uneasy about it. In 1907 the Board of Education had tried to make the declaration a legally enforceable contract, while the 1921 Education Act sought to do the same: and this problem was not finally resolved until after the Second World War.

In the period of freedom from the Board's regulations from 1926 onwards, the final-year professional courses in the university departments of education took on the form which many of them continued to have until comparatively recent years. The school management and theory of teaching courses were differentiated into separate subjects known as principles of education, the history of education, hygiene or health, educational psychology, and the methods of teaching. The elementary school professional courses in music, drawing, physical training and handwork tended, at different rates in different departments, to become perfunctory extras, in some cases entirely voluntary, though compulsory physical training lingered on in some places for a long time. The 'recitation' or 'repetition' element in the early courses tended to become 'speech training', sometimes associated with drama, and needlework and domestic economy disappeared. Some departments retained drawing only in the guise of blackboard practice, though in others voluntary art in a variety of media was still taught, and in at least one department music remained merely as a course in the appreciation of music. Physical training was supplemented by games courses and camps in some departments in quite early years.

The relationship between education departments and the departments in which the teacher training students took their degree courses called for close co-operation at the point of admission, but from then on, except for the minimal requirements of extra courses and vacation teaching practice, the education department merely kept in touch with the student's progress, deferring its major concern with him until the final year. The relationship between the departments and the schools – and by the 1930s practice in secondary schools was as common as in elementary schools, many students having the advantage of both – was close and cordial, whether or not the responsibility for the practice rested mainly with the school. Just as from 1926 onwards it would be difficult to distinguish elementary from secondary training, so it would be impossible without a great deal of detailed enquiry to find out how many students from the university departments went into elementary and how many into secondary schools, and in the 1930s when unemployment was a real risk, many served in both, starting in elementary schools, and moving later into secondary schools.

In conclusion, it is clear that the establishment and development of teacher training in the universities* was the result of a close partnership between the central government and the university institutions, many of which achieved full university status during the period we have been considering. It was a partnership with advantages on both sides: it brought more students and new subjects and a close relationship with the schools to the universities, while to the central authority it meant an upgrading and liberalizing of the whole training system. The principle that teachers should have their secondary education alongside those not intending to teach was slowly gaining ground from 1902 onwards, but was not finally implemented until the late 1920s. The other principle, that teachers should have their higher education alongside those students who are preparing to enter other occupations, which was recognized as a worthwhile goal in 1886 and perhaps even earlier, was realized gradually for a growing minority of students in the period from 1890 until 1939; but it still remains to be realized for the teaching profession as a whole. A special feature of the developments we have been studying is that all the universities took part in them, for all presumably recognized not only that there was a contribution which they alone could make, but also that in the long run there is value in an association between a seat of learning and the humblest elementary school in the land.

* For accounts of individual departments of education see:
 i. *The Department of Education in the University of Manchester 1890–1911* (containing also a brilliant essay by M. E. Sadler on the day training colleges), University of Manchester Press, 1911.
 ii. University of London Institute of Education: *Studies and Impressions 1902–52*, Evans Bros., 1952.
 iii. *The Education Department through Fifty Years*, University of Reading, 1949.
 iv. *The Training of Teachers at a University*. D. W. Humphreys, University of Bristol, unpublished typescript.
 v. *The Origins and Development of the Training of Teachers in the University of Newcastle upon Tyne*, J. C. Tyson and J. P. Tuck, Department of Education, University of Newcastle upon Tyne, 1971.
 vi. 'Oxford University and the Training of Teachers, 1892–1921', L. Tomlinson, *British Journal of Educational Studies*, Vol. XVI, No. 3. 1968.

CHAPTER 6

# The University Departments of Education: their Work and their Future

JOHN TUCK

When full activity in the departments of education was resumed after the Second World War they were still providing for two kinds of student, the four-year grant-aided student who had decided to enter the teaching profession on admission as an undergraduate, and the one-year student, also usually granted-aided, who had decided to become a teacher in his final undergraduate year. The one-year students consisted of those who had held state scholarships or local education authority awards for their undergraduate years, and of a further temporary group of ex-service students who on discharge from the forces had taken up 'Further Education and Training' awards for their undergraduate courses, some of which had been shortened to two years because of the war. All the one-year students had decided to take training voluntarily; for, although before the war graduates had been required to train if they wished to be recognized as certificated teachers in the elementary schools, the reorganization of schools following the 1944 Act and the consequent disappearance of the elementary schools had strangely enough resulted in the freedom of graduates to teach untrained in all kinds of school: of course, training had never been a condition of service for graduates in the prewar secondary schools. The shortage of teachers was so severe in the early postwar years that a considerable number of graduates sought and obtained posts without training not only as before in grammer schools, but also in the newly reorganized primary and secondary modern schools.

This situation raised two problems of policy: the first was whether it was desirable to continue the four-year grant system when the number of students who obtained unconditional grants for undergraduate courses was rising rapidly and the schools were appointing them to teaching posts freely without training; and the second was whether a training requirement should not only be restored for service in the primary and secondary modern schools, but also instituted for the first time for service in the grammar schools. The National Advisory Council on the Training and Supply of Teachers, established as part of the postwar reorganization of education, recommended in 1948 both that the four-year grant system should be discontinued and that a training requirement for graduates should be introduced. The Ministry of Education acted on the first recommendation, the last four-year students being admitted in 1950, completing their courses in 1954, with a few who had missed a year or two going on until 1955 or later. An announcement had been made by the Ministry of Education as early as 1945 that a training requirement would ultimately be introduced, and in 1948 the date 1951 was actually mentioned, but the matter was deferred for the incredibly long period of twenty years presumably because of fears that compulsory training would adversely affect the supply of graduate teachers. The university departments of education were kept in a state of suspense, wondering whether and when they would have to plan for a large influx of students, and whether the money to expand staff and enlarge buildings would be available. Ultimately, after a later report of the National Advisory Council had recommended 1969 as a suitable date, it was decided to introduce a training requirement for graduates in primary schools in 1970, and in secondary schools in 1974.

The graduates of postwar years had a choice, not (like their prewar predecessors) between elementary and secondary school teaching, but between primary, secondary modern and grammar school teaching. The number who chose primary and secondary modern schools was by no means negligible, though the majority of those who chose primary school teaching took their training courses in the colleges of education. As specialized teaching in the secondary modern schools developed, the demand for graduates grew, so that it can be said that the university departments of education have never lost their original connection with the elementary schools and the institutions which succeeded them, i.e. the secondary modern and later the comprehensive schools. The advent of comprehensive schools in recent years of course removes the need for a choice between secondary modern and grammar school teaching, but requires the graduate teacher to be more versatile in adapting his subject matter and methods to a wider ability range.

The removal, through the abolition of the four-year course, of any influence by the education departments on the choice of undergraduate courses by their students meant that a considerable number of graduates began to enter training courses who had degrees in 'non-school' subjects, such as philosophy, sociology, psychology, law, agriculture and some of the applied sciences. This tendency was a valuable one in increasing the variety of the subjects in which graduate teachers were qualified to make a contribution, but it also meant that the education departments were in no position at the point of admission to encourage students to take degree courses in subjects which were in demand in the schools, and in which there was a shortage of teachers. Mathematics and physics are obvious examples. The four-year arrangements had the advantage that the number of places in degree courses available for intending teachers could be controlled.

Student numbers during the immediate postwar years rose rapidly,* making up for the lost years of the war; but they settled down afterwards to a steady rate of increase until the planned expansion following the Robbins Report between 1964 and 1970, when a rapid rate of increase was resumed. During this period the university departments of education were unable to finance expansion to meet the demand, and the Department of Education and Science decided to expand graduate training in the colleges of education instead. The origin of this policy is hard to establish: it was put forward by the ATCDE for the benefit of the colleges at a time when they were disappointed at having to offer eighty per cent. of their places to intending primary school teachers, in order to meet the staffing demands of the primary schools. It appeared to be a way of developing high-level academic work in institutions which were academically ambitious, but in fact it offered the opportunity for higher-level work in education alone; the only way of fostering more advanced work in the other subjects would have been to develop degree work, in the tradition of the period from 1900–30, from a basis in the certificate course. This is of course the opportunity offered by the B.Ed. degree, established in 1966 as a further outcome of the Robbins Report (Robbins, 1963). It may be that the move to develop graduate training in the colleges came also from local education authorities (though voluntary colleges also participate in the work) and was motivated in part by a desire ultimately to concentrate all teacher training in the hands of employing authorities. This desire has been apparent in various policy documents issued by the Association of Education Committees and in the proposals of certain local education authority members of the National Advisory Council; and it has appeared in evidence† to the Robbins Committee and more recently‡ the James Committee (James, 1972). In a sense it is a move to undo the decision of 1890 (discussed in the previous chapter), and to establish a system more closely resembling that which obtains in Scotland.

* Statistics of Education, 1947–69. Ministry of Education and Department of Education and Science.

† Evidence of the following bodies to the Robbins Committee, published in Volumes of Evidence: Conference of Heads of University Departments; Association of Education Committees; the ATCDE.

‡ Evidence of the following bodies to the James Committee, published in pamphlet form: Universities Council for the Education of Teachers; ILEA (Appendix to Report No. 1 of the Further and Higher Education Sub-Committee, 12 May 1971); the ATCDE.

Table 6.1

| Year | Four-Year Students in Professional Year | One-Year Students | Total | Year | One-Year Students |
|---|---|---|---|---|---|
| 1938–9 | 1,140 | 668 | 1,808 | 1957–8 | 2,902 |
| 1941–2[1] | 553 | 237 | 790 | 1958–9 | 3,112 |
| 1942–3 | 541 | 267 | 808 | 1959–60 | 3,500 |
| 1943–4 | 566 | 246 | 812 | 1960–1 | 3,432 |
| 1944–5 | 605 | 337 | 942 | 1961–2 | 3,155 |
| 1945–6 | 535 | 363 | 898 | 1962–3 | 3,203 |
| 1946–7 | 1,035 | 1,058 | 2,093 | 1963–4 | 3,339 |
| 1947–8 | 1,212 | 1,147 | 2,359 | 1964–5 | 3,642 |
| 1948–9 | 1,454 | 1,169 | 2,623 | 1965–6 | 3,612 |
| 1949–50 | 1,356 | 1,334 | 2,690 | 1966–7 | 3,850 |
| 1950–1 | 1,324 | 1,562 | 2,886 | 1967–8 | 4,197 |
| 1951–2 | 1,223 | 1,890 | 3,113 | 1968–9 | 4,633 |
| 1952–3 | 1,079 | 1,942 | 3,021 | 1969–70 | 4,648 |
| 1953–4 | 932 | 1,876 | 2,808 | 1970–1[2] | 4,929 |
| 1954–5 | 271 | 2,447 | 2,718 | | |
| 1955–6 | 82 | 2,500 | 2,582 | | |
| 1956–7 | 69 | 2,624 | 2,693 | | |

[1] No figures available for 1939–40 and 1940–1.
[2] Provisional.

It raises anew the issue of whether the universities should engage directly in the training of graduate teachers: whether the work could be better done, or more appropriately done, by some other agency, and a fuller discussion of this important issue will be found later in this chapter.

Tables 6.1* and 6.2† illustrate the development of the university departments of education in the period from 1938 onwards, showing the rundown of the four-year course, the growth of graduate training in the colleges of education and the increase in the entry of untrained graduates into the schools. It should be borne in mind that the period from 1946 to 1950 was one of rapid expansion of general university student numbers,

* Source: *Annual Reports and Statistics of Education.* Board of Education 1938–1944, Ministry of Education 1945–62, Department of Education and Science 1963–70.
† Source: *Annual Reports and Statistics of Education,* Ministry of Education 1952–62, Department of Education and Science, 1963–69.

Table 6.2

| Graduates in Training in Colleges of Education | | Entry of Graduates (Untrained) from Degree Courses into Maintained Schools | |
| --- | --- | --- | --- |
| 1952–3 | 269 | | |
| 1953–4 | 242 | 1958–9[2] | 1,181 |
| 1954–5 | 204 | 1959–60 | 1,364 |
| 1955–6 | 210 | 1960–1 | 1,472 |
| 1956–7 | 219 | 1961–2 | 1,534 |
| 1957–8 | 276 | 1962–3 | 1,409 |
| 1958–9 | 340 | 1963–4 | 1,302 |
| 1959–60 | 314 | 1964–5 | 1,373 |
| 1960–1 | 296 | 1965–6 | 1,356 |
| 1961–2 | 340 | 1966–7 | 1,611 |
| 1962–3 | 385 | 1967–8 | 1,620 |
| 1963–4 | 501 | 1968–9 | 1,670 |
| 1964–5 | 591 | | |
| 1965–6 | 558 | | |
| 1966–7 | 655 | | |
| 1967–8 | 976 | | |
| 1968–9 | 1,424 | | |
| 1969–70 | 1,845 | | |
| 1970–1[1] | 2,781 | | |

[1] Provisional.    [2] Figures for earlier years are not available.

that from 1950 to 1958 they rose slowly, and that from then on the rate of increase was so rapid that the university population was doubled in ten years.

During the period from 1947 to 1961 the annual output from the colleges of education of two-year students rose from 6,800 to 13,000, from 1963 to 1969 the annual output of three-year students rose from 12,500 to 25,000, so that the output of the university departments of education fell at first to about twenty per cent. and later to seventeen per cent., figures which it is interesting to compare with the somewhat higher percentages of the total number of students in training which were given in the previous chapter for earlier years.

The decline in the number and still greater decline in the proportion of graduates taking training courses from 1952 to 1957 can be directly attributed to the abolition of four-year grants, though it may have been slightly offset by the untrained entry into the schools, for which figures are not available. The comparatively low figures in the early 1960s, however, are fully offset by the untrained entry, and on the whole the proportion of university graduates entering the teaching profession has in recent years remained sufficiently constant to make predictions of future entry reasonably reliable. There are however signs that a decisive increase in the proportion will have taken place in the years 1970 and 1971.

The question which arises in a time of rapid expansion of numbers is whether the universities can accommodate greatly increased numbers of graduates seeking training. Since they have accommodated them as undergraduates, there seems no good reason why they should cease to do so when the students require a kind of professional training which the universities have traditionally provided. The issue of expansion raises the question of the optimum size of an education department, just as it raises the question of the optimum size of the university itself. There is no doubt that university departments of education, which need to be staffed with Method specialists in all the school subjects and with specialists in all the branches of professional studies, and which have to be staffed in proportion to the number of students, can be more efficiently and economically staffed when student numbers reach the level of 250 or 300; and the opportunity generally to reach this size in the last few years has unfortunately been missed. Only two departments, Leeds and the London Institute, have 300 or more students; five, Oxford, Cambridge, Cardiff, Nottingham and Leicester, are in the region of 250, and the average size is about 180.

The period from 1950 to 1970 will in retrospect be seen as the third phase in the increase in the number of university departments of education, for in 1950 the foundation of the University of Keele was accompanied by the establishment of an education department with an entirely new approach: the institution of a four-year concurrent degree and diploma course; and since 1963 departments which offer postgraduate training have been established in the following institutions: the University of Sussex (established 1961), the University of York (1963), Bath and Brunel universities (former colleges of advanced technology, which became universities in 1966), and the Chelsea College of Science and Technology (which became a constituent College of the University of London also in 1966). Brunel and Chelsea admit only graduates in science. In addition Chairs of Education have been established at the Universities of Warwick (1965), Aston and Loughborough (both former colleges of advanced technology which became universities in 1966), and although these three universities are embarking on the undergraduate teaching of education, they have not yet undertaken postgraduate training. At Warwick there is a joint degree course in education and philosophy or mathematics, and at

Loughborough a four-year joint sandwich course in education with engineering or mathematics, while at Bath and Aston education is offered as a component of certain four-year sandwich degree courses. In all three of the last-mentioned universities, the four-year course includes professional training, which in the case of Aston is taken at a college of education.

Whereas in the period from 1900 to 1930 it was possible to say that every university had established a department of education, the recent increase in the number of university institutions has been characterized by two different attitudes to educational studies. Some universities, of which Essex and Kent are examples, have not established education departments at all, while other universities, like Bradford (1966), Lancaster (1964) and Surrey (1966), have established research departments in education (in the case of Surrey limited to educational technology) or, like East Anglia (1964), a department with a limited teaching function (in this case in chemical education). Lancaster, however, offers certain undergraduate courses in education, while Surrey offers a four-year sandwich course of which the education and professional training components take place at a college of education.

No explanations of the assumptions behind these policies have as far as is known been published, but in two cases (Kent and Lancaster) recently founded Church of England colleges of education exist in the area, and are presumably intended to fulfil the role of a training department for the university, while it is understood that Warwick has an arrangement with Coventry College of Education, Aston with St Peter's College, Saltley, and Surrey with Gipsy Hill College. In all these cases the opportunity of establishing a Chair of Education tenable in a college of education was missed. The only university so far to establish such a Chair is the University of London, which has recently done so at Goldsmiths' College. This was facilitated by the special relationship which exists between the university and the college, which is close enough for Goldsmiths' to be regarded as an exception to the general rule that the universities have relinquished their interest in the direct provision of non-graduate teacher training.

The result of the fact that a few universities have no interest in teacher training is that by implication some universities are understood to be saying that this is not a university function: and graduates of the universities in question, having no 'home' education department, are forced to seek places in the departments of other universities or in colleges of education. This is not a situation which can be regarded as satisfactory in the long run in the interests of proper co-operation between universities and schools, unless the colleges become integral parts of the universities.

Those new university foundations which have undertaken the training of teachers have made a valuable contribution to experiment in the combination of degree and training courses. The concurrent four-year course at Keele, already mentioned, was the pioneer. Not surprisingly, the experiment encountered the difficulty from which the three-year concurrent course of the early years of the century, discussed in the previous chapter, had suffered. The existence of the Foundation Year at Keele meant that the four-year course for a degree and a diploma in education was largely concentrated in the three following years, with the difficulty that teaching practice had to take place in university vacations. The idea of combining full professional studies with a degree course has not been fully worked out and established elsewhere, although as mentioned above, four of the former colleges of advanced technology are interested in it, and may well find that the sandwich principle, with release from university courses for periods of teaching practice, will solve the problem.

The inclusion of education in the subjects which may be taken in a degree course, however, is a different matter. This is the principle of the novel arrangements at the University of York, which provides a specially organized postgraduate year, with two terms of teaching practice, for students who have taken education as an undergraduate subject. The University of Warwick, as mentioned above, is beginning to experiment with this idea (and possibly others are doing so too). As was stated in the previous chapter, it was an expedient adopted by a number of the nineteenth-century foundations in the early twentieth century. It was subsequently abandoned by most of them, probably for the good reason that it reduced the time available for the study of other subjects and was thought to be incompatible with the special honours degree. The University of Wales, however, has continued to provide undergraduate courses in education, except at Swansea, though apparently they are not taken by large numbers of students and are in no sense a substitute for postgraduate training. Similar arrangements existed some years ago in the ordinary degree courses in both arts and science at the University of Sheffield. An interesting development of recent years is the establishment of a one-year education tripos at Cambridge, which may be taken as a Part II following a two-year Part I in another subject or subject group, provided that the student has qualified by intercalating in his third year to take the course for the certificate in education. This is a by-product of the arrangements made for the B.Ed. degree for the colleges of education, and it remains to be seen how attractive it will prove to Cambridge undergraduates. But it is an interesting feature of this arrangement that the normal postgraduate training course is built into it.

The developments which have been mentioned must suggest to the universities which confine their teaching of education to the postgraduate year and to advanced courses, that at least they should re-examine the desirability of undergraduate teaching in this subject. One way of compensating for the lack of time available in the postgraduate year would be to provide a preliminary course in education in one of the undergraduate years, preferably the final year, for those who have by this time decided to enter the teaching profession. But another device could be adopted to achieve the same purpose, and that is to prolong the study of education into the probationary year of teaching, establishing what amounts to a two-year period of training with a higher proportion of work in the schools. It will be remembered that the training of teachers in its early years was built on the pupil teacher system, so that all students entered the colleges with prior experience as teachers. The student teacher system associated preliminary practice as teachers with the final years of secondary education, and the concurrent three-year course in the colleges of education associates it with the whole process of higher education. Under the four-year grant system preliminary teaching experience was often gained in the vacations of the undergraduate years, but in recent years the postgraduate training system has relied on teaching practice concentrated in the one year of training, except for those few departments which still require their students to undertake a preliminary period of teaching practice in the long vacation preceding the beginning of their training course.

It would seem a natural development to extend the postgraduate training period by a further year, including in the whole course a total amount of teaching practice equivalent to about one year, thus gaining time for a more thorough study of education and more continuous and satisfactory practice in the schools. Proposals to this end have been made from time to time in, for instance, the evidence of the Conference of Heads of University Departments of Education to the Robbins Committee, and of the Universities Council for the Education of Teachers to the James Committee, while some interest has been expressed by the organizations of headmasters, and a small-scale experiment was tried at the University of Newcastle upon Tyne. The principle of extending training into the first year of teaching has in fact been accepted in the Report of the James Committee, though in a form which removes unity from what the committee call the 'second cycle'. In the long run it may be recognized that to extend training to include the probationary year is likely to be a more constructive development than to include educational studies in undergraduate courses.

An interesting and unrecorded chapter in the history of education is the change in the subject matter and organization of courses in education in the university departments during the period 1950–70. These changes have happened as a result of staff discussions and the development of courses by interested lecturers and have in general not been reported in journals or regarded as new contributions, yet they have influenced the courses in the colleges of education and have revolutionized the nature of educational studies. It would not be a caricature to describe the average university department of education course in the immediate postwar years as being on the whole uniform for all students, with compulsory papers in the history of education, the principles of education, educational psychology and methods of teaching. The major difference between such courses and those of the 1930s would be the dropping of health or hygiene and physical education as compulsory subjects.

The first important change, of which there were some signs in prewar days and during the war, was the emergence of social studies, often called sociology of education, as a major separate subject of study. The second was the subdivision of the subject called the principles of education into courses in educational thought, or in the theory of education, or in fundamental philosophical ideas applied to education, and of courses in school organization and in elementary educational administration. Similarly educational psychology tended to be subdivided into separate courses on the theory of learning, child development and the applications of mathematics to testing and examining (often called mental measurement). In many departments courses in health returned in connection with studies of the School Health Service and the education of handicapped children, while the history of education was frequently subdivided into the history of educational institutions on the one hand and of educational ideas on the other. Comparative education was also frequently introduced as a separate study, and in some departments speech was studied as a separate and important aspect of the work.

The effect of subdividing the subject matter of educational studies in this way was to make it possible to teach more advanced material and to enable courses to be offered by lecturers who had made a special study of the subject and had research experience in it. It became impossible to require all students to take all subjects, and increasingly departments offered their students a choice of options or special subjects instead of a uniform course. In some places, the lecture courses became even more specialized and numerous than has been indicated, and were grouped in order to require students to cover a reasonable variety of subject matter, some topics being chosen from a psychological or social and others from a philosophical or historical group of courses.

Since variety of this kind was less easy to develop in the colleges of education there was a tendency for their courses (and perhaps those of some departments of education too), to be based on the view that there are four major disciplines in educational studies, philosophy, history, psychology and sociology, and to require all students to take general courses in all four. This has been the basis of a number of B.Ed. syllabuses, but it has had the unfortunate consequence that studies in the health and physical development of children have been reduced, comparative education has found little place, while educational administration, the law of education and school organization (all important studies) have not readily fitted into this pattern: and Method courses have been less fully developed in the colleges than in the departments.

In the departments of education during the same period the study of methods of teaching, normally undertaken in separate subject divisions, of which most departments require students to take two, has been substantially changed. First, the philosophy of each subject and its place in the curriculum are generally studied, secondly, practical work in connection with each subject, carried out in rooms specially equipped for the purpose and with separate laboratories for the sciences, serviced by technicians, is now the common practice; thirdly, the amount of time devoted to this work, which was formerly one period per week, has been substantially increased. In special subjects like primary education, art education, music and physical education the amount of practical work is exceptionally large, and the same is true of drama in the few places where it is offered as a separate course. It should be added, however, that all these subjects are more fully covered in specialized courses in some of the colleges of education and in the graduate art teacher training centres; four of the latter, however, are incorporated in university departments of education.

At the same time the approach to examining has been radically changed. The University of Bristol department of education gave up a formal examination as long ago as the 1920s, and Leicester moved in the same direction soon after the Second World War. The growth of the system of options chosen from a long list of specialized courses makes the normal three-hour examination paper unsuitable, and a large number of departments now examine by means of essays or other written exercises instead. In some the long essay or dissertation has been used for many years.

In conditions like these, with the growing specialization of the teaching of education, and professionalization of subject teaching with large collections of material and apparatus with which the student has to become familiar, the old system of employing versatile members of staff who could turn their hand to everything cannot survive; and for adequate provision the large department is essential. Even within one subject or subject group it is frequently necessary to appoint more than one member of staff to cover all the necessary specializations: for instance, in work in English, specialization in the teaching of the language is sufficient to occupy one lecturer, while drama, if it forms part of the English course, calls for specialized attention, and English at the primary stage, including the teaching of reading, is also a specialized topic.

Enough has been said to illustrate the fact that postgraduate courses have changed remarkably in recent years. The same may be said of the approach to school practice. Greater care than was taken formerly is observed in allotting students to schools, in ensuring that they make preliminary visits and are well prepared when the practice begins. Relationships with schools are closer, and more schools are appointing both general and specialized subject supervisors of students (frequently called teacher tutors) while shared appointments between departments and schools are becoming more common. The departments are exploring the further development of co-operation between training institutions and schools in ways which would make it a comparatively easy step to institute a two-year course with shared responsibility between department and school.

During the period when the expansion of the departments to accommodate the influx of students was under active discussion, the suggestion was frequently canvassed that economies in staff and buildings could be obtained by devising a course in which half the student's time was spent in the department and half in the school, thus reducing the need to enlarge accommodation, since the course could be duplicated, and each half of the year group would alternate with the other half. In at least one department an experiment of this kind was tried. It will be clear from what has been said above about specialization that it is not easy or efficient to offer a full range of specialized options to small groups of students twice a year, but as a department increases in size, the more feasible it becomes to make arrangements of this kind. There is, however, a fundamental objection to what was known as a 'box and cox' arrangement within the one-year course. The principle that half the time should be spent in the department and half the time in the school would make it necessary either to break the course up into alternating periods of time which would be too short to be effective, or to give some students a long period of teaching experience before, and others after, the major part of the theoretical course. This does not make sense, as most trainers of teachers would agree, for one pattern of alternation and its exact converse cannot be equally good. However, it is clear that within a two-year framework the situation could be transformed, for more and longer blocks of time could be effectively alternated. It is possible, therefore, that two-year training in large departments with student numbers of 300 or more would be the most efficient in terms of the use of staff and accommodation (and teaching practice places) as well as the most beneficial academically in providing the specialized teaching which is required.

Hitherto in these chapters little reference has been made to the higher degree work of the departments of education and to their contribution to work with serving teachers. The University of London first awarded the degree of M.A. in education in 1916, and of Ph.D. in education in 1925. The University of Durham established the degree of M.Ed. in 1929, while the University of Reading awarded its first M.A. degree in education in 1930. Other universities no doubt instituted higher degrees in education during the same period, but this does not necessarily mean that theses in aspects of educational studies were not successfully presented for master's and doctor's degrees in the faculties of arts and science at earlier dates. Indeed H. Thiselton Mark, who was a lecturer at the Manchester Day Training College from 1899 onwards, was awarded the D.Litt. of the University of London for work in educational psychology as early as 1911, while Godfrey Thomson was awarded the D.Sc. of the University of Durham for work in the same subject in 1913.

During the 1930s the number of theses in educational studies which were presented increased rapidly, nearly all of them no doubt awarded to full-time teachers whose research was undertaken in their spare time. But it was only after the Second World War that the development of this kind of work assumed very large proportions indeed, as is clear from the lists first published by the late Mrs A. M. Blackwell of King's College, London, and continued in recent years by the National Foundation for Educational Research. The University of London established the academic diploma in education in about 1950, as the first higher diploma for research training in education, and since then a large number of diplomas designed to be the first stage of higher degree work have been established. Some universities continue to regard a first degree in an appropriate subject as sufficient qualification to undertake a thesis for a higher degree in education, and practice is by no means uniform. Recently a number of diploma qualifications have become higher degrees by examination, and some universities have required either examination or thesis as alternatives, while others have required both, for the award of a higher degree. But whatever the system, the volume of such work has grown enormously, and has been aided and encouraged recently by the generosity of the Department of Education and Science and the local education authorities in seconding teachers with pay to undertake such courses full-time.

The absence of a first degree qualification in education, since most of the initial study of education is undertaken as part of the 'training year', has made the normal progression from first to higher degree impossible in the case of educational studies. The advanced or academic diploma was intended to bridge the gap and to raise the level of the study of education from that of the initial training qualification (whether in the university department or in the college of education) to first degree standard. The introduction of undergraduate courses in education, and particularly the introduction of the B.Ed. degree, has tended to confuse the situation, particularly where the standard of educational studies in the B.Ed. is below that of the advanced diploma, as it sometimes is. The proposals of the James Committee for two new degrees in education, the B.A.(Ed.) and the M.A.(Ed.), do little to clarify the situation, since one is merely the equivalent of a deferred postgraduate certificate while the relationship of the other to existing degrees of the same name is not apparent from the casual references to it which occur in the Report.

There remain, therefore, a number of problems to be solved before an orderly and more uniform series of academic qualifications in education can be established. It seems to be necessary to establish a first degree of honours standard in education alone, of which the qualifying stages could be taken not only concurrently with undergraduate studies in other subjects, but also as part of a reorganized postgraduate training course, while the major part would consist of a one-year full-time or two-year part-time qualification taken by those with teaching experience. Some of the present masters' degree courses in education by examination are really of this kind (the prototype being the former Scottish Ed.B. or B.Ed.) and are called masters' degrees because the title B.Ed. is now unfortunately associated with a general degree or joint degree including education.

Some of the university departments of education have offered advanced diplomas or higher degrees of another, specialized type in subjects such as educational psychology, or the education of handicapped children, or the teaching of specialized branches of the curriculum. In some cases, however, work of this kind has been undertaken not by the departments but by the institutes of education, which we shall shortly be discussing. The provision of shorter non-qualification courses for teachers has also been an activity of departments of education in some places, and of institutes of education in others. It is a consequence of the overlapping of functions between departments and institutes in the provision of advanced courses and short courses that in some universities there has been a movement, encouraged by the Robbins Committee, to combine department and institute in one organization, known as a school of education, although there are important reservations about the extent to which colleges of education can be said to be 'included' in a school of education.

In the previous chapter reference has been made to the setting up of Joint Examination Boards for training colleges between 1926 and 1929. The McNair Committee on the Training and Supply of Teachers and Youth Leaders, which reported in 1944, proposed the extension of these arrangements by two alternative schemes, either Scheme A, which involved establishing university schools of education, of which both the training colleges and the departments of education would be members, and for which the universities would assume responsibility (though the question of financial control was left open); or Scheme B, which involved merely a slight reorganization of the Joint Boards, widening the membership of their committees and increasing the co-operation between their constituent institutions, while making them responsible for the examination of students in the departments of education as well as the colleges.

In the event, a variant of Scheme A was devised and adopted by all universities except Cambridge, where an organization was established which is constitutionally and financially independent of the university. The variant was called an institute, and differed from Scheme A mainly in the fact that the university departments of education retained their separate identity and were not merged in the headquarters of the school.

Each institute of education was staffed by a director, and by both administrative and teaching staff. All developed elaborate committee systems which, while they differed in many respects, yet had the common feature that financial responsibility for the headquarters organization was undertaken by the universities, and academic responsibility rested ultimately with the university senates.

Almost twenty years later the Robbins Committee on Higher Education endorsed the Scheme A system, but proposed that the logical next step should be taken, first, by uniting the departments of education and the institutes into schools of education (thus returning to the original McNair proposal) and secondly, by instituting a block grant for all the colleges in each school, to be administered by the university, which would thus undertake not only academic supervision of the colleges, but also financial responsibility for their maintenance. It would have been easier to adopt the first of these suggestions if the second had been implemented, but some universities devised a formula for their schools of education which was compatible with lack of financial control of the colleges.

The advocates of McNair Scheme B, the Joint Board scheme, wished to limit the responsibility of universities for teacher training, and even to divert some graduates to the colleges for their postgraduate training, on the ground that the numbers who would be seeking training in the long run would be so large that the universities would have too high a proportion of their total student numbers in training as teachers. In practice, in the present situation, with about 7,700 graduates in training, increased perhaps after allowing for the introduction of the training requirement by a further 1,600, and with a total university population of about 200,000, the modest proportion of at most five per cent. does not look excessive. But it is interesting that those who wished to safeguard the independence of the colleges from the encroachment of the university, also wished to protect the university from too great an involvement in work that, they appeared to suggest, was not consistent with the fundamental duty of the university which 'properly consists in teaching basic subjects and in the advancement of knowledge' rather than in professional training. In passing, it should be noted that the advocates of Scheme B spoke with approval of the Scottish arrangements for the training of teachers and no doubt this made them anxious not to commit themselves too far in the opposite direction.

The outcome of McNair was that the university departments of education provided, in the first place, most of the academic manpower when directors of institutes were appointed, and secondly, a large number of experienced staff to man the institutes' committees, though other departments of the universities also provided a great deal of valuable help, while vice-chancellors and senior professors devoted time and trouble to serve as chairmen of Institute Delegacies and other committees. The institute headquarters were staffed generously with lecturers or tutors for teachers' courses, and a very large number of diploma courses was established; research schemes, in some of which teachers participated, were developed, publications produced, members of the teaching profession joined institute committees, and links between university and college teachers became much closer than they had been in Joint Board days.

It was this newly developed organization which made it possible on the one hand for some universities to move fairly soon after the Robbins Report was issued to the establishment of schools of education, and on the other hand for all universities with institutes of education to establish, in the remarkably short space of about three years, the degree of B.Ed. In retrospect, it can be seen to have been a pity that this degree was not entitled B.A.(Ed.), but nevertheless the speed and unanimity of the universities in setting it up is testimony to their desire to make a reality of a further step in the direction of co-operation with the colleges of education. The contribution of the departments of education to the establishment of the B.Ed degree has consisted of a tremendous amount of committee work in hammering out regulations and syllabuses, of serving on boards of visitors to the colleges, and of doing a great deal of examining, since education is the one subject common to all B.Ed. courses.

The relationship of the colleges with the universities is closer now than it has been at any time in their history, and there are many people in both universities and colleges who hope that the constructive work of the last twenty-five years will be preserved in the reorganization of the training of teachers which will result from the recent recommendations of the James Committee on the Education and Training of Teachers. It must be added, however, that the recommendations of the majority of the Committee do not seem to offer the prospect of continued development on the basis of past achievements.

Just as in 1944, in the deliberations of the McNair Committee, the question of the continued independent existence of university departments of education as internal university departments responsible for the training of graduate teachers, as well as for the promotion of advanced studies and research in education, was raised, and settled by a compromise, so again today it is necessary to devise a constitutional arrangement which permits the colleges to undertake more work at university first degree standard without threatening to displace or disturb the activities of existing university departments. It is customary to hear terms like amalgamation or integration into comprehensive units applied to situations where some kind of federal principle, but a loose one, is what is really required. This principle would tolerate overlapping functions and respect the traditions and differences of contributing institutions. The institutes of education have felt their way towards this kind of federation, not without success, and organizations like the University of London and the University of Wales have long experience of it. It is not difficult to arrange a relationship between universities and colleges of education based on the principle that each organization retains responsibility for the students whom it admits in the first place and in the case of the training of teachers sees the student through to the final stage of his qualification.

By their action over the years the universities have made it clear that generally they do not wish to resume the training of non-graduate teachers, which they did formerly. Indeed many of the local education authority colleges of education came into existence during the period from 1905 to about 1930, when the universities were abandoning two-year training, on the clear understanding that this work was no longer appropriate to the universities. In recent years, when degree courses have become available in non-university institutions, the universities have made no claim to a monopoly of the postgraduate training of graduates of other institutions, and would presumably say without hesitation that the polytechnics and technical colleges should undertake the professional training of their own graduates, and that the colleges of education should undertake the training of students who have taken courses in the colleges for degrees either of the University of London or of other neighbouring universities. This is in accordance with the tradition established in the early years of the century, the only exception apparently being the unusual arrangements in the University of Durham, where the department of education has been responsible for the postgraduate training of students from the colleges of education who have taken degrees of the university.

The question which is put to the universities by those who would wish to transfer all training of graduate teachers to the colleges is therefore not whether it would be reasonable to bring to an end a monopoly which the universities have never claimed, but whether it is right and proper that a monopoly situation should be established by asking them to surrender their interest in the training of graduate teachers to specialized institutions not maintained by them, though possibly still in some academic relationship with them. All the authorities which maintain colleges of education do so as agencies which also maintain or participate in the maintenance of schools, and therefore are employers of teachers. This may give them an understanding of the needs of the schools, but it is undeniable that it also tends to make their conception of the education and training appropriate to a teacher rather different from that of the university. It makes them reluctant to abandon the segregated higher education of the teacher and inclined to apply the test of immediate relevance to the classroom not only to the professional studies of the teacher but also to his general education and his degree studies (if he takes a degree). The history of the training of teachers bears out the truth of this statement, and the influence of the universities was recognized, in the early years of their participation, as providing a disinterested approach at least to the teacher's non-professional studies. It is, however, becoming more and more clear that the professional studies of the most highly qualified teachers also need the support of subjects which can be successfully undertaken, with a research component, at the highest standard, only in institutions of university rank: the question is whether the teacher's access to teaching in such subjects should exist at the stage of initial postgraduate training, or only at the stage of advanced postgraduate studies in education.

The issue seems to turn entirely on the value and intellectual standing of the educational studies undertaken by graduates taking initial post-graduate training courses. If such studies should be mainly practical and closely related to classroom problems (which, incidentally, appeared to be the view of the James Committee), and should involve no higher enquiry into the philosophy of education or educational psychology, no social or historical studies or studies in the physical and mental development of children designed to throw light on educational issues, then obviously the university is not the place for them. The contribution of the university to the training of teachers has been in the development of these studies and their use in the initial training of graduate teachers, whose first degrees are guarantees of their ability to work at the appropriate level and to under-stand the need for this approach to professional studies. Since a great deal of research and enquiry with a bearing on education is now undertaken in university departments of psychology, sociology, history, philosophy, linguistics, physiology and even law and medicine, a department of educa-tion which has a relationship with such departments is more likely to provide informed teaching, even at the initial training stage, than one which has not: this then is the main argument in favour of providing not only the academic training and the advanced postgraduate studies in education, but also the professional training of graduate teachers in a university environment. It is an argument which has been appreciated and accepted by the colleges of education themselves, and is the mainspring behind their desire to establish undergraduate teaching and research and to retain close relationships with university institutions, until in the long run they obtain some satisfactory federal relationship with the universities and are recog-nized as full university institutions.

There are, however, other important arguments. Traditionally, the relationship between universities and schools has been based on the twofold movement of students from schools to universities, and of teachers from universities back into the schools. At one time the universities had a role in the inspection of schools, and still have a role in school examinations, though not without a certain amount of critical complaint about their influence on school curricula.

The original role of degrees in arts was that they conferred a qualification to teach, and no system which does not involve the abandonment of the recruitment of graduate teachers can possibly remove the role of the university in providing the academic and specialized education of the teacher, even if professional training takes place elsewhere. But where would the trainers of teachers, if they stood outside the university, look for the development of the subjects they teach in professional courses, if not to the university?

It is also necessary to consider the effect which changes of a radical kind may have upon the supply of graduate teachers at a time when training is about to be made compulsory. Very little thought has been given to the consequences of introducing compulsory training, and the first principle is that the courses should be popular and that they should be provided in the institutions which can attract students and provide them with the kind of professional course they want. The evidence of the success of the university departments in attracting graduate students under a voluntary system is clear from the figures already quoted. And there is no doubt that graduates enter the colleges very largely not by free choice but because the universities cannot accommodate them. The cost of providing graduate training is, if anything, higher in colleges, which on the whole are more generously staffed and have (so far) smaller teaching groups in graduate courses. There is therefore little to recommend the policy which has recently been adopted. It may work temporarily in a period when university graduates find it difficult to obtain employment, but in a period of full employment the effect on the supply of graduate teachers may be unfortunate.

From the point of view of the universities, which are becoming more interested in the study of higher education and in the training of their own staff, an education department firmly based on the teaching of education in initial teacher training courses, and therefore large enough to contain specialists over the whole range of educational studies, can be a source of strength and an important agent in liaison with schools.

We have already emphasized that it is unlikely that many universities would wish directly to undertake once more the training of non-graduate teachers (although the New University of Ulster at Coleraine appears to have decided to do just this); but there is no good reason why the affiliation of colleges of education with universities should not be organized in such a way that the colleges are autonomous in their training of non-graduate teachers, subject only to such minimal requirements as Area Training Organizations feel inclined to impose, and are in close and intimate relationship with the university as far as the undergraduate and postgraduate studies of their graduating students are concerned. In the long run they could supersede non-graduate training entirely, as the universities did early in the present century, as the teaching profession eventually becomes an all-graduate profession. This process may well take a long time, and it may involve stages similar to those which the university departments of education went through: the separation of the general from the professional education of the teacher (i.e. abandonment of the concurrent course), the removal of the commitment to teaching at the beginning of the course, and therefore the provision of academic courses with an independent status of their own, and finally perhaps also the provision of training courses for professions other than teaching. But it would certainly be premature and unwise to attempt any of these things without extending the three-year course to four full years. It is unfortunate that the James Report failed to recognize this.

These developments do not require the colleges of education to take over a substantial share in the training of graduates from the universities themselves: but they do imply that the training of graduate teachers is a natural activity of the college, and a growing one as its graduating students increase in numbers. One envisages in the long run, therefore, that a university which has accepted colleges of education into this kind of affiliation will retain its own education department, still engaged in the professional training of its own graduates and such graduates of other universities as wish to transfer, for whatever reason. The education departments of its constituent colleges, engaged also in the professional training of their own graduates, would have the same kind of association with the original university department of education as the college undergraduate departments would have with the original undergraduate departments of the university. It could even be that the development of the colleges would reflect that of the university departments of education in another respect also: that for the time being the non-graduating students would take the same professional courses as those who graduate.

It has been said that the building up of graduate training courses in the colleges of education has been undertaken in order to fill vacant places since the number of applicants for three-year courses has fallen off, and in any case will be necessarily reduced in the next few years as the size of the teaching profession reaches the point where the staff-pupil ratios will at long last be satisfactory. If this is true, the action taken has been based on mere expediency, without reference to the long-term benefit of the students or the institutions concerned. Although there has been a good deal of movement in recent years from one university to another for postgraduate teacher training, partly because some of the large universities have not expanded their departments of education, while some of the smaller ones have, and partly because students wish to take training courses either in their home area (having been away from home to take their degrees) or in the area where for personal reasons they wish to obtain posts, on the whole the principle of the four-year course was a sound one. It may in future be found that the present fashion of postponing vocational choice will die out, and the movement to reintroduce four-year courses in some universities may spread to others. If the fashion does change, there will be a wider opportunity to design university degree courses which have special value for teachers, even if they do not consist of school subjects or of early instalments of studies in education. It is particularly important, for instance, that thought should be given to the designing of degree courses appropriate to women who will teach in primary schools, and to students who will specialize in the teaching of languages, mathematics and science. In order to develop arrangements of this sort successfully, it is essential that the final stages of training, whether or not they are associated, as is suggested above, with what is now the probationary year, should remain in the hands of the institution responsible for undergraduate work. Otherwise the possibility of designing the university education of the teacher not necessarily as what we now call a concurrent course, but as what could be called a related whole, will be seriously impaired.

It is a disappointment that the James Report has failed to appreciate the strength of these arguments, and has thought of the consecutive principle as implying disconnection, in the sense not only that there would be no relationship between 'first-cycle' and 'second-cycle' courses (with certain rare exceptions mentioned in the Report as afterthoughts), but also that the two 'cycles' would commonly take place in different institutions. It is possible that the James Committee have failed to appreciate that the university four-year course was for years only consecutive in the sense that the *final* teaching practice was postponed, and professional studies deferred, while the student's choice of degree studies was made under the guidance of the department which admitted him to the first year and which ensured that there was some rational connection between his degree course and his professional intentions.

Our experience of an entire disconnection between 'first-cycle' and 'second-cycle' courses in the universities is recent and incomplete, having lasted for all entrants to postgraduate training for little more than twenty years. The reversion in some universities to the concurrent principle may be evidence of dissatisfaction with this disconnection, and might have impelled an important Committee of Enquiry to hesitate before advocating a restructuring of the training system which assumes disconnection and discontinuity to be a virtue.

From the point of view of the university departments of education (at least of those which are conscious of their history) it may seem a little odd, too, that it should be assumed that because the training of four-year university students has been based on the consecutive principle, therefore the training of three-year college students can be advantageously moved in the same direction, but in completely different circumstances. The university course remained a concurrent course as long as it lasted for three years: the introduction of the consecutive pattern took place only when a further year was added, and only for students who were accepted for degree courses. The lessons of history are that one-year professional training is appropriate only for the ablest students, and that the best way to make effective use of a three-year period is to extend the academic studies of students beyond two years and their professional studies beyond one year. This was the view taken by the colleges when three-year courses became general in the early 1960s. A possible pattern for a reformed three-year course would thus be three years of academic studies in the last two of which professional training would take place. But the very structure recommended by the James Report makes this pattern difficult to achieve.

Again, the university departments can scarcely rest content with a Report which recommends that while some of them might be allowed a marginal expansion (apparently up to a maximum of 200 places) the movement to transfer graduate training in massive proportions to colleges of education, few of which are equipped to do it effectively, should be encouraged, presumably as part of the policy of strengthening the 'third sector' of higher education to which it is proposed to consign the colleges. It might make sense to encourage the development of carefully planned and large-scale graduate training in colleges of education which would act as second university departments of education, retaining a close relationship with universities, and establishing Chairs of Education. But to fail to recognize the leadership of the universities in the field of graduate training and to set going a movement which might lead eventually to the compulsory training outside the universities of two-thirds of all the university graduates who wish to teach is scarcely acceptable as a constructive policy for the future.

# CHAPTER 7

## The Future of Teacher Education in the Polytechnics

### ERIC ROBINSON

A striking feature of the debate on the James Report and the subsequent White Paper was the sudden general recognition that was given to the polytechnics and the Council for National Academic Awards. Although the polytechnics have hitherto had only a minor role in the training of teachers, the development of polytechnics is, for several reasons, of major importance for the future of teacher education in this country. As the polytechnics are little known to, and greatly misunderstood by, teachers and students in the other sectors of higher education it is necessary to explain this in some detail.

The polytechnics were formed from existing colleges – mainly the regional technical colleges but also a number of colleges of art, colleges of commerce and colleges of education. It is natural to assume that the polytechnics are predominantly technological in their scope and, indeed, some of the polytechnic governors and teachers believe this, but in fact most of them are not so and their technological element is rapidly decreasing in importance. When the 1966 White Paper proposed the setting up of polytechnics a number of the technical colleges involved had already developed non-technological studies (particularly in business studies management, public administration, social science and the humanities) to a greater volume than that of their studies in science and technology. The polytechnics have responded to the pressure from students for more places in the social sciences and the humanities so that now, in many of them, non-technological studies are dominant and in some of them, again as a consequence of the pattern of student demand, technological departments are struggling for survival. Thus the widespread idea that the polytechnics have a similarly narrow academic spectrum to the colleges of advanced technology of ten years ago (now the technological universities) is wrong. Polytechnics generally have an academic spectrum as wide as most universities and considerably wider than some. Thus it is not true, as is generally supposed, that the polytechnics train people for work in industry by means of narrow technical 'hardware' studies. Large numbers of their students obtain degrees in arts and science. They obtain a liberal education (even

5—EOT  *  *

the technologists have a more liberal education than many of their contemporaries in the universities) and they proceed to work in all branches of employment open to graduates in industry, commerce and the public services. And many of them become school teachers. For the future the polytechnics must at least be considered as an important source of graduate school teachers in virtually every subject of the curriculum. They will of course need to have professional education as teachers in addition to their degrees. Where will they obtain it? Some are already getting it in the polytechnics but I will return to this question later.

The polytechnics are developing in parallel with the universities; they are not subordinate to universities. This is the academic significance of Mr Crosland's 'binary' modification of the Robbins Committee's recommendations now reinforced by the 1972 White Paper. Whereas Robbins conceived of the Council for National Academic Awards as the academic validating and awarding body for small cadet universities (rather in the way the University of London fostered university colleges at home and in the colonies in the first half of the twentieth century) the Council has developed as a permanent major degree awarding body for very large institutions (with as many as 3,000–4,000 full-time students) of a new kind. This has far-reaching implications that people in other sectors of education have been slow to appreciate. At first many people simply would not believe that colleges and polytechnics would prefer CNAA facilities to those of university patronage: this is now proved beyond doubt. Even if some polytechnics were to be given university charters (and it is far from certain that they will) the huge impact and success of the CNAA remains. The significance of the CNAA is that the universities of Britain are no longer the apex of the whole educational system. They now share this position with the polytechnics and the CNAA, through which a student may proceed by first and higher degrees to the highest levels of academic opportunity. This has significance for the teaching profession in two ways – that the universities must now expect to share with the polytechnics their influence over the school curriculum and their role in the education for the professions, including teaching. Each of these points needs further explanation.

For too long the curriculum of the senior forms of the secondary schools has been dominated by the requirements of university entrance expressed in the syllabuses of university scholarship papers, matriculation regulations, school certificates and, latterly, the GCE – in spite of the fact that the majority of secondary school pupils never enter a university. Recently the Schools Council has begun to challenge this domination with an effectiveness never achieved by its predecessor, the Secondary Schools Examination Council. Unfortunately its efforts hitherto have been hindered by the conservatism of some sectors of the teaching profession and the university representation in its membership. We will, however, soon see a breakthrough based on the undoubted success of the certificate of secondary education (CSE). In the development of the new curriculum of the secondary school a major part will be played by the further education sector – the colleges of further education, the technical colleges and the polytechnics. It is significant that the CNAA was recently asked to nominate a member of the Schools Council. This is only the start. The essential contribution to be made by representatives of the further education sector derives from their concern with the post-school education of young people of all abilities, not only the prospective academics. Apart from the school teachers of children of all abilities none have a more important contribution to make to the design of the new secondary curriculum than the teachers of the further education sector.

The polytechnics are the senior members of the FE family just as the universities are the senior members of the public and grammar school family. The FE colleges that are giving school head teachers such a challenge across the country do not share the orthodox misconceptions about the polytechnics and, most important, they share with the polytechnics an important range of new ideas and approaches in education. In the review of the secondary school curriculum, serious account will have to be taken of the distinctive views of the teachers of sixth-form-level courses in FE colleges and the closely allied but equally distinctive views of entrance requirements of the teachers in polytechnics.

The technical colleges, not the universities, are the experts in professional education. The universities have never paid much heed to any but a small select group of professions (traditionally the church, the law and medicine, with a small number added recently). To say the least they have always been ambiguous about the teaching profession. The technical colleges, on the other hand, have always recognized the needs of all professions, big or small, whatever their pretensions, and the typical college prospectus is evidence of this – courses in law, accountancy, engineering (many varieties), physics, chemistry, pharmacy, biology, mathematics, management, estate agency, chiropody, catering, librarianship, work study – the list seems never ending. In each profession there is a long history of difficult negotiation to reconcile professional demands and requirements with the needs and ambitions of students and with the pedagogical ideas and ambitions of the colleges. In particular there is the difficult problem of weighing the demands of professional autonomy against those of academic freedom. Many features of the present controversy about the professional education of teachers are familiar to the polytechnics in many other fields of professional education: demands from the profession for control of the curriculum, for higher entry standards, for teaching only by experienced members of the profession, for longer courses, for the restriction of courses to high status institutions, for greater emphasis on professional techniques and less on general education.

During the past decade there has been rapid change in the attitude of many professions to the method and route of qualification. There has been a widespread tendency to seek to raise the status of a profession by the insistence upon full-time higher education at university level; this is often accompanied by a demand for a two A-level entry to professional courses and sometimes by the objective of a 'graduate profession' entirely educated in universities. Thus, for example, the Council of Engineering Institutions was formed in 1965 to co-ordinate the efforts of the engineering profession to this end; it has succeeded in almost closing the route to professional status by part-time study; it has almost succeeded in excluding the area technical colleges from participation in the education of professional engineers. The Royal Institute of British Architects made tentative moves towards the limitation of all professional courses to the universities; it has succeeded in closing departments in some technical and art colleges and in 1971 hit the headlines by its attempt to close departments of architecture in four polytechnics and one technical college. The Institute of Chartered Accountants is making steady progress towards two A-level entry and compulsory full-time education for all articled clerks. The professions of law and pharmacy have adopted similar policies.

Such attempts to achieve a graduate profession have coincided with the development of the polytechnics as substantial centres of university-level education. These professions, sometimes rather belatedly, have realized that their ideal of the exclusively university route had to be extended at least to accept the continuation and development of a polytechnic route. Once the polytechnic route was acknowledged even the two A-level principle had to be compromised at least to the extent of the acceptance of the characteristic technical college alternative route into higher education – that of the ordinary national certificates and diplomas. Although some professions were reluctant to accept these qualifications for entry into courses for the professional institution examinations, they were generally unable to resist the policy of the Council for National Academic Awards in accepting these qualifications for entry into degree courses which in turn led into the profession.

The story of the struggle for the status of the teaching profession runs parallel to this. During the 1960s the clamour for two A-level entry into teacher training courses was dampened by the problem of teacher shortage (although it can be expected to grow again now that the crisis in teacher supply is apparently over). It was in the mid-1960s while the teachers in the colleges of education were most adamant about attaining university status that the government by a deliberate act of policy extended teacher training into the technical college sector by opening education departments in five colleges (Sunderland Technical College; John Dalton College of Technology, Manchester; Nottingham Regional College of Technology; Barking

Regional College of Technology and North Western Polytechnic, London). The opening of these departments was a major setback to the objective of limiting teacher education to the universities. It was followed in 1967 and 1968 by the government's decision, with the co-operation of the local authorities concerned, to incorporate existing colleges of education into the polytechnics of Leeds and Huddersfield (even though this had not been anticipated in the proposals for these polytechnics in the 1966 White Paper on polytechnics). Thus by 1970 there were seven polytechnics* with education departments. In addition a new polytechnic established in Ulster had a school of education.

This was not the full extent of teacher training in the polytechnics at the time of their formation. In addition to the courses for teachers, other than formal teacher training, that existed in most polytechnics there were: (1) courses leading to the Art Teachers' Diploma in several art colleges that were incorporated into polytechnics; (2) a small number of part-time teacher training courses of ATOs leading to PGCE; (3) in-service certificate courses for FE teachers run in collaboration with colleges of education (technical). The polytechnic that took longest to come into being was the Middlesex Polytechnic incorporating the Enfield and Hendon Colleges of Technology and the Hornsey College of Art. Although it was not one of the seven polytechnics with an education department it had teacher training in all these categories. In addition Enfield College had a part-time degree in the sociology of education designed for practising teachers which was approved by the Council for National Academic Awards in 1967.

It is in the seven polytechnics with mainstream teacher education that we should look in some detail to anticipate the main impact of the polytechnics on teacher education and it is worth tracing the history of their development in some detail.

The post-Robbins discussion of teacher education in the National Advisory Council for the Training and Supply of Teachers was dominated by the crisis in the supply of primary school teachers. In meetings of the Council the representatives of the Association of Teachers in Technical Institutions expressed reservations about the Robbins' Committee's recommendations for the future of teacher training and urged the recognition of a role in teacher training for the then regional technical colleges. The Council's response to this was to include a statement in its ninth report† calling for a role (unspecified) for the technical colleges. This was

---

* The five technical colleges with education departments previously listed had been incorporated in polytechnics as follows: Sunderland Technical College in Sunderland Polytechnic; John Dalton College of Technology in Manchester Polytechnic; Nottingham Regional College of Technology in Trent Polytechnic; Barking Regional College of Technology in North East London Polytechnic; North Western Polytechnic in The Polytechnic of North London.

† *Ninth Report of the National Advisory Council on the Training and Supply of Teachers* (1965). *The Demand for and Supply of Teachers 1963–1986*, HMSO. See also note of dissent.

commonly interpreted, inside the Council and out, in terms of the use of technical college accommodation and staff, mainly in science and technology, to assist in the work of nearby colleges of education.

However, this was not the idea of the Secretary of State, who, aware of the proceedings and recommendations of the NACTST, defined his emergency programme for teacher education in his speech at Douglas at Easter 1965. This included a declaration of intent to establish education departments in a small number of regional technical colleges. This proposal was firmly defined in a letter to five local authorities in 1966 after discussion with the interested parties. From the start it was clear that these departments were to be new units and not mere extensions of colleges of education housed in technical college buildings.*

The teachers in colleges and departments of education had no enthusiasm for the whole 'experiment' and rightly saw this as part of Mr Crosland's binary policy that threatened to associate the colleges of education with the technical colleges in a public sector of higher education. They also had another objection to it. To many people the obvious contribution the technical colleges could make was in the education of teachers of science and mathematics. But these would generally be prospective secondary school teachers and this was the time of the strict application of the policy of 'balance of training' in the colleges of education: the colleges were permitted to accept only a strictly limited proportion of prospective secondary teachers so as to ensure the training of enough primary teachers to meet the immediate shortage. When it became clear that the government was determined to establish these new departments, the Association of Teachers in Colleges and Departments of Education argued strongly that they should not have privileges that were denied to the colleges of education generally: in particular, that they should not be exempted from the rules on the balance of training. In effect this prevented the new departments from specializing in science and mathematics and compelled them to concentrate mainly on primary training. It undermined the government's declared intention of requiring the departments to make use of existing teaching resources of the colleges. In so far as these were conceived as resources in science this made sense because a number of colleges of education during this period had good facilities and staff for science teaching that were underemployed because few students recruited into the colleges were choosing to study science. It was not so clearly the case in mathematics because the colleges of education were seriously deficient in staff and facilities for teaching that subject.

Any prospect of the new departments quickly making a distinctive contribution to teacher education was destroyed by the DES when it

---

* As, for example, an outpost of Trent Park College of Education, North London, that had been established in Southend Technical College in 1959.

selected the technical colleges that were to house them and when it defined the terms of reference for the departments in the 1966 letter. This letter effectively ensured the establishment of conventional day colleges offering a conventional curriculum to conventionally recruited day students.

Although a small number of technical colleges at that time had, through the Council for National Academic Awards, taken academic initiatives that suggested they might make a distinctive contribution* none of these colleges was among the five selected. The DES letter specified that the new departments were to undertake only the three-year certificate course. In the first instance they were not to undertake B.Ed. work. They were not to participate in the experiments in part-time courses of teacher education that were then about to be launched. They were not to engage in the training of teachers for further education.

The letter from the DES promised one important innovation. The local authorities were advised that the colleges might choose to operate either under the supervision of the appropriate Area Training Organization or the Council for National Academic Awards. This implied that the DES was willing to extend to the CNAA the recognition as a 'relevant body' for teacher certification that was enjoyed by the universities (such as York) which did teacher training but had no ATO. The Secretary of State made no secret of his hope that some of the colleges would choose the CNAA. But he handled this badly and all the colleges chose to work with the ATOs.

The reasons for this were (1) the government made no attempt to obtain in advance the co-operation of the CNAA; (2) the technical colleges chosen were not those suitable, at that stage, for such a development; (3) the DES conception of the curriculum and student body of the departments virtually precluded significant innovation and there was no point in involving the CNAA unless there was a prospect of significant innovation. The key to this confused situation is that the DES was divided and the Secretary of State misjudged the matters he could safely leave to the decision of his officials. Mr Crosland envisaged the role of the new departments as primarily innovatory whereas the officials of his teacher training branch interpreted it as mainly numerical. His FE branch displayed neither interest nor understanding in the project and permitted one complete absurdity. This was that the new departments, although housed in FE colleges, were supervised primarily by the teacher training branch rather than by the FE branch, while the Department was paying lip-service to the importance of the new departments being thoroughly integrated with the colleges in which they were housed. As a result the five departments were established as

---

* Notably Enfield College of Technology, which was preparing to establish its part-time degree in the sociology of education and Hatfield Polytechnic which had an outstanding record with the CNAA and for several years had done substantial work in mathematics and science for Balls Park College of Education.

conventional teacher training enclaves and were staffed almost entirely by recruitment from the staffs of colleges of education. Their initial development coincided with a period of upheaval in their host colleges during the negotiation for their incorporation in the new polytechnics. Only when the polytechnic dust had settled did the departments emerge as potential innovators.

In 1970 the heads of the departments, together with representatives from the colleges and departments at Leeds and Huddersfield, began to meet regularly. One of their first decisions was that the future of teacher education in the polytechnics lay with the CNAA rather than the ATOs. Throughout 1971 the departments, generally with the support of their polytechnic academic boards, started planning new courses for submission to the CNAA to replace their ATO courses. Sunderland Polytechnic opened a part-time degree course, approved by the CNAA, in September 1972 and some polytechnics may convert their full-time initial training courses from ATO to CNAA, by September 1973.

What is the CNAA? What will the polytechnics do in teacher education under the CNAA umbrella?

The Council for National Academic Awards has a Royal Charter enabling it to award degrees to students in colleges outside the universities who have followed courses and taken examinations designed and run by the colleges themselves. It operates by inviting colleges, within a very broad framework of Council policy, to submit detailed proposals for courses for inspection and approval by boards of university, college and professional representatives of the appropriate expertise. This procedure is significantly different from that used by the universities and Area Training Organizations in supervising degree and certificate courses in the colleges of education. Under this system, universally used in England and Wales for the colleges of education, the initiative and responsibility for the courses and examinations rests with the ATO and the university rather than with the individual college. Experience in the technical colleges during the past fifteen years of working with the CNAA (and its predecessor the National Council for Technological Awards) has proved that its system radically changes the college's approach to the planning and operation of courses. It is significant that some of the technical colleges that had most experience of running university degree courses (usually for internal or external degrees of London University) have found great difficulty in adapting themselves to the responsibility thrust on to the college by the CNAA.

The record shows that the CNAA has recognized a wide range of courses expressing many different educational ideas. It has facilitated a great variety of innovation in degree courses that contrasts starkly with the uniformity of concept expressed by the B.Ed. courses developed for the colleges of education by the universities. Many of the polytechnics have had opportunities to continue their university degree courses or to participate in new ones but there is in the polytechnics an overwhelming preference for courses developed under the CNAA.

The substantial development of sandwich courses since 1955 (including most of the courses now located in the universities) has been mainly under the CNAA and, before its foundation, the NCTA. Nearly all the first degrees in business studies in this country have been developed under the CNAA. CNAA courses in science and technology (the courses longest established because the NCTA was restricted to these fields) include many new developments—new course structures, new areas of undergraduate study, new forms of integrated education and professional training. Through the CNAA and NCTA the colleges led the way in this country in the development of liberal studies integral to technological courses, in the introduction of modern computing in undergraduate courses and in the inclusion of substantial project work in first degree courses. Currently there is a huge volume of new development in courses in the humanities and the human sciences: of particular significance are those which anticipate the formidable problem of finding employment for the arts graduate. Enfield College of Technology, for example, has an annual intake of 150 students into a sandwich course in social science who are systematically placed for training in industry and the public services.

Finally, and perhaps most significantly of all, a very rapid expansion of part-time degree opportunities is in progress under CNAA auspices. This expansion is taking place concurrently with the development of the Open University while the universities have remained uniformly indifferent to part-time first degree courses. These courses are generally designed expressly for mature students who have a vocational commitment – they are not merely the full-time courses adapted for part-time students – and the demand for places in these courses is coming predominantly from serving teachers in schools and FE colleges. In sharp contrast to the conventional initial teacher training carried out in their education departments, these part-time degree courses in the polytechnics are generally in areas of special needs of the education service and the teaching profession – in mathematics, physical and biological science and in educational studies of an applied nature.

The potential of the CNAA in the education and training of teachers has yet to be realized. There are two basic reasons for this: the Department of Education and Science has based its policy for teacher education in the 1960s upon the isolation and control of colleges of education in a manner difficult to reconcile with the measure of freedom assumed under the CNAA system; and those concerned with teacher education (school teachers' unions, teachers in colleges and university departments of education) have persisted in their determination to bring teacher education under university control.

The Robbins Committee which recommended the establishment of the CNAA considered its use by colleges of education but decided that this was not the best route for the colleges.* Its recommendation and the government's action on the CNAA did, however, leave open the possibility of teacher education under the CNAA. Probably only a minority of members of the Robbins Committee realized this. It is commonly assumed that this possibility was realized only several years later, but this assumption is untrue: as early as May 1964 *The Times Educational Supplement* had published arguments for and against it.† Almost certainly the distaste for the CNAA possibility helped to persuade the universities quickly to establish their B.Ed. courses.

Although the CNAA has generally tried to avoid entanglement in political conflict, it was forced into the fray of teacher education by the decision of the Secretary of State in 1966 to offer to the five new technical college education departments the prospect of certificate validation by the CNAA. In response to this the Council established its Committee for Education. Before doing so its representatives had an unpublicized contact with representatives of the Universities Council for the Education of Teachers (UCET). UCET expressed strong opposition to teacher certification by the CNAA outside the ATO structure, and forcefully pointed out that if ATO co-operation was withdrawn from a college that sought CNAA certification that college would encounter serious difficulties in finding teaching practice placements for its students. The CNAA quietly submitted to this rather crude threat and in setting up the Committee of Education resolved that this Committee should not for the time being validate the certification of teachers and should restrict its work to the consideration of degree courses. This was done in such a way that for several years most college teachers remained under the mistaken impression that the validation of teachers' certificates was not within the powers of the CNAA. For several years, despite the stated preference of successive Secretaries of State, the officials of the Department of Education and Science made little effort to correct this impression. They were aware that CNAA consideration of courses in teacher education would clearly reveal that the prevailing scale of financial provision for colleges of education was inadequate by CNAA standards.

The popular image of the CNAA amongst teachers in the colleges of education was that it consisted of technical college and university teachers who were unqualified to make judgements about teacher education. This was, and remains, quite wrong because the Committee for Education, which

* See Robbins, p. 118.
† See TES 24 May 1964, Niblett, and 31 May 1964, Robinson.

had discretion to approve degree courses in education with very broad
CNAA policies, consisted almost entirely of professionals experienced in
teacher education. Certainly it had a much higher proportion of people so
experienced than any university senate.\* The Association of Teachers in
Colleges and Departments of Education and the Universities Council for
the Education of Teachers were and remain very strongly represented on
this Committee but they made no great efforts to publicize the fact,
perhaps because they were not anxious for the existence and nature of the
Committee to be widely known. The only published comment of the
Committee's chairman that I can find during these early years was to the
effect that it was less liberal than people might imagine – a strange libel on
himself and his colleagues. Rarely in history was a committee so modest
about itself!

The first and only colleges to put proposals to this committee during the
first two years of its existence were one college of education and one
college of technology. The first of these has been widely misunderstood
and misrepresented. One of the largest and strongest colleges of education
in England is attached to one of the most rigid and conservative universities.
The university was prepared to offer only a pass B.Ed. degree under
excessively rigid regulations and procedures; it was not willing to recognize
for degree purposes some practical subjects.

The college asked for CNAA approval for a B.Ed. honours degree that
was to be superimposed on the structure of the ATO certificate course.
It did not seek CNAA validation of a teachers' certificate course. After
protracted negotiations the CNAA gave its approval to a B.Ed. honours
course but this was limited to certain subjects. The college felt unable to
begin the course without the approval of all the proposed options and the
proposal became a dead letter when the university modified its policies.

This college was to some extent the victim of a failure by the CNAA
to adapt its procedures to the unique characteristics of a college of
education. The technical college curriculum typically consists of numerous
independent courses – quite separate degree and diploma courses in this
and that, very similar to the curriculum pattern of the departmental university. A technical college can thus revise its curriculum in a piecemeal fashion,
course by course, department by department. In contrast, a college of
education typically has a unified curriculum structure which is not susceptible to piecemeal reform. Whereas a technical college can, and many do,
run distinct courses for London degrees, CNAA degrees, Higher National
Diplomas, for the college of education it must be all or nothing unless a
completely new structure of the college is contemplated.

The course proposed by the college of technology was a part-time B.A.

\* Half of its members were teachers in colleges and departments of education.
This proportion was increased when the committee was reconstituted in 1971.

course in the sociology of education. The Council's Committee of Education participated jointly with the Council's sociology board in the consideration of this and it was approved in 1967. This course was designed for qualified teachers and did not raise the delicate question of teacher certification.

Several colleges of education explored the possibility of CNAA proposals but were discouraged by the formidable task of satisfying the Council and carrying out delicate negotiations with Area Training Organizations.

In 1969 and 1970 there was a perceptible change in the attitude of the DES and, most significantly, the Scottish Education Department towards CNAA submissions from colleges of education. In 1970 a proposal for a B.Ed. course superimposed on a certificate course was made by Notre Dame College of Education, Glasgow and was approved in 1971 for a start in September 1971. This college, in common with several Scottish colleges of education, did not have a B.Ed. arrangement with a university. Furthermore this did not raise a problem of certification because there is no ATO system in Scotland and college certificates are validated directly by the Scottish Education Department. The approval of this course firmly established the Council in the field of initial teacher education.

During 1971 the question of submitting the whole teacher education curriculum – certificate and degree – was raised with the Council by one of the largest and strongest colleges of education in England and, collectively, by the eight polytechnic education departments. In response to this, after verifying that the DES was not only willing to permit but anxious to encourage this the Council agreed to consider proposals for certification just in time to include this in its evidence, written and oral, to the James Committee.

There was general acceptance by the end of 1971, both inside the Council and out, that at least the education departments of the polytechnics would apply for transfer from validation of certificate and degree from the universities to the CNAA. In acknowledgement of this, when the CNAA Committee for Education was reconstructed in the autumn of 1971, its constitution was revised to include five representatives of the polytechnics. At the end of 1971 it had, for the first time, a long agenda of proposals for courses, mostly, but not entirely, from polytechnics.

The proposals emerging from the polytechnics at the end of 1971 indicate the likely pattern of development of their contribution to teacher education. During 1972 and 1973 the first new courses will be mainly part-time courses for B.Ed. and B.A. in education. (The demarcation between B.Ed. and B.A. is as yet uncertain. Polytechnics work from strength in these courses because of the huge experience that the institutions already have in part-time education. The polytechnics will take advantage of the fact that the CNAA

has a much more liberal attitude than most universities to entry qualifications for such degrees. They will generally be open to all qualified
teachers, permitting them to take a longer or shorter course according to
their academic level on entry and according to the intensity of the effort
they can give to their studies. The courses will differ from those so far
offered by the universities in that (1) they will have a curriculum purpose-
built for experienced teachers – they will not be the initial training B.Ed.
adapted for part-time students; (2) they will concentrate heavily on professional studies in education and much less heavily than most university
B.Ed. degrees on academic 'main' studies. Many of them will include
practical and development studies related to the problems of teachers in
particular types of school and some will include training for educational
research by the school teacher. It is possible that a national network of
compatible courses will be established so that a teacher can continue his
studies uninterrupted by a move of home and job from one part of the
country to another. (Hatfield Polytechnic has already taken an initiative
towards this in degrees in mathematics for teachers and Sheffield Polytechnic
in degrees for businessmen.) Some of these courses will be run in collaboration with colleges of education and will probably be followed by similar
initiatives by the larger colleges of education going it alone. A welcome,
and long overdue development, is the collaboration of polytechnics with
the Open University in this work. Some of the polytechnics are planning
to give credit in their courses to students who have achieved partial success
In Open University courses and it is likely that the Open University will
reciprocate.

The next stage of polytechnic development, a much more difficult operation, is the design and submission to the CNAA of new courses for initial
education and training. The notable characteristic of these courses will be
the abandonment of the traditional structure of main studies, professional
studies and curriculum studies which is incompatible with the philosophy
of the CNAA. This philosophy demands a much closer integration of the
professional, academic and liberal aspects of the curriculum. New forms
of experience in the field (i.e. in the schools) will be developed, drawing
upon the polytechnic's experience of training in other professional fields
and breaking away from the traditional strait jacket of the concept of
teaching practice. Experiments at Trent Polytechnic are only the start of
new work in this direction.

In the early 1960s several colleges of advanced technology (including
Aston and Brunel) were keen to experiment with sandwich courses of
teacher education, including both industrial and teaching experience, but
got little encouragement from the DES. Both the technological universities
and the polytechnics are likely to make such experiments with official
encouragement during the 1970s. They will be anxious that the James

Report should not be used by the government or the teaching profession to reimpose a rigid pattern of field experience and training in the colleges and universities. One of the great difficulties will be the rigidity of the teaching profession on the question of unqualified and partially qualified people working in the schools, particularly if they are paid for this work. But the polytechnics will fight this battle armed with their experience of the great value of the sandwich method in other fields of professional education. They will exploit the contradiction by which school teachers are desperately in need of assistance in the classroom and yet regard students as a nuisance and a burden under the conventional 'teaching practice' situation.

In some of the new polytechnic courses of initial education and training the performance of the student in the school will weigh, in a way not yet contemplated in any university, in the final assessment for a degree award. The concept of the teacher tutor will develop nationally in institutions that already have experience of analogous roles in the education of technologists, scientists and businessmen.

It is likely that more colleges of education will be incorporated into polytechnics. Even where a marriage is not arranged, co-operation between colleges of education and polytechnics in course development will become more common, particularly when the college of education decides to prepare courses for CNAA approval. In some cases co-operation will be established on a limited basis in the design of part-time degree courses; the mutual respect and confidence established by this co-operation will facilitate subsequent co-operation on the full-time curriculum. In some large towns such as Portsmouth, Plymouth and Sunderland the polytechnic is rapidly becoming the local 'university' and the amalgamation of it with the neighbouring colleges of education seems the almost inevitable outcome of the major change in national policy for teacher education set out in the 1972 White Paper. It is likely that the education schools, faculties or departments of education that emerge from such amalgamations will follow the precedents established by the eight pioneering polytechnic education departments.

Concurrently with this development there will be new course proposals to the CNAA for the education and training of further education teachers. In the first instance the initiative in this will come from outside the polytechnics – from the colleges of education (technical) in Bolton, Huddersfield, London (Garnett College) and Wolverhampton. At first these will be part-time courses and will be followed by the transfer of the full-time courses from university to CNAA supervision. It is a paradox of the government's polytechnic policy that although several colleges of education have been incorporated into polytechnics none of the colleges of education (technical) has been included even though two of them are located in the same towns as polytechnics (Wolverhampton and Huddersfield). All four of them will probably be incorporated into polytechnics sooner or later, and several more polytechnics will develop work in the education and training of FE teachers. The government during the 1960s has demonstrated a remarkable indifference to the training of FE teachers (most of whom have no professional training whatsoever) but substantial advance in this work must soon be made if only for the prospective teachers of the sixteen to nineteen age group in the FE colleges. The anomaly of training being compulsory for the teachers of this age group in secondary schools but neglected for teachers in FE colleges will grow steadily worse during the 1970s unless action is taken to correct it.

All these developments anticipate the continuation of a system in which students in education and training for teaching are isolated from other students. Although for practical reasons this isolation will continue for some years one consequence of the White Paper will be its gradual erosion. There will be a growth of many courses of education and training which enable a student to defer his vocational decision. The polytechnics with education departments will play a major part in developing such courses. They are particularly well placed to do so because they can call upon the resources of other polytechnic departments to broaden the initial educational experience and the subsequent range of vocational opportunity. Soon after the James Report was published several polytechnics began exploratory studies to develop a programme for the Diploma in Higher Education (the Dip.H.E. recommended by James) on a polytechnic rather than departmental basis.* One polytechnic already has plans for a degree course based on the study of social science that provides a delayed option for professional education and training for teaching, social work and social administration.

Many polytechnics have courses based on studies in technology, physical science, biological science, mathematics and social science that incorporate an element of professional education and training for a variety of vocations. Some of these would require only a fairly simple amendment to make provision for one of the available professions to be that of teaching.

It is now generally agreed that teacher education should be more closely integrated into higher education as a whole. There is little agreement on how it should be done. While the educational world debates the question the polytechnics can make their most useful contribution by action to demonstrate one of Lord James' most important points: that in the present situation the necessary radical change is more feasible outside the university system than inside it.

* See, for example, *Diploma of Higher Education. A Proposal*, October 1972, North East London Polytechnic.

# *Part 3*

## TEACHER EDUCATION AND THE COLLEGES OF EDUCATION

CHAPTER 8

# The Development of Teacher Education in Colleges of Education

ALEC ROSS

What are today known as colleges of education in England and Wales have their origins in a tradition which may be traced back to the second quarter of the nineteenth century. It would be tedious to recount in this chapter details of the story previously told in other accounts (Jones, 1924; Rich, 1933). The significant points about what might be called 'the training college tradition' are, however, important, for tradition has a powerful effect in all educational systems and not least in that of England and Wales.

The story of the training colleges is always told separately from that of the education and training of the graduate destined to teach in what would now be regarded as a secondary school. The training college tradition has its roots in the need to provide a means whereby the poor could be educated and trained to educate the poor in elementary schools. The fact that it was education as well as training that was provided is to the credit of Dr (later Sir James) Kay-Shuttleworth whose contribution to early thinking about teacher education is well known. His time as an Inspector of pauper schools and the experience of running a private venture training establishment with his friend and fellow Inspector E. Carleton Tufnell led him to realize that what was needed was a system which provided both education and training (Smith, 1923, Judges, 1952, Pollard, 1956).

> To select from the common drudgery of a handicraft, or from the humble, if not mean pursuits of a petty trade, a young man barely (if indeed at all) instructed in the humblest elements of reading, writing and arithmetic, and to conceive that a few months' attendance in a Model School can make him acquainted with the theory of its organisation, convert him into an adept of its methods, or even rivet upon his stubborn memory any significant part of the technical knowledge of which he has immediate need, is a mistake too shameful to be permitted to survive. . . . (Kay-Shuttleworth, 1862)

An inspection of the examination papers and answers which the students at the private venture college at Battersea had to face provide evidence of the extent of the general education provided during the course of a year in fulfilment of this aim. The students could extract the cube root, parse poetry, prove from the New Testament various items of Christian belief, describe the hydrostatic press, write a full account of various counties and do much else besides. The education provided had, however, a utilitarian purpose – and one which impinged upon the training side.

> The general principles on which the education of children of all classes should be conducted are doubtless fundamentally the same; but for each class specific modifications are requisite, not only in the matter, but in the manner of instruction. The discipline, management, and methods of instruction in elementary schools for the poor, differ widely from those which ought to characterize schools for the middle or upper classes of society. (Kay and Tuffnell, 1841)

The fact that both tasks had to be done simultaneously, or the one through the other, gave rise to a debate about what is now called 'concurrency', i.e. providing both education and training at the same time. An Inspector in the 1840s was criticizing a college in terms almost identical with those still being heard.

> I am simply insisting on the necessity of making teaching as an art the subject of study in a training college, in respect to each subject taught; of viewing each such subject under a double aspect, as that which is to become an element of the student's own knowledge, and as that which he is to be made capable of presenting under so simple a form, that it may become an element of the knowledge of the child.*

In 1923 the principal of Whitelands Training College was protesting that 'the concurrence is not so administratively tidy as the separation, but in my experience the strength of the Two-Year Course lies in that concurrence' (Jones, 1924). The Select Committee of the House of Commons which met in the session of 1969–70† to discuss teacher training received much conflicting evidence on this topic. The Committee of Inquiry (Chairman, Lord James of Rusholme) which reported in 1972 considered what it called the 'virtues and weaknesses' of the concurrent courses but decided that the disadvantages outweighed the advantages and proposed 'a radical solution' (James, 1972). This was to make the courses consecutive, i.e. to deal first with the general education and then to follow it with concentrated professional training. Close reading of the Report reveals that the Committee

---

* Committee of Council on Education, *Minutes, 1847–8*, Vol II, p. 440.
† Select Committee on Education and Science (Session 1969–70), *Teacher Training* (30, i to xv; 135, i to iv; 136, i to ii; 151, i to iv).

was clearly aware of some of the problems associated with the proposed reform especially in the case of students committed to teaching from the start of their higher education. 'The . . . consecutive pattern now proposed, involving a cycle of personal education followed by a cycle of training, would have to give such students similar opportunities to make early progress towards their occupational goal.' It is unlikely that this latest contribution to a debate which has lasted almost as long as the training college tradition will be settled by the recommendations of a single committee. The concurrent course is regarded as being a significant contribution to the practice of higher education and the proposals of the Committee of Enquiry would, if accepted, bring this to an end; the colleges would in this respect be brought into line with usual practice in the sector concerned with the professional training of graduates.

The view taken of the consecutive/concurrent controversy is to some extent influenced by considerations stemming from an examination of the content of the college course. The course lengthened from one year to two years in 1856, to three in 1960 and, for some, to four years in the late 1960s. Yet the main constituents remain much as they were in the nineteenth century. The traditional elements can be characterized as subject study (sometimes, to the dismay of education lecturers, called 'academic' subjects), theoretical studies of education, method courses and teaching practice. A college time-table for the 1920s would not be unduly out of line with what is current practice. The subject study was, till recent years, almost entirely restricted to subjects which had to be taught in schools. The now defunct National Advisory Council on the Training and Supply of Teachers declared as late as 1957 that 'the spread of subjects in the colleges must be related to the subjects taught in the schools'.* Yet when the Select Committee of the Commons carried out its enquiry in 1969–70 the subjects taught to degree level (B.Ed.) in the colleges were as the list shown in Table 8.1.

The list of subjects taught to levels lower than degree was no doubt longer and even more varied. Non-school subjects such as psychology, sociology, philosophy (in their own right and not as a part of a study of education) have become commonplace; other non-school subjects are becoming increasingly common, and in places problem-centred (as distinct from discipline-centred) courses are emerging. Furthermore within the 'subjects' there is often scope for students to follow – for part of the time at least – individual interests. This movement does not reflect an indifference to providing the knowledge needed to teach subjects in schools but realization that in many schools, especially those for younger pupils, subjects as such are not taught. A more significant reason was the view that subject study

* NACTST Sixth Report, HMSO, 1957, p. 4.

Table 8.1    Subjects taught to degree level in Colleges of Education 1969–70.

| | |
|---|---|
| American studies | Handicraft |
| Applied mathematics | History |
| Applied plant science | Home economics |
| Applied science | Housing |
| Art | |
| Art and craft | Music |
| Art and design | |
| Art of movement | Natural science |
| Beginnings of the modern world | |
| Biblical studies | Philosophy |
| Biology | Physics |
| Business studies | Physical education |
| | Physical science |
| Chemistry | Psychology |
| Commercial studies | Principles of religion |
| Computation | Pure mathematics |
| Craft and technical studies | |
| | Rural science |
| Dance | Russian |
| Domestic science | |
| Drama | |
| Dress and design | Science technology |
| | Science, household management |
| Economic organization | (Part I only) |
| Education | Social administration |
| English | Sociology |
| Environmental studies | |
| European studies | Theology |
| Evolution and prehistory | |
| | Welsh |
| Field biology | Welsh literature |
| Fine art | Wood and metalwork |
| Food and nutrition | |
| French | Youth leadership (Part I only) |
| German | |
| Geography | Zoology |
| Geology | |

Source: Select Committee on Education and Science (Session 1969–70), *Teacher Training*, 30, xv, p. 609.

was the principal vehicle for the general education and that if it provides the means for what has often been called the 'personal education' of the student, it is irrelevant whether the subject is taught in school or not.

The counterpart to the 'subjects-for-personal-development' view is the assumption that the studies (sometimes called 'professional') more closely connected with education did not provide such opportunities. This has been vigorously opposed; it has been pointed out that an intending teacher is as likely to find opportunities for self-development, self-realization and personal fulfilment within the theoretical studies in education and in the practice of teaching as in 'subject' studies. A significant experiment has been set up in the north of England (with the financial support of the Department of Education and Science) which provides a college course without subject study at all; the course provides the usual education and practice elements but replaces the subject study with an applied education course strongly directed towards work with children in primary and middle schools.* Elsewhere similar schemes are being developed as 'third area' studies. Another development worthy of note is that of linking or bridging studies designed to explore the relationship between the subjects studied and education.

These problems, and those relating to the link between theoretical studies and experience in school, are explored elsewhere in this volume. What is significant about these developments is that they represent an approach to solving the problems posed by concurrency. They reject the idea of a sharp distinction between, on the one hand, 'subjects' studied for reasons of personal development and, on the other, 'professional' courses followed for vocational purposes. It is claimed that a young person committed to a teaching career is as likely to facilitate personal development and find self-fulfilment in the study of material directly relevant to teaching as in material less remotely so. This enlargement of claims has been matched by those who teach subjects; if the subject is taught in school it can include matter relevant to teaching and if it is not it can be shown to provide an essential perspective. In both cases the personal/professional dichotomy can be shown to have broken down.

The phrase 'personal development' includes, in the field of higher education, the development of critical powers, of analytical and synthesizing skills of sensitivity and of feeling. When the subjects studied are well-recognized academic disciplines it is assumed without question that such powers are developed by studying that subject. Some of the subjects listed above (Table 8.1) are not, of course, disciplines of knowledge or even subjects in the traditional sense; but even universities are today familiar with area and theme-centred studies. The case of educational studies has,

---

* The applied education project is centred in the University of Lancaster school of education.

however, till recent years been different. These studies were first developed to provide a rationale for the method classes which figured so strongly in the curriculum of the nineteenth-century college. As will happen with scholars, courses intended to be practical developed lengthy introductions which recapitulated the ideas and methods of former days (Quick, 1895), analysed the steps by which knowledge could best be imparted (Herbart, 1901; Adams, 1912), and produced theories of education (Adams, 1922; Nunn, 1920). The work of Binet, Stanley Hall, Spearman and Burt, not to mention Freud, gave the study of education an orientation towards psychology which lasted until the 1950s when sociology provided a new dimension of thought on education within which we still operate. The postwar period saw the development of what have been called the foundation disciplines of education – history, philosophy, sociology, psychology (Tibble, 1966). These were developed and were an undoubted improvement upon the undisciplined combined theory courses which preceded them. The price paid for intellectual discipline was fragmentation. In so far as these studies were intended to apply directly to teaching, the student had to make the multi-disciplined application. Moreover, since all students studied them and since education departments commonly work on a staffing ratio much inferior to that enjoyed by 'subject' departments, the way was open for the James Committee to declare its doubts about the procedure. 'It must be doubted ... whether such studies, especially if presented through the medium of lectures to large groups of perplexed students are, in terms of priorities, a useful major element in initial training.'

A more recent trend has been to reduce the fragmentation by distinguishing the empirical approaches (psychology and sociology) from those which are of particular significance in the area of judgement (history and philosophy). In particular the study of behaviour in school learning situations is neither purely psychological nor purely sociological, yet it can be studied with all the rigour normally used in the pursuit of those disciplines and it is seen to be more directly relevant. Similarly, the study of history and philosophy, particularly in relation to the background against which a choice of aims and objectives for a school curriculum is made, has been shown to be highly pertinent. It would appear that two approaches, the empirical and the evaluative, are in some cases replacing the four separate foundation disciplines of psychology, sociology, philosophy and history.

A further step has been taken by those who espouse the theory and practice of curriculum development. The phases of curriculum theory, moving through aims and objectives, learning experiences and the ordering of content and resources to evaluation, involve all the foundation disciplines and in addition require a grasp of the structure of the subject material being taught. It might be thought that the wheel has come full circle in as much as it is now possible to see 'education' being taught in a unitary and not a fragmented way. There has been a return to a more co-ordinated approach which can more surely be continued now that suitably rigorous standards of disciplinary enquiry have been established as a result of the 'foundations' approach.

The most significant development from these advances is that educational studies are now increasingly regarded as capable of being studied in an orderly and disciplined way. They are now being taught in universities, especially as a subsidiary or joint honours subject, even to students who have no particular ambition to teach. It could be said that educational studies have begun that march towards academic respectability already trodden by politics, economics and, more recently, sociology. Like them they draw upon prior disciplines; like them they also have something distinctively their own. This addition to the university's curriculum was made possible only because of the work of the colleges of education. The university departments of education had as their 'base' the one-year graduate course with its notoriously short period for the study of education. The three-year college course gave much greater scope and it is from this tradition that universities developing educational studies as an undergraduate study have drawn their inspiration. Educational studies, as a subject of worthwhile study, appear prominently in *Teacher Education and Training* (James, 1972), and in the Note of Extension* it is seen as part of an honours degree course.

The fact that the study of education is now seen as being capable of providing all the intellectual stimulation which traditional disciplines can offer and can at the same time be shown to have direct relevance to the tasks of teaching has made it possible for the education side of the college course to justify itself on academic as well as professional grounds. Given at the same time the development in the colleges of new subjects and of new content for old subjects, some of it highly relevant to teaching, it is apparent that the professional/academic division is no longer as firm as it was. This does not mean that the problem of 'concurrency' has ceased to exist but it does mean that it has taken a different form. That which was meant to introduce the practical having, for good reasons, developed into a theory, the problem of transmitting the practicalities of day-to-day work in the profession remains. The experimental course already referred to† seeks to do this by developing what it calls 'applied education' and teaches this in addition to the education theory course which all students take.

The powerful development of the academic aspects of both the education and the subject courses has done much to establish the claims of the colleges to be providers of higher education in the full and non-vocational sense. The response to the challenge of the Robbins Report (1963) which asked the

* P. 78, paragraph 4.
† The applied education project, centred in the University of Lancaster.

colleges to undertake teaching to degree level has been more than met. The validity of the B.Ed. degree especially in the honours form which is now all but standard may be judged by the willingness of university departments to accept for higher degree courses students with an appropriate standard of honours in the B.Ed. degree. Clearly the level of teaching and of student attainment in academic studies has risen far beyond the level which Kay-Shuttleworth envisaged when he made such a strong bid for general education as well as professional training. The gulf which in mid-nineteenth-century England and Wales separated the university man from the college-trained schoolmaster had, for some teachers, been bridged by the mid-1960s.

The development of the colleges as institutions of higher education has, however, been said to put at risk their development as institutions of professional formation. A paper presented to the Select Committee on Education and Science (session 1969–70) on teacher training put the point thus:

> When staff appointments are made, too often excellence in theory or in a subject is preferred to excellence in educational practice and too often is the increasingly invalid assumption made that excellence in practical applications can usually be allied with excellence in one or other of the remaining aspects. The introduction of the B.Ed. degree has made the task of appointment committees even more difficult. Is it really possible to find experienced schoolteachers capable of lecturing and tutoring an academic subject at degree level and at the same time conducting lower level courses on how to teach the subject in schools as well as supervising teaching practice mostly in primary schools? There is a growing body of opinion which claims that this particular emperor has no clothes.*

*Teacher Education and Training* took up this point even more strongly:

> The concurrent form of training within the colleges of education suffers from a conflict and confusion of objectives. ... The problem is illustrated by the diffuse role which tutors in colleges are expected to fulfil. Lecturers appointed for the qualifications, ability and teaching skill in an academic discipline may, for example, have to take responsibility for the professional preparation of teachers of young children.†

The solution offered by the committee was to abandon the tradition of concurrency and to divide the preparation of a teacher into a first phase of general education and a separate second phase of 'sharply focused' professional training. This solution has been criticized as being over-simple. It has been pointed out that professional formation needs time, particularly if

---

* Select Committee on Education and Science, Teacher Training Session 1969–70. 30, viii, p. 262. Paper presented by J. Booth and A. M. Ross.
† James Report, HMSO, 1972, para 3.16 p. 23.

that formation depends on the acquisition of a range of competences, sensitivities and insights which require cultivation rather than implantation. The James report has clearly failed to differentiate between those aspects of a professional formation which are capable of being provided in terminal 'crash' courses and those aspects which require longer to be communicated. The latter are, of course, less tangible and are, therefore, less likely to be mentioned in evidence. Many of the critics were anxious not to destroy the concurrent course so much as to change it by introducing a strongly practical additional element taught by experienced practitioners. The case for reform rather than revolution is strengthened by consideration of the content of educational studies in so far as it is distinct from applied practical studies and the relationship of such studies to those which have a practical outcome. Educational studies are developing as a social science subject worth study in themselves like politics, religious studies, environmental studies and economics, even if the student does not intend to join the profession or calling related to that study. The argument that it is wrong to give students a higher education which commits them to teaching does not, therefore, follow. Nevertheless, as a 'set' in the mathematical sense, educational studies overlap to some extent that other 'set' of practical training which intending teachers require. The area of overlap will, of course, vary according to the content of the syllabus; it is an important area since it may well be regarded as making possible a reduction in the amount of training needed by a student who has read educational studies as part of his higher education. Though the 'sets' overlap they are separable and the assumption that all lecturers are sufficiently competent in both areas is clearly unwarranted. An awareness of the significance of the overlap area in terms of the other 'set' would undoubtedly be a requirement; competence in both would not. The tradition which began with Kay-Shuttleworth appears to have failed therefore, first, because of the rising academic standards expected and secondly, because of the more diffuse nature of the practical requirement. The solution may well lie, however, not in a complete rejection of the distinctive feature of the college's work but in its reformulation and restructuring.

Studies involving the application of several disciplines clearly involve problems over and above those met within studies which can be pursued for the most part within a single discipline. It is inevitable that multi-disciplinary studies run a greater risk of losing that degree of intellectual rigour which higher education requires. The very complexity and difficulty of managing the concepts required for a study involving many interacting disciplines may cause the less skilled to clothe their confusion with catch-phrases which in turn supplant reasoning. The standard of the study of education appropriate to a profession in a country which gives to its teachers remarkably wide powers of decision ought, therefore, to be of the highest. Done well there is no reason for believing that educational studies cannot extend the most able students. The colleges have, however, failed to attract their fair share of the able; they have remained – as befits institutions founded to train the poor to teach the poor – the institutions of second and even third choice. A relatively large survey conducted in the department of educational research in the University of Lancaster in the late 1960s investigated the attainments of students admitted to higher education; the level deemed to indicate good academic promise was reached or surpassed by only 7·4 per cent. of the college of education entrants as compared with 68·5 per cent. of those who went to university (Entwistle *et al.*, 1971). The colleges have maintained entry standards if these are expressed in terms of the proportions holding various numbers of 'A' level qualifications but this has been done at a time when the proportion of the population obtaining 'A' levels has risen sharply and in a period when selectors have increasingly taken into account level rather than number of 'A' levels.* This differential flow of ability away from the colleges of education at a time when ever increasing intellectual demands are being made upon teachers is a serious matter. Teaching does not require all the best talent available but it does require its reasonable share if the schools staffed by teachers educated in the non-university sector are to throw up the leaders of the future. The fact that colleges of education have always recruited from the band immediately below those entering university was of little importance when universities took such a small proportion of the age group; now that the numbers entering university have grown and that polytechnics offer another – and some might think a better – alternative, there is a grave risk of a decline in the intellectual quality of the college of education student.

Since the college of education student is more likely to move towards infant and primary school work than the student who approaches teaching from the university, it is sometimes suggested that the fact that colleges recruit less able students is of no great concern. There is no evidence to support the assumption that the personal qualities which the successful teacher of younger children must possess are not to be found coupled with academic ability. Furthermore it is apparent to those who are close to primary school work of the best kind that the developments now needed are ones which call upon those teaching skills that belong to the cognitive rather than the affective order. There can be no doubt that infant and primary education in England and Wales has developed an atmosphere for learning appropriate to the age range concerned and worthy of imitation. There can be no doubt that to exploit these advantages fully, especially in relation to children who for environmental or other reasons are not apt learners, a form of teaching must be developed which seeks out the structures of knowledge, identifies the concepts needed and links these together

* See annual reports of the Central Register and Clearing House and of the Graduate Training Registry.

in order to construct networks of ideas, skills, attitudes and values. This is work which calls for teaching of the highest order. The intellectual demands of such a task are as great as any to be found in teaching.

It is necessary to turn next to the question of numbers. During the 1950s and 1960s the colleges of education have acted as an adjustable regulator to the higher education system, providing teachers in response to ever increasing demand and at the same time supplying higher education (in the form of teacher training) to many – especially girls – unable to get it elsewhere. The demand for teachers is declining and will probably continue to decline throughout the 1970s since the numbers staying at school longer are unlikely to counterbalance a birth rate which has declined steeply since 1964. But as the demand for teachers is declining, demand for higher education is increasing, and governments are always quick to notice that college places are cheaper than university places. It should be pointed out, however, that if the comparison is made between similar types of teaching the differentiation in cost is not as great as Education Planning Paper No. 2* would seem to imply. Furthermore, in the 1970s it is the cost of *additional* places which must be computed and these are cheaper if they do not involve creating new institutions. Be that as it may, college of education places remain attractive to governments seeking to provide more places for less money. The somewhat slow expansion allowed for in Education Planning Paper No. 2. (from 118,000 places in 1971 to 129,600 in 1981) reflected caution about the demand for teachers. An alternative view could be developed from the standpoint of *Teacher Education and Training*. This report develops the higher education side of the college's work, though it sees this in terms of a two-year non-degree course. Clearly a lower level award in British higher education is needed; clearly the colleges can provide an available facility for this purpose. Nevertheless, it is unfortunate that at a time when the colleges have developed honours degree courses they should again be pulled back to less demanding academic work and be confirmed in their function of reserve institutions charged with taking up the slack whenever more prestigious institutions are full. This is unfortunate not because the task of teaching at sub-degree level is an unworthy one; it is unfortunate because it links teaching – especially the teaching of younger children – with the less demanding forms of higher education.

It is possible to develop from the position adopted in *Teacher Education and Training* an alternative plan which saves teacher education from being associated firmly with lower-level higher education though it does so at the cost of up-grading only some of the colleges. Such an alternative plan begins by looking at the growth in the numbers of graduates being trained for entry to the teaching profession. These have grown rapidly to close on

---

* *Student Numbers in Higher Education in England and Wales.* Education Planning Paper No. 2. HMSO, 1970.

10,000 in 1971, they will double in the 1970s and in each year there will be an increasing number of graduates willing to train but unable to find a place. The profession could probably meet all its needs from graduate output by the end of the decade if sufficient training places were provided. Despite the fact that many degree courses now include educational studies, such a development would imply that the consecutive pattern of education and training had become standard. The colleges would be entirely devoted to training and to two-year higher education courses. It would be wrong, however, to cast away the experience (much criticized) and value (much misunderstood) of the concurrent tradition. If – to take round and approximate figures – it were decided that the number of new teachers needed per annum were 30,000 it would be reasonable to recruit only 20,000 of these from the polytechnics and the universities (including, of course, the Open University). The remaining 10,000 could be recruited from three-year degree courses taught in up-graded colleges of education affiliated to universities and polytechnics which had entry standards at the same level as those applying to the major institution and which were developed as major centres of pedagogical research. Courses in such colleges would, perhaps, be more attractive to school leavers and because of their orientation towards teaching might well merit a shortened period of training. To provide the 10,000 per annum hypothesized above, only one-quarter of the existing colleges would be needed. The remainder would provide training courses (pre-service and in-service) or provide the two-year courses of general higher education from which a few students might cross over to join the degree courses which by then would have become the only entry to the teaching profession. Teaching and the study of education would thus have 'arrived' but at the expense of redeploying the resources of the colleges of education.

Colleges of education were created because there was nowhere else for student teachers to receive the post-elementary education they required. In the age of secondary education for all they continued to train teachers while providing higher education for those who had failed to gain entry to what was considered a superior form of higher education. This has not been in the best interests of teaching. If teaching is to find its rightful place in the most prestigious forms of higher education it can do so only if the colleges cease to be used as inferior providers of education. This means that some colleges should find their future within the framework of a university or polytechnic and others should position themselves within whatever structures are created to provide a much-needed pattern of sub-degree higher education. When the country decided to move towards providing higher education for the many rather than the few, part of the case for a college of education sector disappeared. At the same time the colleges had developed their curriculum to the point at which it has become acceptable to regard many of the things done in colleges of education as suitable for degree courses. The college of education has so far made its contribution to higher education practice if not from outside the walls of the university at least from outside most faculties. The time has come for that contribution to be made from within. The college of education has rendered itself superfluous. The best of its academic work can now be done within the major institutions; the lower levels of academic work have still to be done but now have a different purpose; the training work can be done in professional centres. In a binary system there is no place for a third force.

# CHAPTER 9

# The Area Training Organization

## JOHN TURNER

The question, 'Who controls the schools?' is one of the most important questions to ask about any country's educational system, and in Britain it is one of the most difficult to answer. A visitor from overseas who asks such a question about the education and qualification of teachers is likely to receive such confusing and sometimes contradictory replies that he may wonder whether the teacher education system (if indeed the word 'system' can be justly applied to it) has not been designed deliberately to confuse the answer. There seems to be a considerable number of agents claiming the right to control the sort of preparation which teachers should receive and the sort of institution in which they should receive this preparation.

The Department of Education and Science, which bears the ultimate responsibility for the formulation of national educational policy and for financing much of the nation's education from the central exchequer, naturally claims the right to a voice in teacher education. The local education authorities, which employ the teachers and own the great majority of the schools in which they will teach and the colleges in which the teachers receive their own professional education demand the same right. The universities have been charged with establishing and maintaining the standard of the awards given in the colleges and clearly have the right to speak on the academic policy of the colleges. A similar right can hardly be denied to the staffs of the colleges themselves, who, as the professionals most closely involved with the actual work of preparing the teachers of the future, may feel the most competent to exercise control over it. The teaching profession may well challenge that competence, however, and claim the ability to regulate entry into the profession as a basic professional right. More recently students throughout higher education have felt justified in seeking a share in the determination of their own curricula and study methods. Parents too are beginning to take a deeper interest in a matter which so closely concerns the future of their own children.

The Area Training Organization has evolved to draw together these different claimants to the control of teacher education and to give them an opportunity to express their different views, in the hope that a coherent policy will emerge from the discussion. Having formulated the policy, the ATO also has to give effect to its decisions; its role is not only consultative but also executive. The ATO may not be able to pay the piper but its power over the qualifications of the teachers enables it to produce very compulsive music of its own.

This way of attempting to balance the conflicting interests concerned in teacher education was developed as a result of the McNair Commission Report of 1944.* The Commisison had been set up by Mr. R. A. Butler, President of the Board of Education, in March 1942, during the dark days of the war, under the chairmanship of Sir Arnold McNair, then Vice-Chancellor of the University of Liverpool, 'to investigate the present sources of supply and the methods of recruitment and training of teachers and youth leaders, and to report what principles should guide the Board in these matters in the future'. Their report determined the shape of teacher education in Britain for the following twenty-five years.

Two distinguishing marks of the training colleges at the time of the McNair Report were their poverty and their small size. 'What is chiefly wrong with the majority of the training colleges', said the Report, 'is their poverty and all that flows from it.'† Of the eighty-three training colleges in 1938, sixty-four had fewer than 150 students and twenty-eight of those had fewer than a hundred. The paragraphs in the report on conditions in the colleges made depressing reading.‡ In fifty per cent. of the colleges it was judged that laboratories, studios, workshops and gymnasia were inadequate. In more than twenty-five per cent. the assembly halls, libraries, lecture rooms or dining accommodation were considered inadequate. In some colleges even the washing and sanitary arrangements were insufficient or unsuitable.

Since 1926 the colleges had been grouped together under Joint Examination Boards in a relationship with the universities for examination purposes.§ The McNaire Report noted that:

> The fact that the several colleges of a group are all represented on the same Joint Board has not, in general, resulted in their having any closer relations with one another, save in the matter of examinations, than they had when they were more directly under the Board of Education.¶

* Board of Education: *Teachers and Youth Leaders*. Report of the Committee appointed by the President of the Board of Education to consider the supply, recruitment and training of teachers and Youth Leaders. HMSO, 1944.
† P. 13, para. 34.     ‡Pp. 13–15, para. 34–9.
§ The 1925 Board of Education Report, which recommended this grouping, still makes interesting and relevant reading. (Board of Education: Report on the training of teachers for public elementary schools, HMSO, 1925. The Chairman of the Committee was the Right Honourable Viscount Burnham of later 'Burnham Committee' fame.)
¶ McNair Report (1944), p. 16, para. 44.

It is interesting to note that, although the Joint Boards were responsible for formulating syllabuses for the examinations, and in this way exercised a considerable influence over the courses in the colleges, the Board of Education had to approve the syllabuses and retained direct control of the practical examination. Moreover, these arrangements concerned the training colleges only, the departments of education in the universities not being involved in the Board's work. The prefatory note to the McNair Report also noted that 'a large number of teachers now in the secondary schools have not pursued any course of professional training', a reference to the fact that the Board of Education accepted a university degree as a sufficient criterion for the award of qualified teacher status. Not until 1973 will this practice cease, a time lag of nearly thirty years, which is remarkable even in educational reform.

The McNair Committee was divided in its recommendations for changing the organization of teacher training colleges, though it was united in recommending that all teacher training institutions should be brought together in groups to provide 'an integrated service for the education and training of teachers'. This service would break down the clear lines of demarcation between the provision of teachers for primary and secondary schools, and would further reduce the power to control education which belonged to the Board of Education and which had been initiated in 1926 when the responsibility to examine students passed from the Board of Education to the examining boards.

The equal division of opinion among the committee members about the type of 'Area Training Authority' (a term used to describe either form of organization) which should be set up, was caused by a disagreement about the relationship of universities to the colleges of education. One group of committee members favoured the creation of university schools of education in which the universities would accept responsibility for the general supervision of the training of teachers, both graduate and non-graduate. It was assumed that under this scheme 'there would be no separately organized university training departments'. The colleges would become affiliated institutions of the schools of education which would thus be the units 'which would provide the courses required for students entering at about 18 years of age and for those entering after graduation'. The schools' role in the continuing education of teachers and in the planning and conduct of educational investigation and research was also foreseen.

In some ways this part of the report was extraordinarily perceptive, though excessively optimistic, in its delineation of the desirable outcomes of the school organization. The sharing of resources between the affiliated institutions of the school was seen to be of great importance, not only as a way of economizing but also as a way of breaking down the isolation of the staff of the colleges and thus raising the standard of college provision.

'To break down the isolation of staff is even more important than mitigating the segregation of students.'* Recent criticisms of the mono-professional colleges, especially of those which are too far from the parent university to share fully in its cultural and educational life, were anticipated and the interesting assumption made that:

> Of course a university School of Education would not admit to affiliation a distant institution unless the authorities of the School were satisfied that the institution was co-operating with other educational institutions in the area, for example, technical colleges, schools of art, agricultural institutions, in such a way that it became a centre of cultural interest for the neighbourhood and was not merely an institution for the training of students isolated from the community.†

In this way the influence of the university could be seen as permeating the whole of the tertiary education of the district. Is it too fanciful to detect here a distant foreshadowing of the idea of the 'comprehensive university'? The proposals of this part of the committee arose from a belief that 'in years to come it will be considered disastrous if the national system for the training of teachers is found to be divorced from the work of the universities or even to be running parallel with it'.

The second group of committee members, which included the Chairman himself, favoured rather a development of the Joint Board scheme. It was not appropriate for the universities to undertake all kinds of professional training. The fact that they participated in certain kinds of professional training was ascribed to 'a variety of reasons, historical and other', but such training was a subsidiary function, the university's main duty consisting in 'teaching basic subjects and in the advancement of knowledge'. The universities, faced with an increasing variety of demands, should 'exercise a high degree of discrimination, accepting only those tasks which they are best fitted to carry out and rejecting those for which they are unsuitable instruments'.‡ One task which should be rejected was the responsibility for the training of all teachers. 'We do not consider it to be either practicable or desirable that they should accept responsibility for the training of all teachers.'

In place therefore of the schools of education recommended in the first scheme, the second recommended the development of the Joint Boards: the relationship between the colleges and the universities would be that of a 'partnership between equals' which would not lead to 'the universities having a predominant influence in the training of the students in the training colleges'.§ The existing Joint Boards should therefore be expanded to include 'persons interested in the well-being of our educational system,

---

* P. 51, para. 174.　　　　† P.51, para. 174.
‡ P. 55, para. 184.　　　　§ P. 56, para. 188.

such as directors of education, teachers, parents and other representative citizens'.* They should aim at creating a training service organized on an area basis, and establishing relations with technical colleges, art colleges and schools, agricultural institutes and other educational institutions in their areas.

These enlarged Joint Boards, which would be linked with the Central Training Council, would have a small executive committee and staff. 'In some of the areas it may be necessary to appoint a whole-time officer of considerable standing.' The Joint Boards would take over the arrangement of teaching practice and the final assessment, including practical teaching, of students of the university departments as well as the training colleges. They should be active in in-service education and provide an educational centre for the area.

It can thus be seen that in many ways the intentions of the alternative recommendations within the McNair Report were similar. The main point at issue was the place which the universities should play in the scheme. The first group rejected the dichotomy between education and training and believed that the only way in which it could be removed was for the universities to accept responsibility for the preparation of teachers. The second group, however, feared that the control of the teacher training system by the universities would concentrate the future growth of training colleges in urban areas and cause the training to become too academic. The predominant qualities required by the vast majority of teachers 'in addition to a good general education' are 'qualities which have no necessary connection with university standards at all and are apt not to receive due recognition and encouragement in an academic atmosphere, but will be adequately safeguarded in the training colleges'.† The argument was an argument not only about the control of the system but also about the qualities necessary for the members of the teaching profession during the ensuing years.

After the publication of the report universities were asked to consider the extent to which they would be able to assume the responsibilities outlined in it. Their response ensured that the school of education scheme would be adopted in preference to the Joint Board scheme and seventeen Area Training Organizations were established, thirteen of which were integral parts of the universities or university colleges and four of which were not. The latter group was financed directly by the Ministry of Education. The term 'school of education', proposed by the McNair Committee, was in fact adopted by only two of the new organizations.‡ The great majority used the title 'institute of education', though the title 'delegacy for the training of teachers' was also used. The Ministry of Education used the neutral title 'Area Training Organizations' to describe

* P. 56, para. 189(a).          † P. 61, para. 195(d).          ‡ Manchester and Wales.

all these bodies and it is by that title that they will subsequently be described in this chapter.

In the intervening years there have been changes in the number, titles and organization of the ATOs. As more universities were established new ATOs were developed, in some cases dividing excessively large ATOs and to some extent rationalizing the geographical area for which the ATOs were responsible. At the end of 1971 there were the following ATOs:

University of Birmingham School of Education, with fifteen constituent colleges and three associated colleges;

University of Bristol School of Education, with eight constituent colleges;

Cambridge Institute of Education, with ten constituent colleges;

University of Durham Institute of Education, with eight constituent colleges;

University of Exeter Institute of Education, with three constituent colleges and one associated college;

University of Hull Institute of Education, with two constituent colleges;

University of Keele Institute of Education, with three constituent colleges;

University of Lancaster School of Education, with four constituent colleges;

University of Leeds Institute of Education, with thirteen constituent colleges;

University of Leicester School of Education, with five constituent colleges;

University of Liverpool Institute of Education, with eleven constituent colleges;

University of London Institute of Education, with thirty-two constituent colleges;

Loughborough University of Technology Institute of Education, with one constituent college;

University of Manchester School of Education, with nine constituent colleges;

University of Newcastle upon Tyne Institute of Education, with five constituent colleges;

University of Nottingham School of Education, with eight constituent colleges;

University of Oxford Delegacy for Education Studies, with four constituent colleges;

University of Reading School of Education, with three constituent colleges;

University of Sheffield Institute of Education, with six constituent colleges;

University of Southampton School of Education, with six constituent colleges;

University of Sussex School of Education, with six constituent colleges;

University of Wales School of Education, with ten constituent colleges;

University of Warwick, with one constituent college.

It should be noted that, with the exception of the Cambridge Institute of Education, all the organizations listed above are now integral parts of their universities. Each of these organizations includes the department or departments of education of its own university. For example, the London Institute includes the Central Institute, the faculty of education of King's College, the Chelsea College of Science and Technology Centre for Science Education, and the education courses of the Goldsmiths' College. The University of Manchester School of Education includes the university departments of education, of audiology and education of the deaf, of physical education and of adult education. There is no need to prolong the list beyond these examples. In a number of cases education departments of polytechnics and of other non-education colleges which are pursuing courses of the Institute or School are included as 'constituent colleges'.

It will thus be apparent that there are many differences between the ATOs. These differences become more striking when one compares the sizes of the geographical areas covered by the ATOs, the number and size of their constituent colleges, and their constitutions and schemes of government. Nevertheless, all of them fulfil the same basic function, which could briefly be described as the supervision of the initial and further education of teachers within the geographical area of the ATO.

The ultimate responsibility for ensuring that the supply of teachers is adequate for the statutory school system lies with the Department of Education and Science. The Department therefore has to ensure that the constitution of each ATO fulfils the statutory requirements of the DES, especially with regard to the representative nature of its governing body. Once such recognition has been given, however, the DES is scrupulously correct in refraining from interfering in the academic control of the courses within the ATO. The DES retains the right to ensure that the number of teachers produced nationally is adequate for the needs of the schools, and that the balance in preparing teachers for the various sectors of the educational system is properly maintained, but here too it acts through the ATO. The DES is represented on the governing bodies of the ATOs by assessors who act as the eyes and ears of the Department rather than as its mouthpieces, and rarely attempt to influence the decisions taken. Even decisions about the award of qualified teacher (QT) status, which remain the prerogative of the DES, are normally only taken on the advice of the ATO concerned.

The DES is extremely careful, its detractors would say excessively careful, to respect the autonomy of the ATOs in matters of academic control and recognition for QT status. For example, if a teacher failed a certificate examination in, say, the Leeds ATO in 1950, he may subsequently have taught as an unqualified teacher for twenty years, at the end of which Her Majesty's Inspectors may have concluded that, by virtue of the teaching which they have observed over a long period, he was worthy of qualified teacher status. The DES would not normally confer this status, however, without seeking the advice of the Leeds ATO, even if the teacher had actually been teaching for the whole period outside the Leeds area. The principle of the separation of the academic control of teacher education from the central Department of Education and Science is such an important one that it is easy to tolerate occasional cases of this sort in which some would see an element of absurdity.

The supreme authority of the ATO is a governing body, generally called a Delegacy. The chairman of the Delegacy is usually the vice-chancellor of the university, and the body will contain representatives of the council and senate of the university, of the local education authorities of the area, of the constituent institutions and of teachers. Assessors of the DES will also attend. Unfortunately the boundaries of the ATOs are not congruent with LEA boundaries so that in some cases one LEA may have membership of several Delegacies. This prevents the LEA concerned from participating fully in the work of the Delegacy and also prevents it from formulating a comprehensive teacher education programme for the whole of its area. Derbyshire LEA, for example, is divided between the ATOs of Manchester, Sheffield, Keele and Nottingham and may find its teachers who wish to take part-time courses leading to an academic diploma or a B.Ed. degree treated quite differently by the ATOs in which their own part of the county is situated.

The Delegacy will be advised by a professional or Academic Board which will be primarily concerned with the academic conduct of the initial teacher's certificate of the constituent institutions of the school, including the admission of students, the recognition of courses, curriculum and syllabus matters, the appointment of internal and external examiners, the conduct of examinations, recommendations for QT status and related matters. The membership of the Board will typically consist of representatives of the university senate, the director and professional staff of the school of education, and the principal and other representatives of each of the constituent colleges or departments of the school. Many such Boards will also include representatives of the teaching profession, of students and of local education authorities and assessors appointed by the Department of Education and Science.

The Professional Board will itself have a very considerable number of sub-committees. These may include a Sub-Committee or Board of Studies for each subject taught for the teacher's certificate, which will consider proposals for the syllabus and examinations in that subject and will advise the Professional Board about them. The Boards of Studies will consist of representatives of each of the institutions which teach the subject concerned (in some cases all the tutors are entitled to membership) and of the appropriate departments of the university: in an increasing number of cases serving teachers and students are members of the Boards. There will also be Boards of Examiners concerned with the conduct of the examinations in each subject. Other committees of the Professional Board may be a Committee of Principals and an Awarding Committee which will advise the Professional Board on the award of its certificates.

The academic control of the B.Ed. degree sometimes followed the pattern which had previously been established for the teacher's certificate. In other cases a completely separate pattern was established to take account of the more direct interest of the senate of the university and its departments in this degree. The variety of the degree structure itself in different universities, from a four-year degree programme to a one-year programme following the award of the Certificate, led to a corresponding variety of organizational framework. In all cases, however, the student on the B.Ed. programme has at some stage to be awarded a teacher's certificate or certificate in education and has to be recommended (or not recommended) for qualified teacher status. Both of these matters remain the concern of the Delegacy of the ATO.

The authority structure within an ATO is therefore a very complex one which becomes more complex as an effort is made to involve in fruitful consultation all those who are concerned in teacher education. This complexity can hardly be said to work in favour of rapid change within the system.

Indeed it is at this point that one of the most serious attacks on the ATO structure is made by some tutors in colleges of education. As has been noted elsewhere in this volume, considerable changes have recently been effected in the structure of the colleges of education. A great deal of power formerly exercised by the LEAs and by the principal himself is now exercised by the college Academic Board and there is no doubt that the colleges will become more properly autonomous as they learn to use the powers which are now theirs. As they do so they tend increasingly to resent the restrictions on their academic freedom which the ATO principle seems to impose on them. For example, a proposal to integrate the study of history and geography in one college of education may involve the establishment of a new Board of Studies in Integrated Studies, which in turn will have to persuade both the existing Boards of Studies for History and Geography before the proposal can be implemented. A suggestion that all the studies which bear on the professional preparation of the students should be integrated into a coherent professional studies programme might lead to the setting up of a special ATO committee for this purpose, which in turn would have to take soundings of a number of existing Boards of Studies; and when agreement has been reached by all those concerned within the colleges the Professional Board will still have to consider and approve the proposal before the actual teaching can begin.

Any major change in the structure of the teacher's certificate course would be likely to meet with an even lengthier process of consultation. The advocates of such fundamental reform would in any case have to undertake very considerable work in persuading vested interests within their own college that such a fundamental reappraisal of their work was necessary and would have to hold many meetings with groups representing different interests within the college before any scheme could be put before the Academic Board of the college itself. When this had been done and the internal discussion brought to a satisfactory conclusion, the whole issue would have to be raised with the ATO. This would be a prospect which would cause the most enthusiastic to quail if the discussion within the colleges had been at all lengthy and passionate. In those ATOs where there is expected to be close similarity between the courses offered by the different colleges the proponents of the new scheme would have to set about persuading the staff members of the other colleges in the area that their proposed new scheme was worthy of adoption by them. The battles which they had fought in their own colleges would be duplicated in the other colleges concerned and not only in the colleges themselves but in committees established by the Professional Board of the ATO. The Professional Board itself would have to be satisfied that there was no lowering of the standards in the new proposals as compared with the form of professional preparation already in use and as compared with the courses offered in other colleges throughout the country. The teacher members of the Board would be concerned to ensure that an adequate professional preparation was being given to their members and that no one who was already qualified was being disadvantaged by the new proposals. The methods of examining the new courses would have to be seen to be efficient. The road which must be followed before the Professional Board was prepared to accept the new arrangements might seem to be interminable.

Even in ATOs where the individual colleges are allowed to adopt their own individual courses of study and syllabuses, a college wishing to propose fundamental changes of the sort envisaged here would generally be expected to justify itself to the other colleges in the area and to show that the new courses were adequate for the purpose for which they were established. The Boards of Studies could be expected to subject the new proposals to a very close and perhaps lengthy scrutiny before they were prepared to recommend them for adoption to the Professional Board.

When these requirements had been fulfilled, changes of this sort would have to be approved by the senate of the university which would wish to be satisfied that a proper academic scrutiny of the courses themselves had already been carried out by people qualified to undertake that task, that the proposals were acceptable on general educational principles, that as far as could be judged the level of entry to the certificate course and the level of attainment at the end were broadly comparable with those of other certificates within the university and that the proposals were not too far out of line with national trends.

It is hardly surprising that some colleges, and especially the larger ones, find the elaborate checks and balances imposed by this ponderous process of mutual consultation irksome and would like to escape the restraints imposed upon them. In most cases college Academic Boards would agree that a case which is academically well-prepared, well-presented and well-argued will normally be accepted with little or no modification. On the other hand, the time taken by this preparation and discussion is felt to be a heavy burden in addition to the normal responsibilities of teaching within the colleges. The hard-won liberty of students and practising teachers to speak on matters of teacher preparation may seem to college tutors to be eroding their own freedom to control the teaching within their college. The more closely colleges approach genuine integration with a university the less acceptable some of them find the degree of control which university government imposes on them. The higher the status which they seek for the awards given by their institutions the more unwelcome seem the increasingly difficult requirements which they are expected to meet.

The question of the nature of academic autonomy is therefore central to the whole discussion about the future of the Area Training Organizations. The new universities which have been established in recent years have been given charters which enable them to grant their own degrees as soon as they have been established, even when their number of students was small. Colleges of education are asking why they may not be allowed to issue their own certificates when they have been engaged in the work of teacher education for many decades, during which their staffing and their physical provision have gradually increased in standard. This is a question which is not asked only by colleges of education. The polytechnics which have been established recently and many of which are of a size considerably in excess of some universities are asking why they are not able to give degrees of their own but have to continue to give degrees of an external examining body, the Committee for National Academic Awards.

It was partly because some considered that the process of effecting change through the machinery already described was unnecessarily slow that departments of education were established in a number of poly-technics. It was thought that these polytechnics would be likely to wish to take degrees and perhaps also certificates of the CNAA and that CNAA courses might also be attractive to those colleges of education which were dissatisfied with their university relationship. In the event, however, all the polytechnic departments of education associated themselves with their local school or institute of education, though some departments and colleges are holding preliminary discussions with the CNAA. Up to the present time the CNAA has not seemed to offer an acceptable alternative to the school or institute of education as a method of accrediting qualifications in teacher education.*

Another responsibility which is exercised by the ATO relates to the in-service education of teachers. A later chapter of this book deals in full with the subject of in-service teacher education. It is sufficient therefore to draw attention here to the important role which the ATO has of co-ordinating the provision which is made for teacher education within the geographical area which is its concern and in providing for needs, perhaps of a specialist nature, which can be met more economically in a large area than in an area covered by a single local education authority. The ATO also has a particular responsibility to provide longer courses of study leading to named awards of the university or of its school of education, and to acquaint the teachers of its area with the results of recent research and with recent developments in educational theory and practice.

A type of activity which belongs, at least in part, to the field of in-service education is co-operative work on curriculum development. One example of this which has been particularly well documented is the North-West Regional Curriculum Development Study Group Project of the University of Manchester School of Education. This project and its in-service education role is described in Chapter 17, in which the integrative role of the ATO becomes very clear.

The ATOs have also attempted to serve teachers in their area by providing some form of education centre. This has generally included a library of educational materials which is open to all teachers in the area; a postal library service is also generally provided. In addition the education centre may include workshops for the preparation of teaching aids and suites of rooms for teachers' meetings as well as the normal provision for lectures and discussions. In some ATOs the education centre is intensively used, though the welcome growth of LEA Teachers' Centres throughout the country has ensured that such provision is not concentrated only in the main population centres which form the headquarters of the Schools and Institutes of Education. The ATO now has a new and important role in providing a meeting ground where those concerned with the work of teachers' centres may consider the principles of their work.

Another responsibility of ATOs is to undertake research and this is a responsibility which most of them have taken very seriously. Many major pieces of research have emerged from schools and institutes of education but these have generally been undertaken by the permanent staff of the schools or by research workers specially appointed for the purpose.

* The CNAA has agreed to validate a B.Ed. degree at Notre Dame College, Glasgow, and an in-service B.Ed. degree at Sunderland Polytechnic. It has not yet, however, agreed to validate any initial certificate courses or full-time B.Ed. courses in England or Wales.

One of the responsibilities of the Professional Board of the Manchester School of Education, in common with many other schools and institutes, is 'to encourage and facilitate educational research in the constituent institutions and among teachers and others'. Generally, however, the emphasis has been on individual pieces of research within the central institute rather than on the encouragement of research by those in the colleges and in the schools, though it would be wrong to attempt to draw too close a line of demarcation between the two different kinds of research. Most research in education, even though it may be initiated by one individual, requires the co-operation of many teachers in its execution. Nevertheless, one must say that the volume of research undertaken by teachers with the help of specialist advice in the schools of education has been smaller than one would have wished. Some teachers may even feel that they are being used simply to supply data for research undertaken for the personal qualification or prestige of a distant researcher.

Similarly, the volume of work in fields specific to the work of ATOs, such as the methodology and aims of teacher education, the organization and value of school practice, the predictive value of teacher qualifications, and problems of changing teacher behaviour, has not been great, though even in these fields some valuable pieces of research have been done. The opportunity of forging long-term relationships of increasing depth between ATOs and selected schools in their areas for research purposes has generally not been taken, nor have we seen the creation of data banks containing information about these schools and the pupils attending them. Moreover, the rich quantity of research material which has accumulated in schools of education during twenty-five years of guiding students' work and conducting examinations remains largely unstudied.

Although many valuable pieces of individual and group research have emerged from schools and institutes of education, and some schools have been successful in organizing group research by teachers and tutors in colleges of education, it is not unfair to say that most schools have not been successful in establishing a systematic and comprehensive study of educational processes within their geographical area. Nor should one underestimate the problems of group research. Most academics consider it a restriction on their academic freedom if the type of work on which they are to engage is selected for them. Even when it has proved possible to engage research assistants for a particular piece of co-operative, large-scale research there is a tendency for them to find the restrictions of such work irksome and to seek promotion through moving elsewhere or by undertaking research for a higher degree which tends of its nature to be individual research.

This review of the activities undertaken by Area Training Organizations has shown that they are involved in every aspect of the provision of initial and further education for the teaching profession. Much of the work is shared by many other partners. In the case of initial training, for example, the national policy for the colleges is determined by the Department of Education and Science, while the colleges are owned and financed through local education authorities. In-service education for teachers is provided not only by the ATO but also by local education authorities, by the Department of Education and Science through its inspectorate and by the teachers' professional organizations themselves. Increasingly, LEAs are providing teachers' libraries and Teachers' Centres for meetings and practical activities. Nevertheless the ATO is regarded by most of the participants as having a co-ordinating function which at the least may prevent waste of scarce resources by overlapping provision and ensure that important ground does not remain uncovered. One is sometimes tempted to say that if the ATOs did not exist it would be necessary to invent them. It would not be necessary, however, to plant them so firmly in the university and there is no doubt that the close university connection imparts to the ATOs their distinctive ethos. Is this desirable?

The Robbins Committee on Higher Education, whose important and influential report was published in 1963, was in no doubt about this issue. Having recommended the establishment in the colleges, which in future should be called colleges of education,* of the bachelor of education degree with the assumption that 'by the middle of the 1970s provision should be made for twenty-five per cent. of the entrants to training colleges to take a four-year course'† the committee considered the administrative arrangements which were desirable consequent upon this measure.

First they considered the possibility that the responsibility for the administration of the colleges should remain with the LEAs and voluntary bodies while the links between the colleges and the university senate were strengthened to enable the new bachelor of education degree courses to be introduced within the colleges. This solution the Robbins Committee decisively rejected before considering a radical alternative.

This alternative, in some ways an attractive one, was that the college of education system should be separated from the universities and made analogous to the technical education structure. The colleges would remain under their 'LEAs or voluntary bodies and awards, including the new degrees, would be made available through a central body on the model of the National Council for Technological Awards. The leading colleges would become autonomous, either on their own or as constituent parts of a university new or old'. The committee was unable to recommend this change. 'For many years [the colleges] have turned their eyes towards the universities and we do not believe that they would now willingly look

* P. 119, para. 351.
† P. 116, para. 339.

elsewhere even if there were other means by which degrees could be made available to their students.' This was a remarkably prophetic statement as the initial reaction of the colleges to the CNAA has indicated.

The Robbins Committee proposed a different solution which it considered to be in line with the proposals of the McNair Report, and recommended a return to the basic conception of the university school of education which would take over all the functions of the institutes of education and would also establish arrangements for the award of the new bachelor of education degree. The committee went further, however, to suggest that 'academic and administrative responsibility should go hand in hand'. The colleges of education should have independent governing bodies related federally to the school of education and through the school of education to the university. The financial support of the colleges should now come not from the LEAs but from a special earmarked grant made available to schools of education by the University Grants Committee. The schools of education would have their own well-qualified administrative and financial officers who would relieve the central administration of the universities from a considerable burden.

The Robbins Committee therefore suggested that academic and financial authority for the colleges of education should go together and that the colleges should become an integral part of a university school of education, being financed through the University Grants Committee. Some of the bigger colleges might become individually constituent parts of a university or might combine with a leading technical college to form a new university or to become part of one.* In the event this solution to the problems of administering teacher education was rejected by the government. The universities accepted the suggestion that they should establish bachelor of education degrees with readiness and indeed, in many cases, with eagerness, and the new degrees were being taught in a remarkably short space of time. The fact, however, that the colleges of education, although working for university degrees, have not come fully within the university structure, has led in many cases to a 'we and them' attitude which has caused resentment and misunderstanding. There is a widespread feeling among colleges of education that they are unable to influence decisions which are vital to their own future because they are not members of the university bodies at which the decisions are taken. Many of the excellent and enlightened suggestions of the Robbins Committee about the future of the work of colleges of education have been implemented: the colleges have been renamed, the degree of bachelor of education has been established – in most cases as an honours degree – and the government of the colleges has been liberalized as a result of the Weaver Report on the government of colleges of education which gave detailed consideration to some of the proposals in this field

* P. 108, para. 314.

of the Robbins Committee. Nevertheless the fundamental Robbins' recommendation that the colleges of education should become integral parts of the universities themselves through a new relationship with university schools of education was not put into effect.

The years which followed the publication of the Robbins Report were years of extraordinary achievement for colleges of education, as has been stated elsewhere in this volume. The raising of the level of teaching in colleges from certificate to honours degree level was accompanied by a doubling of the number of students in the colleges and a consequential massive building programme. Principals and staffs were concerned simultaneously with developing new courses of study, recruiting increasing numbers of tutors and students, developing structures capable of dealing with financial and administrative problems of an unfamiliar size and complexity, and planning library, laboratory and other plant for purposes not previously undertaken in colleges of education. These changes were being accomplished at a time when the school system itself was undergoing striking changes and facing new problems, and when there was intensifying debate about the purpose of the school and the role of the teacher. Higher education saw the formulation of the binary system, the creation of the polytechnics and an increasing demand for higher education for the increasing numbers of qualified school leavers which threatened to overwhelm the existing institutions and called into question the purpose and cost of higher education.

In early 1970 the then Secretary of State for Education, Mr Short, asked all the ATOs to enquire into their own work and, in particular, the content of the initial teacher education course. After the Conservative victory at the general election of June 1970, the new Secretary of State for Education, Mrs Margaret Thatcher, established a committee under the chairmanship of Lord James of Rusholme with the following terms of reference:

In the light of the review currently being undertaken by the Area Training Organizations and of the evidence published by the former Select Committee on Education and Science to inquire into the present arrangements for the education, training and probation of teachers in England and Wales, and in particular to examine:

    i. what should be the content and organization of courses to be provided;

    ii. whether a larger proportion of intending teachers should be educated with students who have not chosen their careers or chosen other careers;

    iii. what, in the context of i and ii above, should be the role of the maintained and voluntary colleges of education, the polytechnics

and other further education institutions maintained by local education authorities, and the universities;
and to make recommendations.

The Report of the Committee was published at the end of January 1972 and provided immediate and widespread discussion. It contained 133 recommendations some of which, if adopted, would radically change the system of teacher education in England. In order to understand its implications for the ATOs it will be necessary to give a brief account of its main recommendations.

The Report claimed to be based on two principles.

First, proposals should be capable of speedy implementation and should relate to the immediate future, since it would be unrealistic in the extreme to attempt to construct a system capable of lasting indefinitely... Secondly, the proposals should reflect and help to enhance the status and independence of the teaching profession and of the institutions in which many teachers are educated and trained. For too long the teaching profession has been denied a proper degree of responsibility for its own professional affairs. For too long the colleges of education have been treated as junior partners in the system of higher education. It is hoped that the implementation of this report would do much to encourage both the profession and the colleges to move forward to a new degree of independence and self-determination.*

The Report takes as its basis the assumption that the teacher's professional education will continue throughout his life and divides this education into three parts or cycles. The first cycle would consist of the personal higher education of the student, the second cycle of his initial professional education, and the third cycle his in-service education.

The first cycle for many intending teachers would be provided by a university or CNAA degree programme, though the committee would 'welcome and would encourage those degree courses in which Education is studied as part of a joint degree'. Such a degree programme, however, would not prove the most suitable form of first-cycle preparation for all teachers. It is therefore proposed that a two-year course should be established leading to the award of a diploma in higher education. This diploma course could very suitably be provided by colleges of education though it would not be exclusive to those colleges. The entry level for a diploma course should be two 'A' levels in the GCE though there should be generous provision for exemptions from this requirement. The diploma itself should combine the advantages of study in depth with those of a more broadly based education and should thus inter-relate 'special' and 'general' studies,

* P. 1, para. 1.2.

one-third of the total time of the course being devoted to general studies. Each institution should be free to devise its own diploma in higher education courses though there should be some form of external validation. Education should be available as a subject of study for the diploma in higher education irrespective of whether or not the student intends himself to become a teacher.

Following the first cycle the intending teacher should be admitted to second-cycle training. This would be a common course of professional training extending over two years which, as we have seen, would have been preceded for some by a two-year diploma course and for others by a three-year degree course. Some students admitted to the second cycle would already have undertaken a study of education for two or three years while others would not. The first year of the second-cycle course would be taken in a college of education, a university department of education or the education department of a polytechnic (though the committee recommended that polytechnic departments of education should concentrate on the preparation of teachers for the older age groups in schools and FE colleges).*

The second cycle should itself be divided into two years. The first year would be within the college or department of education and the emphasis should be 'unashamedly specialized and functional'.† It should 'concentrate on preparation for work appropriate to a teacher at the beginning of his career rather than on formal courses in "educational theory"'.‡ The emphasis should be on specialization and a sharp focus on the particular tasks which the student will undertake when he enters the school. There would also be a period of at least four weeks' teaching practice, with the aims of providing 'a basis for the illustration and reinforcement of theoretical studies', of 'familiarizing the student with the teaching situation' and of 'satisfying regional bodies of student suitability to undertake the next stage of training'.§

At the end of the first year the student would take up a post in a school and begin to receive a salary. He 'would be, in most of the senses important to him, a "full" member of the staff', though he would not be a 'qualified teacher' but a 'licensed teacher'. The second year of the second cycle was viewed as 'an essential part of the initial training course', and the 'licensed teacher' should be released for attendance at special professional centres for the equivalent of not less than one day a week of further training.

It is important to note that this 'licensing' would be provisional and 'would do no more than admit him to the second year of the cycle and allow him to undertake for a year four-fifths of a normal teaching commitment in the post for which he had been selected and for which he was

* P. 35, para. 3.44.          † P. 23, para. 3.14.
‡ P. 23, para. 3.16.          § P. 25, para. 3.19.

receiving a salary'.* At the end of a successful second year the teacher would be admitted as a 'registered teacher'. The Report stated clearly that such registration would be far from automatic; it would be possible for a further year of work and study within the second cycle to be prescribed or, in exceptional circumstances, for registration to be refused.

Any student who had completed satisfactorily both the first and second cycles would be awarded a general degree of B.A. (Ed.) on the recommendation of the regional body in the region in which he had been working as a 'licensed teacher', which would not necessarily be in the region in which he had undertaken the college course in the first year of the second cycle. In this way all new teachers would enjoy graduate status.

On registration the teacher would enter the third cycle of his training and the Report stated emphatically that 'much of the argument of this Report depends upon the proposals made for the third cycle'.† It was a fundamental principle of the Report that 'the best education and training of teachers is that which is built upon and illuminated by growing maturity and experience'. Third-cycle training would cover:

> a wide spectrum, at one end of which are evening meetings and discussions, weekend conferences and other short-term activities, with limited and specific objectives and taking place usually, but not always, in the teacher's own time. At the other end are long courses leading to higher degrees or advanced qualifications, and requiring the release of teachers for full-time attendance at suitable establishments. At this end of the spectrum, too, may be periods of release to take part in curriculum development and evaluation, or in other projects and investigations. For some teachers there may be periods of secondment to fields outside teaching, so that they may widen their experience and thereby enrich their contribution to the schools.‡

The intention of this part of the Report was that the teacher throughout his career should have opportunities of refreshment and further training to fit him for the continually changing demands of the school situation. Its main weapons were two, the first being the network of professional centres to which reference has already been made and the second an entitlement to secondment for every teacher.

The latter recommendation was most important; it would, however, depend for its implementation on an improvement of school staffing ratios. The entitlement which was suggested was release with pay for a minimum of one school term or the equivalent (a period of, say, twelve weeks) in a specified number of years; initially, perhaps, one term in every seven years

* P. 31, para. 3.33.  † P. 5, para. 2.1.
‡ P. 5, para. 2.2.

but later one term in five years. No teacher should be required to undertake further training if he did not wish to take advantage of the opportunities available to him.*

Every school should have on its staff a professional tutor who would co-ordinate the second- and third-cycle work of the school and be the link between the school and other agencies engaged in that work. 'Among the responsibilities of the professional tutor would be that of compiling and maintaining a training programme for the staff of the school which would take account both of the curricula needs of the school and of the professional needs of the teachers.' The professional tutor would have a special responsibility for the licensed teachers serving in the school and for ensuring that they undertook a satisfactory programme of studies.

The Report suggested that the existing degree of B.Ed. should be abolished as an initial training degree but that it might be retained as an in-service qualification in the third cycle. It also recommended that some training institutions might offer a course leading to the award of an M.A.(Ed.) which would be taken either immediately after the second school-based year of the second cycle or after more years of additional teaching experience.

The Report also suggested a radical reform of the administration of teacher education, involving the abolition of the Area Training Organization system. In its place would be a two-tier organization. Locally there would be a Regional Council for Colleges and Departments of Education which would fulfil many of the functions of the ATO which it would replace and would have a composition broadly similar to that of the Delegacy of the ATO. The borders of the regions would be redrawn in a more rational manner. The main purpose of the change would be to abolish the domination of the regional organization by the universities and to replace it by an 'open partnership of institutions of higher education'.† The governing council of a RCCDE would consist of one member from each professional institution, an additional member from each university or polytechnic, a representative from each LEA within the RCCDE, five teacher representatives from schools and FE chosen for their professional standing, one representative nominated by the CNAA, one from the Open University and two members nominated by the Secretary of State. There would also be two assessors appointed by the Secretary of State. The RCCDE would have two strong committees, an academic committee and a professional committee, to advise it and to undertake its work.

Above the structure of RCCDEs there would be a national agency, perhaps called the National Council for Teacher Education and Training. This would be a small committee of about twenty members all chosen by the

* P. 12, para. 2.22.    † P. 52, para. 5.12.

Secretary of State from amongst several prospective members nominated by each of the RCCDEs. To make clear the relative duties of these bodies it will be necessary to quote fully from the Report:

In its very important professional role the system of RCCDEs and the NCTET would be directly responsible for establishing and safeguarding the standards of nationally recognized professional qualifications in the second and third cycles. The RCCDEs would establish, on the basis of guide lines provided by the NCTET, the academic awards acceptable for entry to the second cycle, including recognition for the purpose of existing awards, such as university and CNAA degrees, the diploma in art and design and higher national diplomas, and of course the diploma in higher education. They would also have to make decisions on those special cases where the normal entry requirements to the second cycle might be modified. Arrangements for the assessment of students and licensed teachers in the second cycle would also fall to the professional committees. The RCCDEs would transmit to the NCTET recommendations for the award of 'licensed teacher' status to students who were to be admitted to the second year of the cycle, for the acceptance of successful licensed teachers as 'registered teachers' and for the award of the B.A.(Ed.) at the end of the cycle. They would also make recommendations to the NCTET about the recognition for professional purposes of all specialist diplomas and other third cycle qualifications, including the B.Ed. Applications for such recognition of courses and qualifications, and of the institutions in which they were offered, would be channelled through the RCCDEs to the NCTET. The National Council would have the responsibility for the recognition of all these qualifications. It would award the B.A.(Ed.) and decide, in the light of appropriate advice, whether or not to recognize initial teaching qualifications awarded by other bodies. It would make recommendations to the Secretary of State for the licensing and registration of teachers and it would award the M.A.(Ed.). On the advice of the RCCDEs, it would approve the other third cycle qualifications and would determine which courses could be counted against teachers' entitlement to release for third cycle activities.*

The planning responsibilities of the new agencies would be an important part of their professional role.

It would be for the NCTET to advise RCCDEs on the provision of second and third cycle facilities in the training system as a whole and to satisfy itself that national needs were being met.... Acting within the guide lines provided by the NCTET, the RCCDEs would be

* P. 57, para. 5.28.

responsible for planning the total provision within their regions. They would have to ensure that the size and composition of their student population accorded with the national indicators and would have to make recommendations, in consultation with LEAs and other providing bodies, on the development of individual colleges and on the distribution of first, second and third cycle places, together with the number and location of any places leading to the award of degrees other than the B.A.(Ed.).*

As far as the first cycle was concerned the NCTET would be 'empowered to make the award of the Dip.H.E., although the responsibility for ensuring that the arrangements were satisfactory would be delegated to the RCCDEs. The colleges themselves, subject to approval by the RCCDEs, would conduct the examinations and appoint examiners.'†

The committee hoped that the main academic responsibilities of the NCTET would 'quite rapidly be assumed by the CNAA or in some cases by universities'.‡

It was recognized that in order to allow the RCCDEs to plan the work of their regions effectively they must be given a considerable degree of control over the allocation of resources to the different institutions within their areas.

It seems to us to be essential that once decisions had been taken centrally, after consultation with the NCTET, on the total level of resources to be committed, and had been interpreted by that body, the RCCDEs should be responsible for making recommendations to all their constituent members on the allocation of resources within their regions. Their power to make these recommendations would have to be fully recognized.§

Ranging as it did over the whole field of teacher education the Report contained a number of important recommendations which have not been touched on in the above summary. For example, the recommendation that teachers in FE institutions should be required to take courses of professional training as soon as this became practicable gave considerable encouragement to workers in that branch of the educational system.‖

It is interesting to note how the Report echoed some of the recommendations of earlier reports. In a number of interesting ways the Report reached conclusions similar to those of the 'memorandum of dissent' of the 1925 Report of the Departmental Committee of the Board of Education on the Training of Teachers for Public Elementary Schools. Not only did the

* P. 58, para. 5.29.     † P. 59, para. 5.30.
‡ P. 59, para. 5.31.     § P. 60, para. 5.34.
‖ P. 14, para. 2.27.

1925 dissenting note separate very carefully the academic from the professional preparation of the teacher, emphasizing 'that the content of training college courses should be strictly professional, and based upon subject method rather than upon philosophic theory' but it also interestingly suggested a precursor of the diploma in higher education:

> Nor do we altogether exclude the alternative of a shorter university course for those unable to aim at a degree, although we think it important that this shorter course should be complete in itself and not a mere truncated degree course, even if it is accepted as a stage towards certain degrees.

The same note of dissent also recommended what the James Report came to call third-cycle training.

> After a few years' teaching there should, at any rate for ambitious teachers, be a break to be spent either in renewed academic study or in a more fundamental study of educational principles and their application on the basis of the experience gained.*

With regard to the control of teacher education the James Committee adopted the solution of separation of the Regional Councils from the universities which was proposed in the McNair Report by the group which was headed by McNair himself. The James Report recognized, however, as did the Robbins Report, that control over teacher education cannot be exercised by any regional body unless it also has the responsibility of dispersing to the colleges the funds which they need for their development. It therefore placed this important power not in the hands of a university ATO on the Robbins pattern but in the hands of the RCCDE. While its solutions to the vexing problems of teacher education and of its regional control were not therefore entirely novel, they were contained in a pattern different from any that had been seen in previous reports.

In an attempt to provoke swift and decisive action the James Report outlined a programme for the rapid implementation of its policy. Recognizing that final decisions on Regional Councils could not become effective until the reorganization of local authorities had taken place and the reorganized authorities had assumed office in April 1974, the Report recommended that an interim national body should be set up as soon as possible to provide interim solutions to the problems of the new award structure. Similar interim regional agencies should be set up for the same purpose with the intention that those students who entered college in 1973 would be able to take Dip.H.E. courses and subsequently be awarded the degree of B.A.(Ed.). Indeed, it was hoped that even students enrolling in 1972 would be able

---

* Board of Education: Report of the Departmental Committee on the Training of Teachers for Public Elementary Schools. HMSO, 1925, pp. 177–83.

to get this degree. The Committee felt that from the academic point of view also it was desirable to take urgent decisions. 'A decision in principle to proceed along the lines suggested here could release considerable energies and immediately initiate a great deal of essential preliminary work.'*

In the months that followed the publication of the Report, however, it became clear that action was unlikely to be taken with the speed envisaged within the Report itself. The proposals for in-service education and especially for an entitlement to periods of secondment were universally welcomed but some other recommendations of the Report received extensive criticism, especially from members of the teaching profession and from those engaged in the training of teachers. The proposed B.A.(Ed.) degree, for example, was said not to be genuinely comparable to other British bachelors' degrees. Those students who entered the second cycle as graduates would obtain their B.A.(Ed.) degree after a two-year period. Moreover, the first of these two years would be spent in a college of education under the tutorial supervision of the college staff and the second period in a teaching post, not necessarily accessible to the college, where the student would be under the tutorial supervision of the professional tutor of his school and the tutor in a professional centre. It would be as a result of a recommendation from the area in which he was spending his second period of study that the Regional Council would award him his bachelor's degree.

Not only was this plan criticized on the ground that the degree would be so dissimilar to other degrees that teaching would still not really be an all-graduate profession, but also on the grounds that it fragmented the second cycle into two disparate parts. The entire four-year period of training for the student who took a diploma in higher education in the first cycle would be even more fragmented. It would be possible for this student to spend his two years of the first cycle in one college, to move to a second college for the first year of the second cycle, and to a different area altogether for his period as a 'licensed teacher'.

Again, although in theory the student would have an opportunity to delay the selection of his career until he had completed his Dip.H.E. the parallel disadvantage would exist that a student intent on teaching would not know until he had completed his diploma whether or not he would find a place in the second cycle. Moreover, unless the Dip.H.E. permitted the student to transfer to other forms of professional training or to move to different educational institutions to complete a degree, the balance of advantage to the student in delaying vocational choice would be very doubtful. If the number of places in the second cycle became considerably smaller, as may be anticipated, the colleges may well insist on students who wished to take a teacher's course declaring their intention at the beginning of the first

* P. 64, para. 5.43.

cycle so that they could take education courses in their diploma or degree.

The concept of a 'licensed teacher' also came under serious criticism. The NUT, in particular, rejected the idea of an unqualified teacher having control of a class of children. It was also pointed out how difficult it would be for schools to organize their teaching in such a way that a licensed teacher could be free either for one day each week or for the equivalent of this period in a block. Even if it proved possible to employ other teachers to take care of the children while the licensed teacher was undergoing further training, this would seem hardly satisfactory for them.

Nor did it seem likely that all schools would easily find teachers whom they could appoint as 'professional tutors'. This would be particularly difficult in the small schools where it was presumed that the headmaster would have to undertake these duties. In large schools, on the other hand, the supervision of ten or more licensed teachers and the arrangements for the further training of the remainder of the staff would be a task which would be likely to take the greater part of the time of anyone undertaking it. The relationship of the professional tutor to his colleagues on the staff also caused a good deal of concern.

The proposal for a diploma in higher education aroused a great deal of interest. For some years there had been discussion about the desirability for an award between the present GCE at advanced level and a university degree. There was a general reluctance, however, to establish such a diploma primarily for intending teachers: if, on the other hand, it was intended for wider use, it seemed inappropriate that it should be awarded, even initially, by a National Committee for Teacher Education and Training rather than by the universities and the CNAA. The examples of the curriculum for the diploma given in Appendix 6 of the James Report also failed to carry conviction.

As far as the Area Training Organizations themselves were concerned it was noted that while the James Report recommended their severance from the universities and indeed their abolition in their existing form, the new regional bodies had great similarities both in composition and function to the ATOs which they would replace. Indeed in some respects (for example, in the number of teacher representatives recommended for the Regional Councils) they seemed to be less representative than the Delegacies of the ATOs. The removal of the Regional Councils from the universities organizationally, even if not necessarily physically, would, however, represent a major change. Whether this was viewed with favour or with disapproval depended on one's view of the pre-James situation which could be considered either as domination by the university, stifling the colleges' willingness and ability to develop in a variety of different ways, or as a fruitful co-operation of institutions and authorities fulfilling a usefully complementary role.

At the time of writing it is not at all clear which of the recommendations of the James Committee will be accepted or what the future shape of teacher education in Britain will be. It can be said, however, with confidence that the ATO concept has proved itself to be of immense value and that whether as an ATO, a Regional Council or some other form of regional organization it will continue as the basic unit of organization in teacher education for many years to come.

# CHAPTER 10

# A Principal's View of College Administration

GERALD COLLIER

## Historical Background of a Particular College

There have been fundamental changes in the structure of administration in the colleges of education in England and Wales during the decade of the 1960s. These have arisen from a variety of causes, which will be discussed in the course of this chapter. The brief for the chapter, however, is 'A Principal's view of college administration' and the variety of pattern among colleges being very great, it would be as well to begin from the operation of a particular Principal – the present author – in a particular college – the College of the Venerable Bede, Durham.

In law, the responsibility for the proper conduct of the college lies with the Board of Governors. The decision to establish in Durham a diocesan college for training schoolmasters was taken in 1839, a few years after the founding of the university. A few years later a second college was founded in the university as well as a diocesan college for training women teachers, and for many years these constituted 'the Durham colleges', between which various links were gradually formed. The training colleges began to take students who followed degree courses in the university alongside their teacher training courses, but student numbers in the various colleges rarely exceeded 150.

At the time of writing, in July 1971, the official number of students in Bede College is 730, these including 630 students taught by the college staff for a teacher's certificate, a B.Ed. degree, or a postgraduate certificate in education, and a hundred students attending courses in the university for a B.A. or B.Sc. degree or a separate postgraduate certificate in education, or working for a higher degree.

Since the university students are governed by the regulations of the university in regard to curriculum, discipline, organization and finance, and the college finance is controlled by the Department of Education and Science, the administration of the college is a good deal more complex than in most colleges of education in England and Wales. But if, as the

James Committee has proposed (James, 1972), the colleges begin to teach for qualifications other than those designed for the teaching profession it may well become less atypical.

The membership of the governing body of the college has been revised from time to time and at present includes representatives of the diocesan and cathedral authorities of Durham and Newcastle, together with representatives of Durham University, the local education authority associations, the association of former students of the college, and the staff and students of the college, as well as a number of co-optative governors who include members of the teaching profession. The accession of staff members followed the publication of the Weaver Report (Weaver, 1966) and that of student members after negotiations which took place in 1968–9. The Chairman and Vice-Chairman are respectively the Bishops of Durham and Newcastle. There is thus a fairly even distribution of representation between churchmen's interests and educational interests.

The Weaver Committee was set up in 1965 as a result of the governmental decision to leave the control of the LEA colleges in the hands of the LEAs: the Robbins Committee reporting in 1963 had recommended their moving into the university sphere. Many colleges had felt that LEA control was often restrictive, being based on inappropriate criteria, and the Association of Teachers in Colleges and Departments of Education (ATCDE) pressed for a review of the procedures of control. Hence the DES invited the bodies representing the LEAs, the voluntary colleges and the teaching staffs of the colleges, and a little later of the universities, to join a working party under the chairmanship of a senior DES officer. Much of the report consisted of proposals for a structure of control by LEAs which would give the degree of autonomy that was felt to be suited to institutions of higher education and had only previously been enjoyed by the voluntary colleges and a minority of LEA colleges.

One matter which was particularly emphasized by the Committee was that the control of staff appointments should rest with the governors rather than with an LEA committee, and this pattern is now built into college schemes of government. Heads of departments are usually nominated by a joint committee of staff and governors, the rest by the staff. At Bede College the procedure is perhaps more elaborate than usual. The short-list is made up by the Principal, Vice-Principal and Head of department in agreement. At the interview stage a candidate begins with one to one-and-a-half hours with the department, followed by forty-five minutes each with the Vice-Principal and Principal. This procedure has provided a fuller and better balanced picture of a candidate's potential than the usual board interview and has been felt by the participants to make a very material contribution to staff solidarity, which will be discussed more fully later.

## A Principal's Reports to his Governors

The annual general meeting of the governors is held in the autumn of each year and at this meeting the annual report for the previous academic year is presented by the Principal and the annual financial statement by the Bursar. Two other meetings are held in the other terms of the year and at all these meetings the Principal presents a report on the events that have occurred in the college since the previous meeting. A 'House Committee' meets each month to keep in touch with the day-to-day running of the college and to receive reports from the chief officers.

The contents of the Principal's report are classified under three headings: buildings, academic work, and community. During the 1960s they have been heavily weighted by the extensive building programmes necessitated by the rapid expansion of the college. At every meeting there has been discussion of congested accommodation, of plans for new buildings and for the adaptation of the old, of meetings with representatives of the DES, of negotiations with architects and estate agents, or of visits from the landscape consultant, quite apart from reports on the routine maintenance of the existing property. In a voluntary college of modest size with a correspondingly small administrative staff this has entailed a heavy additional burden of administration which in LEA colleges has been carried by the officers at County Hall.

### Financial Structure

The financial year for the college runs from 1 August to 31 July. Annual estimates are drawn up by the Bursar and his staff, in conjunction with the Principal, during January and February for the following financial year. These are scrutinized by the governors and submitted to the DES in March. The Principal and Bursar usually visit the DES in London in June or July to take up any problems or queries and agree the final figures for the following year. Adjustments are made during the course of that year where necessary: new agreements on salaries or wages, unforeseen changes in student numbers and so on may call for modifications.

The estimates are classified, according to detailed DES instructions, under six headings: teaching staff; other tuition costs; catering; catering overheads; residential costs; and lodgings for students. The object of the classification is to separate out the costs of tuition, catering, residence in college buildings, and lodgings. Thus the category, 'other tuition costs', includes not only the cost of technical and library staff but that of books, equipment and materials for teaching, the maintenance, heating, lighting and cleaning of buildings used for teaching, and school practice. Similarly the categories of 'catering overheads' and 'residential costs' include expenditure on the maintenance, heating, lighting and cleaning of the corresponding buildings. The whole of the cost of administration is included under 'other tuition costs'.

A college is permitted to exercise 'virement' within a category but not – unless permission is obtained from the DES – between categories (except that for this purpose 'catering' and 'catering overheads' are regarded as one group); that is, saving may be made under one sub-heading and the money spent under another. The latitude is reasonable.

In order to control expenditure on administrative and domestic staffs the DES issue notes of guidance which show 'notional' staff structures for colleges of different sizes. These set out the numbers, grades and salary ranges of the staff considered appropriate, from which a total of expenditure can be calculated. A college then has the total expenditure fixed but is at liberty to organize its administrative and domestic staff in any way it wishes. Circumstances vary greatly from college to college and the concept of a notional but not dictated structure allows reasonable flexibility. In fact at Bede College the staffing on this side diverges considerably from the notional pattern. Academic staffing is calculated according to the number of students, the student/staff ratio being fixed within narrow bands laid down by the DES. Adjustments are possible in special circumstances: the existence of a hundred university students at Bede is recognized by the DES as entailing additional tutorial supervision and therefore additional staff allowance.

During each year the DES issue an analysis of the cost per student of individual colleges in respect of a considerable number of items of expenditure, and calculate cost-bands within which colleges must keep their expenditure in each section. These show college authorities where their own expenditures stand in relation to the general levels; they are also used by the DES to give guidance to individual colleges to reduce particular estimates where these exceed the norms. However, in fairness to the DES it must be said that their officers are always prepared to listen to a special case and on occasion to accede to it.

At Bede College current expenditure is monitored by means of a monthly 'barometer' submitted to the House Committee. Expenditure by academic departments is planned ahead when the estimates are prepared: an Estimates Committee of the College Academic Board gets budgets from academic departments for equipment and materials, assesses the overall requirements of the college, and sends forward a sum for inclusion in the estimates. The Bursar is a member of the Estimates Committee and advises the Committee on the current averages of expenditure in the colleges as a whole. When the DES make their decision on the estimates the Committee sends forward to departments proposals for their allocation and after gaining the agreement of departments submits an award to the Academic Board for their approval. The structure works well on the whole; in early days the Committee had difficulty in establishing agreed criteria by which to judge the relative claims of departments teaching, for example, physics, history, metalwork, and physical education. Similar problems arose in the allocation of the grant for field work.

Before the publication of the Weaver Report a very large part of the financial administration of LEA colleges, including the work connected with the erection and maintenance of buildings, was carried out in LEA offices. Since the establishment of governing bodies with more substantial powers LEA colleges have appointed administrative staffs to handle finance, maintenance and so on, and the procedures are analogous to those described above.

Capital projects not exceeding £1,000 can be undertaken by a voluntary college on its own responsibility; it has to find twenty per cent. of the expenditure itself. Larger projects require detailed negotiation between the college authorities and the DES: the advice of the inspectorate is available to the colleges and is always sought by the administrators in London on the educational soundness of the schemes put forward and the DES architects have a code of standards for accommodation for different purposes. Here again the standards are notional rather than prescriptive and colleges have considerable latitude in adapting the overall measures to their own needs. LEA colleges work closely with the educational and architectural departments of the Council.

Another aspect of administration in the areas of routine maintenance and domestic management at Bede College which is of considerable importance is the consultative structure. The traditional structure, of a linear chain of command for the Principal into the various sectors of the college organization, proved quite inadequate to deal with the tensions and misunderstandings that began to arise, inevitably, when the three-year course of teacher training was introduced in 1960 and extensive programmes of building, adaptation and reorganization were launched. An Administrative Committee was set up, consisting of Principal, Vice-Principal, Bursar, Domestic Supervisor, Housekeeper and Catering Officer. Within a year or two it was found to be convenient and economical of time to invite the President and Vice-President of the JCR (Junior Common Room or student body of the college) to join the Committee for part of the meeting and this pattern has proved invaluable in improving the understanding between representatives of different sectors of the community and developing a more global view of the interests of the community as a whole. This is not an automatic result: it only arises through the efforts of some members of the committee in consistently using appropriate criteria of judgement in the many matters that are dealt with.

## Administration in the Academic Sphere

The primary purpose of a college of education is to prepare students to enter the teaching profession and the curriculum has since 1945 been conceived in terms of four elements: one or two 'main' subjects studied for their own sake; the principles of education, including psychology and the other underlying disciplines; practical work in schools; and the basic subjects or 'curriculum courses' needed by teachers in primary schools and the lower classes of secondary schools. The introduction of the three-year course in 1960 and the bachelor of education degree in 1965 and onwards have served to extend and deepen existing patterns. The James Report has set out proposals for further radical departures from the inherited patterns but these have yet to be decided.

Thus the main problems in the academic sphere are four: the improvement of students' knowledge and conceptual grasp in all the academic aspects of their studies; the better integration of college-based studies with professional practice; the initiation of students into the full range of teaching/learning methods now used in the best primary (and secondary) schools; and the development of a positive attitude to innovation. All these have been the subject of many experiments and researches among those engaged in higher education, the second, third and fourth having particularly preoccupied those who prepare students for professions; the established results to date are thin.

Thus one of the over-riding needs in considering the administrative aspects of the college curriculum is how to establish a policy-forming and decision-making structure that facilitates development in the above four areas while safeguarding the position of those who do not wish to take part in particular schemes. At Bede College the structure adopted has been based on a fairly high degree of departmental autonomy combined with a fairly elaborate network of committees which involve members of different departments in collaborating to develop policy.

At the peak of this grid structure is the College Academic Board (CAB), which is the decision-making body on academic matters. Its authority is legislated for in the scheme of government of the college. In the early 1960s colleges experimented widely with such decision-taking bodies, usually at first with the staff as a whole constituting the CAB. With the expansion of numbers this was felt to be cumbersome and time-wasting and the Weaver Committee proposed a membership of about twenty-five in which roughly two-thirds were senior members of staff and one-third elected. This is now the usual, though not universal, pattern. As a result of strong representations made by student bodies during the later 1960s there is now on many CABs an element of student membership.

To refer once again to the college best known to the present writer, the sub-committees of the CAB are of some significance and it is worth outlining their composition and duties.

The Academic Programme Committee is responsible to CAB for the time-table, the pattern of courses in basic subjects and the structure of the curriculum as a whole; all proposals on changes in the curriculum coming forward from other committees are automatically referred to APC, which accordingly has representatives from all departments and ex officio membership of those responsible for the organization of practical work in schools. Being large, it rarely initiates changes itself but refers fresh ideas to other committees or sets up ad hoc working parties.

The Qualifications Committee is responsible for policy on qualifications for entry and for completion of the course (within the policies laid down by the Area Training Organization), and for reviewing the progress of students. These duties call for departmental representation.

The School-based Experience Committee has a wider brief than might be supposed, since first-year curriculum courses in environmental studies, the teaching of reading, art, and discovery learning, take place to a considerable extent within the schools, and second-year students work a group practice in schools, over and above the normal 'block' practices of three to six weeks. In addition the arrangements for an experimental system of teacher tutors (teachers in schools appointed to take responsibility for the students practising in them and paid by the college in respect of attendance at regular seminars with college staff) are the responsibility of this committee. Another committee not directly responsible to CAB but concerned with practical work in schools is the Consultative Committee with teachers' organizations. This consists of three representatives of each of three teachers' organizations and nine senior members of staff. It represents a further aspect of the machinery for tackling the second and third of the curriculum problems listed above.

A related committee is the Teaching Methods Committee, whose brief is not the teaching methods used by students in schools but the methods used by staff in teaching students. An ex officio member is the head of the audio-visual service, which, like the library, ranks as a department. The membership of this committee, as with all the small committees of CAB, is based on 'faculty' representation: one member represents the practical subjects, one the sciences and mathematics, one the arts subjects, and one the education department. This makes for economy in manpower and helps to foster inter-departmental linkages.

Two other committees of senior standing are the Staffing Committee and the Development Committee. The former is concerned with the balance of staff between departments and is – like the Estimates Committee – therefore involved in the problem of assessing the relative claims of departments doing very different jobs. A 'faculty' membership keeps the committee small; a practice of inviting any department with a complaint to send members to meet it has helped to keep relations sweet in a very sensitive part of the college life.

The Development Committee is responsible for forward planning of college development in so far as policies may cut across the boundaries of other committees. The establishment (for example) of new subjects or departments involves not only the balance of the curriculum but staffing, recruitment and finance.

In the college there is no student representative on CAB: in the negotiations which led to their joining the governing body they considered that a small staff-student sub-committee of CAB which saw all the papers both of CAB and of the JCR Council would be a more effective way of handling delicate issues if at the same time a system of staff-student committees were set up in the departments. This pattern has proved reasonably effective. Student membership has been introduced in 1972–73.

Some readers may be dismayed at the number of committees and the resulting expenditure of time. Others will rather ask how many members of a staff of sixty feel unable to make an effective contribution. It may be that the existing structure is over-formalized and more of the work could be done by ad hoc working parties, or by informal talks over cups of coffee. The drawback of the latter approach is the lack of authority of such groups. To guard against the other criticism the Staff Council, which comprises the whole staff and is free to debate any matter it wishes, has drawn up a list of members not overburdened by committees and willing to serve on working parties when needed.

Those familiar with the work of such authors as Etzioni, Burns and Stalker, or Guest on the sociology of organizations, may recognize in the above description a machinery designed to promote what Burns and Stalker termed an 'organic' structure in the academic sphere, in which communication is effective upwards and laterally as well as downwards, and where a great deal depends on certain shared values and attitudes spreading through the organization: 'The sanctions which apply to the individual's conduct in his working role derive more from presumed community of interest with the rest of the working organization . . . and less from a contractual relationship between himself and a non-personal corporation, represented for him by an immediate superior' (Burns and Stalker, 1961). This concept is the basis of the elaborate procedure described earlier for the appointment of staff. It may be questioned whether an organic structure necessarily favours innovation (as is suggested by Burns and Stalker); but it does demand a conscious orientation of the senior members of staff towards shared decisions. The Principal in particular must eschew the traditional decision-taking function of the head of a college and rely partly on his work in small committees and in informal personal relations, but more especially on his role as a chairman who obliges decision-making bodies to probe into the implications of their proposals in the most detailed manner and thus to avoid sliding into ill-considered policies.

A further aspect of administration on the academic side is the need to ensure that staff members have adequate opportunities for improving their qualifications and skills. Important contributions to this can be made by encouraging members to embark on more advanced qualifications, for which the DES provide financial assistance; by facilitating their release for short periods of additional study or research; by financing attendance at conferences; and by devolution of responsibilities within the committee structure of the college. Much in this respect almost inevitably depends on the Principal's attitude.

The above account is heavily based on the practice in a single college, but it probably shows more convincingly than a set of generalizations the kind of thinking at present current in the colleges.

## The College Community

The dominant values of the English tradition of teacher training have been stigmatized by Professor William Taylor as those of 'social and literary romanticism', including 'a suspicion of the intellect', 'a hunger for the satisfactions of inter-personal life within the community and the small group', and 'a flight from rationality' (Taylor, 1969). The English tradition in politics has, however, been described by Butterfield as based on 'a respect for the other man's personality, a recognition of what is due to political opponents, a certain homage to what the other man may think to be a political good. This is the ground and logic of political compromise . . . and without it democracy can only destroy itself in a conflict of divine right versus diabolical wrong.' (Butterfield, 1945.) The English tradition, again, was described by Sir Fred Clarke as characterized by a very widespread and deeply felt sense of the importance of human relationships within a community, of membership in a community (Clarke, 1948), which underlies the persistence of institutions as contrasted as the public house and the public school. It may be argued that the dominant tradition of teacher training in England has been influenced not so much by 'social and literary romanticism' as by this feeling for community. There are inevitably, perhaps, tensions between the values which focus on positive relationships within a community and those which focus on a rigorous impersonal discipline of the mind. There is no doubt that the small size of educational institutions in England has reflected the high priority accorded to the first of these clusters of values, and that the trend towards larger schools and colleges is widely felt to be sacrificing something precious. On the other hand those who are struggling in the colleges to cope with the demands of work for the B.Ed. degree and the postgraduate certificate of education know that in the 'knowledge explosion' of the present time high academic standards cannot be achieved by college staffs unless departments are large enough to permit some degree of specialization. Yet it is also possible for the demands of academic courses in the colleges to rise without either achieving any intellectual rigour or improving the quality of those who enter the teaching profession. What is probably needed is a rethinking of what is involved in intellectual 'rigour' and how detailed 'academic' thinking is to be related to first-hand experience.

The above notes outline the dilemma that faces many members of college staffs at the present time. The multiplication of student numbers in the colleges was necessitated by the desperate shortage of teachers in the schools; but it also created larger, more varied staffs and led to a great reduction in the proportion of resident students. Colleges have become much less intimate places; often they have become more outward-looking, less parochial; but sometimes also they have lost their sense of community and gained little else. The problem for those who value both the sense of community and the intellectual vitality is to create, in a college of 800 or more students, on the one hand a sense of enquiry and a discipline of the mind, and on the other a structure and a climate of opinion in which there is mutual respect between staff and students and in which relationships can become personal when this is desired (Shipman, 1969).

With the above objects in view, the following aspects of organization are widely shared in the colleges. A 'Freshers' Conference' is held for two or three days before the beginning of the students' first year and opportunities created for informal contacts. A 'personal tutorial' system is maintained in which the personal tutor is a member of the student's main-subject department but there is sufficient flexibility to enable the student to change to another tutor if this is considered desirable. Many teaching groups are small enough for a student to get to know, and to be known by, perhaps six or eight tutors during his college career. A bar or other suitable space is shared by both staff and students. Standing and lightweight camps and field-work courses as well as sports clubs, dramatic societies and so on offer opportunities for tutors and students to make close personal contacts. A Founder's Day or Open Day is held in a student's final year to which his parents are invited and where they can meet his tutors. The college chaplaincy – in a Church college – provides a pastoral and social link. At Bede College staff seminars on the counselling of students have been conducted with the expert assistance of the university health officer, mainly on a case-study basis.

A suitable climate of opinion cannot be created at the drop of a hat. One of the consequences of the student disturbances of the late 1960s has been a decline in mutual confidence between staff and students: there appears to be more mistrust on both sides and this calls for a more conscious forbearance on the part of staff than formerly. The tact and understanding of resident tutors may have a special importance. Standards to which the great majority of tutors adhere may be openly flouted by militant students, particularly in regard to sex, to drugs, and to dress, while yet the great majority of students remain rather conservative on many fundamentals.

Faith and personal experience, reinforced with evidence provided by work on the sociology of organizations, maintain that the appropriate climate of opinion depends in some degree on the customary relationships established in the institution in the past, but in a greater degree on the way in which the Principal and Vice-Principal of a college treat their colleagues and treat the students: the extent of their personal concern and consideration, their success in maintaining a just and dependable structure of authority. This point indeed brings us to a topic whose importance requires separate discussion.

## The Structure of Authority

Etzioni in his study of complex organizations (1961) distinguished three forms of power in society. Coercive power depends on the use or threat of force and utilitarian power on the use of economic rewards or penalties, while normative power is that which an idolized party leader, or a loved teacher, exerts over his followers, or which a small band of close friends exert over one another. Etzioni's delineation of coercive power is perhaps too restrictive, since many people can be coerced by verbal pressures of various kinds which cannot easily be included under utilitarian or normative power. Coercive power tends to evoke negative reactions, of resentment or over-submission, termed by Etzioni 'alienative involvement'. Utilitarian power tends to evoke a calculative form of involvement, a concern with the 'nicely calculated less or more'. Normative power tends to evoke a co-operative attitude, a 'moral involvement'. All three forms of power are to be seen at work in the colleges of education: the college governors have the power to expel a student from the college or to require him to withdraw on account of inadequate performance in his studies. Degrees and certificates are awarded which qualify the holders for certain occupations and salaries. And there is a normative element: college authorities try to run their institution in such a way that the students develop a genuine attachment to it and/or to the staff members they know and/or to the student body.

A college Principal is here then faced with some formidable problems. To what extent is coercion necessary? or desirable? What forms should it take? If it has to be used, how can one minimize the alienation which is likely to result and which may neutralize the normative influence of the institution? How far is it desirable to emphasize the qualifications to be obtained? In what way is it, on the one hand, legitimate, and on the other practicable, to create a climate of relationships in which students form an attachment to the institution and imbibe some of its values? What values should a college be committed to? How far can a whole college, as distinct from a department or a separate residential section, be committed to particular values or clusters of values? Here again it seems sensible for the author to describe some of the principles adopted at the college he knows best.

First, with regard to coercive measures. A series of cases in various parts of the country over the last few years in which students have challenged the legitimacy of the procedures and/or the penalties adopted by university or college authorities has led to a great deal of rethinking on such matters, both in universities and colleges and at the DES. Articles of Government of colleges of education now state explicitly that a student may be required by CAB to withdraw on account of an 'unsatisfactory standard of work' or expelled by a disciplinary committee for misconduct. The composition of the disciplinary committee requires equal numbers of staff, of students, and of governors who are neither staff nor students. No member of the disciplinary committee may take part in the governors' meeting which hears an appeal, nor any member of CAB who was present at the initial hearing of an academic case. A student may be accompanied by a 'friend', which may be interpreted as a solicitor, at either hearing. Thus students have a safeguard against arbitrary penalties and governors have powers to get rid of unsuitable students.

There are, however, real problems as yet in the definition of the offences. At Bede College, in order to establish criteria for the assessment of an 'unsatisfactory standard of work', a system of weighting for the various courses taken by any one student has been drawn up in conjunction with student representatives; but the balance of judgement between the academic body, CAB, and the largely 'lay' body of governors who hear an appeal may take one or two test cases to establish clearly. With regard to 'misconduct' there is no doubt that public opinion expects certain standards of teachers which it does not necessarily expect of other people, and that young people in general tend to question the validity of these standards, particularly in regard to relations between the sexes. Here again the new procedures will probably require a certain number of test cases to establish criteria.

The element of coercion is to be assessed, however, not only in terms of the handling of extreme cases but in terms of the nature and source of ordinary college regulations and the manner of their enforcement. In this particular college the formulation and revision of the college regulations have been handled by staff-student committees for a number of years. Even here problems can arise if the student representatives on such committees are not in sufficiently close contact with the student body, and when large numbers of students are non-resident much depends on the structure of management *within* the student body. In this college the JCR Council consists of thirty members elected on a geographical basis by all sections of the student body; the president has a year's release from academic studies to devote his full time to JCR business and he is responsible therefore not only for keeping in close personal touch with all shades of opinion but also for giving stimulus, encouragement and guidance to student representatives.

Again, the manner of enforcement of regulations includes not only the procedures but the justice of the decisions, and especially the existence of a positive attitude on the part of the college officers to the offenders, and the absence of any atmosphere of recrimination or vindictiveness. As has already been noted, this is thought to be related to the way in which the Principal and senior members of staff treat other members as well as students. But the changes in student attitudes that have taken place in recent years have made patience and objectivity more difficult to maintain; these changes, however, could be interpreted as having occurred originally through inadequate sensitiveness or awareness on the part of the older generation to the changing needs of society and of young people.

What in effect is being said here is that the element of coercion needs to be handled without arousing negative reactions which will prejudice the normative influence of the college. The latter, as has been noted, raises two questions: what values is it legitimate to try to communicate? and what means can be employed to create this influence?

Much discussion has been held at many staff and staff-student meetings about the values and standards this college stands for, both as a teacher training institution and as a Church-sponsored institution. In effect the values on which all agree can be summed up in terms of personal concern and respect of members of the community for other members of the community; of adherence to such traditional ideals as justice, integrity and hard work; and of a conscientious application to academic and professional studies. Some members would add the academic ideals of rationality and dispassionate enquiriy; others would add what is the present ideal of many young people: freedom to act in any way which they personally consider does not injure another person. But these two latter views would not command general support, the former being too high-falutin', the second being felt by staff to be too egotistical. We turn to the practical problem of how to create an appropriate influence.

This depends on the identification of the student body with the college community and its ideals (Etzioni, 1961). This consensus in turn depends on several factors: the confidence of the student body in the genuine concern of the college authorities; the effectiveness of the communication system; the extent to which the college satisfies such student aspirations as the desire to be treated as adults; and the extent to which the college course is felt to be realistic and satisfying. In effect, therefore, much of the structure that has been described earlier regarding the involvement of both staff and students in administrative decisions and in the development of academic policy, as well as in matters of community discipline, is part of a more general structure designed to embody in the life of the institution the values of the community as a whole, without bringing pressure on an individual to conform over and above the agreed standards (Collier, 1969).

How far the structures and procedures outlined above would be recognizable in these terms to an outsider, or to a lecturer or student, or how far they are successful in achieving their purposes, is debatable. But at this point 'a Principal's view of college administration' inevitably contains a subjective, personal element. However, the evidence assembled by Professor William Taylor (1969) indicates a fairly wide currency for similar views in the colleges of education at the present time.

### External Relations

The internal structure of college organization has been described at some length. But colleges of education also have links with a variety of outside bodies: a university, an Area Training Organization (ATO), the DES, LEAs, teachers' organizations, schools, student organizations, churches, not to mention the press and the public.

At the level of practical administration – of school practice, of B.Ed. syllabuses and certificate examinations – it is necessary to spend more time and effort on collaboration with outside bodies than before. But over and above these needs there lies the fact of the rapid and radical changes now taking place in society and the implications of this situation for the colleges. The colleges believe they have something valuable to contribute both to the schools and to higher education; that despite their shortcomings they offer a better model for a general and humane education for non-specialists between the ages of eighteen and twenty-one than (for example) the general degrees in arts offered in English universities. The James

Committee evidently also held this view. They hold a strategic position in relation to schools and to universities in regard both to innovation and to the preservation of valuable elements from the past. But this situation demands far more attention than has been customary to the establishment of understanding and respect between the colleges and the other institutions listed above. At Bede College some experiments in relation to teachers' organizations, to schools and to the churches have been set up but much more experiment is called for, together with evaluations of the experiments.

## Innovation

Finally it is necessary to look at the problems of evolution and adaptation. Indications have been given regarding the machinery for forward thinking in a particular college and the extent to which it is hoped that an 'organic' pattern of organization can facilitate change and development. It would, however, be too optimistic to suppose that the structure in itself will produce a highly innovatory institution; or that innovations will necessarily take place in significant ways. One can easily picture a highly organic institution which is also highly resistant to change in any but trivial matters. Somewhere there must be senior members of staff who can encourage fresh thinking; somewhere there must be members who can see which areas of the college curriculum or organization are most in need of re-examination. At any one moment this is a matter of hunch or speculation; the rightness or wrongness of the hunch may only become apparent a decade later. What is thought of as a valuable innovation in a particular college may turn out to be positively damaging; it may turn out to be 'old hat'; it may turn out to be a significant growing point.

Possibly the two areas in which most colleges are lacking in creating the conditions for innovation are in the formulation of aims and objectives and in the evaluation of experiments. In the college we have looked at in some detail there has been a good deal of discussion of values and standards in the community life but relatively little in relation to academic or professional work, and some procedure is needed for exploring and making explicit the assumptions which underlie the work of staff and students. Probably also closer attention needs to be given to the more specifically intellectual values of dispassionate inquiry.

With regard to the evaluation of courses the CAB has an 'advisory committee for evaluation' which has done some initial thinking on the problems of evaluation. But evaluation in itself is a form of action-research, which notoriously tends to elude efforts to introduce objective techniques and which has not yet come to terms with the subjective elements in the formulation of aims and objectives. Possibly the three aspects of college life that have most significance for effective innovation are the establishing of an organic type of organization, the specification of aims and objectives, and the development of a machinery for evaluation.

The James Report may well lead to radical changes in the structure of the curriculum and the nature of the external controlling authorities of the colleges of education. Thus many details of the above picture may become obsolete in a few years. I would maintain, however, that the underlying principles which have been set out in this chapter will retain their validity.

In conclusion I would like to record my warmest appreciation to my former colleague, subsequently Secretary to the Council of Church Colleges of Education, Canon J. S. Robertson, for very kindly reading and commenting on this chapter.

# *Part 4*

## VALUES, CURRICULA AND TEACHING METHODS

## CHAPTER 11

# On the 'Educated' Person and the Problem of Values in Teacher Education and Training

### DAVID ASPIN

It is interesting to speculate as to what might happen if one were to pose the question, 'What *is* education?' to a representative group of pupils and students from our schools and colleges. One suspects that some of the answers one might receive – from 'Education is learning' to 'It's all indoctrination' – would bring to light some intriguing notions in our young people's grasp of what it is that teachers are about when they profess to be 'educating' their charges. It also seems probable that others would hesitate as to the meaning of the question.

In many adult circles, by contrast, there would be no such diffidence: 'education' is about going to schools and other places to get some sort of qualification, some preparation and training for the real business of living. We are all familiar, for example, with such assertions in newspaper correspondence columns as, 'What these students ought to do is get on with their education', and with the idea that sending children to 'good' schools to get the 'best' education is a matter of the highest social importance.

From public expressions of such views we may infer that in some quarters education is envisaged as a commodity, for the acquisition of which it is sufficient only that access be open. The student in full-time education is thus represented as a species of raw material for processing. On the successful completion of his courses of study he is considered as a sort of artifact 'turned off' as though by a conveyor belt, the marketable outcome of programmes conceived to ensure the continuing availability of a certain product for consumption, application and use.

That such is a humdrum, strictly utilitarian conception of education as providing personnel for industrial or commercial deployment scarcely needs to be stated. Of course one has to earn a living. But to be able to perform one's duties as the functionary of some agency within the capitalist economic system, one would not need, presumably, to be more than merely well-informed or highly trained. It would not be necessary to be *educated*.

And, on the opinions which such a person would bring to the world outside his particular commercial or industrial interest, A. N. Whitehead (1932) remarked that, 'The merely well-informed man is the most useless bore on God's earth'. In that respect, it is not necessary, either, for the commercially successful or industrially efficient employee to exhibit anything which might make people describe him as 'cultivated' or 'sophisticated' in any wide sense. On the other hand, it is equally possible for the 'cultivated' person to be accepted in society without in any way possessing the detailed mass of information or complex technical skills which the employer would look for in his work force. Folklore again refers us to those who, while being consummate embellishers of social intercourse, were minuscule contributors to the real business of living. Thus on the one hand, it seems likely that the merely well-trained person will possess little more than a narrow range of information (however deep) and skills (however complex), while on the other, the merely cultivated would seem to be capable of a wide range of discourse, but, in certain respects, only on something of a superficial level. What we seem to require is both depth and breadth of cognitive repertoire. John Passmore (1967) sees differences between the labels 'cultivated', 'well-informed' and 'educated' which we attach to persons.

> An educated man – as distinct from a merely 'cultivated' man – must be, let us agree, independent, critical, capable of facing problems. But these qualities, while necessary, are not sufficient. . . .

We may perhaps take such a differentiation as a starting point in the attempt to characterize a person as 'educated'. There is, of course, a difficulty here: to construct a lexical definition which will allow all those people we may regard as being 'educated' to be included in any general description. It might be, perhaps, less problematic if one were to be frankly stipulative; but then it would be open to anyone simply to refuse to accede to certain stipulations as to what constitutes the educated person. In general it would seem to be much easier to attempt to work out in terms of ordinary language usage what we mean when we call someone an educated person – and thus to try to establish a set of criteria by which we judge whether a person might be regarded as educated. It would seem to be a cardinal feature in any explanation of calling someone educated that 'standards' of some sort are involved. For, as we use the term, to call someone 'educated' is to load them with value of some sort. Either it is a term of approval or regard (in which case 'educated' functions as a 'medal-pinning' expression) or it is a term with pejorative overtones (so to say that someone has been 'educated' may be to evince distance or disapproval). At all events, any concept of an educated person is almost inescapably normative (Langford, 1968; Bantock, 1964; Peters, 1966; Daveney, 1970; Oakeshott, 1971).

One of *our* societal norms would be that the educated person *knows* something. And in any account of what is involved in knowing something, certain minimal conditions of warrantable assertability for the use of the claim to know will be in operation. Broadly speaking, this will necessitate some such concatenation of conditions for satisfaction as that offered by Scheffler (1965) or Ayer (1956) of propositional knowledge as a disposition of justified true belief.* Thus the educated person will not only act and speak as if that which he asserts to believe is in fact true, but the style of his belief will be evidential: he will be able to give adequate grounds for his claim to know which all sane and sensible people would be disposed to accept as rational and sufficient warrant of his right to say 'I know'.

This 'evidential style of belief' will involve something else, however. For the different kinds of evidential ground which can be given for knowledge propositions, depending upon whether they are factual or evaluative utterance, a priori or empirical, will impose an additional requirement on the educated person's claim to know – namely, that he be conversant with the nature of the varying types of *rationales* and their distinct types of application. As Aristotle pointed out, 'It is the mark of an educated mind to expect that amount of exactness in each kind which the nature of the particular subjects admits'.† It was perhaps on some such basis that Professor P. H. Hirst (1965) endeavoured to analyse what is involved in the claim to know. He concluded that:

> To acquire knowledge is to become aware of experience as structured, organised and made meaningful in some quite specific way, and the varieties of human knowledge constitute the highly developed forms in which man has found this possible.

Hirst's explication of his postulate of logically distinct 'forms of knowledge' is open to some epistemological objections (Wilson, 1969; Gribble, 1970; Hindess, 1972); nevertheless, there seems to be fairly wide agreement among a number of educational thinkers that we can only talk properly of knowing in terms of different 'ways of knowing', 'modes of understanding', 'ways of looking at things' (and so on), dispute how we may about the number of these various ways (Peterson, 1960; Reid, 1961; Phenix, 1964; Dearden, 1968; Schwab, 1964).

It seems, then, that our use of the term 'educated' of a person who, *inter alia*, knows things, carries certain important implications; first, that his claims to knowledge can be supported by the giving of reasons and, secondly, that these reasons will be such as can be publicly observed to be appropriate as substantiations for the claim in the particular 'realm' of knowledge in question. This further implies that the educated person will be aware of and versed in the various distinct realms of knowledge and ways of knowing, so that he may assess whether the account offered or called for is in fact adequate and appropriate. It is in these terms that

* See also Ryle, 1949.    † Aristotle, *Nichomachean Ethics*, I, iii, 4, 1094 b 25.

Passmore (1967) fills out his description of the educated man: 'To be educated one must be able to participate in the great human traditions of critico-creative thought: science, history, literature, philosophy, technology ...'.

It is not sufficient to be aware of, or versed in the various cognitive realms, the different bodies of propositions in each of the distinct ways of knowing. As Passmore states, the educated person can also participate in them, or at least some of them. And this will involve his being able, to some extent, to understand and apply the various procedural skills of verification or validation, evaluation and testing that are relevant and appropriate to the different modes, to operate within the cognitive contexts and frameworks that are required. This necessarily implies, to use Professor R. S. Peters' language, his being 'initiated' into and becoming 'on the inside of' the various disciplined forms of thinking involved. Thus our educated man will have some grasp of and ability in these forms; and if he is not as far 'on the inside' of some of them as he is in the case of others, at least we may expect that he will know what it is that, for example, distinguishes mathematical from scientific philosophical or moral thinking and that he will be able to make out the body of propositions that are variously mathematical, scientific, philosophical and moral in his cognitive repertoire. What we are after is, in fact, both depth and width of cognitive capacity and concern.

Perhaps we may establish, then, as one of our criteria for the allocation of the title 'educated' the observation that an educated person has, *inter alia*, gained some understanding of the major areas of organized knowledge, together with some grasp of the modes of thinking through which each type of knowledge is acquired.

Having achieved such grasp and understanding, however, our educated man does not let it lie inert. We would, one imagines, be most reluctant to regard as 'educated' the new graduate who on returning to his rooms throws off his gown and hood with the comment, 'Thank God I need never read another book!' It is more likely that we should conceive of our educated person as thinking of his being educated in the same way in which a former archbishop is said to have formulated an answer when asked the question, 'Are you saved?'; 'If you mean,' he is reported to have replied, 'σωθείς, then I am far from it, but if you mean σωζόμενος, then I most certainly am!' In simpler words 'education' and 'being educated' is not a state which we reach and sink into gratefully, nor is it an achievement; rather it is a propensity to engage in activities of a certain kind and in certain ways rather than certain others – it is a whole pattern of activity, a whole form of life that one is continuously engaged in. Peters summed up this point in a memorable aphorism: 'To be educated is not to have arrived at a destination; it is to travel with a different view.'

How is it different? It is different by virtue of our regard for the various modes of reason-giving involved in the extraction of distinct ways of knowing from the notion of what it is to know something, which we delineated as characteristic of the educated man. The various procedures by which we acquire knowledge in the different realms become, as it were, built into our way of looking at things, become ingrained in us, as one of the chief distinguishing features of the particular form of life we associate with 'being educated'.

Thus the educated man never gives up learning, reflecting, considering, reasoning, or deliberating on questions – both the nature of the real business of living and what he ought to do in respect of it. He throws further light on the knowledge he already has by being interested in and by mastering new methods of enquiry, by being willing continually to examine and re-examine his assumptions and to test and retest his hypotheses. Indeed, as Passmore points out, the person who is 'educated' according to these criteria is going to have a difficult and embarrassing time, because he is constantly ready to expose himself to criticism and refutation. His chosen form of life is made up of activities susceptible to these sorts of harassment; and A. Phillips Griffiths (1965) spells out its consequences for the teacher:

At every stage [such activities] require the stance of doubt: the readiness to meet challenge. Every step must be questioned and must always be prepared for – indeed look for – refutation. One cannot be prepared for refutation unless one knows what refutation is, and that means knowing what it is to refute ... From the beginning the pupil must take an active part: it is the teacher's cross to bear with initially simple-minded and half-baked objections so that he may eventually be proved wrong with good ones.

Why does the teacher/educated person do this? It is because he places value upon knowing and understanding, because he considers them pre-eminently worthwhile. Indeed it is by virtue of his care and concern for these knowings, understandings and other cognitive skills that in our society at any rate we mark out such a person as 'educated'. He is different from people who are not 'educated', according to these criteria, in the sense both that he cares about and values such cognitive concerns, and also that his form of life will, it is suggested, necessarily have been transformed in the acquisition of the educated person's cognitive repertoire by the value which he places on the various ways in which he claims to have acquired it and to be able to justify it. For, in addition to the particular modes of verification and evaluation operative in each of the kinds, the very notion of 'substantiation' is underpinned, as has just been argued above, by certain general principles of procedure, such as those of tolerating and respecting other people's points of view, of giving pride of place to reason and fact rather than emotion or prejudice, of restraint in making claims and drawing conclusions, of weighing matters impartially and objectively. Our educated man is committed to these sorts of values, and the adherence to such features of life as reason-giving and open-mindedness is, arguably, his principal distinguishing characteristic. It is, at any rate, for some such feature of his life that the man of science can be properly described as 'educated' in that he '... not only knows that evidence must be found for assumptions but knows also what counts as evidence and cares that it should be found'.*

Here then might be how our analysis of the educated person would break down: an educated man is one who has gained some understanding of the major areas of organized knowledge, together with some grasp of the various modes of thinking through which each type of knowledge is acquired. He holds all these knowing procedures, and the bodies of propositions and skills to which they can lead, to be valuable, cares about them, and is committed to them. Indeed this value commitment may be said to be the mark of the educated man.

It might be objected at this point that what has been said so far relates to the notion of the 'educated' somebody, but that the notion of 'person' is still vacuous. Such a criticism might add that the analysis has involved a particular concept of personhood which has not in fact been defined. There would be some justice to such a charge, for there is a fairly clear conception of personhood underlying what has been said so far – of what it is that characterizes and constitutes the person. To enter into a discussion on the concept of the person at this juncture, however, would involve an undertaking of some length, and would also be hazardous. For the question 'what is a person?' is one that involves controversy. We should quickly, if we were to embark upon such a project, elicit dubieties concerning the admissibility of the equation of 'person' with 'human being' or of 'person' with 'civilized being' (Collins, 1972). Some would argue, for instance, that hottentots and cannibals, very small children, insane human beings, people who as a result of some dreadful accident or handicap lived out their lives in some vegetable-like existence, should be excluded from the class of 'persons'.

We may perhaps best solve this problem by having recourse to the same sort of negative principles that some moral philosophers have employed in other matters: by making the initial presumption that the two concepts 'person' and 'human being' are co-extensive, and by inferring that for this reason we may discount other forms of animal life from the class of persons; and by concluding that, again for this reason, the onus is upon anyone who wishes to discount such cases as have been described

* Peters, 1966, p. 31.

above from the class of persons, to present reasoned and relevant arguments
for so doing.

What then is the concept of personhood implicit in the foregoing analysis
of what it means to us to describe someone as 'educated'?

The connotation of 'man' as 'rational animal' may provide us with *some*
pointers, for it lies at the root of our idea of the person as a being with
an identity that persists, of individual consciousness and rational nature.
This basic principle of permanence – the persisting personal identity – is
characterised and distinguished by a predisposition towards a particular
pattern of activities in which it is pre-eminently asserted and exhibited, and
in which it habitually and characteristically tends to engage, such as reflecting, appraising, judging, estimating, valuing, deciding, and so on. The
individual is nevertheless developed by a whole range of experience and is
capable of being further developed, so that he comes to know new things,
attains to certain levels of understanding and exhibits certain attitudes,
qualities of mind, beliefs and values with respect to what is desirable and
worthwhile. All this, and the knowings he continues to acquire, help the
individual to direct and control his own existence, to take account of things,
to make appraisals, and responsible choices – in sum, to engage in rational
activity. Indeed it is these things that, together with the idea of independence,
stand out as the principal distinguishing marks of our notion of what it is
to be a person in one's own right – the ability of the individual to act
rationally and to exercise freedom in his choices. Other qualities and
characteristics would also operate along with those of autonomy and
responsibility in the exercise of will and making of decisions, for we must
not forget that the idea of *individual* identity implies the existence of the
person in a setting and points to its relations and interdependence with its
environs. For us these would, perhaps, involve the awareness of self and of
others, emotional stability and control, and the capacity to form satisfying
inter-personal relationships.

It is readily conceded that this is a culture-bound conception, loaded
in terms of those values which we cherish in our particular society and,
maybe pre-eminently, in the teaching profession. It is suggested that a
concept such as this underlies much of our work as trainers of teachers,
in our striving for 'personal education' and the 'personal development' of
our students. But at least the frank avowal of a preference for knowledge,
rationality, and certain moral ways of proceeding enable one to anticipate
and provide for the charge that this analysis is in fact a prescription for
education (Cooper, 1966). For we are taking as one of our determining
criteria of applicability for the term 'educated' the notion of commitment
to some value or set of values. It would thus make equal sense, on this
analysis, to talk of the 'educated hottentot', 'the educated communist', or
the 'educated Spartan' (Peters, 1970), for those in such social systems to
whom such titles might meaningfully be ascribed would all have a particular

cognitive repertoire, certain cognitive perspectives, a commitment to a set of values or societal or cultural norms.

The concept which we have endeavoured to describe here, however, is one which has a particular substantive content packed into its value and knowledge frames – those procedures and activities which *we* regard as being especially worthwhile. And, it is suggested, it is this concept of the 'educated' person to which all our activity as educators is directed, whether it be in schools or in colleges or departments of education; and the activity involved is that of 'initiating' another person or persons into a particularly valued form of life. Such an endeavour and aspiration might be regarded by some as their 'aim' of education.

It is, however, interesting and perhaps instructive to note that in many of the recent publications concerned with the problems of and issues in the training of teachers in England and Wales there is little extended or rigorous consideration of much that could, even loosely, be called 'aims'. The principal areas of controversy seem rather to be those of, first, the organization and construction of courses in the various training institutions, secondly, the content and internal relationships of the different parts of the syllabuses of such institutions, and thirdly, the external relationships and connections of the different stages of the work of the institutions with each other. It may also be observed that the pages of some periodicals devoted to topics in tertiary education are not often distinguished by the frequency with which the questions of 'aims' or 'objectives' in higher education are expatiated upon; much more consideration seems to be given there to such important matters as cost-effectiveness, productivity and economic value.

Yet a close examination of the schemes of organization and curricula of teacher training institutions indicate that these are, in fact, shot through with 'aims and objectives' of one sort or another, with particular concepts of 'education' or 'personhood', whether these are made explicit or left latent. Indeed, in the final analysis, the adherence to whatever aims or objectives can be extracted from such publications is, in itself, based upon considerations not necessarily or merely restricted to those of economic acceptability and viability. It seems fair to say that the chronological order in which the four issues of organization, curriculum, aims and values are often dealt with in such works, can, in terms of logical priority, be reversed. This then puts the consideration of the problem of values as first in any reflections on the construction of an optimum model for the education and training of our future teachers.

It is, of course, precisely at this point that such reflections become complicated, even almost intractable. One of the basic difficulties is that one can never be sure whether the term 'value' has the same meaning even for all those engaged in reflection and discussion on such issues as those

of 'values' in teacher education – much less that their values are similar.
Thus even the most elementary steps in such activities may be awkward.
For the problem of meaning here is so fraught with ambiguities and
dubieties that the serious student can hardly begin to treat the problems
for preoccupation with the meta-problems.

The various questions with which that student must deal in his considerations on value theory are well set out by W. K. Frankena (1958):

> ... value-theory is concerned both with the property of value and with
> the process of valuing. About the former it asks various questions.
> What is its nature? Is it a quality or a relation? Is it objective or
> subjective? Is it a single property, or is it several properties, value
> being an ambiguous term? Is its presence in a thing dependent on or
> reducible to the fact that the thing is valued by someone? About the
> latter it has also various questions. Is it a mere feeling or desire? Or
> does it involve judgment or cognition? And if so, is this cognition of
> a value already there independently of the act of valuing or knowing?

To these knotty problems we need only add others, such as those concerning the question of different types of value, and of the justification of values
and value judgements, to see that much work has to be done in the matter
of ground-clearing before ever the problems of substantive differences in
values in teacher education, or of value as existent and value as procedure,
can begin to be tackled. Add to this other realms of value discussion, such
as those engaged in by our fellow-workers in the social sciences or
psychology – differences, for example, between 'value', 'belief' or 'attitude'
– and one can perhaps begin to understand why this is an area that has
been the subject of relatively little rigorous investigation. And even if we
look at the various incursions that have been made into these wider fields,
we find that there is not only a lack of any general consensus concerning
the nature and properties of values and valuing but also concerning even
the most appropriate ways to approach the basic value problems.

One of those who has hazarded a foray into questions connected with
the various values in teacher education has been Professor G. H. Bantock
(1969). In a paper given to the Colston research symposium he sees the
basic issue as one arising within the context of changing values in society
generally, and, in particular, in the changing evaluations made of the
teacher's role and function by members of our society, by those responsible
for training teachers, and by the trainee teachers themselves.

Bantock seeks to point up the transformation which is, he alleges,
taking place in the public conception of the teacher's role as an agent of
modern society and, to a lesser extent, the change which is taking place in
his actual role. He sees the latter in terms of an expansion from what was
an essentially limited task – the transmission of a limited cognitive content

and the cultivation of intellectual virtues and 'conformist' values – to a much more global one – the all-round development of children as persons and as members of a 'new' society. He insists that such a shift from a traditional limited conception to a much wider all-embracing one has taken place and is still taking place in the versions of the teaching concept and the teacher's role which are currently being presented to students in training. These, he argues, are either poorly analysed or just simply confused; he points out that no one has ever taken time to consider whether, and to what extent, the large-scale (and, he alleges, pretentious) claims for the influence of schooling on children's development have any chance of being realized in practice, and he accuses the modern predilection for 'theorizing' in education of failing to take account of such crucial inhibiting factors as the enormous inertia of existing educational institutions, and failing to understand what might be involved in the attempt to change the character of an institution like the school.

His solution to this conflict is that in our training establishments we should evade the confusion inherent in a changing value system by reverting to ones which are more traditional, tested and quite limited. The purpose of schooling is, he claims, 'to induct young people into some important areas of understanding, certain refined modes of feeling and a few complex skills. The emphasis should vary with level of ability.' We must cease resolutely refusing

> to face up to the unmistakable fact of unequal aptitude and ability in the school population.... If we could grant that the job of the school is with certain very specific and limited types of learning only, we could, perhaps, give our students a more rigorous professional training for their jobs, and, by seeking to achieve less, accomplish more.

In the colleges therefore we must 'undertake a rigorous and unsentimental sort out of possibilities within the time available... in relation to the competence of the people involved'.

A number of criticisms could be levelled against this argument and most have already been voiced. Professor Ben Morris (1969) in his reply to the paper points out that Bantock's version of the teaching concept is one of very limited currency and not one that many teachers would actually subscribe to. Bantock's value preferences are deeply conditioned by his (usually avowed) intellectualist bias and his unwillingness to admit more than an irreducible affective element in learning. These preferences have made it inevitable that he has contributed little to clarifying the underlying issues. It might be thought, moreover, that he has taken no account of some important historical and sociological evidence which would count strongly against his case. Yet, as Morris seems to suggest, our feeling about

Bantock's view is the uncomfortable one that, although we may disagree with his solutions, there is more than a grain of truth in his analyses. And in this connection, he has clearly brought out the conflicts of value that are often present in public views on the nature and function of teacher education.

But apart from the difficulty and confusion arising from the changing and conflicting values (Bantock suggests) in the teacher's conception of his role in society, it appears that we can detect, in many of our training establishments, a deeper and more fundamental conflict. One side of this conflict supported a view long held in the training colleges of the educative function of such institutions, a view that was strikingly reflected and given formal approval in the recommendations of the Robbins Report (1963) concerning the future organization and administration of the training colleges. It was recognized that there were many students in the colleges

> who know while they are still at school that they wish to become teachers and who ... prefer a course of combined education and pro- fessional training. ... For many students .. . a strongly felt professional purpose is a great incentive to the education that should accompany training in a liberal profession.

It was for these reasons that: 'In recent years the great effort of the Colleges has been to improve the general education of their students'. They now had 'an educational opportunity for which they have long pressed. The teachers of the future will have had the opportunity to be better educated than their predecessors.' It was in recognition of such a feature in the activities and aspirations of the training colleges that the Robbins report recommended 'that the colleges should be known in future as Colleges of Education'.*

This, then, is one version of the dominant function of the teacher train- ing institutions at that time. The other is more difficult to isolate, in Robbins at least. In that report there are only odd hints:

> ... a young woman with no great desire to take a degree in psychology but with a genuine interest in children may study their psychological development *with an enhanced sense of relevance* when it is combined with observation of children in school *and practice in her future vocation* ... (my italics).

This is the other side: the idea of the colleges' principal function as a con- centration upon what has been regarded as their main task, definable as 'giving good training, in the narrower sense of the word'. This is the version, too, that still appears to be the one tacitly adhered to in the organization and activity of many colleges of education, the emphasis in them being on the production of highly-trained and skilled personnel to function in

* Robbins, paras 310, 311, 351.

certain specific ways in a specific situation – that of teaching children in a classroom.

The predominance of this latter currency in the thinking and planning of educational legislators and administrators interested in the future orientation and development of teacher education and training in this country is nowhere more strikingly reflected than in the recommendations recently published by the James Committee. The approach suggested in the Report produced by the committee, described variously as a 'nuts and bolts' approach or as a 'sell-out to practice',* can be seen, if examined closely, to bear out the view that there does exist a dichtomy of values in the models for the future organization of teacher education presently being constructed and proposed.

It is, of course, true that the Report seeks to make specific provision for 'personal education' and 'continuing general education', especially in the first, and, to an extent, in the third cycles it proposes. Its concept of 'personal education' or 'general education' may be examined in Chapter 4, in particular paragraphs 4.2 to 4.11 (but also elsewhere). The authors of the Report consider that two elements can, in theory, be sharply distinguished in the initial preparation of the teacher, one of which is the acquisition of theoretical and practical expertise, the other is the personal education of the student.

Lord James and his colleagues believe

> that there are general principles which should give shape to that 'personal education' . . . and that the work of the students following a first-cycle programme . . . should combine the advantages of study in depth with the merits of a more broadly based general education. (4.2)

They go on to lay down that:

> These elements must be combined and inter-related. . . . In special studies the aim will be to encourage the student to pursue his chosen subjects in some depth and to acquire some degree of mastery of them. In general studies the aim will rather be to stimulate individual thought and discussion, to enable the student to realise the kind of problems and experiences that exist in fields outside his own, to make good the deficiencies in his intellectual and cultural awareness, and above all to tempt him to further efforts of self-education in directions which he had not previously considered. (4.8)

This concept of a 'more general education' is spelled out in greater detail in para. 4.10:

---

* See the letters from R. S. Peters and G. H. Bantock in the *Times Educational Supplement* (11 February 1972 and 18 February 1972).

The aim of a course in general studies should be to provide stimulus to the student, an incentive to self-education, and an attitude of critical awareness. Studies of this kind provide an opportunity to raise and discuss issues of importance with an obligation to pursue each one in all its specialist connotations. One of the main tasks of general education is to make good some of the cultural deficiencies of those who propose to be teachers of others. The course must therefore aim at providing some essential background in the main areas of human thought and activity, i.e. the humanities ... mathematics and the sciences (including their applications in practical situations), the social sciences, and the arts ... (4.11) ... ideally every student should follow a course made up of elements selected from all or most of these areas ... [though]. ... In the hands of the skilful and enthusiastic teacher many apparently narrow and irrelevant courses can become vehicles for an authentic general education.

Such a course of 'more general education' is to be regarded as complementary to the course of studies of a more specialist character occupying about two-thirds of the college student's time in the first cycle.

If there is to be this balance between special studies and general studies in a student's 'personal education' in the first cycle, however, it is odd to find that the nature of the former is nowhere spelt out so clearly as that of the latter. Hints here and there give the clue that special studies will be approached 'in depth' and will lead to 'mastery' (neither of these concepts ever being explained in detail, however, despite the difficulties their ambiguous nature entails*); they will, it is hoped, stimulate thought and interest and lead the student to work independently and to read widely for himself. But we see too, from the supplementary function of the 'general studies' element in what will be 'the right kind of education', that there is a danger that such special work will become 'narrow and irrelevant'.

This consideration and reflection on those paragraphs in which the aims of the 'general studies' are adumbrated might give some insight into the nature of the James Report's concept of the 'right kind of education'. It is one that has to do with the idea of 'relevance', of 'width' or 'breadth' of interest, of cognitive inventory; the cultivation of such 'breadth' having the (clearly instrumental) function of enabling the student to 'consider the applications of his [special] subject and to widen his horizons beyond his special interests' (4.3); to be aware of various kinds of 'problems and experiences' in fields outside his own, to make good his own cultural deficiencies – in a word, to get him to undertake further 'self-education'.

Presumably, this means he must go further and endeavour to exhibit greater and greater breadth of interest, to engage in further thought and

* For a conspectus of such difficulties see Ennis, 1967, and Broudy, 1961.

further discussion of 'questions of importance' – though this will be 'only as background' and 'without the obligation of pursuing each one in all its specialist connotations'. But it can be objected to this model of the 'right kind of education' that it is open to exactly the same charge as that which A. N. Whitehead brought so many years ago against the notion of education being concerned with the production of 'merely well-informed persons', and that its concern for 'breadth' and 'relevance' admits precisely that sort of distinction which Passmore makes between the notions of the 'educated' and the 'merely cultivated'. For 'breadth', while undoubtedly laudable in itself, is, it might be argued, not sufficient to characterize our notion of the 'educated person'; such an emphasis in any activity might lead to charges of superficiality, parochialism, or eclecticism. We might prefer to see other necessary conditions satisfied before we could agree that we were talking meaningfully about a notion of 'personal education' (such as the element of coming up to standards of a certain minimal sort in each or any particular area of interest or discipline), before we would be willing to admit that our hypothetical 'educated person' had any sort of understanding of what might be involved in or actually constitute various kinds of 'problems and experiences in fields outside his own'. We might require that such a person's 'special and general' educational studies had had the effect of 'initiating' him into a certain form of life, had 'spilled over' (Peters, 1966) and transformed his cognitive awareness of other areas of human living and concern, or had committed him to act in accordance with certain principles of procedure involved in knowledge-getting. None of these conditions appears to be present in the James concept, or, if they are, they are latent and only to be extracted with considerable stretching from the sub-concepts of 'breadth' and 'attitude of critical awareness'. For the well informed or the cultivated can discuss, think and be interested in the wide range of matters which the James writers allude to, but their approach to them would not necessarily be that which we would expect to see in our 'educated' person.

Quite apart from the reservations which one may reasonably entertain concerning the heavy emphasis in the James Report's notion of the 'right kind of education' on 'breadth' as the (evidently principal) defining characteristic, there are also points to be made with respect to the other element upon which it lays so much weight – that of 'relevance', 'utility', 'applicability'. This, it may be said, is the 'nuts and bolts' approach of the whole Report, pre-eminently to be observed in the proposals for the work of the second cycle, discernible as the major element in the rationale for the third cycle, and present as an overtone in the detailed account of the whole area of 'personal education'. Thus:

... the intending teacher [must] ... consider the applications of his subject ... educational studies can be a broadening influence on development. ... (4.3)

For very many teachers a different kind of preparation is needed. ... [The Dip.H.E.] would be a more appropriate foundation ... for many non-specialist teachers of adolescents. (4.4)

... the course should be suitable for those students intending to teach as well as for those with other objectives. ... (4.13)

Paragraph 4.15 gives examples of 'the ways in which the "committed teacher" may be helped to see the relevance of either his general or his special studies to the career he proposes to follow'. (4.15) The third-cycle proposals display similar concern with the practical utility of theoretical activity and study: it comprehends 'the whole range of activities by which teachers can extend their personal education, develop their professional competence and improve their understanding of educational principles and techniques. ...' (2.2) Some of these will enable teachers to 'widen their experience and thereby enrich their contributions to the schools ...'. While:

> ... a much expanded and properly co-ordinated programme of in-service education and training is essential to the future strength and development of the teaching profession (2.3),

> ... some teachers [may] be asked to teach subjects for which their education and initial training has not prepared them. (2.9)

Indeed the key paragraph 2.7 makes it clear that the whole orientation of what the Report has described as 'inservice education' is the applicability of knowledge, which is, in the third cycle for serving teachers, pursued only for its functional usefulness. Nothing here about the 'joys of scholarship' or knowledge worth pursuing for its own sake, no mention of the educated person's characteristic *modus vivendi*, the idea of standards and academic excellence, of studies which are rigorous and demanding and transforming, the idea 'that education is not a matter of habit and improvisation but of thought based on knowledge and understanding – and that these should be the orientation of the teacher from the beginning' (G. H. Bantock).

In the approach suggested by the James Report's proposals, as against the analysis of an educated person, the emphasis is upon the side of 'training' in the institutions for the preparation of teachers, everything being underpinned by the idea of function – of practicality, relevance, utility. In these terms the only justification offered for the inclusion of such subjects as philosophy, psychology or sociology on the curriculum of the education department of such institutions is for reasons of their applicability and the only important consideration in the minds of some educational administrators within such places is the instrumental purpose of placing a piece of 'plant' in a setting to function, like a machine, as efficiently as possibl in achieving those goals which it has been designed to reach.

The point which it is sought to establish is that there is a potential con flict of values in the ideas upon which our teacher preparation institution rest, particularly evident in many of the proposals currently being can vassed, and that this conflict arises from two concepts of function concern ing such establishments. The first concept is the 'educative' notion, con nected with the intended activity of the future teacher as an educated person 'initiating' his charges into the 'educated' form of life, which is (for us) taken up by a concern for worthwhile activities that are largely cognitive in char acter and which are valued for their own sake – and whose justification i therefore in terms of their own intrinsic value. The second concept is the 'training for teaching' notion, which is conditioned by the belief that the future teacher is going out into a particular situation with a set of fairly specific tasks to fulfil – largely, it would seem, those of vocational training and socialization. The latter is a view of school life as a preparation for placement in a society geared principally to production and consumption regarding all things in terms of their utility and 'relevance', and whose justification is therefore largely instrumental in emphasis.

Even within these frameworks there are possibilities of subsidiary clashes of value. One thinks of the differences, with which many teachers and parents are familiar, in contemporary assessments of what it is that con stitutes a worthwhile activity of what things are instrumental to what else, of what C. L. Stevenson (1944) distinguished as 'disagreements in attitude' and 'disagreements in belief' between values and value systems. Add to this such differences as there may be concerning the relative importance over the various principles of procedure in educational discourse generally, or the substantive content of values and value systems, and it can be seen that the discussion of values in teacher education and training is beset with potential difficulties of a fundamental sort. For if we accept the view that education is inescapably a value-laden enterprise (Professor T. F. Daveney, 1970, goes further and argues that 'education' is a specifically moral con cept) then we shall readily admit that investigation into the nature of its values, an examination of their justification and some appraisal of the various models of educational decision-making based upon them is indeed a matter of prior logical importance and that consideration of other matters will logically depend upon such analysis, justification and appraisal.

To this extent then it would seem that, for our purposes, the initial ques tions raised in any discussion concerned with the place of values in teacher education are likely to be of a meta-theoretical kind, concerning, as they will, the nature of value, the complex inter-relationships of values, value sets and value systems, and – perhaps the crucial issues – the justification of our value judgements. In this chapter it has been argued that in current

eflection on teacher education there are two views of function – the one
oncerned with intrinsic, the other with instrumental values – and that,
vhere the two are not conflicting, the latter is the dominant emphasis. This
•rings with it questions concerning the nature and possible modes of justi-
ication for intrinsic and instrumental values. The word 'instrumental' is
ised here in a loose sense instead of 'extrinsic', although one is aware that
his is itself a problem requiring much more exhaustive treatment. In this
connection it is interesting to note one account (Taylor, 1961) which claims
hat at least three elements can be discerned in a notion of extrinsic value –
values may be held to be contributorily extrinsic, instrumentally extrinsic
or inherently extrinsic. This is, perhaps, to attempt to unpack the concept
a little too extensively; but for our purposes, at any rate, the distinction
between 'educative' and 'training' functions in teacher preparation is
sufficient.

It is not, of course, intimated that the two are distinct or irreconcilable.
The James Report makes it clear that the two emphases can be conjoined;
of the proposed Dip.H.E. it remarks:

> The course described here would provide a higher education of value
> in itself . . . [such a course] would provide a more satisfying educational
> experience for many [students]. . . . (4.19)

> The Diploma in Higher Education, given its content and character,
> would not only be a terminal qualification for many students and the
> basis for the professional training of many teachers, but could also
> increasingly provide an appropriate educational basis for training in
> other professions. (4.20)

And in his paper at the Colston Symposium Bantock appears to believe that
'education' and 'training' are connected; he argues that the student in training 'should be taught, first, to instruct . . . then to teach . . . and only finally,
to educate' (though we may consider that his concept of education is more
restricted than that with which we are more familiar). Indeed, it might be
maintained that the connection between these two notions and their value
justification is, in terms of the aspirations and functions of the school, much
more fundamental.

What is of key importance here is a point that is often overlooked in
public debate upon the structure and objectives of those institutions where
such potential conflicts of value may be observed – namely, that instrumental values, in the final analysis, depend on and are derived from some
form of 'first order' value or set of values, in which the notion of 'intrinsically valuable' or 'worthwhile for its own sake' is the keynote, functioning
as an ἀνυπόθετος ἀρχή from which all other considerations as to what is
valuable may be ultimately judged to originate. In terms of teacher education

this involves a significant distinction such as that postulated by Professor R. S. Peters in his reflections on the nature of the activities and values to which the educated person is committed: education 'implies the transmission of what is of ultimate value' (1966) and again: 'Education ... has norms built into it, which generate the aims which educators strive to develop or attain' (1967). Peters and Hirst (1970) set this distinction squarely within the context of our particular view of civilization:

> ... [perhaps] the knowledge conditions are the only proper logical conditions, and the desirability condition is dependent upon them. ... Because knowledge and understanding are valued in our culture, both for their own sake and [instrumentally]. ...

It is hoped that the point will not be laboured if it is suggested, diffidently and tentatively, that those engaged in teacher preparation who insist that their primary duty lies in the formulation of 'educational aims' betray a lack of awareness, perhaps even a misunderstanding of this very point. As J. H. Gribble (1969) writes:

> The sort of model they have in mind is of something to be gone through in order that some desirable outcome will ensue. And while this model is appropriate to a number of skills which are usually learned very early on, it is entirely inappropriate to see an engagement in activities which are valuable in themselves as merely the means to achieving extrinsic ends. One familiar example of this kind of thinking is the view held by a number of sociologists and men in the street, that education has vocational aims – that [it] is the means of providing people with the training which will enable them to get a suitable job.

The latter may well be a very proper object of schooling, but it is not immediately obvious that it is an educational activity. Education we would rather take to be a term connoting, *inter alia*, values which belong to that 'first order' set already referred to. Professor R. F. Atkinson (1965) summarizes this point thus:

> Statements about the aims of education are better to be understood as expressing views about *how* rather than *what* we should teach, views about the procedure rather than the content of education. Values are involved in education less in the shape of goals or end products than as principles implicit in certain manners of proceeding.

This being so, it is inescapable that the basic form of justification for 'education' will itself be concerned with intrinsic values, whereas the accounts of the place given to 'training' in our teacher preparation will be of an instrumental character.

It is not being stated, or denied, that there may be tension or even conflict between these two emphases in all models of teacher education and training. It is argued merely that they may be observed to be there; that the nature of the two ideas is such as has been described; and that the problem of their justification, if and when tackled, is a matter that is likely to be easier in the case of the instrumental values of the 'training' concept rather than in that of the ultimate values of 'education'. But at all events such an analysis enables one to view with a clearer understanding the Robbins Report's account of our teacher colleges as both educative and training institutions, although elevating the former emphasis, implicitly, in its recommendation for the change of title.

Having examined this difference in value preference, we may now go on and consider briefly the question of the justification of the (potentially conflicting) values. Ultimately, it can be contended, both value choices and the manner of their justification are matters of individual decision. There are – though doubtless some would disagree – no 'right' answers to problems of valuation and value justification to be obtained from the relevant source of authority such as a manual or text-book. For this reason, we may think, the individual, as the final arbiter in such matters, must become, at the very least, familiar with the appropriate methods of enquiry and capable of applying them, and must develop a disposition to exercise those powers of deliberation, evaluation and judgement that facilitate discussion and decision-making in the various problems of seeking and communicating meaning and of giving a justification. It is, of course, precisely at this point that philosophy has a role, promoting the clarification of our own ideas and an understanding of the various sorts of reasons and reason-giving that are necessarily involved in the public making of decisions not based upon prejudice, emotion, whim or arbitrary power. One might, with Dewey, contend that in such deliberations 'improved valuation must grow out of existing valuations, subjected to critical methods of investigation that bring them into systematic relations with one another'.

One matter which some people may consider important in the question of value justification is that concerned with the substantive content of value sets and value systems. In this connection it is also important that we distinguish between things which we value and our value sets or systems. Carlton H. Bowyer (1970) points to the danger of confusion here:

> Granted that one's theory of value may be *related* to the things he deems valuable, it would be a mistake to confuse our worldly possessions with our value structure, and we must be wary of the danger of equivocation when we speak in terms of value.

For example, he points out, primitive man, being primarily concerned only with his own survival, must have valued things which he could use as instruments to further that end, but it could scarcely be posited that he subscribed to any theory of value. Rather it would seem that value theories are an outgrowth of societies and have evolved with human society – perhaps, we might add, with a similar or corresponding degree of sophistication.

Thus, even in terms of the dichotomy of values that has been here outlined, there are likely to be differences of viewpoint over substance. It may well be that there are different and distinctive notions of extrinsicality; and in the case of first-order value theories we may observe differences between, say, honour ethics and those of religious duty. It might even be argued that activities which might *prima facie* be regarded as dominated and directed by instrumental considerations could properly be placed among those which are intrinsically worthwhile doing. Dr Harold Entwistle (1970), for example, has recently maintained that work has a cultural value and that for the individual it can be an intrinsically satisfying experience. He concludes that

> work is a fundamental human need. The paradigm of the good life is not that of the gentleman of leisure: it is, rather, the life which derives from intelligent, skilful and responsible involvement in the world of work. It is self-evident . . . that earning a living is a central factor in living.

Or, it might be alleged, R. S. Peters' restriction of the concept of 'worthwhile activities' to the realm of intrinsic values cannot be supported since, for one thing, he has not produced any argument to prevent the use of instrumental purposes as criteria of worthwhileness.

Be that as it may, the foregoing examination of our concept of education has picked out certain criteria as being necessarily involved when we describe someone as 'educated', the chief of these being a commitment to values associated with, and pre-eminently present in, things which are considered worth doing for their own sake. These particular values are, in our culture, those which are firmly bound up with a concern for cognitive activities and the rational way of going about things.

Now our selection of, and adherence to, these values as the pre-eminently worthwhile ones is a matter that can be justified in a number of ways. But if we are going to demand that the justification of our value preferences must involve, apart from the notion of individual commitment, public discourse of some sort, then certain consequences follow.

We do not need to spend much time on the methodology of conducting such a discourse, though there are some interesting and important things written and said in this field. R. B. Brandt (1959), for example, has set out a method for discriminating between and deciding about our value judgements, springing from his dissatisfaction with the naturalist, non-naturalist and emotivist approaches to this question, by setting up a *modus operandi* which is in some respects similar to that of induction. He describes is as the 'qualified attitude method' and employs it to highlight the procedure which, he contends, thinking people generally follow in some form or other when assessing whether an ethical statement is justified or not.

(1) We decide particular problems both by appeal to principles that we have already more or less explicitly in mind and by appeal to our preferences, feelings of obligation and so forth (which kind of attitude depending upon whether the question is one about what is desirable, or what is obligatory and so on). (2) We correct our principles if they are incompatible with our criticized (undiscounted) attitudes (feelings of obligation and so forth), and we rely on our criticized attitudes in filling out and weighing our principles. (3) Judgments ... must be consistent, and particular ones must be generalisable. (4) Attitudes are discounted if they are not impartial, informed, the product of a normal state of mind, or compatible with having a consistent set of general principles not excessively complex. Ethical thinking, then, is a complex interplay of attitudes, principles, formal requirements for principles, and rules for discounting. None of these can be submerged in the other three.

This account of methodology has two virtues. It lends support to the contention set out above that one of the key features in the justification of value judgements is that the activity must, in principle at any rate, be capable of being carried on in form of public discourse. But it also suggests another crucial feature of such an activity: namely, that it involves evaluation, judgement, the giving of reasons, as distinct from straightforward descriptions of factual states of affairs, on the one hand, and from mere expressions of personal taste, on the other. This seems to follow both from the first feature – public discourse – and also from the particular procedures usually followed by sane and sensible people in value thinking.

Now in respect of our particular interest – the claim that all models of teacher education and training are underpinned by value considerations of intrinsically worthwhile activities – some attempt has to be made to provide a justification for those particular first order values we have here elevated. One of the forms of argument that may be deployed to provide such a justification is the well-known Kantian-type of 'transcendental deduction' of worthwhile activities, employed by philosophers such as P. H. Hirst, A. Phillips Griffiths, and R. S. Peters. The latter's version of it is set out in his *Ethics and Education*, Chapter 5:

Anyone who is thinking seriously about how to spend his time cannot but go for activities which afford rich opportunities for employing his wits, resources and sensibilities in situations in which there is a premium on unpredictability and opportunities for skill – and a sense of the fitting.

8—EOT  *  *

The evaluation of, and decision-making concerning the worthwhileness of various courses of action is just such an activity. The very posing of questions in this connection is like the attitude of the questioner who in all seriousness demands to be given one good reason for being rational: it presumes a commitment to the central feature of the activity whose existence is thus called into question. It is at this point, argues Dr J. P. Powell (1970), that the 'transcendental deduction' really gets a grip, for

> if someone questions the pre-eminent worthwhileness of scholarship he must already possess to some degree the deep concern for truth which characterizes all scholarly activity.... The justification of the pursuit of knowledge is thus pre-supposed by any serious attempt to question it.

This point was precisely one of the consequences referred to above, following from our notion of what is involved in the justification of value judgements. For if the principal features of the activity of judging and justifying our substantive value preferences are that it will be public and involve the giving of reasons, then it seems that we do have a prior commitment to the procedural principles of rationality and rational discourse and that this therefore constitutes the major component of our first order set. And the argument here is that it is our subscription to those sorts of principles that conditions our concept of the educated person, and that this is the model that we project into our work in teacher education and training.

There have been attempts to call this form of argument into question (Wilson, 1967; Powell, 1970). Dr Powell's counter-argument rests upon a consideration of the implications for education of the presuppositions of the society in which it is established – in our case, a democracy. Powell contends that Peters' case

> amounts to a vindication of the status quo as far as the curriculum is concerned ... his whole approach to the problem ... is dominated by a concern for the cognitive, the literary, the theoretical, the traditional. ...

Instead Powell proposes that the notion of 'education for democracy' be adduced as an alternative valid justification for a broad educational curriculum (Harrison, 1968). He claims that

> democracy cannot function if most of the citizens are ignorant since there would be then no possibility of informed and responsible discussion ... any democrat therefore is bound to do all he can to maximize educational opportunity and to ensure that educational programmes are sufficiently broad in scope to provide preparation for critical discussion of the major types of political issue with which the

student will be confronted during his adult life. . . . Preparation for democratic action [however] demands more than knowledge on a broad front; it requires the development of a commitment to action based firmly upon understanding and values.

Thus the curriculum must include opportunities for action; it must aim at fostering a predisposition to engage in activities which will secure and perpetuate those values which are pre-eminently involved in the democratic form of life.

Indeed Mrs P. A. White (1971) argues that 'An examination of what is involved in an education for democracy actually establishes a large part of what must be the common content of the curriculum', and this, in her view, will involve

(i) the values of tolerance, fraternity, justice and consideration of interests;
(ii) the knowledge of particular political and social institutions, embodying the values outlined, and how to operate them;
(iii) and a liberal education covering all the forms of knowledge.

The argument from the 'public interest' and from the concept of 'education for democracy' is extremely interesting and persuasive. These matters cannot, unfortunately, be gone into more fully, both for reasons of space and also because our concerns are not so much with various forms of justification but with the problem of values and their justification as such. It is, perhaps, sufficient to notice that the arguments of an 'education for democracy' type are, to an extent and as presented by some writers, open to rebuttal. One line of counter-argument might be, for example, that the 'democracy and public interest' case might be seen as covertly advocating or implicitly including an instrumentalism of the sort already criticized. The claim that educational programmes must provide *preparation* evidently involves extrinsicality as a major emphasis; while the notion of 'preparation for critical discussion of the major types of political issue with which one will be confronted in one's adult life' seems to admit of the possibility of implementation on a 'lowest common denominator' basis by the educational organizers and administrators in the democracy, as far as the content of the curriculum is concerned. And, quite apart from the dubieties of a public interest requirement to proceed in an area of knowledge only 'as far as one needs to' to gain 'understanding' the same dangers of eclecticism and superficiality as were noted in the James Report's concept of a 'general education' would also appear to be present here: such a requirement, in any case, being evidently based upon considerations of utility. There is the further point that the argument for the importance of activities in promoting democracy may fall into the fallacy of analogy, of the microcosm-macrocosm type. And even if this is not the case, it is possibly not without some significance that the argument for a 'democratic' education evidently involves some sort of commitment to similar sorts of procedural principles as those held to be of value by those who seek to establish criteria for the content of the curriculum of an educational institution by means of a transcendental deduction of worthwhile activities. For the very notion of informed and responsible public discussion and decision-making presumes a predilection for and an acceptance of those features of public discourse that R. S. Peters' (1966) argument seeks to show as fundamental in our version of the civilized life, and which he finally associates with the principles implicit in the idea of education for democracy.

For these reasons, then, it is maintained that, although there are criticisms that can be levelled against this particular form of justificatory argument, it is incontrovertibly the one to which, in virtue of our form of life and the values of our culture, we inevitably incline. This is a procedural point; it does not enjoin any prescriptions about the substantive content of our value systems. Indeed in this connection it may well be that there is further work to be done in investigating and mapping out substantive differences in the values in teacher education, as, for instance, between those held by teacher trainers, teacher institutions and teachers; those held by parents and members of society generally about teachers and 'education'; and those held by pupils and students about teachers and institutions of teacher preparation; and in examining whether there are any tensions between these various views. What is beyond doubt is that while we, as teachers and educators, remain committed to the idea of 'initiating' our students and pupils into 'first order' procedural principles, we must be prepared, in view of the changing structure of social conditions and perhaps also of value systems in society generally, to be willing continually and radically to reappraise the substantive content associated with them, and, by exhibiting this willingness to our pupils, to get them started on the same path too.

It will be observed that the notions of 'education' and 'society' are here closely associated. Indeed it may be supposed that there is as strong a case for education being a social concept as has been made out for its being inescapably a moral one; it is probable that there is in fact a high degree of interconnectedness between the two aspects. Indeed it would be paradoxical, as C. H. Bowyer notes, if the values elevated by a society were not reflected in its educational objectives and institutional procedures, and if the curriculum and organization of its educational establishments were not specifically directed towards the induction of its young into the complex structure of those values.

Thus it is that in our universities, colleges and schools we may expect to see reflected the tensions and conflicts of differing values and value systems that exist in society at large. But it is also comforting to reflect that schools and colleges are, in their devotion to proceeding always in a framework of first-order values, agencies of stabilization and that they have, in many respects, the same sort of task as that which some political commentators ascribe to our instruments of government: that not only of innovation in changing value commitments, but also that of the reassertion and promotion of what might be regarded as the traditional values in our culture. And it is in respect of the latter – of the maintenance of such principles as tolerance, sympathy and fraternity, justice and impartiality, consideration of other people's interests, respect for persons, 'patience, prudence and hard work' – that our institutions of teacher education have the right, even the duty to be assertive.

For if open-mindedness and reason-giving are the good things of life, the whole of the above activity is a matter that is infinitely worth the while. It is this that makes the task of acting as 'midwife' to other people's minds the most rewarding one there is for the teacher.

# CHAPTER 12

# A Flexible Curriculum for Teacher Education

PETER RENSHAW

## The Underlying Principles

The central argument of this chapter rests on the premise that if we wish to meet the growing needs of future generations of children, it is necessary to raise the standard and quality of the professional education of teachers. This could be achieved by developing and promoting a viable body of professional knowledge, which would also help to enhance the status of the teaching profession and to change the nature of those institutions responsible for the education of teachers. At present, about eighty per cent. of British teachers are trained in monotechnic colleges of education, but evidence is mounting* to support the view that teacher training ought to develop within the wider perspective of tertiary education (Willey and Maddison, 1971). It is proposed that many colleges expand into multi-purpose institutions which could establish a flexible curriculum designed to cater for a variety of student interests and vocational goals. This would enable students to keep their career options open at the age of eighteen and it could break the current academic, professional and social isolation of student teachers. As early as 1924 Lance Jones suggested that the prospective teacher ought to be associated for as long as possible with students preparing for other professions (Jones, 1924). Much later, the Robbins Committee on Higher Education recommended 'experiments with institutions that bridge the traditional gap between colleges for the education of teachers and institutions of further education which prepare their students for other professions' (Robbins, 1963). But very little progress has been achieved in this direction. Several polytechnics have embarked on teacher training programmes, while a few colleges of education have started courses for youth leaders and teacher-social workers. Nevertheless, pressure is growing for many colleges to develop into multi-vocational institutions. For instance, in its policy

---

* See ATCDE, *The Professional Education of Teachers*, London, ATCDE, 1971. UCET, *The Education of Teachers: Looking to the Future*, London, UCET, 1971. NUT, *The Reform of Teacher Education*, London, NUT, 1971.

statement *Higher Education and Preparing for Teaching*, the Association of Teachers in Colleges and Departments of Education supports the concept of a 'federated group of colleges associated with a parent university' (ATCDE, 1970), in which a variety of first degree and professional courses could be offered through the faculties of arts, sciences and social sciences. In its more recent evidence to the James Committee of Enquiry into Teacher Education the ATCDE (1971), along with the Universities Council for the Education of Teachers (UCET, 1971), makes explicit the advantages of developing colleges into multi-purpose institutions. On another front, the National Union of Teachers has urged that colleges should become full constituent members of a comprehensive university (NUT, 1971), in contrast to which the Committee of Vice-Chancellors, in *University Development in the 1970s*, envisages that some colleges might expand their activities into social work or into the liberal arts, thus enlarging their role beyond that of the training of teachers.\* If the idea of a multi-purpose college is to become a viable proposition, it will be necessary to develop a flexible curriculum, possibly through a modular system† in which different types of concurrent and consecutive programmes are offered to students, leaving open a range of possible options both within and between courses (Renshaw, 1971). Again, this notion is entertained seriously by the ATCDE in its evidence to the James Committee of Enquiry, while the James Report itself encourages colleges to strike out in new directions and to develop along their own particular lines (James, 1972).

Although changing the nature of teacher training establishments and adopting more flexible curricular programmes might help to enhance the status of both the colleges and the teaching profession, in themselves these developments would not necessarily raise the standards and quality of the education received by children in schools. This can be achieved only by a fundamental reappraisal of the objectives, content and methodology of our teacher education curricula. For instance, it is imperative that all teachers are sensitive to the demands of education and society in a rapidly changing world. They must recognize that children are entering a dynamic society in which the pace of technological advance is accelerating, bringing in its wake new social and economic pressures, new organizational structures, new modes of thought, new concepts, values, roles and patterns of behaviour. Children need to understand these new social and economic systems, but on the other hand, if we are committed to the idea of a rational notion of morality, we will also respect the need for all children to develop an autonomy of mind that will help them to control and to master technology

---

\* Committee of Vice-Chancellors and Principals of the Universities of the United Kingdom, *University Development in the 1970s*, London, 1970.

† For an example of a modular system see: Report of the Royal Commission on *Medical Education* (Todd Report), London. HMSO, pp. 92–5.

rather than to be enslaved by it (Reimer, 1971). At the moment many schools are being criticized for processing their children into the passive acceptance of the ideology and norms implicit in a technocratic state. In their searching discussions on the myth of traditional schooling, Ivan Illich and Paulo Freire see this process as one of conforming 'domestication' (Illich, 1970, 1971; Freire, 1970), in which children fail to evaluate the inheritance into which they are being initiated. But such critical reflection on the past, present and future can arise only through education that is, through building up in children a differentiated and structured awareness of the world in a way that goes far beyond the mere amassing of facts and the acquisition of skills; for it involves transforming the way they think, feel and conceive of themselves and of the world.

In the present system of schooling, teachers are at the heart of the educational process. The demands on them are considerable, and these can be met only by creating a scientifically-based profession which is supported by a body of relevant theoretical and practical knowledge. Without this knowledge, children's future education will be impoverished. It is this systematic body of theory, in which abstract principles are formulated through scientific research and logical analysis, that forms the basis of the professional's authority and autonomy. Together with the ideal of service, a professional code of ethics and strict control of recruitment, training and entry into the occupational group, it is knowledge that constitutes one of the distinguishing characteristics of a profession (Becker, 1962; Cogan, 1953; Goode, 1969; Greenwood, 1966; Lieberman, 1956). But it is sometimes questioned whether the so-called profession of teaching does possess the necessary esoteric knowledge to support its professional status. Etzioni views teaching, along with nursing and social work, as a 'semi-profession', because its members receive a shorter training and have a less legitimated status resting on a limited body of specialized knowledge. This results in teachers having less authority and weaker autonomy than the members of such established professions as medicine, law, university teaching and the church (Etzioni, 1969). The central point arising from this criticism is whether teachers have an arcane corpus of technical knowledge with which to assert their professional status (Lortie, 1969). Does teaching pedagogy rest on a set of research-based theoretical principles which are distinctive to education, or are they rather the property of those scholars working within the behavioural and social sciences? Do teachers rely too heavily on an unreflective pragmatism, which tends to spurn rational self-evaluation and theoretical controversy arising from research activity? Can the criticism be met that the knowledge underlying educational practice is intellectually shallow and that it is unlikely to develop much over the next generation (Goode, 1969)?

It cannot be denied that there has been a vast increase in educational research in both Britain and the United States during the past few years.

There is a growing body of knowledge directed to solving educational problems in such areas as curriculum development, language and social class, human development, learning and concept formation, social interaction in group learning situations, and the administration and management of organizations. Although the basic disciplines involved include the behavioural and social sciences and philosophy, the theoretical principles formulated need to be applied to problems unique to education. For example, teachers need a general frame of reference relating to race relations and colour prejudice, but they need more specialized knowledge if they are to teach immigrants effectively. Again, an understanding of the general principles underlying the communication arts and media needs to be directed towards specific situations arising from children's learning in school. In other words, all empirical study and logical analysis conducted by teachers and research workers in education must draw on the general modes of thinking and methods of inquiry of those disciplines which contribute to educational theory, but they must also be focused on real educational problems. Furthermore, the judgements and actions of teachers in the classroom must be informed by this theoretical knowledge, otherwise their claim to professional status would be severely weakened. I would suggest that there is a growing body of valid professional knowledge which should form the basis of a curriculum for teacher education, and that students need to be initiated into this if they are to attain those objectives crucial to a modern teaching profession. These objectives are:

1. To gain the authority and autonomy fundamental to the making of rational professional judgements;
2. To acquire professional autonomy within a world of increasing bureaucratic control;
3. To perform their various roles within a dynamic, organic social system;
4. To understand the nature of the educational process;
5. To understand the structure of educational institutions;
6. To participate in the decision-making machinery;
7. To develop managerial and organizational expertise;
8. To apply technology to educational situations;
9. To contribute to an on-going process of curriculum development in schools, colleges, universities and teacher centres;
10. To formulate and to implement strategies for planned change and innovation in schools;
11. To participate in the initial training of student teachers;
12. To work as a link in a supplemented teaching force.

These objectives could not possibly be realized fully during the initial period of training, but they could form the basis of a distinctive professional education in which initial training, the induction period and in-service education are viewed as an on-going continuum.

## The Idea of a Supplemented Teaching Force*

This chapter has emphasized purposely the need for the teaching profession to be supported by a systematic body of theoretical and practical knowledge. But another closely related priority is the need for teachers to adopt an occupational structure which is based on an objective appraisal of varying levels of competence (Maden, 1971, Lieberman, 1956). The teaching force should contain different levels of function in which a distinction should be made between the professional teacher and his sub-professional assistants. One of the reasons why teachers are often invested with a low academic and economic status is that skilled professionals, semi-professionals and non-professionals have been encapsulated under the single umbrella of the teaching profession (Anderson, 1962). It is one of the characteristic features of the professional doctor or lawyer that he is supported by sub-professional help. The more routine occupational tasks can be mastered by subordinates who have had less training and who are allowed to practise only under professional supervision.

The same principle could be applied to a supplemented teaching force in which the different levels of function might comprise:

1. *Fully professional teachers* (with graduate status) who, by virtue of their long training, specialized knowledge and skill, could manage a team of supplementary staff and plan the curricular programmes for a school. The more senior personnel could act as co-ordinating directors of studies and leader teachers responsible for certain organizational tasks or specific areas of activity, such as teacher training or liaison officer to the local teacher centre, college of education, polytechnic, university of curriculum development unit.
2. *Specialist teachers* (fully professional with graduate status) who could offer some specific professional expertise in areas like the teaching of backward children or immigrant children. Some of these teachers might also be able to assume such important supporting roles as school counsellor or teacher-social worker.
3. *Teacher assistants* who are qualified only to act in a sub-professional capacity under the guidance of a fully professional or specialist teacher. They would have gained Part I of the degree in teaching, awarded after two years of training, but this could be up-graded into a degree after

---

* I am indebted to Dr Joan Tough of the University of Leeds Institute of Education for the use of the term 'supplemented' teaching force.

further full-time or part-time study. Teacher assistants would never be allowed to plan or to initiate teaching programmes in schools, but they would be equipped to guide children in activities like reading, writing and number, and they could give invaluable assistance in the supervision of small mixed-ability groups operating within a flexible system like an integrated day. Their responsibilities could also include the preparation of teaching aids and materials, as well as conducting some of the more routine educational measurement and evaluation.

4. *Aides* who would provide the type of technical, clerical and administrative support which many schools lack at present. This category could include technicians whose assistance will be required increasingly as schools move more into the area of educational technology, e.g. audio-visual aid centres, resource centres, language laboratories.

5. *Ancillaries*, who would be largely unqualified part-time helpers.

This notion of a supplemented teaching force would necessitate a re-appraisal of three main areas: the levels of knowledge required by the various personnel, different types of training programme and qualifications, and an adequate provision of in-service education. First, it is possible to distinguish between three levels of knowledge, only two of which could conceivably be considered *professional* knowledge. At the pre-theoretical level there is an area of recipe knowledge* which is limited to achieving practical competence in routine performances. It comprises largely a set of non-critical skills and facilities which become habitualized in practice. As good teaching ought to entail rational judgement and intelligent action, guided by theoretical rules and principles, recipe knowledge is hopelessly inadequate not only for the professional leader teacher and specialist teacher, but also for the teacher assistant.

The initial teacher education programme is bedevilled by colleges attempting to achieve too much in too short a time, and a sharper focus needs to be placed on curricular priorities during this period. There is growing evidence to support the view that much of the theoretical knowledge selected for initial training needs to be directly related to those practical experiences likely to be encountered by teachers in the first few years of their professional work (Hilliard, 1971). At present, many of the theoretical insights presented to students are too abstract and divorced from the realities of teaching, as seen by many students and teachers (Hannam *et al.*, 1971). There is no doubt that some theorists resort to an empty verbalism which has little reference to practical action and to the solution of significant educational problems (Bereiter, 1971). Instead of preparing students

---

* The term 'recipe knowledge' is derived from Alfred Schutz. See P. L. Berger and T. Luckmann, *The Social Construction of Reality*, London, Penguin, pp. 56 and 83.

for the world in which they will have to work, many theoretical programmes are related more to an idealized conception of reality – almost a 'folk concept' (Becker, 1962) which, although highly valued by some educational innovators and theoreticians, fails to meet the conditions of the young teacher in the classroom. One implication of this is that during initial training emphasis should be given to a middle-range theory of instruction designed to help students establish confidence and technical competence in the classroom. The focus should be on such areas as teaching within an integrated day, teaching mixed-ability groups, teaching reading and language skills, class control and discipline, classroom organization and management, co-operative teaching, classroom interaction, the utilization of audio-visual material and different methods of keeping records. This approach should be the joint concern of colleges and schools operating through a teacher tutor or professional tutor system (Baker, 1967; Tibble, 1966; Hollins, 1969; Collier, 1969), because the theory needs to be studied in conjunction with direct observation and group work with children, assisted by closed-circuit television and micro-teaching. This second level of knowledge, which draws on the contributory disciplines of educational theory, would be necessary for anyone concerned with the teaching and supervision of children. Therefore, it should take a central position in the first two years of the students' professional education.

But this middle-range area of theory needs to be underpinned by that body of higher-order theory which constitutes the fundamental core of professional knowledge for teachers. If the skills and insights developed by the students are not supported by a sound theoretical frame of reference, their teaching will soon slip into a series of routine performances. This fundamental point seems to have been ignored by the James Report (1972) which, in its discussion of the second cycle, recommends that the pre-service training year should be 'unashamedly specialized and functional'.* It considers that this initial training period should focus largely on a rudimentary introduction to educational theory, with the implication that the development of the teacher's theoretical insights should take place only during subsequent in-service education. This would suggest that the B.A.(Ed.) degree proposed by the James Report† resembles a low-level certificate masquerading as a professional degree, designed to propagate unreflective pragmatists. Apart from the fact that the in-service proposals for the third cycle could hardly be implemented for some time to come due to the prohibitive cost, we have already questioned the desirability of allowing student teachers to be given a meagre apprenticeship based on a recipe-type training. On the one hand the report sees the role of educational studies 'as contributory to effective teaching', but its proposals successfully deprive

* P. 23, para. 3.14.　　　　　　† P. 31–2, para. 3.34.

the student 'of the conceptual framework within which he may integrate his learning and experience'* – although this is denied earlier in the same paragraph. The James Report is right to criticize the excessive formal courses in educational theory which can be found at present in many colleges and university departments of education. But because it sees the pointlessness of much of this theory as it is taught at present, it does not necessarily follow that 'a rudimentary introduction is all that can realistically be attempted at this stage'.† The fully professional teacher needs to be given the conceptual expertise with which to reflect on teaching before he enters the profession. Thus during initial training he needs to be initiated into the logical, psychological and sociological principles underlying learning and teaching. He needs to understand the conceptual and practical relationships between the theory, different areas of the curriculum, and practice, because it is this awareness of concepts, structures and validation procedures, together with the ability to grasp interconnections, which lies at the heart of professional knowledge for teaching. Nevertheless, it must be recognized that this higher-order theory can be studied at many different levels, and that during initial training students cannot be expected to master this rapidly expanding body of esoteric knowledge. They need to be sensitized to the language and methods of inquiry of the different disciplines gradually throughout the whole college course, thus laying sound foundations for more systematic study later. This demands skilful imaginative teaching conducted in a context that is meaningful to the students.

So far the argument has focused on the different levels of knowledge which might support a supplemented teaching force, but it is also important to question the validity of the present undifferentiated training which is related to a single common qualification. In Britain there is a large measure of support for the concept of 'a teacher' who can be trained to fit into any teaching job. A common certificate might appear to give the profession a degree of unity, but a much stronger sense of 'professionalism' could be achieved through a body of more highly skilled and knowledgeable teachers operating in specialist areas within a supplemented teaching force. Admittedly, there is a core of common professional knowledge required by potential leader teachers, specialist teachers and teacher assistants, but sometime during the period of initial training this needs to be related to a specific context such as the teaching of young children or the education of the early school leaver. In such a scheme students would leave college as authorities in certain fields, equipped to operate at different levels of competence. For instance, in the curricular proposals to be discussed later, those students who successfully complete a four-year course would gain full professional and graduate status, whereas the two-year student would be awarded a teacher assistant certificate qualifying him to act in a

* P. 23, para. 3.16.                    † P. 23, para. 3.16.

sub-professional capacity. Flexibility within such a structure would be attained through a coherent system of in-service education in which teachers would attend regular retraining and adjustment courses.* The implementation of this idea could strengthen the claim for a knowledge-based, rationally constituted profession, in which a strong sense of unity could be achieved through diversity of function.

The principle of an undifferentiated training leading to a common qualification has been upheld by the National Union of Teachers for a long time, but it is interesting to note a slight shift in its position recently. Although still committed to the idea of one qualification, in its policy statement *The Reform of Teacher Education* (NUT, 1971) the Union recognizes the need for initial training to be directed towards the teaching of specific stages – that is, for first, middle or secondary schools. It comments that 'this sectionalized approach, coupled with the principle of one qualification, has great significance in educational development in schools'. It is tempting to speculate whether the Union's next move will be towards a more developed concept of a supplemented teaching force. The James Report also fails to radically reappraise the structure of the teaching profession, but along with the NUT it does recognize that 'we should abandon the pretence that it is possible to train, during the initial training period, a "teacher" '. It suggests that students should be trained to work within a defined area, such as the age of pupil or the subject to be taught.

### The Relationship between Academic and Professional Studies in a Professional Degree

Given a reformed occupational structure supported by a viable body of professional knowledge, it would then be necessary to establish a genuine professional degree in which academic study is viewed within a broad professional frame of reference (Higginbotham, 1969; Renshaw, 1969; Wheeler, 1971). But what do we understand by 'academic' and 'professional' study, and in what way might they be related? The idea of 'academic study' implies the objective systematic study of one or more areas of knowledge pursued in depth for reasons intrinsic to the activity. With its emphasis on developing a clear perception of a particular mode of experience, academic study enables a person to reflect critically and imaginatively on the nature of a discipline, to master its methods of inquiry, and to view its distinctive characteristics in relation to other forms of understanding. Serious engagement in academic study sensitizes a student to the similarities

---

* The need for 'a much expanded and properly co-ordinated programme of in-service education and training' is recognized by the James Report in its discussion of the third cycle.

and interconnections between different structures of thought, and it gets him to focus on their central underlying principles. As its primary concern is the development of certain qualities of mind, powers of reasoning and the capacity for general ideas, academic study brings a student to the point of raising fundamental questions as to the value, assumptions, standards and scope of one or more disciplines. Thus it enables him to build up a personal commitment to an area of activity so that it becomes significant to him.

On the other hand, the notion of 'professional study' implies a partnership between a systematic body of rationally determined theoretical knowledge and the practical skills which form the basis of professional competence. The development of these critical skills, acquired through training, needs to be informed by theoretical principles distilled through academic study, otherwise a student is unlikely to build up the authority, autonomy and breadth of understanding which are central to the formation of professional judgements. Professional study does not limit itself to the acquisition of specific technical expertise fed by a restricted number of recipes. Its aim, rather, is to initiate students into a profession, as distinct from training them for a trade or occupation. To achieve this end a balance must be maintained between theoretical and practical knowledge in the course of professional study. But, as the theoretical concepts, principles and insights can be gained only through academic study, there must always be a close relationship between academic and professional studies. The central point of this analysis is that at whatever stage a student opts for a professional education in teaching, academic study must be viewed as an integral part of professional study.

This view has been challenged by Professor Hollins in his paper 'Desirable changes in the structure of courses'. In a discussion of the design of curriculum courses he questions whether it is sound to have teaching methods as part of academic study. He continues:

> ... educational philosophers tend to argue that theory and practice should go hand in hand. No doubt they should in those parts of the course which consider classroom practice. ... But an academic study has its structure, without which it is not fully intelligible, and it is unsound to bend it too much to immediate practical needs. (Hollins, 1971)

It is true that academic study has its own distinctive structure and that this should not be distorted. But when it is suggested that academic study should be conceived within a professional frame of reference, this is not to imply that it should be geared to meeting merely the 'immediate practical needs' of the classroom. The concept of 'professional relevance' which underlies the following curricular proposals is very broad in character, and it necessarily entails disciplined academic study of theoretical principles if students are to become reflective autonomous teachers.

There is a growing body of opinion which supports the view that academic and professional study are not dichotomous but rather complementary (Anderson, 1962; McGlothlin, 1960). McGrath (1962) considers that in the United States 'majority opinion favours the preservation of undergraduate professional curricula, which include both technical and general education offered concurrently.... On balance, the weight of the evidence seems to rest with those who favour an integrated programme.' In Britain the National Union of Teachers (1971) firmly supports the principle that 'degrees in education should be structured with the aim of achieving a synthesis of the academic elements and the professional elements of the course'. Similarly, in another sector of higher education, the Ormrod Report on Legal Education (1971) urges 'the integration of academic and professional teaching resources into a coherent whole'. A minority view in the Report supports the idea of a concurrent professional education for law students. On the principle that 'a dichotomy between theory and practice is not inevitable', it proposes that 'instead of handling vocational training after the academic stage, the two should be merged by sandwiching the practical training within the academic, so that the practical training becomes an integral part of the academic stage'. Finally, the Todd Report on Medical Education (1968) stresses the need for greater integration between 'preclinical' and 'clinical' training in order to avoid the gulf between academic and professional studies. In its proposals for a flexible course structure, based on a modular system, the report suggests that the clinical aspects of medicine should be introduced into the course at an early stage thereby helping to relate theory to practice.

This combined evidence would appear to make a strong case to support the view that in a professional degree academic and professional study should be intimately related. And yet the James Report has in effect abandoned the principle of concurrence, thus losing the opportunity of promoting a genuine professional degree for teaching. Although it recognizes that personal education and professional training are not logically incompatible, it suggests that 'their simultaneous coexistence as valid objectives for the whole of the three-year course must be seriously questioned'.* Admittedly, the present system in many instances has produced tensions, conflicts and diffusion of effort, but if teachers are to be given a high-quality professional education, we ought to be working towards a newly constituted concurrent course. Perhaps something can be salvaged from the Report's statement that the committed student teacher should not be denied the opportunity of pursuing a programme of studies which 'is similar in many important respects to the concurrent courses now offered

* P. 19, para. 3.2.

Table 12.1
Four-year Concurrent Course for Prospective Teachers

| Year | Education | | Subjects |
|---|---|---|---|
| | Middle-range Theory | Higher-order Theory | |
| *Year I* | 1. A theory of instruction designed to help students establish confidence and competence in the classroom<br>2. Joint concern of college and schools operating through a teacher tutor system<br>3. Theory to be studied in conjunction with observation and group work with children, partly through micro-teaching, film and closed-circuit television<br>4. All students to gain some experience of first, middle and secondary schools<br>5. Content to include teaching an integrated day, mixed-ability groups, vertical groups, reading, language skills, organization, discipline, co-operative teaching, record keeping, audio-visual material, etc. | Introductory courses in:<br>(a) Philosophy of education<br>(b) Educational psychology (with special reference to human development)<br>(c) Sociology of education (to include a historical perspective) | 1. A general education gained through academic study conceived within a professional frame of reference.<br>2. Each student to study one core subject, supported by two or three related contextual subjects.<br>3. Each subject to comprise the following inter-related elements:<br>(a) The nature of the discipline (e.g. facts, concepts, principles, validation procedures)<br>(b) Conceptual relationships between the different areas of knowledge<br>(c) The place of the subject in education (e.g. aims and justifications)<br>(d) The psychological aspects of learning the subject<br>(e) The sociological dimension of teaching the subject<br>(f) Subject-matter for schools and teaching methods<br>4. Possible combinations of subjects:<br>Language —English literature and drama, movement<br>Geography —history, science, sociology<br>History —English literature, art, history of ideas<br>Mathematics—science, geography<br>Physics —chemistry, mathematics<br>Music —literature, art, social history |
| *Year II*<br><br>*Part I Qual:*<br>Teacher Asst.<br>Cert:<br>(Sub-professional | Continuation from Year I including more extended school experience | A central core of topics to be studied in a multi-disciplinary approach (i.e. through philosophy, sociology and psychology of education) e.g.:<br>(a) The nature of the educational process | Continuation of study of core and contextual subjects as in Year I |

*Year III*

Optional Courses (A) e.g.:

(a) Education of immigrant children
(b) Education of backward children
(c) Education of socially disadvantaged children
(d) Education of the early leaver

Optional Courses (B) e.g.:

(a) Philosophy of education
(b) History of education
(c) Sociology of education
(d) Social psychology
(e) Human development
(f) Curriculum theory
(g) Research methods in education
(h) Statistics and educational measurement

Optional Subjects (C)—Academic study conducted within a professional context e.g.:

(a) Language
(b) English literature and drama
(c) History
(d) Divinity
(e) Art and craft
(f) Movement and P.E.
(g) Music
(h) Geography
(i) Mathematics
(j) Physics
(k) Chemistry
(l) Biology

(c) Learning and motivation
(d) Thinking and concept formation
(e) Language in education
(f) Interpersonal behaviour
(g) Education and society
(h) The nature of educational institutions
(i) Curriculum development

*Principles underlying third-year programme*
(a) Programme differentiation in the initial education of prospective first, middle and secondary school teachers
(b) The provision of optional courses which permit a student to extend either the breadth or depth of his knowledge

First-school students
1. Compulsory courses in mathematics and language
2. Three optional courses: *Either* one course from A, B and C
   *Or*    three courses from A and B
3. An extended period of teaching practice in a first school

Middle/secondary school students
1. Continuation of study of core subject
2. Four optional courses from A, B and C (one course could include a previous contextual subject)
3. An extended period of teaching practice in a middle/secondary school

Part II
Qual.
Ordinary
B.Ed. degree

Year IV
1. School-based continuation of professional training instead of the present probationary year.
2. The graduate trainee's teaching experience to be supported by tutorials and seminars under the co-operative guidance of head teachers, teacher tutors, college lecturers and advisory staff.
3. This continued training to be conducted in conjunction with schools, colleges, teacher centres and curriculum development units.
4. Aim – to fuse both the middle-range and higher-order theory with practice, thus helping the trainee to gain the authority and autonomy necessary for a professional teacher.

Qual:
Cert. in Education

in the colleges of education'.* Furthermore, the Webster-Porter Note of Extension in the Report recommends that a four-year degree course for teachers be built on the unit structure of the diploma of higher education.† This could include the study of education as well as incorporating the professional training which forms the first year of the second cycle. It would be hoped that those institutions concerned with raising the standard of teaching in schools will seek to establish a valid professional degree, in which academic study is conducted within a professional frame of reference.

### Towards a Flexible Curriculum for Teacher Education

If the arguments in the previous sections are valid, it follows that a curriculum for teacher education must be flexible enough to meet both the demands of a modern teaching force and the diverse needs of students, with their different abilities, interests and destinations. In a multi-purpose institution it should be possible to provide a range of courses, some of which would give students who are likely to enter a variety of professions the opportunity to study alongside each other. This could help to break down the academic and professional parochialism of many existing colleges of education. Nevertheless, although flexibility is an important general criterion, it must be recognized that those programmes devised for the professional education of teachers need to be guided by the principles discussed previously. The central condition is that when a student opts for teaching as a career, his academic study must be conducted within a broad professional context. The curriculum also needs to be related to a reformed occupational structure which would necessitate some programme differentiation according to the level of function and to the different stages of teaching (i.e. first, middle or secondary schools). In the proposed concurrent and consecutive courses parity should be achieved, in the sense that all students could gain a Part I qualification after the second year, and those continuing their study could receive an ordinary degree at the end of the third year and a certificate in education at the culmination of the fourth year (see Table 12.1).‡

### Scheme A: Four-year Concurrent Course for Prospective Teachers

An outline of this concurrent course can be seen in Table 12.1. It is divided basically between the study of education and those subjects that are likely

---

* P. 42, para. 4.6.     † A Note of Extension, p. 78, para. 4.
‡ For further discussion of course structures in teacher education see: Browne, 1969; Conant, 1963; Hollins, 1969; Renshaw, 1971; Robinson, 1971; Taylor, 1969.

to appear on the school curriculum; but it is intended that a close relationship be maintained between both of these main sectors. During the first two years the emphasis would be on a general education conceived within a professional frame of reference. Each student would study one core (or main) subject, supported by two or three related contextual subjects, each of which would comprise six inter-related elements:

1. The nature of the discipline, including basic factual knowledge of selected areas of study, the central concepts and principles underlying the subject, and its distinctive methods of inquiry and validation procedures.
2. The conceptual interconnections between the different areas of knowledge.
3. The place of the subject in education, including the aims underlying the teaching of the subject and the justification for including it in the school curriculum.
4. The psychological aspects of learning the subject.
5. The sociological dimension of teaching the subject.
6. Subject-matter for schools and teaching methods.

In the area of education a structural distinction is made between the middle-range theory of instruction and the higher-order theory, but as was discussed earlier the two should be closely related to each other. Given sufficient adequately trained lecturers and teacher tutors, students could be sensitized gradually to philosophical, psychological and sociological questions during the middle-range theory and practice sessions. To help the students build up the necessary analytical and empirical skills with which to identify these distinctive questions, this area of study in Year I could be supported by short introductory courses in the methodology of the contributory disciplines. In philosophy, for instance, the focus would be on questions of meaning and justification. Students could be guided in the use of conceptual analysis, in the recognition of logical contradictions and inconsistencies in argument, and in the examination of the assumptions and presuppositions which underlie the statements they make. In psychology special attention could be given to human development, while the sociology could include a historical dimension, as it is difficult to justify an extensive course on history of education and administration for all students during initial training. It is important for teachers to view the educational system, the nature of educational institutions and the curriculum in a historical perspective, but as this dimension can hardly be ignored in a sociological analysis of systems, organizations, institutions, roles and the social determinants of curricula, a separate course on history of education does not seem legitimate.

With this background, the second year could be geared towards developing further the students' insights into philosophy, psychology and sociology. As a basis for this work, a central core of topics could be studied through a multi-disciplinary approach in an attempt to see educational problems within a related coherent conceptual framework. Such a system would entail some joint consultation and co-operative teaching, but it is not always feasible or even desirable for three tutors from the relevant disciplines to be engaged in combined seminars for every session. This can produce discontinuity and confusion in the thinking of the students. Nevertheless, it is important for them to view certain fundamental topics through a variety of conceptual perspectives (Table 12.1, Year II, examples (a) to (i) ).

On the satisfactory completion of this two-year course of professional education a student could leave college with a certificate of competence to act in a sub-professional capacity as a teacher assistant. This qualification would form Part I of a professional degree in teaching and it could be up-graded after further full-time or part-time study.

Two basic principles underlie the structure of the third-year course. First, at this stage of the training there should be some programme differentiation for students intending to teach in first, middle or secondary schools. Secondly, a variety of optional courses, chosen from a number of subjects, middle-range and higher-order theory, should be provided which permit a student either to extend the breadth of his knowledge or to go more deeply into an aspect of a particular discipline. In this scheme, first-school students would drop their core subject and attend compulsory courses in mathematics and language. In addition, they would select three optional courses (see Table 12.1, Year III) and engage in an extended period of teaching practice under the guidance of a college lecturer and a teacher tutor. Both the middle and secondary school students would continue the study of their core subject, but they would select four optional courses, one of which could include a previous contextual subject. They would also pursue a substantial teaching practice in either a middle or secondary school. On the successful completion of Part II of the course a student would be awarded an ordinary B.Ed. degree, but he would not achieve full professional status without having passed the certificate in education. This could be gained at the end of the fourth year, which should be regarded as an induction into the profession rather than the nebulous probationary year it now is.* During this largely school-based continuation of professional training, the graduate trainee's teaching experience needs to be supported by tutorials and seminars under the co-operative guidance of head teachers, teacher tutors, college lecturers and advisory staff. This continued training should be conducted in conjunction with schools, colleges, teacher centres

* Criticisms of the probationary year appear in the James Report, pp. 20–21, paras. 3.8, 3.9, 3.10.

and curriculum development units, the central aim being to fuse both the middle-range and higher-order theory with practice, thus enabling the trainee to gain an authority and autonomy based on professional knowledge.

## Scheme B: Four-year Consecutive Course

At present there is a growing awareness in many professions that their work ought to be viewed within a broad social and human perspective. It is recognized that greater attention should be given to the role of the social and behavioural sciences in professional education programmes. Furthermore, the possibility of more interprofessional training between such related professions as education and the social services has received a measure of support (Tibble, 1967; Craft, 1967; Craft, 1970). For example, in the Seebohm Report on the Personal Social Services (1968) it is urged that teachers and social workers ought to have an informed understanding of each others' roles. In an attempt to establish a wider concept of generic training, it discusses the possible provision of a common basic training for the social welfare, probation, child care and health services. This proposal is taken further by the ATCDE in its evidence to the James Committee of Enquiry, where it suggests the desirability not only of developing the professional education of teachers and social workers alongside each other but also of providing some courses common to both.* In the domain of medical education, the Todd Report (1968) places considerable emphasis on the social and behavioural sciences, as it supports the principle that 'the student should learn about man in all his aspects, not only as a patient but also as a social being'. In its specimen syllabuses for psychology and sociology, there is a marked similarity between the topics recommended for medical students and those that already appear in the curricula for teachers and social workers. The Ormrod Report on Legal Education (1971) also urges co-operation with other disciplines such as psychology, sociology, psychiatry, medicine, economics and business studies, so that lawyers will know when 'to call in expert assistance; to be able to communicate with other experts; and to use the help which they can give to the fullest advantage of the client'. Elsewhere, an American source suggests that new links should be established between law and such supporting disciplines as science, the social sciences and philosophy because the lawyer needs to view his task in response to changing social, psychological and moral problems (McConnell et al., 1962). This principle could be applied to any modern profession.

The proposals for a four-year consecutive course embodied in scheme B must be interpreted in the light of the above evidence. The first year would comprise a multi-disciplinary academic foundation programme centred on

* Appendix III, p. 32.

the disciplines of psychology, social psychology, sociology and philosophy. It is intended for students entering a range of professions including not only education and the social services, but also medicine, law and business. In Year II students would opt for a specific professional area and a joint course could be planned for prospective members of the education and social services. The central disciplines would continue as before, but whereas in Year I all four subjects would be studied without any special professional orientation, in Year II the higher order theory would be related more to practical school experience, case work and field studies. A variety of optional topics could be offered within each discipline, and certain selected themes could be approached in a multi-disciplinary way (e.g. language, human development, the family).

At the end of the second year those students wishing to terminate their study could gain a Part I qualification, but those going on into the third year would pursue a curriculum designed especially for a particular professional group. The principles underlying the programme for prospective teachers would be largely similar to those underlying the concurrent course. Due to limited time there would have to be some programme differentiation for first, middle and secondary students from the start. Optional courses should be provided, and all academic components in both the compulsory and optional subjects should be studied within a professional frame of reference. This should include an examination of:

(a) The nature of the discipline;
(b) The place of the subject in education;
(c) The psychological aspects of learning the subject;
(d) The sociological dimension of teaching the subject;
(e) Subject-matter for schools and teaching methods.

The basic structure of this third-year programme would comprise:

1. *Compulsory subjects* First-school students should study mathematics and language, as both are so central to the education of young children. Middle and secondary-school students would select one core or main subject from a range of school teaching subjects.
2. *Optional subjects* First-school students could select three areas of study from science, environmental studies, human movement studies, art and craft, music and religious education. Middle-school students could take two contextual subjects, which would be designed to set the core discipline in its cognitive frame, while secondary-school students could limit themselves to one contextual subject.
3. *Study of the curriculum* All students should be introduced to some of the higher-order educational theory underlying the study of the school curriculum. This could consist of four components:

(a) Philosophy: the concepts 'education' and 'socialization', the development of mind, the nature and structure of knowledge, curriculum objectives, curriculum integration, educational justifications.

(b) Psychology: human development, children's levels of thinking, concept acquisition, the place of language in learning experiences, learning and motivation, evaluation procedures and testing.

(c) Sociology: socio-linguistic factors in learning, the 'hidden' curriculum, the social organization of knowledge, the distribution of knowledge in schools, problems of power, order and control arising from different types of curricula.

(d) Practical application in schools.

4. *Middle-range educational theory and practice* All students should study the middle-range theory of instruction as discussed in the details of the concurrent course (see Table 12.1, Year I). This should include some school experience and thus become the joint concern of colleges and schools operating through a teacher tutor system.

5. *Middle-range educational theory options* All students could select one optional topic, in which the emphasis would be on learning about the teaching of children in one of the following problem areas. In general, the development of practical expertise is probably best left for in-service education programmes. Topics could include:

(a) Education of immigrant children;

(b) Education of backward children;

(c) Education of socially disadvantaged children;

(d) Education of the early leaver.

On the satisfactory completion of this third-year course a student would be awarded an ordinary degree, but before gaining fully qualified teacher status a further year of school-based professional training leading to the certificate in education would have to be taken. The details of this fourth year would be similar to those discussed in the concurrent course.

## Scheme C: Four-year Consecutive Course

The idea underlying this scheme is that for two years students would engage in the academic study of one core and two contextual subjects designed to extend their general education. As in the other schemes, this would lead to a Part I qualification, after which students could opt for a specific programme of professional education as discussed under Years II and IV in Scheme B. Possible combinations of cognate subjects that could be studied include:

| Core Subject | Contextual Subjects |
|---|---|
| History | politics, economics |
| English | sociology, philosophy |
| Art | literature, philosophy |
| Philosophy | history, politics |
| Language | psychology, sociology |
| Mathematics | computer science, physics |
| Physics | chemistry, mathematics |
| Business studies | economics, statistics |
| Biology | geography, geology |
| Language | mathematics, philosophy |

The structure of Scheme C contains some similar features to the proposals in the first cycle of the James Report. For instance, at the heart of the diploma of higher education lies the principle that study in depth and in breadth 'must be combined and inter-related, as "special" and "general" studies'.* It is suggested that for a third of their time students should follow a general studies course which draws on the humanities, mathematics and the sciences, the social sciences and the arts.† In the time available, however, this general studies component would be so broad and disparate that it could result in a very superficial *smorgasbrod* academic programme. There is some merit in the idea of combining study in depth with that in breadth, but as I have already indicated, it would seem more logical for a student to study one core or special subject supported by two or three related contextual subjects, which are designed to set the different disciplines in their cognitive frame and to draw out possible conceptual relationships. This type of structure would be more consistent with the principles implicit in the idea of higher education, and as such it might be more acceptable in terms of its academic standards and status than the proposed Dip.H.E.

## Some Possible Implications of These Proposals for the Professional Education of Teachers

These curricular proposals are not revolutionary, but they are innovatory in the sense that they question many of the assumptions underlying existing teacher education programmes. If adopted they would demand fundamental changes in the overall structure of the college of education curriculum and of the graduate certificate in education. For instance, the four-year concurrent course would involve three major changes. First, the idea of the integral relationship between academic and professional study challenges both the structure and status of the present main subject, which in many

* P. 42, para. 4.8.        † P. 43, para. 4.10.

cases has taken the traditional university undergraduate course somewhat uncritically as its model. Secondly, as the whole curriculum is viewed within a global professional perspective, this would entail the sensitive placing of educational theory throughout the whole course. The middle-range area of theory and practice would be emphasized during the initial training period, and there would be a continuing focus on philosophy, psychology and sociology. The third main change is that curriculum courses, as conceived at present, would cease to exist. This dimension of the student's professional education would be catered for more systematically in this new scheme.

At the centre of any discussions about teacher education is the contribution that universities have made to the planning of syllabuses, the control of academic standards and the validation of public awards. This century has witnessed a growing link between colleges and universities, and as Professor Hilliard points out: '... there is no doubt that the efforts of the universities here have been and should continue to be directed towards assisting the colleges to maintain and enhance the academic standards of college courses' (Hilliard, 1968). But has this determination to improve the level of the academic attainment of teachers necessarily resulted in raising the quality of the *professional* education in colleges? Throughout this chapter it has been asserted that teachers need a body of theoretical knowledge which must be supported by research. But some universities seem to forget that the professional is concerned with the *application* of knowledge. The conservative scholastic attitudes which prevail in some university departments have militated against providing a valid professional degree. At present, traditional university thinking has influenced unduly the structure of the main subject, the nature of the B.Ed. degree and the general attitude towards the low status of professional study. Quite often a desire for academic prestige has acted as a stranglehold on the establishment of a professional degree for teaching, in which academic study is conducted within a professional frame of reference. For example, the character and status of the main subject has reinforced the growing separation between academic and professional studies in colleges. There has been a tendency for the academic education of the student to become associated with the main subject, while the study of curriculum courses and education has been identified as professional training. In many colleges this attitude has created an unfortunate gulf between education and subject departments. Another similar problem has arisen in recent years with the emergence of the B.Ed. degree, and with the accompanying recognition that the disciplines contributing to educational theory are worthy of academic study. This has resulted in a rift developing between academic and professional studies within some education departments. In terms of status it is frequently the so-called academic philosopher, psychologist and sociologist who gains the power and prestige, and this can lead to a distortion of the character and relevance of professional study. Therefore I am suggesting that although high academic standards achieved through theoretical study are of central importance, they must be viewed in relation to professional knowledge; that is, knowledge which can be applied to practical action.

Other implications also follow from this suggestion. It has been maintained that the logical, psychological and sociological aspects of learning and teaching a subject constitute the core of professional knowledge for teachers. If this is the case, a very close working partnership must be established between subject and education departments, as well as between schools and colleges. In practice this implies strengthening institutional and inter-departmental links, fostering joint-planning and co-operative teaching, and adopting a teacher tutor system. But this proposal presents a variety of problems, some of which could be resolved only through the greater provision of advanced in-service education programmes for teachers and lecturers. For instance, those subject lecturers who have some responsibility for professional programmes would need to be able to view their disciplines in a broad educational context. Not only would this help them to give students a more relevant training, but it would also enable them to understand the conceptual interconnections between educational theory and the nature of their different subjects, and to see how this knowledge can be related to educational practice. Education tutors would also be confronted with a range of demands requiring a high level of skill and conceptual understanding. Ideally, each lecturer would need expertise in at least one of the central educational disciplines, but in addition he should be capable of placing this particular perspective within a wider global view of educational theory. Furthermore, it would be necessary for him to be able to relate this knowledge to the professional study being conducted in the subject departments. The teaching of the middle-range area of theory needs to be informed by knowledge of the higher-order principles, otherwise the study of education can degenerate into the presentation of tidy recipes based on one individual's experience. In the schools the role of the teacher tutor would have to be made explicit, and the teachers selected for this vital task would have to receive an advanced form of professional education, thus enabling them to reflect critically on the nature of teaching and to be able to articulate and communicate this knowledge to the student teacher.

Perhaps one of the most fundamental difficulties arising from these suggestions is the problem of establishing communication between the different specialist subject lecturers, education tutors and teachers. The conception of professional education which has been proposed presupposes that all tutors share similar assumptions, understand each other's languages and that their intention is to work together towards a common goal. But if one examines the overall structure of knowledge and the distribution of knowledge within an institution, a major problem arises in the provision of 'integrative meanings' or meaningful conceptual relationships between different disciplines or modes of thought. Professor Musgrove (1968) has defined a subject as

> ... a social institution with its sense of identity and loyalty exacted from its members. In conflict with other subjects it defines its boundaries and its sphere of influence. Subjects are highly organized, hierarchic, bureaucratic. They are busy discovering reasons for their existence and importance. They develop their own defensive systems against encroachment.

This definition draws out several important points which are supported by Berger and Luckmann (1969). For instance, each subject can be viewed as a distinctive 'symbolic universe' containing its own language, its own style of thought, its own conceptual machinery and its own practical and theoretical procedures. As people begin to identify with a particular symbolic system, thus gaining security from its institutional order, problems of communication and social interaction arise between the different disciplines. As Berger and Luckman indicate: '... the increasing number and complexity of sub-universes make them increasingly inaccessible to outsiders. They become esoteric enclaves, "hermetically sealed" ... to all but those who have been properly initiated into their mysteries.' For example, outsiders tend to be ostracized through the use of prestige symbols and technical language, which act as a restricted code militating against meaningful communication. Moreover, as each discipline strives to establish its own autonomy, problems of conflict emerge. The existence and development of other symbolic systems often appear as a territorial threat which leads to a power struggle within an institution. The main implication of this analysis for teacher education is that if a professional education for teaching presupposes a meaningful interaction between different experts, considerable knowledge, tolerance and mutual understanding would be necessary for effective communication and co-operative teaching.

Finally, colleges and universities need to establish their curricular priorities for both initial and in-service education. Student teachers cannot possibly be expected to master that specialized theoretical and practical knowledge fundamental to teaching. Continual professional education is of vital importance if teachers are to perform their many roles, which are subject to constant redefinition due to changing social, technological and educational demands. The future is likely to see most elements of the profession contributing to policy decisions on such matters as the structure and content of the curriculum, teaching methods, school organization and teacher education. The knowledge necessary for this high level of participation can be gained only through far greater provision of in-service education.

The James Report is right to suggest that 'a much expanded and properly co-ordinated programme of in-service education and training is essential to the future strength and development of the teaching profession'.* But this shift in emphasis must not be to the detriment of the quality of the professional education received by the student teacher during the initial period of training. Ideally, initial training, the induction period and in-service education need to be viewed as an on-going continuum, within which a variety of curricular structures (i.e. concurrent and consecutive) can be established without sacrificing the standards of the professional education of teachers. If this could be realized, along with a reformed occupational structure supported by a systematic body of professional knowledge, a considerable step will have been taken towards providing future generations of children with an education of quality and integrity.

* P. 5, para. 2.3.

CHAPTER 13

# School Experience and Student Learning

EDITH COPE

## Practice Teaching in Schools: a Survey

Practical experience of teaching in schools has constituted an essential element in courses of teacher training. The principal avenue of entry into the profession in the nineteenth century was via apprenticeship as a pupil teacher, and this preliminary experience was supplemented in the actual training programmes by directed experience in schools. Thus students at the pioneer establishment of Borough Road College attended the attached model school for four-and-a-half hours each day, those at Kay Shuttleworth's Battersea College the adjacent village school for three hours a day. When the redoubtable Miss Beale decided to establish a training department at Cheltenham Ladies College for girls who proposed to enter the teaching profession, she could not, of course, allow them to teach in the College itself ('It is an expensive school and we cannot give them much practice there') but she did arrange for them to practise in a nearby establishment, 'a sort of high school' (Rich, 1933). It was the customary pattern for all the early denominational colleges to have their model or demonstration schools and many of the LEA colleges established after 1904 maintained this system by forging a special relationship with an adjacent state school. In time, however, the model school approach declined, partly because the day training colleges demonstrated the success of an alternative pattern in the 1890s by utilizing a range of existing schools for student practice; partly because the reorganization of state education into separate primary and secondary stages meant that not one model school, but several, would have been required on each campus. The impracticality of this undermined the system just as theoretical doubts on educational grounds were being expressed. Though the model school approach has survived in the United States it has largely disappeared in this country: what has emerged as the standard pattern of organization is one in which the college or university department enlists the co-operation of a range of schools which agree to offer 'school practice places' to the students of the training establishment.

When places were comparatively plentiful in relation to the number of students, the arrangements were carried out on an informal basis through personal contacts between college staff and head teachers. As pressure on places increased and colleges were driven to making raids on more distant territories, the administrative machinery of the new post-McNair Area Training Organizations was frequently brought in to regulate the demands on schools and to distribute the places equitably. Within the three-year course of training inaugurated in 1960 a fairly stable pattern of practice persisted, with procedures carried over by and large from the earlier two-year training course. Thus the amount of time given to school practice was extended by a mere two or three weeks, from a standard twelve weeks to fourteen or fifteen. This was in line with the advice proffered in the Sixth Report of the National Advisory Council (1957), which stated, 'There is no case for a greatly increased allotment of time to teaching practice [since] much practical skill must perforce be acquired after the student leaves college'. The distribution of practice was generally in line with suggestions in the Ministry of Education Pamphlet No. 34 *The Training of Teachers: Suggestions for a three-year course* (1957), which advocated initial visits for observation and small group work, with an extended practice of two or three weeks at the end of Year I, individual and group work with children with an extended practice of four weeks in Year II and a final practice from six to eight weeks in length, or even a term if it were felt the strain would not be too great. Supervision of students was carried out by the college staff on the basis of visits of observation, the number varying according to the needs of the students and the level of commitment of the lecturer. Thus some students over a six-week practice would receive as few as two visits, others as many as fourteen, though the norm was about one a week. The lecturers' impressions were in most instances supplemented by written reports from the schools, and on the basis of all the evidence a final grade was allocated to the student, usually on a five-point scale from A to E. So engrained were the conventions, and so little disturbed by the extension of the course from two years to three years, that as late as 1966 Professor Tibble could complain in an article in *Education for Teaching*:

> We have not engaged in any serious evaluation of the purposes and methods used in this branch of our work. . . . In general it is fair to say that in practical work training we took over a set of procedures from the Board of Education when it gave up its responsibility for running the Certificate Courses and we have continued with these largely unchanged to the present day.

This static situation has been modified to some extent by innovations introduced on an empirical basis by individual colleges and training departments Thus a rethinking of the supervisor's role is apparent in the experiment at Leicester School of Education reported by Caspari and Eggleston (1965), in which some of the techniques of training social workers were employed in the teacher-training situation. The students, instead of being visited in schools, reported back to their tutors, using them as resource persons. Hannam, Smyth and Stephenson (1971), have described the way in which students in the Bristol Department have explored, under tutorial guidance, the kind of learning which results when they encounter adolescent pupils outside the school setting in less structured situations. Also from Bristol, Richardson (1967) has reported on her employment of study-group techniques with students to deepen and extend their awareness of group interaction processes with particular reference to school situations. Many colleges have experimented with forms of 'group practice', where students are placed in twos, threes and fours to work in team situations rather than on the one-student, one-teacher, one-class basis (Downes and Shaw, 1968). Sustained research into micro-teaching as a means of analysing the teaching task and modifying student behaviour has been ongoing at Stirling University since 1968 (McIntyre, 1971). Wragg (1970) at Exeter has reported on his employment of interaction analysis as a means of diagnosing perform-ance and sharpening insights into teaching styles. Many colleges are experi-menting with the use of films, video tapes and closed-circuit television in relation to the practice situation (Collier et al., 1971). Experiments in in-viting certain teachers to act as teacher tutors, sharing in the method and education courses and acting as school practice assessors have been initiated (Bell, 1966; Baker, 1967; Collier, 1969). Some colleges have even developed entirely 'school supervised' practices in which visits from the college staff are strictly limited and the school takes over the direct responsibility for student guidance.

This survey suggests a ferment of activity and it is indeed true that in the area of school practice, as in other aspects of teacher training, existing procedures have been modified by a variety of experiments. Nevertheless, these are small-scale, ad hoc innovations, and the overall pattern is still the traditional one of the student entering the school, simulating for increasing proportions of time the conventional role of the teacher, and being observed sporadically by a visiting lecturer who comments to the student on the particular teaching/learning episode and provides an overall report to the college at the end of the sequence.

There are two main reasons for the failure to modify in any fundamental fashion the provision for practice teaching. One is the scale of the operation. School practice provides the point of interaction between the training institutions, the schools, the administrative machinery of the local education authorities and Area Training Organizations. To inaugurate change is a complex and delicate operation when more than one interested institution is involved. Moreover, because of the tremendous expansion of student

9—EOT * *

numbers and the problem of placing these in existing schools (approximately 110,000 students to 33,100 schools) the strains of maintaining the system have proved so demanding that there has been little energy to spare for large-scale reappraisal. Another factor has been the level of client satisfaction. The practical element in the training course has always been highly valued by students! The existing research evidence, though limited, suggests that in comparison with other aspects of the programme school practice provokes very positive responses (Cope, 1971; Lomax, 1971). In view of the complexities of tampering with the system and of the high level of student satisfaction with this aspect of training it is not surprising that innovation has been comparatively limited.

Indeed, what is perhaps surprising is that for more than a century there has been a sufficient level of co-operation and goodwill to enable schools and colleges to collaborate in this complex school practice enterprise with little overt friction. Admittedly, the goal of both institutions is to foster children's learning. With the schools, however, this is an immediate goal, with the colleges a long-term one. The college's primary aim is to foster student learning, and this is not invariably compatible in the school practice situation with the immediate fostering of children's learning. Moreover, schools and colleges are complex organizations with internal power structures to balance, systems to maintain, human relationships to foster, value systems to exemplify; interaction which briefly transposes individual students from one institution to another will inevitably be delicate. What is remarkable is not that strains are increasingly being manifested, but that the system has stood the test for so long.

### The Liaison between Colleges and Schools

My own research over the last five years has underlined some of the areas of difficulty and confusion and has pointed to inadequacies and inefficiencies in existing school practice procedures. For the rest of the chapter I intend to utilize this material to throw light on the state of the liaison between schools and colleges, to explore the factors which affect student learning in the school situation, and to offer suggestions for improved supervisory procedures. These suggestions, since they are concerned with the processes involved in the supervisory activity, will retain validity irrespective of any new organizational patterns which may result from the James Report and the current reappraisal of teacher education.

This research into school practice has been ongoing from 1965. It was funded by the Department of Education and Science and based in the Bristol University School of Education Research Unit. The first stage was a small-scale two-year enquiry; two colleges which train for both primary and secondary levels collaborated with thirty-five schools ranging from nursery to comprehensive and situated in four LEA areas. Research procedures adopted included discussions, questionnaires and direct observation, and the main findings were published in *School Experience in Teacher Education* (1971). Stage II investigated a 'school supervised' practice which had been operating between a particular college and its catchment of schools for a period of five years; small-scale innovation was introduced which was designed to develop the liaison between school and college and to increase the teachers' sense of participation. A report on this 1968–70 stage, entitled *A Study of a School Supervised Practice,* was produced in 1971. I intend to draw material from both reports to throw light on the issues mentioned.

Both stages of the research provided ample evidence of the problems of maintaining an adequate liaison between the colleges and the collaborating schools. Thus, in discussion, class teachers and head teachers indicated that while contacts were socially pleasant, they did not constitute genuine working partnerships.

'We don't know what the students have done or anything about their courses till they turn up in school and we ask them questions.' (Class teacher)

'We don't have the real liaison with the college. I'd like to know more about the way the students are prepared – how they are sent out.' (Head teacher)

In response to the statement that 'teachers do not have a clear understanding of what the college expects of them on school practice', fifty-six per cent. of the sample of teachers, sixty-five per cent. of supervisors and seventy-five per cent. of students agreed – dangerously high proportions to what is a very bald assertion. Teachers' uncertainty as to their school practice role is apparent in their response to another questionnaire item: 'teachers are in partnership with college supervisors in the assessment of students'. Sixty-seven per cent. of college staff, but a mere thirty-five per cent. of teachers agreed with this item. Now at the rational level teachers know that their opinion of the student's performance is incorporated into the head teacher's report. Indeed, at many schools the class or subject teachers provide a written report which is merely vetted by the head teacher. Thus they make a very real contribution to the assessment of the student. This high negative response, however, shows that many have no real sense of partnership with the college staff; they have too little exchange of opinion with supervisors to feel directly involved. This evidence of the teacher's incomplete sense of participation in school practice responsibility is underlined by their response to an open-ended question which asked what they found rewarding in school practice. The majority said the influx of new ideas: only fourteen per cent. of the responses expressed satisfaction arising from guiding and helping a student. This surely indicates that many teachers feel only a partial responsibility for the student's progress.

There was ample evidence not only of the teachers' confusion and uncertainty about their school practice responsibilities, but of a certain degree of wariness and mistrust between schools and college staff. Six out of eighteen head teachers, representing secondary, primary, infant and nursery, had quite specific anecdotes to contribute which related to the inexperience of supervisors. 'Three years ago a man supervisor came in. He just said that he'd never been in a primary school – "I can't help her. I'll have to ask you." That's unfair to the head.' As another remarked, after describing a similar incident, 'I don't mind the responsibility of writing a report, but it's too much for a head teacher if the supervisor has no idea.' The head teachers made it quite clear that the lecturers' honest admissions of ignorance and inadequacy, far from being disarming, provoked a breakdown of confidence.

At a non-anecdotal level, the replies to one particular questionnaire item strikingly demonstrated the suspicion which can exist between the two agencies collaborating in the training of teachers. Only twenty per cent. of the sample of teachers, only seventeen per cent. of the college staff, and only six per cent. of students agreed with the statement that 'Teachers approve of the methods advocated by college lecturers'. If this response indicated the extent of genuine disagreement in specific areas of work then the students' school practice position would be untenable. Experience shows, however, that there are substantial areas where lecturers and teachers are advocating similar approaches and where students function without undue strain. What the item is doing is, of course, triggering off an emotive response which indicates the unease and suspicion which can exist between the teachers, lecturers and students involved in the school practice enterprise.

What accounts for this situation when social contacts are courteous and amicable? One can put forward a complex of causes. There is the unresolved dichotomy within the colleges between those who see their role as fostering the students' academic education and those who see it as developing professional expertise. This dichotomy has been intensified with the introduction of the B.Ed. degree and an increase in the appointment of staff members who may be highly qualified in an academic discipline but who have no experience of and little interest in aspects of primary teaching, or even in the teaching of pupils of varied ability at secondary level. Such lecturers find themselves required, under present organizational arrangements, to supervise students in school situations which they have not themselves experienced. They lack the expertise to give the necessary advice and guidance and this is apparent to both school staff and students. A further source of difficulty is the rapid expansion of the colleges in the last three decades. Instead of their utilizing a tight little catchment of schools, physically close and visited by a small and therefore familiar group of lecturers, the colleges are now compelled to draw upon schools over a wide geographical area, some so distant that students have to be billeted. The team of lecturers is so large that schools may be visited by different individuals on virtually each practice. In such situations a close liaison is difficult to maintain and mutual understanding may diminish.

More fundamental than current staffing or organizational inadequacies are the inescapable tensions which arise between training institutions and institutions which work directly in the field. Schools are very exposed to social pressures, being expected at one and the same time to preserve values which society still considers important and to prepare children for new and unknown future situations. Teachers have not worked out how far they are preservationists, how far agents for change. They are conscious of the strain of their ambivalent position when the speed of change increases, when values are questioned and the educational situation is in flux. They may feel the need of a scapegoat and the college of education may be chosen for this role. Training institutions can then be stigmatized as the source of avant garde impractical approaches. Their staff, who receive higher salaries and status, but who escape from daily encounters with a coerced clientele, may be regarded with a certain envy and suspicion. This kind of depersonalized tension which may not colour individual relationships but which emerges clearly in the stereotyped and emotive responses to itemized questions is to some extent inescapable. Indeed, it would not be desirable, even if it were possible, to achieve identity between the ethos, processes and goals of institutions serving different clients and purposes. Somewhere in the tensions and counter-tensions between the aims and processes of two different organizations, the college and the school, the student finds freedom to move and ultimately to settle on his personal location. What is undesirable, however, is a situation where useful tension degenerates into suspicion, where communication is garbled and confused and energy dissipated. There is evidence in the research that under the pressures of college expansion these symptoms have sometimes been manifested.

## Student Learning on School Practice

Students find school practice a highly valued learning experience. Thus, from a sample of 322 students, ninety-five per cent. felt they learned a great deal or a reasonable amount from it, and only five per cent. felt they learned little or nothing. Such a generalized response, however, conveys nothing of the kinds or sources of learning. There is no doubt that some of the learning is negative, and can in extreme instances be traumatic. Positive learning is derived in a great many instances from the responses of the children and would occur even if no formal arrangements were made for fostering it. The sources of increased student learning are, of course, the professional adults who by their supervisory guidance supplement the students' own insights. The research disclosed that of the sample of students, twenty-three per cent. felt that the class/subject teacher contributed very little or nothing to their learning, thirty-four per cent. of students felt they learned little or nothing from the visits of general supervisors and forty-two per cent. felt they learned little or nothing from the visits of education lecturers. These responses may, in a few instances, reflect a personality characteristic of certain students, that is, an inability to acknowledge others as a source of their own learning. Observation and discussion evidence, however, suggests that in the main these responses are likely to be quite realistic. A number of factors may frustrate learning. A tiny minority of students experience personality clashes with their supervising teachers; rather more are placed with teachers who are amiably disposed but lack the capacity to be explicit about their own teaching behaviour or to analyse that of the student; there is even evidence that teachers who may have this capacity are so confused about the college's expectations and their own school practice role that they withhold advice on the grounds of not wanting to interfere.

As to the comparatively high proportion of students (more than a third) who learn little or nothing from visits of college staff, again this may be a realistic appraisal of the current situation. A minority of lecturers, as has been pointed out, lack both commitment to the supervisory role and relevant expertise. Others are prevented from providing adequate supervisory help by the pressure of time-table engagements in college and the travelling distances to be covered. A quick suggestion, a hasty word of reassurance or even a few written comments left behind may be all that they can offer in infrequent and tightly-scheduled visits. In addition to these obvious factors, other more subtle elements may operate to limit their contribution to student learning. College staff assert that the main purpose of their visits is to provide students with support and guidance. Nevertheless, an inescapable responsibility is to ensure that unsuitable students withdraw from the course: moreover, their one obligatory duty is to provide a report and a grade on the student's school practice performance. The research provides ample evidence that the lecturers' dual responsibility for both guidance and assessment constitutes an area of unresolved difficulty. For instance, thirty-nine per cent. of the student sample agreed with the statement that 'Students are afraid to approach college supervisors with real problems because of assessment', whereas only twenty per cent. of the college staff thought this to be the case. Only fifty-two per cent. of students agreed that 'Students use college supervisors for help in dealing with problems', whereas eighty-six per cent. of lecturers affirmed that they did. Comparison of replies on these and linked items indicates that college lecturers are to some extent self-deceived as to their success in reducing the effect of assessment pressures. A great many must believe that the power of good personal relationships has largely overcome the problems inherent in their dual role. Their replies suggest an inadequate recognition of the powerful factors which inhibit students from fully utilizing their help.

The reduction of the school practice grades to a simple two-point pass/fail would simplify assessment procedures and would represent a rational recognition of the arbitrary variables which affect student performance. It would not, in itself, resolve the fundamental difficulty. Some students refrain from approaching college lecturers with real problems not only because of grades, but because they wish to preserve self-esteem. Supervisors and teachers have a problem not only in grading students, but, more fundamentally, in evaluating them as part of the process of assisting their learning. Grades can be simplified, but evaluation will still remain part of any educational programme and an inescapable responsibility of all adult groups involved in the school practice enterprise. Two of these groups, the students and the teachers, project most of this responsibility on to the college staff. If, however, students are to achieve the maximum learning from their experiences in school and are to continue to learn after emerging as qualified teachers, then they must be educated in the skills of self-evaluation at a deeper and less facile level than is manifested in the school practice file. Supervisors must face the relationship problems imposed by the fact that guidance can only be effective if based on the critical evaluation of weaknesses as well as strengths. Teachers would need to share in the onus of accepting part of the responsibility for this evaluation. Within the present system guidance, which is seen as supportive, is split off from assessment, which is seen as threatening. Adequate student learning depends on a sophisticated understanding by all participants in the school practice enterprise that guidance and evaluation are inseparable, and mutually reinforcing. The simplification of the grading system would be a useful first step towards clarifying these deeper issues.

## The Case for Differentiated Practice Provision

A development which would also contribute to student learning would be the organization of more differentiated forms of practice. For the student to acquire a measure of conviction in the simulation of the teacher's role, a fairly lengthy practice conducted at a reasonably leisurely pace would seem desirable. If a student is to develop the flexibility and versatility to

*[handwritten: What should a student be trained?]*

meet changing situations, however, he must not only acquire specific skills and techniques. He must acquire the capacity to analyse a task and adopt appropriate procedures, the willingness to subject behaviour to critical appraisal, and the ability to modify behaviour in the light of theoretical insights. This kind of learning, instead of being diffused throughout block practices, might be accelerated by providing different kinds of school experience, conducted at a different pace and through different approaches. There is nothing original in this advocacy of differentiation. Indeed John Dewey, as early as 1904, was careful to distinguish between 'apprenticeship' and the 'laboratory point of view' and to emphasize that 'the method of conducting it [practical work] of supervising, criticising and correlating it' will differ according to the viewpoint which predominates.

> On the one hand, we may carry out the practical work with the object of giving teachers in training command of the necessary tools of their profession: control of technique of class instruction and management: skill and proficiency in the work of teaching. With this aim in view, practical work is, as far as it goes, of the nature of apprenticeship. On the other hand we may propose to use practice work as an instrument in making real and vital theoretical instruction, the knowledge of subject matter and the principles of education. This is the laboratory point of view ... there is a fundamental difference in the conception and conduct of the practice work according as one idea or the other is dominant and the other subordinate (Dewey, 1904).

*[handwritten: Conventional block]*

Exactly forty years later the McNair Committee recommended two types of school practice, one continuous and school-based to provide 'a situation in which the student can experience what it is to be a teacher, that is, to become as far as possible a member of a school staff', and the other 'comparatively discontinuous periods of teaching and observation in the schools, minor investigations and so on' (McNair, 1944).

My own conviction of the necessity for differentiated forms of practical work has been reinforced by the findings from the second stage of the Bristol research, where a 'school-supervised' practice was the focus of study. Students could discriminate quite clearly and consistently between the opportunities provided by this particular school-supervised system and those provided by the orthodox 'college-supervised' (Cope, 1971). The strengths of the former in this instance resided in its firmly rooted practicalities, the opportunities for student identification with the orthodox teaching role, and for the assimilation of professional skills and mores. The strength of college supervision lay in its potential for innovatory drive, diagnostic power, and tutorial exploration of the students' experiences. The relevance of this research to the argument for differentiation is that, given these complementary experiences, very few students opted for either one or the

*[handwritten: NB]*
*[handwritten: Conventional NB]*

other exclusively. Out of a sample of 158 third-year students in 1968, and 159 third-year students in 1969, eighty-five per cent. and eighty-four per cent. wished to retain both the school-supervised and the college-supervised practices. In other words, they wanted more than one type of practice provision.

It is easy, of course, to fall into a false dichotomy which presents school-based, continuous practice as mere apprenticeship and college-initiated, college-supervised practical work as exemplifying the laboratory approach. This is a gross over-simplification. I am not advocating crude differentiation, nor a simple duality, but varied and flexible practice arrangements to meet varied student needs. We need to clarify objectives more stringently, to specify certain learning goals more accurately, and to designate the kinds of supervisory behaviour and types of practice provision which are likely to enable us to achieve those goals. I suggest that the substitution of the term 'school experience' for the traditional 'school practice' may help us to move towards this more dynamic and varied approach.

It may be argued that if the suggestions put forward in the James Report were implemented, then Stage I of the second cycle, or a single year of professional training, would be too compressed a period to allow for differentiated practice provision. But the very compression of the course would strengthen the argument for differentiation. If the 'block practice' provision were to be a 'minimum of four weeks' then this would be supplemented by school experience of an intensive kind which exemplifies the laboratory approach. Moreover, if Stage II of the second cycle or, abandoning the James terminology, if the probationary year were genuinely to be incorporated in the process of professional training, then inevitably it would be regarded as an 'extension and deepening of what is now called teaching practice' even though the report warned against the 'over-simplification' that this viewpoint could represent.

Currently, though reactions to the specific James proposals are mixed, there is a good deal of support for drawing teachers into more direct responsibility for student training. The National Union of Teachers (1971) and the Head Masters Association and Head Masters Conference (1970) have all made policy statements advocating increased school participation. The James Report advocated teacher involvement in the selection and guidance of both students and 'licensed' teachers and claims that 'if these proposals were accepted, the teaching profession in this country would have a share in training its own members and establishing its own standards which would be almost certainly greater than that enjoyed by teachers anywhere in the world'. Whatever reservations may be held about the total Report, and whatever organizational pattern ultimately emerges from the current reappraisals, I am convinced that the movement towards increased teacher participation in professional training will continue. It constitutes a healthy development which could lead to a more effective deployment of resources and the blurring of the unhelpful division between initial training and the probationary year. Provided colleges retain opportunities for initiating certain forms of practice, this increasing interest in student guidance manifested by the teachers' professional organizations could be a powerful means of achieving that variation of practice provision which I have proposed.

If any shift of responsibility is to prove beneficial, however, the complexity of the task must be recognized, the members of both organizations must be educated for the change and certain safeguards must be built in. The second stage of the Bristol research throws some light on the complexity and pitfalls of the operation at primary school level. An instrument was devised which asked respondents to allocate the level of school practice responsibility which they thought head teachers, class teachers and college tutors ought to assume. On twelve out of twenty items class teachers allocated to themselves a lower level of responsibility than was ascribed to them by heads, college staff and, particularly, students (Cope 1971, b). This under-ascription could arise from two causes. Either class teachers feel unnecessarily diffident about taking on school practice responsibility, or they see it as peripheral rather than central to their role and ascribe responsibility to those who are paid to assume it, namely the head teacher and the college tutors. These reservations would need to be overcome if any restructuring of the practice situation were to operate effectively. I have argued in the research report that the existing pamphlets advocating 'school supervision', teacher tutors, etc. gloss over the complexities – as does the James proposal for 'professional tutors'. The effects on the career structures of teachers, the internal organization of the schools, the relationship patterns between staff members have been largely ignored. It is no small task for college tutors to rethink their role and deflect some of their energies from direct student guidance to oblique guidance via the teachers. It is even more demanding for teachers to rethink their role and accept student training as an essential element in it. The research evidence indicates that many individual teachers as yet lack both the confidence and commitment necessary for carrying out the task.

If teachers as a profession accept an increased responsibility for student guidance in certain practice situations, then, because of student numbers, this is likely to involve the majority of qualified practitioners. If supervision is not to go by default what will be needed is a broadly spread commitment and expertise which is possessed by all teachers with whom the students are working. Such expertise can only be developed by more generous school staffing coupled with sustained programmes of in-service education which will enable the staffs of training organizations and the teachers to pool their knowledge and tackle in functional working partnership the task of increasing student learning.

## A Survey of Various Types of Supervision

One difficulty is that we have, as yet, made very little study in this country of the activity designated by the term 'supervision'. In this, our situation differs from that in the United States. There, supervision is not restricted to the guidance and evaluation of students in training but is also applied to fully fledged teachers, who may be invited or required to expose themselves to supervisory programmes designed to increase their effectiveness. Should the James proposals for professional tutors be instituted, then these tutors will be concerned not only with students but with 'licensed teachers' and we shall be nearer to the pattern within the United States. In the English system as yet, however, the role of supervisor exists only in relation to students. Theoretically, the activity is considered an important one and is carried out by all the staff members of the training organizations, including the most senior. Yet, in practice, because of the narrow focus of supervision in this country no formal training for the role is as yet available. So the process may be ill performed by individuals who can have had no training for the task and may feel little interest in it. Because in the United States teachers in employment as well as students are subject to supervisory procedures, theories of supervision exist, a variety of practices has been developed, a literature has been constructed, and special training in the 'profession' of supervisor is available. If we in this country are to maximize the learning which students derive from school experience, and if we are additionally to arrange that probationers receive adequate guidance and help, then we, too, need to ensure professional standards and expertise in those who carry out this task.

Already certain promising approaches have been developed and a brief survey will indicate the range of strategies now available. Stanford University has been developing the process known as 'micro-teaching' since 1963, and this with various modifications was being utilized in the United States in a third of the accredited colleges for secondary education by 1969 (Allen and Ryan, 1969). In this country its employment has been very limited, but Stirling University has mounted a rigorous long-term research project, and the new University of Ulster, training departments in polytechnics and a number of colleges of education are experimenting with the utilization of micro-teaching techniques. Micro-teaching is characterized by:

1. *A systematic simplification* of the complexities of the normal teaching situation. This constitutes the micro-element. Simplification is achieved by:

(a) reducing the time span to a period of between five and twenty minutes;
(b) reducing the number of pupils to between three and ten;
(c) reducing the number of skills to be employed by the teacher to one or two specified ones, e.g., asking open-ended questions.

2. *Feedback* Feedback on performance is an essential element. This can be supplied by a written version of the episode provided by an observer, by an audio-taped version, or by a video tape. It can be supplemented by feedback from questionnaires, schedules and inventories filled in by the 'pupils'.

3. *Replanning and Repeat* After an analysis of the 'feedback' information, it is customary to replan the teaching episode and repeat the performance with a new group of pupils.

Underlying the technique are the basic assumptions that the process of teaching involves the utilization of a number of skills which can be defined; that in a complex task the simplification of certain elements may lead to more insightful analysis of the nature of the task; and that objective feedback enables supervisor and student teacher to analyse, organize and direct changes in behaviour, effective behaviour being reinforced by praise and further practice.

Micro-teaching as developed at Stanford has increasingly emphasized the importance of models, and model tapes of teacher-pupil interaction and interaction situations from other professions, e.g. doctor-patient and social worker-client, have been produced in a variety of training programmes. Modelling has its theoretical as well as specific dangers. It presupposes in the teacher training situation that there are appropriate 'models' of teacher behaviour which can be imitated by a wide range of student aspirants. The two fundamental problems are, of course, deciding what constitutes an appropriate model, and implementing in individual teaching behaviour the desired characteristics of the model. Investigation into these issues, and into variations in the length of sessions, the kind of feedback, the teach-critique-reteach cycle, and the transfer into the total teaching situation of skills developed in micro-teaching, is being pursued on a fairly wide scale in the United States and is beginning in this country.

Another process which is widely utilized in the United States and has been introduced on a small scale in this country is 'interaction' analysis. This term is used to designate systems of categorization by means of which the processes of human interaction can be described and analysed. One of the pioneer studies on classroom interaction was the paper by H. H. Anderson (1937), 'Domination and integration in the social behaviour of young children in an experimental play situation'. In this Anderson discusses the problem of measuring dominative and integrative behaviour of teachers in their contacts with pupils. The categories he designates serve as forerunners to some of the later categories developed by researchers in the 1940s and 1950s. Withall (1951) attempted to measure classroom social climate by classifying teacher statements. Bales (1950) employed interaction analysis as a research technique in his studies of the behaviour of small groups and with Strodtbeck presented a system of Interaction Process Analysis by means of which 'phases' in group problem solving could be determined. The most widely utilized system within the field of education is that constructed by Ned Flanders (1970) for analysing the verbal interaction of teacher-pupils within the classroom context. The system was developed at the University of Minnesota between 1955 and 1960 and consists of ten categories. Seven of the categories define teacher talk, three pupil talk.

| | | |
|---|---|---|
| *Teacher talk* | 1. Accepts feeling | |
| | 2. Praises | Response |
| | 3. Accepts and/or uses ideas of pupils | |
| | 4. Asks questions | |
| | 5. Lectures | |
| | 6. Gives directions | Initiation |
| | 7. Criticizes or justifies authority | |
| *Pupil talk* | 8. Pupil talk-response | |
| | 9. Pupil talk-initiation | |
| | 10. Silence or confusion | |

An observer tallies the verbal interaction at the rate of approximately twenty to twenty-five tallies a minute. Alternatively, the individual student or teacher can perform the analysis on himself if a taped record is available. From the tally sheets a matrix can be constructed.

The purpose of the activity is to study teaching behaviour by keeping track of selected events that occur during classroom interaction. One application is to help an individual develop and control his teaching behaviour. A second application is to discover through research how to explain the variations which occur in the chain of classroom events. Though the application of a category-system is intended to supply objective evidence as to actual classroom behaviour, the categories employed carry implicit value judgements and a long term goal is to identify patterns of interaction which are associated with teacher-effectiveness. Flanders and his co-workers have produced some evidence that 'indirect' behaviour by the teacher is more conducive to pupil learning, and this value judgement has received some slight support from other research; although Turner (1967) has posed the 'hen egg" question with his statement that 'bright pupils are more likely to produce certain behaviours (longer, more thoughtful responses, more questions to each other ... which increase the probability that a teacher will appear indirect'.

Although Flanders' system of interaction analysis is the most well known, other systems have proliferated and there are now a plethora of classroom observation instruments. These differ by

1. the particularities of the teaching act observed;
2. the number of categories;
3. the way the data is recorded.

By 1970, *Mirrors of Behaviour*, the Anthology of Classroom Observation Instruments, ed. Simon and Boyer, had reached nine volumes, and covered fifty-three different systems.

Once we are aware of the possibilities of categorizing, of ignoring much of the content in order to clarify modes of interacting, we can profitably utilize or invent category systems to test hypotheses or to bring home certain truths to individual students in training. Their large-scale adoption as a required part of a teacher training programme would seem to me ill advised, however. I believe that the majority of students are capable of more subtle and complex analyses than the pre-set category system allows for and that this holds true particularly for analysis of the behaviour of children, with which category systems deal very inadequately, being invariably teacher-weighted. In other words, a taped record of the teaching event, utilized as evidence to be jointly explored by supervisor and supervisee, is likely to provide a richer learning situation for the student than an analysis limited to pre-set interaction categories. For highly specific purposes, however, in relation to research or the particular needs of a group or individual, interaction analysis is a useful tool.

A form of supervision which has been developed at Harvard since 1956 is that termed 'clinical supervision'. This has received a stimulating and detailed exposition by Goldhammer (1969). Its principles and practices are not dissimilar to those of traditional supervision, inasmuch as they entail a pre-planning session, observation of full teaching sequence, and a post-teaching conference. They represent a more stringent, explicit and coherent implementation of approaches employed in some measure by supervisors of students in this country. What differentiates the system is the stringency of application and the behavioural emphasis. The focus is on the evidence provided by teacher and pupil behaviour, and the supervisory conference is not used for the exploration of diffuse personal and professional concerns. Underlying the approach are the assumptions that teaching behaviour should be conscious, rational action, subject to understanding and therefore control and change by the teacher, and that the supervisor's task is to assist the teacher to achieve this understanding.

Goldhammer, in his developed treatment of clinical supervision, posits five stages, 1. Pre-observation, 2. Observation, 3. Analysis and strategy, 4. Supervision conference, 5. Post-conference analysis.

1. *Pre-observation conference* The actual teaching event to be observed is discussed in advance of the situation. Objectives, content, approaches, and methods of evaluation are explicitly spelt out. This is the element which with English college students is most neglected. Overall plans for the entire practice are vetted, but there is no formal allocation of time for pre-planning sessions between supervisor and student on individual lessons, except in experimental group-practice situations or according to strongly evidenced individual need. One could argue the case that if time is limited, the supervisor could be more useful in pre-planning sessions than in any other activity.

2. *Observation* As full a record as possible is taken. Goldhammer asserts that a written account of the main verbal interaction is as useful as more elaborate procedures. A tape recording or video tape provides a more comprehensive record and is increasingly being employed.

3. *Analysis and strategy* The supervisor and student separately study the evidence looking for salient teaching patterns rather than unusual variables, and making a selection of issues which will form the basis of the supervisory conference.

4. *Supervision conference* The timing is important. It should be near to the teaching event to retain freshness yet a sufficient interval should have elapsed to allow the student and supervisor to have studied the record. In the conference a selection from the evidence is utilized, the student may be made conscious of recurrent patterns, alternatives may be explored which will increase his repertoire, and value judgements may be exchanged.

5. *Post-conference analysis* This consists of the supervisor privately reviewing the supervisory conference, or, as was the practice at Harvard, of a group of supervisors coming together to subject the conference to a similarly searching analysis as was applied to the student teaching episode.

Clinical supervision is a stringent and rigorous way of fostering student learning and, if the fifth element of post-conference analysis by the group is included, of fostering supervisors' learning. Goldhammer, while accepting the behavioural orientation and presenting a meticulously detailed analysis of the strategies involved in the process, nevertheless stresses the vital importance of the relationship between supervisor and supervisee. 'If good teaching requires intimacy, empathy, sensitivity, and psychological investment, and if, indeed, it is the relationship that teaches rather than the text, then supervisees must be experienced as people, not as intervening variables.'

Perhaps the approach which centres most directly on the 'supervisee' as a person is that of counselling. Since supervision entails a relationship of guidance and support between student client and supervisor it is only to be expected that techniques developed in connection with the 'helping' professions should provide useful models. In this country the Leicester School of Education has utilized the client-social worker conference as the prototype of experimental supervisor-student conferences. At a more informal level supervisors have not hesitated to utilize tutorial relationships for the exploration of personal problems related to the student's teaching role. In the United States, where educational counselling is a fully developed profession, it is natural that the techniques of counselling as related to the supervisory conference should have been spelt out more explicitly than in this country.

The advocation of counselling approaches rests on the assumption that students and mature teachers with 'normal' personalities are nevertheless subject to psychological strains which diminish professional competence. These strains arise because teaching involves human interaction within a complex institution. Problems develop when students' or teachers' self-esteem is damaged by specific situations, when teachers have difficulty in responding positively to certain individual children or to certain colleagues, or when teachers' goals and aspirations do not match those of the school. Successful teaching entails the acquisition of an appropriate self-image, and this is a process involving more than the rational development of a range of specific skills. An adequate supervisor must be prepared to explore the 'feeling' as well as the 'cognitive' elements involved in the process of becoming an effective teacher. Counselling offers an appropriate model for the supervisory conference in that it is client-centred: the client brings his personally-felt problems forward and is encouraged to share responsibility for their solution. Carl Rogers (1962) has emphasized the crucial importance of the quality of the relationship between counsellor and client in what is essentially a therapeutic process, and has stressed the relevance of his work to teacher training. Coombes (1969) and co-workers at the University of Florida have studied the characteristics of the various 'helping' professions, in which they include teaching, and have stressed the importance of developing in students in training a positive self-image and a sensitive responsiveness to others. Mosher (1972) has advocated 'ego counselling' as a specific model, and has spelt out its characteristics. The counselling approach, with its emphasis on the client-centred conference and the relevance of feeling, offers a complementary process to behaviourally orientated 'clinical supervision'.

One can add to this survey supervisory insights gained from the study of written, taped or filmed case material, from the study of group dynamics, from role playing and from simulation exercises. Of profound importance is some awareness of curriculum theory and theories of innovation and change. Heaven forbid that we should train people to be more effective if the knowledge and attitudes they are promoting are obsolete. It is perfectly possible, given these theoretical foundations and this wide range of strategies, to envisage supervision as a 'professional' activity with particular training requirements and forms of expertise. Practitioners of supervision, whether college staff or teachers, should be familiar at some level with these processes for assisting their own and student learning. Selected teachers and college staff who wish to develop specialized expertise could move on to high-level training programmes which would develop their skills in particular aspects of the supervisory activity.

## Conclusion

If professional learning in the practical teaching situation is to be increased we must assist students and probationers to accept, at a sophisticated level, the necessity for analysis, diagnosis and evaluation. We must develop differentiated forms of practice which will cater for varied objectives. We must involve teachers in a more genuine working partnership with the staffs of the training organizations. We must explore the various strategies for assisting learning which are now available, and ensure that those who are responsible for guidance, whether tutors or teachers, have some level of commitment to the supervisory role and expertise within it. The supervision of students is a teaching task, made more complex by the fact that it is shared by members of two different organizations. At a time when a reappraisal of teacher training is under way, there is a temptation to simplify the process by proposing the handing over of major responsibility for practical teaching guidance to one organization, i.e. the school. This temptation is dangerous, and, in my opinion, to be resisted. Otherwise a dichotomy will be set up between theory and practice: the colleges, cut off from their work in the field, will retreat into irresponsibility, the schools, engaged in a self-perpetuating activity, will sink into complacency. The expertise of staff members of both organizations is needed if variety of practice provision is to be ensured and if students are to be equipped for present professional competence and future professional growth. Increasingly we shall learn more about the teaching process and develop more sophisticated techniques for assisting professional learning. Fundamentally, however, supervision will remain an exercise in human relationships. Just as we recognize the crucial importance of the relationship between class teacher and child in the learning situation, so we must acknowledge at the adult level the importance of the relationship between supervisor and student. Professional expertise in strategies of supervision will be invalidated unless it is combined with sensitivity to the individual student and his unique learning requirements.

CHAPTER 14

# Teaching Methods in Colleges of Education

GERALD COLLIER

## Variations in Curriculum Structure

The curriculum* consists of four elements: a specialist study, or main
subject; principles of education, including the underlying disciplines; practical work in schools; and professional courses in subjects such as English,
mathematics, and environmental studies. These generalizations, however,
conceal a great deal of variation from college to college, and from department to department. Colleges preserve a strong sense of individuality and
guard this jealously. They vary far more widely in the structure and balance
of their courses than might be supposed from outside. The Area Training
Organization will usually only organize official examinations or assessments
in education and the main subjects; other courses are the responsibility of
the individual colleges. The basic courses in English, mathematics and
physical education, and the curriculum courses in art and craft, music and
environmental studies, may be assigned twice, or three times, as much time
in one college as in another. Some colleges differentiate sharply between
courses for teachers of different age-groups, others scarcely at all. To some
extent this depends on the history of the college, whether it was originally
a men's or women's college and whether it had a specialist bias towards a
subject such as home economics, or towards a particular age-group. Partly
it is a matter of the habitual assumptions built up over the course of years,
which may lead one college to adhere to a firmly timed syllabus of work
while another in the same ATO adjusts its pace of work, its syllabus
coverage, and its volume of tutorial guidance to the abilities and special
interests of the students.

* The James Report has proposed radical changes in the colleges of education,
two of which have particular relevance to the present chapter: A broadening of
the curriculum to prepare students for qualifications of general utility, not
restricted to the teaching profession: and a consequent change in the relations of
different components of the existing college curriculum. These changes do not affect
the accounts of recent developments given in this chapter; but they are likely to
have a considerable influence in the future.

Departments too vary widely in their circumstances: an education department, which has to teach every student in the college and has a student/staff ratio of perhaps fifty to one, will organize its work on very different lines from a small music department with few students. A college with a strong science section heavily orientated towards B.Ed. and secondary specialist work will have a very different ethos and pattern of work in its science departments from that of a college where the only science is biology based on nature study.

## Prevailing Practice in Teaching Method

The above outline provides a background against which one can discuss the teaching methods used in the colleges. The Robbins Committee organized a massive survey of higher education in Great Britain and their evidence is important. In 1961–2 students in the colleges in England and Wales spent on average approximately sixteen hours per week in teaching periods, made up as follows:*

| Lectures | Seminars | Tutorials | Practicals | Miscellaneous |
|----------|----------|-----------|------------|---------------|
| 8·8 | 2·0 | 0·1 | 4·8 | 0·5 hours per week |

The Robbins Committee defined its terms as follows. In a lecture, 'the teaching period is occupied wholly or mainly with *continuous exposition by the lecturer*'. Seminars are distinguished 'in giving *more opportunity for the participation of students*'; for example, 'there may be discussion of topics introduced briefly by students or staff,' or 'of any matters or problems on the initiative of students or staff'. Tutorials are differentiated from seminars in having from one to four students. 'Practicals' are held in such subjects as physical education, drama, music, home economics, art and craft. The 'miscellaneous' heading covers, among other things, field work and written-exercise classes (on, for example, language translation).

Average numbers of students are given as follows:

| Lectures | Discussion periods | Practicals |
|----------|--------------------|-----------| 
| 21·2 | 10·2 | 12·7 |

There was 'no evidence of larger lecture audiences in the larger colleges'. A small study conducted by the National Union of Students in 1969 tends to confirm the prepondance of formal instruction. In this case two colleges of education, two colleges of art, two technical colleges and two universities provided data of attendance, which for the colleges of education emerged as follows: †

* Robbins, 1963.                    † NUS, 1969.

| Lectures | Seminars | Tutorials | Practicals | Written-exercise classes |
|---|---|---|---|---|
| 13·6 | 3·4 | 1·7 | 6·4 | 2·3 hours per week |
| 15·4 | 2·1 | 1·4 | 11·4 | 4·3 |

Since the Robbins survey was carried out the college population has become three times greater and there has been much reorganization. The colleges have embarked on undergraduate work for the bachelor of education degree and have greatly extended their postgraduate work for the postgraduate certificate of education, as well as their in-service work with practising teachers. There is no doubt that in these new areas many of the student groups are very small, some even qualifying for designation as 'tutorials', and there is consequently much opportunity for exchange between tutor and student. It must also be remembered that in much of the work designated 'practical', tutors will be circulating among students giving individual advice and guidance.

Moreover, a very useful unpublished survey of college methods of teaching carried out by a working party of the Association of Teachers in Colleges and Departments of Education in 1965–6 demonstrates that a large volume of experimentation was under way in every aspect of teaching methods. Much of the later part of this chapter merely illustrates what has been in progress in many colleges for a number of years. The files of the Association's journal, *Education for Teaching*, over the last two decades contain many accounts of such work in progress.

## Practical Work in Schools

The traditional pattern of school practice, based on a class-instruction model, consisted – in the pre-1960 two-year course – of two 'block' practices, that is periods of four to six weeks of class teaching in primary or secondary schools. The first was usually introduced by a series of 'demonstration' lessons by college staff and observation visits to schools.

With the gradual growth of the more informal approaches, particularly at the primary level, colleges have introduced a variety of other types of work. Observation visits, which rarely seem to yield much fresh insight, have tended to be replaced by work with single children, or groups of two or three, leading up to a first block practice. Group practices have become fairly widespread, in which a tutor with a group of eight to fourteen students will take a certain section of work with a particular school class for one or two terms, spending half a day a week in the school. The tutor and the students plan the work between them, thus making it possible for the students to practise a variety of less familiar methods, such as the use of films and film-strips, field work, projects and displays, improvised drama, and so on, in circumstances where an experienced teacher can ensure effective organization and discipline. The class will be divided into small groups and students will get to know a few children well. Standardized tests can be administered and interpreted; it may become practicable for students to visit the homes of 'their' children and see something of the relation between home circumstances and school performance (Collier, 1969). Similarly, professional or curriculum courses are beginning to take students into schools, and teachers are becoming involved in the teaching and supervision of such courses.

In addition the studies of individual children which have often been an essential part of an education course have been extended in various ways. Many colleges have made arrangements for varying numbers of students to work in approved schools, with probation officers, in schools for the educationally sub-normal, in youth clubs, and in a great variety of other places where they meet children or adolescents, and to get to know them as people. Increasingly also – though still on a small scale – colleges and schools are collaborating in experimental schemes. A school embarking on a new enterprise in connection with the raising of the school-leaving age asks a college for the assistance of a few students who are keen on that particular type of enterprise; and a collaboration of teachers, students and tutors may provide useful assistance to the innovating school, illuminating experience for the students, and a richer scheme than would otherwise have been possible for the pupils concerned.

In general it may be said that colleges and schools are learning to work more closely together, but have some way to go yet before the aspirations of the two sides establish an adequate new tradition of intimate working partnership.

## Field Work

Field work has traditionally been the prerogative of the biologists, the geographers and the geologists, but in recent years other departments have made considerable use of field excursions for studying historical remains, drama, art, architecture, industrial or rural reorganization, museum collections, and so on. There has been some slow development towards a greater degree of independent observation by small groups of students but the usual habit is for a tutor or guide to give a lecture tour.

## Current Developments in Lecture and Seminar Techniques

### Film

The last two decades have seen a steady increase in the use of audio-visual materials in class work. Films are used constantly, particularly by education and geography departments. They may be used to show children's behaviour in classroom or playground, to demonstrate psychological experiments, to present experienced teachers at work, to introduce comparative material on child-rearing (or other) customs in different societies, or to bring forward selected materials on industrial societies to underpin sociological principles. The geographer will use films to bring out in a particularly vivid way conditions in other areas of the world. Tutors are increasingly sophisticated in their use of such material, asking questions in advance, planning with student groups what questions they wish to ask on the material to be shown, or stopping a film at critical points for discussion.

Films are also sometimes used in a rather different manner. One of the inevitable defects of all classroom education is that the material presented to students for analysis and study is an extremely simplified version – usually in the form of a verbal description – of the complex 'reality'. A film, however, can present not only the dialogue used but the expressions on the speakers' faces, the tone and rhythm of their speech, the movement and timing of their bodily gestures. It is valuable for students to immerse themselves in a human situation of this sort and discuss afterwards what they felt to be the reactions and inter-relationships of the participants. Here is a setting in which students can learn how to look at the complexities of 'real' situations and how to see which questions are significant for which purposes (Schwab, 1969).

An extension of the same concept is to study a good fictional film, in which questions about motives and values can be examined. For example, a short film of the American Civil War, *Time out of War*, shows three soldiers on a hot day making a private truce among themselves. The tutor may ask such questions as, 'What do you think were the motives of the soldiers in making their private truce? How far were they justified in doing so? Where do you think their obligations, their duties, lay? Can you make any distinctions between their obligations to their military commanders, their obligations to the sub-nations they represented, and their obligations to human beings generally? What were the writer of the story and the director of the film trying to say about the worth or validity of certain human relationships?' (Collier, 1969).

## Closed-circuit Television (CCTV)

In the last decade there has been an increasing use of CCTV and the video-tape recorder (VTR). A number of colleges have fairly sophisticated one-inch systems; an increasing number are investing in half-inch equipment, which is not only less expensive but also more portable and therefore more readily used in a school or a playground to record material for use in college. Sound recording, however, still presents problems. Mobile units shared by groups of colleges are also used in some parts of the country. Libraries of material are beginning to be assembled and soon, it is expected, colleges will be circulating the most useful recordings widely among themselves. The National Council for Educational Technology has produced a first catalogue of VTR materials made, and available for exchange, within the field of higher education, which will no doubt serve to stimulate the circulation (National Council for Educational Technology, 1971).

Tutors in colleges are also now using the VTR for recording their own lectures when these incorporate film excerpts or other visual material, since the main components can be welded together more effectively in this way. Some studio facilities are needed for this work as well as ciné equipment, and electronic editing equipment is an additional if expensive advantage. Such a studio production also provides an opportunity for a certain number of students to gain further experience, as members of a production team. The production process enables them to see how verbalized concepts can be translated into a richer medium of communication than descriptive language. With experience the actual production process has become simplified into what almost amounts to a self-directing production by the lecturer; but this does not of course reduce in any way the care and discussion needed in the planning of the programme to ensure the effective utilization of the most appropriate media for the communication intended.

The availability of the VTR has considerably increased the use of BBC and ITV educational broadcasts, since these can now (within certain limits) be recorded and played back in lectures and seminars when required. The majority of these are used in professional courses, for illustrating the teaching of different subjects. The School Broadcasting Council has greatly assisted by providing boxes or kits of materials for classwork in the colleges, on the methods of using school radio and television broadcasts. The box contains a filmed version of a television broadcast or a sound-tape of a radio broadcast, the booklet of notes prepared for the teacher, and the booklet of pictures to accompany a sound broadcast for the pupils; in many cases it also contains a sound-tape of a teacher's discussion with the class in preparation for and follow-up after the broadcast and of his comments on his use of broadcast material together with slides of the work produced by his pupils, such as written accounts, stories, paintings and models. These kits are hired out to the colleges.

Some television programmes have been used for academic instruction: an introductory psychology course designed for sixth forms, for example, has been found well suited to the needs of first-year students. The most significant may well turn out – for reasons which will be mentioned later – to be the programmes produced by the BBC for the Open University.

What is particularly noticeable is that many tutors now are wishing to record material from programmes not specifically designated 'educational', and therefore restricted in use by copyright agreements. Many documentary programmes, for example, include sections which are very relevant to history, geography, sociology, psychology, science, religious knowledge and other subjects, and it is to be hoped that fresh agreements will be negotiated which will make this material available for use in the colleges.

Another feature of current thinking in the colleges is the desire of tutors to have audio-visual material, particularly from broadcast programmes, made available in relatively short excerpts – say five to ten minutes. It can then be utilized in a variety of contexts, and in conjunction with a variety of other written materials. Long ready-made presentations of thirty minutes may – even when expertly produced by a national broadcasting organization – be too inflexible for tutors to make use of in the special circumstances of their own classes: most experienced teachers have their own distinctive ways of handling their subject matter and their classwork. A tutor who wishes to build a session, for example, on discipline problems with thirteen-year-old children in an urban environment would be delighted to have a couple of dozen five-minute excerpts to choose from, rather than three or four thirty-minute programmes of sophisticated construction, though the latter may in some circumstances be extremely useful (Collier et al., 1971).

A further use of CCTV is for students to have the opportunity of seeing themselves at work. Experiments are being carried out quite widely in this sphere but little systematic reporting is available as yet. The use of the technique as a general tool for personal guidance is plain, but it also has the potential of three further types of training, namely micro-teaching, interaction analysis, and procedural analysis.

Micro-teaching is a technique developed at Stanford University (Allen and Ryan, 1969) California, in which a student gives a mini-lesson of a few minutes to a mini-class of four or five pupils, practising one specific technique. He sees a VTR of himself, discusses it with his tutor, and repeats the process with different material or different pupils. The pupils may be boys and girls from a school or fellow-students playing a role. A number of colleges have been experimenting with the technique; the drawback is the high demand it makes on time and manpower.

A second form of training is in the analysis of the process of interaction between teacher and pupils, as pioneered by Flanders and Amidon (Amidon and Hough, 1967). A code of analysis is used for categorizing the teachers' and the pupils' behaviour in the class. The process of training students to apply this code is arduous but it is a valuable way of teaching them to make detailed discriminations of teachers' and pupils' interactions. The student who has undergone this training is in a better position to appreciate his own strong and weak points on a VTR. Simplified versions are being used to considerable advantage in English colleges; the defect of the system in the more elaborate form is again the time and manpower required.

A third form of training which is as yet little developed is training in the analysis of the intellectual and imaginative processes that take place in classroom work. When codes of analysis are available for the different subjects of the curriculum they will add a valuable technique for training students in the understanding and discrimination of teaching and learning processes (Smith and Ennis, 1961; Taba, 1962; Bellack *et al.*, 1966).

Yet another use of CCTV is for the presentation of case-studies and other problem materials for use with discussion groups. One independent television company has created a simulation of a school accompanied by documentation and a series of practical 'problem situations'. A modified pattern has been used in some colleges. They have written an outline of a school, assembled incidents reported by their students from school practice, and composed a series of small problems for class discussion in a manner similar to the in-tray technique used by the television company.

Most of the above techniques are used both for importing an added 'reality' and vividness into lectures and seminars and for stimulating more vital and realistic discussion.

### Miscellaneous Other Techniques for Use in Lectures and Seminars

Sound-tape recorders (STR) and record-players are now widely used in the colleges for the study of music, drama and poetry, since many excellent recordings have become available from commercial firms and students can gain a great deal from hearing their own performances. In the shape of a language laboratory the STR is used also for language teaching.

The development of modern reprographic techniques has brought a good deal of material from museums and archives into use in the colleges. This can provide students with striking source material for their historical studies and an opportunity to make judgements and inferences from historical evidence at first hand.

Role-playing is another technique quite widely used for enabling students to gain insight into problems of relationships in schools, particularly perhaps authority relationships. It takes a variety of forms, such as the improvised acting out of adolescent behaviour at home or in school in relation to the adults concerned, the presentation of short spells of teaching to students who place themselves in the position of children, and so on.

### The Development or Independent Learning Techniques for the Individual Student

When programmed learning was introduced into the schools, education lecturers explained the principle of it in their lectures and sometimes asked students to experiment in a school, either with writing short programmes of their own or with using commercially produced programmes. Scarcely anything was available at the level of a student's own studies, academic or professional. As experience has accumulated, however, many of the original concepts have been modified while at the same time material has begun to be produced at adult level for adult studies. A number of colleges now find a place in the education course for a theoretical study and in the school setting for practical trials, while experimental courses are being developed at adult level in all branches of the college curriculum. It is worth quoting examples.

A number of programmed courses are in print form. Several colleges, for example, have produced courses on statistics, particularly as service courses for other subjects. Programmed courses on psychology have been published for college use. The trend, however, is towards a multi-media form, whether a combination of print with photographs, or print with slides, or print with sound-tape and slides, or some other conjunction. A number of self-instructional courses have been developed on the use of audio-visual equipment; a number on sections of main courses in geography; similarly in biology, chemistry, psychology, visual design, and physical education. Programmed video-tapes and films or film-loops have been produced, instructions being given from time to time to switch off the VTR or projector and write an answer on a response sheet. The Science Teacher Education Project is assembling and testing a wide range of modest exercises to form a coherent pattern of independent study of science education and its underlying principles.

Much of this work is in effect an extended and systematized form of the traditional seminar/tutorial methods utilized by skilled tutors, where individuals or pairs of students are required to prepare privately essays or short papers which are designed to contribute to a joint exploration of a complex topic by a seminar or tutorial group. Similar techniques have been used in laboratory and studio work. The difference is that the materials produced to form the basis of the students' studies are developed systematically: the designers work out in detail what factual knowledge, conceptual understanding, skills and attitudes they wish the students to learn; they test the materials on sample groups of students; and they make a methodical evaluation of the effectiveness of the materials in bringing about the desired learning. There is, however, a good deal of suspicion of programmed materials, which are often thought of through sheer lack of experience as 'mechanizing' rather than enriching the learning process. Evidence from the University of California indicates a greatly increased contact between staff and students when courses have been converted to multi-media programmes and the time saved on the preparation and presentation of lectures applied to tutorial work (Fagan, 1971).

With the development of multi-media methods colleges have recently been establishing 'resource centres'. These take two forms. The majority are centres where students can preview films, filmstrips and other audio-visual materials for use on school practice, or produce their own materials for these purposes, and comprise workshops, viewing rooms, sound studio, storage and other facilities. A minority, however, are developing adult study facilities for students to work in multi-media materials, including video-tape recordings, in their main and professional subjects at their own level. There is a good deal of experiment in this respect and the relations with the library vary from college to college.

### The Development of Independent Learning Techniques for Small Groups

As was shown by the Robbins survey, many classes in the colleges number from twenty to twenty-five students. Frequently such classes are divided into small groups of four to six students which are given assignments to be carried out. These groups are the same size as a large tutorial or small seminar group but the degree of independence in which the situation obliges them to work creates a rather distinctive style of outlook and relationships. For this reason it is convenient to use the term 'syndicate' for the sub-groups of a class.

The most frequent use of a syndicate method of organization is for practical tasks, such as conducting a local survey, making models from scrap materials, or producing a mime, within a professional course of some sort.

The technique is, however, being increasingly used for work of a more specifically academic character. Case-study material, for example, may be provided in print form, drawn from records of delinquent or otherwise maladjusted children, and the students required to interpret them in terms of psychological and sociological principles already studied. Or the material may consist of demographic information about a local authority's area and schools, the exercise consisting in the creation of a plan for secondary reorganization. Again, as we noted in connection with the use of television, the case-material may be the data of a simulated school, including information on the staff, the neighbourhood and the pupils. Such exercises may be used as a concrete introduction to general principles, or alternatively as the concrete application of general principles. They have the merit of bringing the general and the particular into close relationship, and both staff and students report a high degree of involvement and effective marrying of the theoretical with the practical, in the great majority of the participants.

In the examples quoted above, the exercises do not themselves add up to a systematic academic course: either they are practical exercises on general principles already expounded, or they are exercises leading into formal expositions. They are essentially ancillary to the formal instruction. The problem is to harness the syndicate mode of organization to a course that involves a systematic conceptual development. This has been solved in some colleges in the following way. In a course on the sociology of education the syndicates have been given assignments consisting of three or four questions on a specific topic, with detailed references to selected books provided by the library, and have been required to hand in reports worked out jointly within the syndicates. The lecturer then summarizes the findings of the syndicates in a formal lecture and holds a plenary discussion with the whole class. Assignments which are indispensable have been worked by all syndicates; others have been distributed among the syndicates (Collier, 1970).

A course on religious knowledge has been taught in a similar way. In a course on kinesiology the syndicates have reported back direct to the class and have been provided with any equipment or demonstration materials required for communicating their findings.

An endemic problem in the colleges is ensuring that students read widely and critically. The writing of essays is the usual technique used by tutors for ensuring that reading is done but where essays are based on books much of the material shown up is derivative and lacking in value. One of the advantages of the syndicate approach is in the stimulus it gives to the students' individual reading and to their desire to make use of books as tools of thought.

An important problem raised by these more student-centred techniques is that of assessment. Methods of examination are an important 'teaching method': what a student gives his greatest effort to is influenced by what he believes his examiners are rewarding him for; and in the academic field this is interpreted largely in terms of the examination technique used. Orthodox written examinations tend to set a high premium on memorized information on facts, concepts and received opinions, and skill in marshalling a complex argument in a short time. The reports of those who have worked with syndicates point to a striking increase in the involvement of the students, a more active and selective attitude towards the books they use, and a quicker appreciation of the bearing of first-hand experience and academic reading on each other. Programmed learning techniques similarly tend to foster certain qualities. If such talents are regarded as important, their development must not be prejudiced by inappropriate types of assessment. A good deal of experiment is taking place in this sphere in the colleges, and indeed a virtue of the ATOs has been the freedom for experiment they have accorded to the colleges. As the colleges extend the variety of techniques available and objectives attainable, so it will become more necessary to make aims explicit and to regard the formulation of agreed objectives as a normal part of college procedure. Correspondingly, it will become necessary to plan systematically the sampling of student activities in various types of academic and professional performance and the adaptation of assessment procedures to the declared objectives.

The evidence recorded above indicates a very general movement of opinion in the colleges towards more flexible, more informal, more realistic methods of teaching in all sections of the curriculum. The breaking of the inherited mould itself, however, raises important problems, which require separate attention.

## Underlying Problems

The most striking features of the above developments are two: the growth of student-centred methods; and the increased use of audio-visual techniques. The fundamental questions posed by this proliferation of fresh approaches are: how is one to choose between them? How can one measure the effectiveness of the different techniques? What criteria is one to judge by? It is useful to quote an example of one attempt to assess the effectiveness of a teaching method, namely McLeish's careful and detailed study of the lecture technique (McLeish, 1968).

McLeish begins by reporting Trenaman's experiments. Trenaman played sound tapes of forty-five-minute lectures by distinguished speakers to volunteer groups of adult students, sixth form pupils, and others. He divided a class into three groups, sending one group out after fifteen minutes and a second after thirty minutes. They were tested on two occasions on the information retained: first after the lecture, and second a week later.

The reader will notice in Table 14.1 the very small percentages of information retained, and the poor results of those who heard the whole lecture. A week later it was found that those hearing only the first fifteen

Table 14.1
Recall of Broadcast Talk: Trenaman's Data

| | Amount Recalled Immediately, Expressed as a Percentage of Material Heard | | | | | |
|---|---|---|---|---|---|---|
| Group Hearing | First 15 mins. | Second 15 mins. | Third 15 mins. | Total | Possible Score | Percentage |
| 45 mins. | 20 | 24 | 15 | 69 | 300 | 20 |
| 30 mins. | 23 | 27 | — | 50 | 200 | 25 |
| 15 mins. | 41 | — | — | 41 | 100 | 41 |

minutes recalled twice as much as those who had heard the whole forty-five minutes.

McLeish gave a lecture to a number of college of education students on a psychological subject with which they were unfamiliar. The students were instructed to make whatever notes they wished, they were supplied with a brief summary, and they were warned of a test. They were divided into three groups on a random basis. After twenty-five minutes Group III were sent out and did a test on the material of the whole lecture. After forty minutes Group II did the same. After the end of the sixty minutes Group I followed suit. The test given was based on multiple-choice questions, true-false statements, and so on; most of the items tested factual information. Two other groups of students completed the test without having heard the lecture but having been supplied with a summary. Each group consisted of five students. The results are shown in Table 14.2.

Table 14.2
Recall of Lecture: Norwich Experiment

|  | Part I | Part II | Part III | Total |
|---|---|---|---|---|
| Possible Score | 270 | 285 | 250 | 805 |
| Group I | 176 | 130 | 153 | 459 |
| Group II | 196 | 147 | 35 | 378 |
| Group III | 169 | 84 | 47 | 300 |
| Group IV | 106 | 94 | 45 | 245 |
| Group V | 48 | 49 | 43 | 140 |
| Totals | 695 (52%) | 504 (35%) | 323 (26%) | 1,522 (38%) |

In order to eliminate the influence of the summary and other incidental factors, shown in the scores obtained by the students who had not heard the lecture, the experimenter removed all those items of the test in which Groups IV and V did as well as Groups I, II and III. The result is shown in Table 14.3. It will be noticed in Table 14.3 that there was no falling off of scores for the groups which left the lecture room later. McLeish explained the lower scores on Part II as due to this being a more theoretical and abstract aspect of the topic. The differences between the groups for Part I of the lecture were not statistically significant. Group I repeated the test a week later, without having had recourse to their notes or the duplicated summaries (see Table 14.4).

Table 14.3
Adjusted Scores: Norwich Experiment

| | Part I | Part II | Part III | Total |
|---|---|---|---|---|
| Possible Score | 181 | 134 | 199 | 514 |
| Group I | 49 (44%) | 34 (25%) | 96 (48%) | 209 (41%) |
| Group II | 99 (55%) | 46 (34%) | 0 | 145 (46%) |
| Group III | 72 (40%) | 0 | 0 | 72 (40%) |
| Group IV | 0 | 0 | 0 | 0 |
| Group V | 0 | 0 | 0 | 0 |
| Totals | 250 (46%) | 80 (30%) | 96 (48%) | 426 (42%) |

But when one looks at the methodology of the experiment one is bound to ask what assumptions are being made. The first appears to be that the object of a lecturer is to communicate information about facts, about concepts, about theories, about the views of various authorities. These are the things that have been tested. It is assumed by both lecturer and students that they should absorb and retain this material. To what extent are these suitable objectives in higher education? How far is it proper, in testing the effectiveness of a teaching method, to *use these criteria exclusively*? How should those objectives be balanced against other objectives which may be pursued and which fresh techniques are bringing within practical reach?

These questions cannot in the present writer's opinion be answered in purely objective terms; they inevitably, and properly, raise questions regarding the values of the academic community concerned and the way that community perceives its task. Different college communities, different individual members, may set very different values on the qualities evoked by different teaching methods; they may perceive the tasks of the students they send into the schools, the qualities of these students, and their own

Table 14.4
Immediate and Delayed Recall: Norwich Experiment

| Group I | Part I | Part II | Part III | Total |
|---|---|---|---|---|
| Immediate recall | 44% | 25% | 48% | 41% |
| Recall after one week | 14% | 17% | 20% | 17% |

functions in very different ways. These elements of *value* and *perception* have inescapably subjective aspects which require to be recognized. This is not to say that objective evidence on the effects of different teaching methods is not required; the availability of a wider range of methods calls for more systematic investigation of their effects.

The fact is that the technical developments of the last two decades have created a new situation in the educational world, in which a vastly greater range of teaching methods have become available than has ever been possible before. In addition, social changes on a global scale have led to a much greater demand among students for effective participation in their own education. It has become urgent for the academic communities of the colleges to embark on the arduous and indeed soul-searching process of making explicit their aims and objectives and ordering their priorities; and on the equally difficult and refractory task of assessing the effectiveness of their courses for achieving the declared aims and objectives. It is in their pioneer work in these two respects that the Open University may have made its most significant contributions. In designing a course a group of perhaps six academic teachers, two specialists in educational technology and two from the BBC have found it necessary to spend a vast number of man-hours on agreeing on the essential concepts, the factual content, and the situational contexts of a course, the major intellectual skills and attitudes to be attained, and the distribution of the material between the media available – television, radio, print, and practical exercises. The problems of creating test instruments for assessing the students' acquisition of the content and the skills have similarly been complex and obstinate. But these appear to be the first attempts of a university body to tackle these problems on a large scale and they have revealed both the difficulty and the practicability of the venture. How much more complex are likely to be the analogous problems where the profession concerned is responsible for a calculated effort to influence both the social and the individual, the personal and the intellectual development of young human beings.

This is not to say that the other problems mentioned are to be set aside: the problem of relating academic studies to first-hand experience; the relations between college courses and practical work in schools; the relation between staff aims and student aims; the adaptation of examination methods to the purposes specified.

The over-riding questions of defining objectives and evaluating courses raise in an acute form the general problem of innovation: how is a college staff to recreate itself as a consciously self-evolving academic community? What part is to be played by the principal? The college academic board? The committee structure? The student body? What becomes quite clear is that the decision-making body, the college academic board, needs to take a long hard look at the college's courses and this probably can only be achieved by setting up working-parties to examine the aims and objectives of the different courses, the teaching methods used in them, and the effectiveness of the courses for achieving the declared aims. What structures are needed in ATOs to facilitate such development, or – on a national scale – in such bodies as the DES, the National Council for Educational Technology, or a professional body such as the ATCDE? NCET has already taken the initiative in setting up a study-team to examine the college's needs for learning materials and to plan a production system for them, and if the resulting proposals (Collier *et al.*, 1971) are implemented they may give an important impetus to the developments here indicated. These are some of the difficult questions which are provoked by the current developments in teaching methods in the colleges of education.

The present author is greatly indebted to Dame Beryl Paston Brown, formerly Principal of Homerton College, Cambridge, for very kindly reading and commenting on this chapter.

# Part 5

IN-SERVICE TRAINING

CHAPTER 15

# The First Year of Teaching

### JOHN TAYLOR AND IAN DALE

The experiences encountered during the first or probationary year of teaching are probably more crucial to the new teacher's future career than is the case in many other professions. Two factors in particular, the suddenness of the break from the work done in initial training and the feeling of a need to master the whole job at once, throw a considerable strain on the new teacher. Moreover, teachers – more than many other professionals – work largely in isolation from one another and may be less conscious of either adding to, or drawing from, an existing and organized body of professional knowledge (Lortie, 1969). This problem of professional induction into a new role and a new setting is likely to remain in existence even if major structural changes (such as those proposed by the 1972 Government White Paper) take place in the present pattern of teacher training.

In this chapter we will attempt to outline the conditions under which teachers serve their probationary year, the policies and practices towards them of agencies concerned with their welfare, and the experiences and problems which they encounter. Only a relatively small amount of writing and research has been carried out in Britain concerning the probationary year but we have been able to draw upon findings arising from the Bristol University probationary year National Survey with which we have both been associated and, unless otherwise stated, any research findings contained in this chapter may be assumed to have been taken from this source. Like most other research data in this field, of course, these findings only suggest the reality of a situation as perceived by either the probationers or their head teachers (Taylor and Dale, 1971).

We have chosen to examine and discuss the probationary year under six headings: 1. the statutory provisions for probation; 2. the appointment and placement of probationers; 3. the probationer's experiences and problems within the classroom; 4. the probationer's experiences and problems within the school at large; 5. the effect of starting teaching upon the probationer's personal life; 6. the in-service training and assessment of probationers. These six aspects of the probationary year are, of course, closely inter-related, and issues or problems associated with them are not, of course, confined to beginning teachers.

## 1. The Statutory Provisions for Probation

While the attitudes and experiences encountered by individual probationers may vary widely, the broad conditions and general characteristics of the state of probation itself are common to all maintained schools throughout England and Wales. The current detail of such policy and procedures are contained in the Department of Education and Science Administrative Memorandum 10/68, the most salient features of which may be summarized as follows:

(a) The initial period of service of a full-time teacher who has successfully completed an approved course of teacher training shall be a probationary period of one year but for other teachers it will be two years. During this time he may be required to satisfy the Minister of his practical proficiency as a teacher; but in exceptional cases the Minister may approve a probationary period which is less or more than one year, or dispense with it entirely.

(b) Probation, as such, relates to teachers employed in maintained nursery and primary schools, secondary (but not direct-grant grammar) schools, and special schools to which the Handicapped Pupils' and Special School Regulations, 1959, apply. No matter how long a teacher may have taught in a direct-grant grammar school, for example, he may nevertheless be required to serve a probationary year if and when he transfers to teach in a maintained school.

(c) There exist two procedures of probation: briefly, under procedure A, the main assessment responsibility for a teacher's probation rests with the employing authority, while under procedure B (which usually applies to untrained graduates) this responsibility is shared by the employing authority and HM Inspectorate.

(d) If at the end of the probationary period the Minister decides that the teacher is unsuitable for further employment as a qualified teacher he shall not be so employed. In borderline cases, however, the period of probation may be extended for a further six months and then reviewed again.

(e) Teachers on probation should be placed in schools where working conditions are favourable to their success and where a head teacher or an experienced member of the staff will help and advise them in their work. It is the authority's responsibility to make arrangements for more general help and guidance to supplement that which the head teacher and staff can give, and to see that the teacher knows to whom he can turn for it.

In fact very few probationers fail completely and have their employment terminated: in 1964–5, for example, only twelve out of some 20,000 probationers. However, about one in twenty-five of these 1964–5 probationers had their probation extended for a further six months' period and this appears to be a fairly constant proportion.

Both government memoranda and reports and a broad consensus of opinion within the teaching profession have long declared that the probationary year should not be seen as only a period of trial but also as a further year of professional training. For example, as long ago as 1944, McNair forecast that

> to make the probationary year an effective part of the training of all students will take a long time and entail considerable development of administrative machinery. [The failures] will be few, and the main purpose of the probationary year is not to catch them out, but to help the young teacher to settle into his profession with the minimum of disappointment and discomfort. The damage done to a young teacher . . . may be irreparable and such tragedies can be prevented only by a properly organised system of probation, which is regarded as a continuation of the teacher's training period.

On the other hand, a number of voices within the profession have long argued that only lip service has been paid to this 'training' concept of the probationary year. Thus Plowden (1967) concluded that 'it is doubtful if the majority of young teachers are given the conditions and guidance in their first posts which will reinforce their training and lead to rising standards in the profession as a whole'. Even head teachers have described the present reality of the probationary year as being, in most cases, a hollow mockery of what it should be (HMA and HMC, 1970), and the James Committee concluded that 'nothing depressed [them] more than the gross inadequacy of the present arrangements for the probationary year'.

Necessarily, the form taken by the arrangements for the probationary year is largely a function of the forms of initial and in-service training. At present, therefore, its main function appears to be that of a filter rather than that of bridge or a springboard. If, however, initial training went on for four or five years and included prolonged periods of internship, then the need for a probationary year in any form might be considerably less than is the case at the present; the converse is also true. In both cases, however, it is likely that many problems associated with induction into a new school and/or professional situation would remain. Thus the discussion on probationary year practice and experiences which follows will inevitably reflect the existing patterns of initial training which have been detailed earlier in this volume.

## 2. The Appointment and Placement of Probationers

In their final year, students in colleges and departments of education begin to look for a job and the process of their application, appointment and placement gives most of them their first specific glimpse of the probationary year conditions and experiences which lie ahead of them. There are a number of elements within this process of probationer appointment which are worth exploring.

If we consider the structure of occupational opportunities available within the profession it is clear that, until very recently, nearly everyone with a teacher's certificate would be able to find a job. Even within this overall sellers' market, however, differences have long existed between more and less popular authorities and regions. Moreover, differences exist between primary and secondary school applicants: most of the former are appointed initially to the service of a local education authority (LEA) 'pool' and only learn the name of their school sometime later. Secondary teachers, on the other hand, more typically apply for a particular post within a school. Thus the openings available to secondary teachers are much more clearly differentiated and in a sense the professional implications of their applications are much clearer than in the case with most primary teachers.

The state of job opportunities as perceived by the beginning teacher himself, however, may be quite different from that suggested by overall national vacancy figures. For research (e.g. Duggan and Stewart, 1970) suggests that personal rather than professional reasons guide the LEA or school choice of most teachers at all stages of their careers and many would simply not consider vacancies in parts of the country distant from their own homes (Taylor, 1967). When a nationwide sample of probationers were asked to state the factor which had most influenced their choice of LEA or school area, then it became clear that most were attracted to their home area (see Group 1 in Table 15.1). Some had applied to areas where their spouse would be working; some seem never to have considered the possibility of working away from their home area; and some stated that they felt an obligation either to their parents or to their own LEA for enabling them to train as teachers. Many other probationers, it seems, return to their home area as a second-best choice (Group 2) with some of these feeling they simply could not afford to live away from home in their first job.

The probationers in Group 3 were attracted by the social and aesthetic amenities of a particular area. Several of these were girls who had moved to London or other large cities and taken a flat with a group of friends from college. Others in this group were teachers with specialized leisure interests, such as climbing, which they could only carry out in a few places, and others were those who exploited the relative geographical freedom available to them to teach in areas which they found particularly attractive.

Table 15.1
Factors Affecting the Job-choices of Probationers

| Interviewed probationers who stated (after six months' teaching) that they were most influenced in their choice of LEA or school area by the following factors | Numbers | Percentages |
|---|---|---|
| Group 1: attracted to home area | 202 | 58 |
| Group 2: attracted to home area – as a 2nd best | 65 | 19 |
| Group 3: a liking for the area | 58 | 17 |
| Group 4: attracted by reputation of LEA/Sch. | 18 | 5 |
| Group 5: random choice | 5 | 1 |
| Total interviewed probationers | 348 | 100 |

A small number of probationers (Group 5) apparently chose quite literally at random (in one case sticking a pin into a copy of the *Times Educational Supplement*). Quite the most striking point about Table 15.1, however, is that only five per cent. of those interviewed chose their first teaching post for educational reasons, i.e. those in Group 4.

One reason for this is the lack of professional criteria by which probationers are able to choose posts. Even where they possess such criteria, they have little knowledge of where more favoured practices are being carried out. There are, of course, a very few exceptions to this general opacity; certain local education authorities, for instance, are considered 'progressive' and certain individual secondary schools have a national reputation. Teaching practice affords an opportunity to get to know one or two schools quite well, and it is significant that several probationers who did choose a particular school had become acquainted with it on teaching practice. But, on the whole, it seems a realistic reaction to the situation for final-year students to say, in effect, 'I'm taking pot luck with the school anyway, so I may as well go somewhere where I'll be happy outside school'.

Another aspect of the appointment process which bears examination is that of the interaction of the college and the LEA (or school) concerning data about the student. Notwithstanding that many colleges differ considerably in their language and standards of assessment, it appears that little is known about which elements in the college's personal report on the student are of most value to the LEA or school and which parts are in need of clarification. It seems clear, however, that if full use is not made by many LEAs of the background data available about the probationer this may mean that many heads receive such limited advance information about their probationers that it is of little value in helping them to decide which classes to allocate to the probationer or how to assist and assess his first year's progress.

It could be argued, of course, that should adverse college reports follow them into their schools, there is a danger of weak probationers too easily finding themselves in the position of a dog given a bad name – although this questions the entire set of assumptions upon which colleges and departments of education devote much time and effort preparing reports on their final year students. However, probationer reports may be written from one point of view but interpreted from another and it seems likely that LEAs and heads pick out what they want from college reports and weight the importance of this data accordingly. Thus a probationer's teaching practice grade or assessment (when available) is valued much more by many LEAs than is the verbal report – even after the probationer's appointment has been settled and his placement is being considered. If colleges became aware of the ways in which their assessments and reports are used, or underused, then they might well restructure their form and standardize their nomenclature to the benefit of both the LEA and the probationer.

An important element in the appointment process experienced by any probationer is the amount of advance notice he is given of the details of his post, the children with whom he will be working and the nature of the teaching he will be expected to carry out. One is, of course, aware of the many administrative problems facing LEAs in their task of informing beginning teachers before the end of the summer term of the names of the schools to which they have been appointed. However, notwithstanding the fact that all established teachers normally have to offer at least three months' notice of an end-of-year resignation, the National Survey data indicates that twenty-one per cent. of probationers only learnt their children's age and ability less than a month before beginning teaching while nearly nine per cent. of probationers only learnt the age and ability of their pupils on the day they began teaching! In most cases, this must mean that these probationers are less able to make adequate preparation for their work in the autumn term. It is interesting to discover the degree to which the heads of these same probationers hold a more sanguine picture of this situation: for example, only three per cent. of heads stated that their probationers learnt of their pupils' age and ability within one week of beginning teaching, whereas in fact sixteen per cent. of probationers stated this to be the case. As far as knowledge of syllabus or schemes of work is concerned, the situation is even more marked: twenty-seven per cent. of probationers only learnt this one week before starting teaching and two-thirds of these (eighteen per cent. of all probationers) only found out on the day that they arrived at the school to begin teaching. Once again, in the light of probationer evidence, the probationers' head teachers appeared to be over-optimistic; for only seven per cent. of them stated that they gave their probationers less than one week's notice of their syllabus.

What is perhaps more important than this data is the extent to which there may exist a climate of opinion among many teachers which accepts this situation as unfortunate rather than unprofessional. At no other stage in a teacher's career will he enter a new situation with as little chance as this of knowing what his tasks will be; a change of school or promotion to a new appointment, for example, will usually be known about months beforehand. But it is now, as a probationer, that he is most vulnerable to the effects of under-preparation. In practice, of course, he usually gets on with the job as well as he can and, because the effects of this lack of preparation cannot easily be measured, it may often seem that the situation has satisfactorily resolved itself in the end. Yet, apart from the children's education, the probationer's own levels of expectation have been affected: in other words, what he expected from his professional colleagues and what he felt that they were entitled to expect from him may now have changed, perhaps even without the probationer being aware of this himself. It may be, of course, that those probationers who do not receive this information until the last minute include many who make little effort to seek it; but this assumes that the onus of action should be on the less knowledgeable probationer rather than on the head, and it still accepts the fact that such a situation can be allowed to develop at the pupils' expense.

The culmination of the appointment process should, of course, lie in the intending probationer's pre-teaching visit or visits to his prospective school and colleagues. The fact that – according to the National Survey data – a higher proportion of probationers (ninety-two per cent.) visited their schools than were invited to visit them (eighty-three per cent.) hardly suggests a picture of probationer apathy, although many of these visits may have been close to the start of term. The function and nature of these probationer visits is worthy of examination. For example, by the time they had begun teaching, only about one in three probationers had previously met their pupils, only half had met their predecessor and even in primary schools one in five had not seen their probable classroom; yet one would have supposed that these three objectives were very important to someone planning his next year's work. The question of the timing and duration of a visit raises also that of expense. Although it appears that only a small minority of probationers at present receive travelling expenses for their visits, an expenses-paid two- or three-day 'teaching-visit' might well prove to be a modest but profitable investment on the part of the LEA in improving the probationer's professional preparation, and the level of work for which he now felt responsible and which his head felt could be expected of him.

It appears that as many as one in five probationers may already be paid for teaching during the last few weeks of the summer term in their prospective

schools. Some LEAs make such appointments primarily for training purposes, which means that the probationer is a supernumerary and can
thus spend some time observing his future colleagues at work. A recent
NUT report (1971) recommends that all probationers should spend a paid
three- or four-week summer period in their prospective LEAs – two to three
days a week in the schools and the remainder of the week at the local
college of education or similar institution, where they would find support
in the form of tutorial, library, workshop and residential resources jointly
organized by the LEA and the Area Training Organization (ATO). In such
a peer-group setting, moreover, many problems of accommodation-seeking
might be eased and friendships established which would lessen the future
experience of personal loneliness during the probationary year.

At present, therefore, it seems that the precise pattern of appointment
experience may vary widely from one LEA or school to the next; what is
clear, however, is that many probationers will have had a longer and more
careful introduction to their last (final teaching practice) school – in which
they may only have taught part-time, for as little as a month, and with all
the care and support of a teacher, their tutors and their college contemporaries – than they will have had to their first full year of teaching full-time,
and in a school with much less support at hand.

### 3. *The Probationer's Experiences and Problems within the Classroom*

The nature of the problems people face in any area of their life is a function
of the way they define the particular situations they encounter. Take, as an
instance, what many would regard as the teachers' central problem, discipline. Discipline is only a problem for teachers where the situation is
defined by them, or by others with power over them, as one in which they
must 'control' the pupils. Empirically, of course, nearly all teachers know
that this is expected of them, but we should not take it for granted that
teachers inevitably experience discipline problems or any other kind of
problem. We should look at their definition of the situation and the various
influences upon it and then ask why they encounter the problems they do.

There are some very clear influences on the way teachers define their
situation. These can be divided into those which derive from broad cultural
expectations of teachers and those which vary with the particular teaching
situation. The broad cultural definitions are mediated to the beginning
teacher in three main ways. The first, and perhaps the most potent of these,
in his own experience as a pupil. The second is his professional training, with
which the other contributors to this volume have dealt in detail. And the
third is his employing authority which, as a public body, officially mediates
to him the views of those who pay his salary. Evidence from a study carried
out by one of the authors on reasons for extensions of probation by local
authorities suggests that good discipline in the classroom, effective teaching

techniques, and some sort of moral rectitude are the major expectations of the teacher held by this group. To oversimplify, in the terms of these cultural definitions of the teaching situation, the teacher is expected to be in control of the classroom, to be teaching, and the pupils are expected to be learning what he is teaching. We should not forget either one further important influence, that of the pupils' own definitions of the classroom situation. One way in which the impact of these is manifested is in the differential salience for primary and secondary school beginning teachers of technical and discipline problems. Thus, primary beginning teachers mention most frequently technical problems concerning the teaching of reading and the teaching of wide ability groups; secondary beginning teachers, on the other hand, are concerned with problems of attempting to work to a syllabus and, above all, in coping with individual and class discipline worries.

When we come to the specific situational influences, the beginning teacher may experience a number of difficulties not only in adapting his general training to a particular situation but may also encounter more problems than do established teachers simply because he may be treated differently from them. For example, it is often stated that beginning teachers are given more difficult or less able classes than are the 'old hands' of the staff. Although the National Survey evidence shows that the majority of beginning teachers felt that their class was about the same in ability as the school's average, twice as many (ten per cent.) felt that they had been given classes of below-average rather than of above-average ability. This in any case raises the issue of whether beginning teachers should be given not merely average classes but those which are better than average in ability or difficulty. This may happen in some schools, but we suspect that many probationers' experiences reflect the wider truth that, in general, the most able teachers are not assigned to the least able children. However, while a number of beginning teachers profess eagerness to undertake posts for which they are poorly qualified in order to obtain an appointment in the city or area of their choice, research suggests that the overwhelming majority teach both the age range and the specialism for which they were trained.

Many LEAs have quite clear placement policies which preclude the employment of a probationer in very large or difficult classes, as a supply or floating teacher, or with backward children. But in areas or times of teacher shortage, such policies are not always easy to enforce. Cornwell (1965), for example, found that seventy per cent. of his Midlands sample of infant school probationers were given a reception class to teach, and the writers learnt of one infant school in a large city which was staffed by six probationers and a head teacher. In such areas a vicious circle of rapid staff turnover can develop with the result that throughout their primary school life some children will never have been taught by other than probationers.

A further research finding suggests that those probationers who find out about their class ability and syllabus at the last moment are more likely to have been given backward classes or classes of below-average ability; indeed, in a number of instances it appears that a small number of probationers arrive at the school on the first day of the autumn term to discover that they will be working with children of well-below-average ability for the majority of their teaching time! This link between inadequacy of notice and below-average class ability levels suggests that some of the probationers who are in most need of preparatory support are least likely to receive it. In fact, it would seem likely to produce a situation of maximum stress as far as the period at the start of the probationer's career is concerned and suggests that circumstances leading to such situations need more intensive study within individual LEAs.

Close examination of individual school situations is required before any assessment can be made of the extent to which probationers in an over-crowded school have to 'work their passage' in makeshift teaching conditions before being given accommodation similar to that enjoyed by most teachers in the school. Nevertheless, whether the most effective (and probably longer-established) teachers should automatically expect to work in their school's poorest teaching accommodation precisely because they are most able to cope with such a situation is another issue worth exploring in greater depth by all members of the profession.

Although heads are more inclined than probationers to perceive discipline as one of the most important problems facing beginning teachers, there is evidence to suggest that few probationers feel that their head teacher is breathing down their neck and closely controlling the quality, pace and emphasis of their work. Certainly it seems that most heads tend towards allowing probationers freedom to work largely along their own lines. One traditional method by which many heads supervise their probationers, of course, is by means of regularly obtaining lesson notes, schemes of work or records, and this is particularly true of primary heads. In secondary schools, there is always the possibility that responsibility for giving support and guidance to the probationer's teaching in the classroom will fall between the headmaster and the departmental head; this appears to be a particular danger in those schools which through reorganization have rapidly changed both their size and their internal structure and conventions. The nature and extent of the support and guidance experienced by probationers within the broader school community is of crucial importance, and to this we must now turn.

### 4. The Probationer's Experiences within the School at Large

The importance to the beginning teacher of the support and stimulation which he receives from his head and colleagues can hardly be over-emphasized. Anselm Strauss and his colleagues (Strauss *et al.*, 1964) have suggested that

> as professionals enter and travel among institutions, their professional identities are likely to be deeply affected by the particular institutional conditions they encounter. Some situations allow them to fulfil and elaborate upon the aspirations with which they entered. Others thwart them – perhaps to the point of forcing withdrawal or induce subtle, even dramatic changes as in conceptions of their professional selves. They may even divert the professional into other career paths. Consequently, institutional affiliations should be regarded as fateful to some degree in the development of professionals.

It seems likely that beginning teachers in particular are lastingly influenced by the conventions and values of their first school, although problems arising from relationships with colleagues are, of course, encountered by all teachers. In their discussion of the dissatisfactions with teaching of a group of teachers with five years' experience, Rudd and Wiseman (1962) suggested that

> the irritations reported by this group of subjects would not have been banished by increased public expenditure on salaries, buildings and reducing the size of classes. Apparently, however, much benefit could accrue at little, if any expense through the improvement of human relations in schools.

While sometimes the beginning teacher alone can resolve his classroom difficulties, a great deal can be done by his head and his colleagues about any school community problems he faces. Although at the beginning of the year some problems – such as shyness and lack of confidence – will be common to most probationers, the importance of others – such as unfamiliarity with his children's home background – will depend both upon the sort of school and neighbourhood in which he is teaching and upon his own class background and training.

It is tempting to assume that a probationer's greatest need for advice and help from his head and colleagues in coping with such problems is at the beginning of his first year and that his needs decrease steadily throughout the year, as his confidence and competence develop. There appears to be some evidence that the opposite situation may obtain, however, for the National Survey findings show that the proportion of probationers who feel the need for more advice from their head and colleagues is half as high again at the end of the first year (twenty-three per cent.) as it is at the beginning (only fifteen per cent.). The more one considers this situation the less surprising it seems; for the more relaxed and competent the probationer becomes then the more he will want to extend and develop his work –

and so increase his appetite for advice and guidance for the best possible reasons. One only needs to support this assumption by extrapolation in time: on an in-service course one expects a group of teachers with four or five years of experience behind them to be much more demanding of advice than would be a group of students or probationers. In terms of a beginning teacher's pace and direction of development, it is obvious that the twelve months of probation constitute a quite arbitrary and irrelevant time period. Further research into this first year of teaching might reveal, for example, that the type of advice which beginning teachers feel they require in their first term differs markedly from the type of questions their experience has led them to ask by the time they are in their third term. It may be that many heads administer to the first order of needs (particularly when the beginning teacher finds himself working in an unfamiliar school environment) but that far fewer of them recognize the gradual development of the second. One suspects that, if this is the case, it forms a good example of the way many teachers regard development and progress within the present probationary year: 'If you don't fail or get extended then you've passed.' Compare this view with that used in colleges concerning student development and progress; the tutors there are not merely concerned with the potential failures and borderline passes. They are also concerned with developing and assessing the strengths of students of both average and above-average ability.

Any attempt to measure something of a school staff's friendliness towards probationers is necessarily a delicate and difficult task, since this comes close to involving probationers in making judgements on their colleagues – albeit as a group. As far as the National Survey data is concerned, however, the overwhelming proportion of probationers find their colleagues friendly and usually willing to take the initiative in offering them help and advice. Allegedly, however, one of their commonest experiences is to be told by an older member of their school staff to forget much of what they have learned at college and this is often taken to refer to the more permissive teaching regimes which may have been advocated during training. That this attitude still exists widely on the part of school staff is open to question, but certainly many probationers still find a sharp difference between the teaching atmosphere pervading their college and that in their first school: for example, the National Survey data suggests that only a minority of probationers initially found it neither more permissive nor more controlled than that which their department or college had led them to consider was most effective.

Evidence from a number of sources, of course, suggests that probationers' attitudes harden and become more conservative during the course of their first year's teaching (Getzels and Jackson, 1963). Thus many probationers, who initially felt that their informal or progressive teaching approaches were being resisted by more authoritarian or formal approaches favoured by their head and senior colleagues may, by the end of their probationary year, have moved, consciously or otherwise, much closer towards these colleagues' views. Where he feels himself to be the odd man out in such situations, the probationer may experience considerable stress. Some of this may be both inevitable and desirable and can be seen as part of the probationer's first-year learning experience. But in other cases it may lead to disillusionment, lowered teaching standards and even wastage from the profession. It is worth remembering that if we wish schools to change their teaching approaches, then probationers are necessarily frail change-agents.

The most pressing research need in this area is for an examination of the exact processes whereby a probationer acquires advice and counselling from within the school setting. The roles of the head and a colleague of the probationer's own choice are at present of over-riding importance when compared with those of inspectors, college tutors or any outside course or agency. But we know little of how the head (or his departmental head) goes about helping both weak (and strong) probationers to develop their professional skills. And while most probationers appear to rate a colleague's advice and support more highly than anyone else's, their comments suggest that the staffroom rarely seems to be used as a deliberate means of facilitating probationer induction; and the National Survey revealed that nearly one in four probationers found staffroom conversation to be of little or no help to their work. Furthermore, a minority of probationers appear never to have attended a full staff meeting throughout the course of their entire first year of teaching.

One solution to the problem of providing the probationer with a more supportive school situation may seem to be fairly obvious: the appointing of a teacher within the school whose special responsibility is designated as that of caring for probationers. Indeed, as many as half the heads in the National Survey sample claimed that such appointments already existed in their school (although fewer than half of these heads' probationers appeared to know of the existence of these same tutors). Yet the creation of such an appointment may create fresh problems of an institutional order. Unless his duties are carefully defined and agreed by all the staff, one can foresee some conflict arising between a 'professional tutor' and, for example, the probationer's head of department. It is important, therefore, that the role and work of such professional tutors should be both defined and developed: in large secondary schools, at least, there would appear to be a case for such teachers meeting with the LEA inspector and local college and department of education tutors to discuss ways in which the progress of their probationers might most effectively be assisted and assessed. If regional networks of such tutors are ever to be developed (either in or out of schools) then their broader institutional allegiances and roles will likewise need careful definition.

## 5. *The Effect of Starting Teaching upon the Probationer's Personal Life*

In most cases, the probationer is becoming not only a teacher but also an adult (and even mature probationers are changing their professional identity). When examining the problems and conditions encountered in the probationer's personal life, therefore, we need to be aware of the mutual influence of what Olesen and Whitaker (1969) call his 'lateral' roles and his professional roles. This is underlined by Becker and Carper (1965) who have pointed out that 'an important part of a person's work-based identity grows out of his relationship to his occupational role'.

How then do the demands implicit in the donning of the teacher's identity affect those entering the profession? Evidence (see Table 15.2) suggests that men and women differ in their perception of probationary year personal problems and we suggest that this may be because men consider their professional role more central to their lives than do women probationers.

Table 15.2

Personal Problems Perceived by Men and Women Probationers

| Personal problems selected by probationers (towards the end of their first year) as being particularly relevant to their present situation: | Men | | Women | |
|---|---|---|---|---|
| | Number | Percentage | Number | Percentage |
| Longer-term financial worries | 547 | 51 | 449 | 18 |
| Immediate financial worries | 392 | 37 | 628 | 25 |
| Nervous stress | 283 | 26 | 996 | 40 |
| Physical fatigue | 247 | 23 | 1,069 | 43 |
| Accommodation problems | 121 | 11 | 200 | 8 |
| Travelling problems | 102 | 10 | 364 | 15 |
| Loneliness out of school | 106 | 10 | 279 | 11 |
| Loneliness in school | 38 | 4 | 158 | 6 |
| Total probationers | 1,071 | 100 | 2,510 | 100 |

For men in our society, it is their occupation which pre-eminently identifies them to others. Thus what 'teacher' conveys to society at large is of great and continuing concern to them. For women, on the other hand, cultural pressures emphasize the centrality of the housewife/spouse/mother role, and play down the importance of what it is imagined will be the temporary occupational role. We might expect to find, therefore, as indeed appears to be the case, that women probationers are more likely to report by immediate or short-term problems (such as physical tiredness) whilst men probationers are more likely to be worried by longer-term problems.

This difference is most apparent on the question of salary. Single men and women must find it equally difficult to live on a small salary, but it is salary as the basic determinant of one's style of life, which, more than any other aspect of a job, bestows identity upon its holder. It is for this reason, we suggest, that men perceive it as a more important personal problem than do women probationers, and this is especially true of long-term salary prospects. Moreover, the perceived and anticipated salary needs of most men differ from those of most women probationers; for instance, few women leave the profession at the end of their first year because they do not earn enough to get a house mortgage.

For both men and women, however, the sharpness of the differences in the roles of student and teacher probably account for much of the fatigue and stress experienced in the first year of work. There is a great difference, for example, between explaining to a tutor one's absence at a nine o'clock lecture (even supposing any such explanation were necessary) and explaining to a head (and then to a colleague who had been deprived of a free period owing to one's absence) that one had overslept. Beyond this there is the responsibility factor; each new teacher suddenly finds himself responsible for the educational progress of a number of children and is accountable for that progress to the children, their parents, his colleagues and his employer. The strain is increased by the isolation of the teaching enterprise and the completeness of one's participation in it. There is no easy escape to the lavatory for a smoke, nor is there usually a confidant at hand when one is needed. Indeed, often there is no other probationer or nearly-new teacher in the same school with whom one can discuss and compare one's progress.

Because no celebrations attend beginning teaching, because nothing marks a beginning teacher, he is expected to behave like other teachers. As Fred Davis and Virginia Olesen (1963) point out when describing student nurses: 'Unable to relate their anxiety ceremonially to an institutional framework outside themselves, they may find anxiety all the more difficult to bear.' The provision of just such an institutional framework – particularly one outside the school – is, of course, very much the concern of the probationer's LEA and/or ATO. The need for such institutionalized provision may be particularly necessary in the case of those beginning teachers who are living away from home and who live alone. Some final-year students may anticipate the stresses of loneliness, fatigue and uncertainty facing them in their first year of teaching and from the comments of many beginning teachers it seems clear that any LEA which manages to establish for itself a reputation of an awareness of, and practical sympathy for, these fears, is likely to acquire a more favourable reputation among final-year college students. Some LEAs have been known to go to the trouble of providing flats and houses for teachers coming to work in their areas, and the existence is known of subsidized teacher social clubs or centres. In many cases, however, much less than this may still prove a valuable investment of effort in attracting teachers and in assisting their progress throughout the probationary year and beyond. Just as beginning teachers often find it difficult to get to know about their new job (until they are actually in the school and doing it), so this must often apply to accommodation, travel distances, salary budgeting and a whole host of other personal and professional matters. Often the mere provision of flat agency addresses or vacancy lists, of school location and catchment area maps, and of useful institutional addresses would serve to reassure many beginning teachers that their employer is visibly aware of, and cares about, their welfare outside school hours. Of course, the dangers of over-emphasizing this approach are obvious: few young adults entering their first financially independent job want to feel that their private lives are being watched over against their wishes or that they are having allowances made for them as far as their work in school is concerned. But there is no reason why the LEA inspector, or university, college or school staff should not be able to present their assistance as something which is readily available but leaves the initiative (and self-respect and self-confidence) with the beginning teacher. Just how much of this supportive work can – and should – be carried out by the LEA inspector, a specially appointed tutor teacher within the school, or by someone more detached from the beginning teacher's immediate professional appointment (such as other teachers, counsellors, or teacher centre, college of education or university staff) is something which both relevant action research projects and professional questioning and discussion should help to answer.

### 6. The In-service Guidance and Assessment of Probationers

As far as most probationers are concerned, their greatest need for support and guidance is inside the school, because that is where the action takes place. But the nature of the support and guidance programmes available to probationers in the local teacher centre, college or university is also important, not least because it can help to influence – both directly and indirectly – the in-school support given to probationers.

If one of the functions of a probationer in-service guidance programme is that of bridging the gap between initial training and future in-service training then its structure, content and setting needs to take account of the strengths, weaknesses, gaps and opportunities which typify these other training experiences. The appropriateness of institutional settings, structures, course content and teaching methods associated with the probationer's initial training in his college or university department of education is at present being questioned. The National Survey findings suggest that although three-quarters of probationers found their initial training to be entirely or reasonably adequate and only two per cent. considered it to be very inadequate, many felt that it contained a number of weaknesses and missed opportunities; in fact, looking back at their college training, most young teachers appeared to want more of everything it offered. Above all, they wanted more teaching practice and method work but also more main subject and more theory of education work. This therefore raises the question: what should a teacher learn in his college and what in his probationary year? Furthermore, what in-service experiences should he be offered or guided towards during his next forty years – and what factors should decide this? Since there will never be sufficient money to permit the adequate in-service training of all teachers then it is important that priorities should be fully thought through by the profession.

It is unlikely that the probationer will hear of, let alone attend, any in-service courses for teachers in general during his first year, the National Survey data shows that, even by the end of their first year, one in four beginning teachers had not heard of such courses. The need for the initiative must therefore come not from the new teacher but from the LEA or other course-organizing agency. Even then, probationer attendance rates at courses held in out-of-school time are often low. National Survey findings show that more than one-third of all probationers – nearing the end of the first year of teaching – had still not met their LEA Inspector or adviser in any setting and nearly four out of ten had not been visited by Inspectors in their schools. A school-time course with one hundred per cent. attendance would thus seem to be economic in terms of everyone's time in ensuring a minimum level of contact with the probationer. It is worth noting also that less than one in five probationers maintain any contact with their old college or department of education, and only one in twenty approach a local college or department for support or advice.

What is also clearly evident (although this varies in extent from one LEA to the next) is that most probationers are ignorant of the procedures and criteria employed in the process of their assessment. The National Survey findings reveal that although nearly half of all LEAs ask for reports on their probationers every term, nearly two out of every three probationers still do not know, towards the end of their first year, in what ways and by which persons their progress is being assessed. Moreover, although extension rates are generally higher in urban than in rural areas, they fluctuate considerably between different LEAs in all parts of the country – suggesting perhaps differences in standards or criteria rather than in quality of entrants. It is worthwhile considering the person or institution most appropriate to carrying out the assessment of probationers. Because they are perceived as threat figures by some probationers the assessment role of Inspectors and advisers may militate against their great potential for organizing and developing the positive aspects of probation. If this is the case, then one long-term solution to this dilemma might be to take the probationary year assessment function out of the hands of the inspectorate and give it to either a General Teachers' Council, or any similar body which might be set up. Although this would raise far-reaching administrative and professional issues which cannot be explored here, such a solution would also result in teachers exercising a greater degree of control over entry to their profession.

In spite of the efforts of unions, subject associations and university schools or institutes of education, it seems clear that the brunt of probationer out-of-school course provision is borne by the LEAs and that little co-ordination exists between LEAs in this field of work. Courses vary in their timing, in their duration, in their pattern, in their contents, and (where any have been consciously developed) in their aims. Although there is evidence to suggest that secondary probationers are less likely than their primary colleagues either to hear of or to attend probationary induction courses, there at present exists only a limited amount of detailed and practical knowledge concerning the development of guidance programmes for probationers.

At present, for example, no one knows whether support for probationers in the form of courses is more valuable if organized before, during or at the end of the first year of teaching, or even whether it is preferable for probationers to get their heads down to the practical business of teaching for a year or two before being encouraged to participate in any form of guidance programme. What appears clear, however, is that whenever the time and whatever the form of the course, most probationers appear to derive benefit from it, if for no other reason than because it enables some of them for the first time to discuss with their peers problems which often seem more personal and intractable when faced alone. For this reason alone it seems essential that induction courses should never be identified as being designed only for weak or for committed probationers; indeed, the larger and more representative the cross-section of probationers, the greater chance there should be of individual probationers examining their own problems or situations in as wide a perspective as possible. Many of these important issues and questions which concern the value and viability of out-of-school courses for probationers have been the subject of a second phase (1968–72) of research carried out at Bristol University. In an early progress report, Bolam (1970) has described this action research programme whereby experimental forms of induction courses have been developed in four very different English LEAs. Inspectors, advisers, college and university tutors, teacher centre staff, and heads and teachers all helped to organize and staff the experimental courses, thus functionally drawing together all the existing institutions and agencies concerned with probationer development. The overall form of the year-long programme normally comprised:

(*a*) A September induction day – held in school time at a local university or teacher centre and during which probationers met representatives of their LEA and other organizations, as well as their prospective tutors;

(*b*) An autumn term series of voluntary afternoon or evening meetings in which small groups of probationers discussed such general problems as discipline and organization;

(*c*) A series of spring term evening or afternoon meetings of tutorial groups who discussed more specialist topics (such as the teaching of reading);

(*d*) An overview day held in school time, in, say, July when probationers were encouraged to review their first year's progress and experiences and to consider their future development.

The entire guidance programme was based upon a curriculum model so that its goals were carefully formulated (thus 'informing the professional judgement' of the probationer was considered preferable to 'increasing his sense of satisfaction' with what might have conceivably been an unsatisfactory situation school or LEA). Likewise, it was considered essential to obtain from both attending and non-attending probationers feedback concerning aims, content, methods, staffing, timing and setting of the course.

In many ways, of course, this programme's greatest value may lie in its function as an 'Aunt Sally' and in its informing and stimulating local developments which will be adapted to local needs and conditions. Indeed, other and quite different models of organized probationer support already exist: in the Leicestershire LEA, for example, a young liaison officer transports probationers from scattered rural schools to an informal early evening meeting at a school in which their host is a fellow probationer. Some other areas have developed other quite different patterns of guidance in which teacher centre leaders exercise a particularly important role.

Notwithstanding any changes made to the pattern of the initial training of teachers, the general problem of professional induction is likely to remain with us, whatever new form it may take. Indeed, as the educational service expands and diversifies, so the backgrounds, working environments, and therefore the induction needs of beginning teachers are likely to become increasingly varied and complex. Yet it is clear that, at present, the positive potential of this year of training and development is not being exploited as fully as it might be. Although it is important that much probationary training must be school-based, it seems questionable whether this task can be carried out by the schools alone; at the very least, the teacher tutors in them need training and support from outside. More importantly, however, it can be argued that there is a case for at least some elements of the probationer's in-service training being carried by tutors who, because they are not fellow employees of the same LEA nor members of staff of the same school, nor officially responsible for his end-of-year assessment, can help him to stand back and evaluate his role and his progress in as wide a professional context as possible. Whether the college, polytechnic or university should be precluded from participating in probationary (as opposed to any other) teacher in-service training is thus another issue of considerable interest and of professional importance. One might speculate also as to whether the probationer response to his in-service courses should ever influence his overall probationary assessment and, if so, what pedagogic and institutional implications might be associated with such a possibility. It may also be worth exploring the desirability of divorcing the support and assessment functions performed by the same LEA personnel.

If improvements in the present situation are to take place, therefore, it seems essential that not only should the findings of relevant research work be taken note of by probationer-course organizers but also that a structure must be created whereby Inspectors, heads, teachers and college lecturers can work together on these courses. For it seems to us that it is only by working side by side that the colleges and school systems will ever get down to developing (albeit only locally) a common language of terms, assumptions, levels and standards. At present, for example, what does the average head know of his nearby college's educational curriculum? And what do tutors know of the declared objectives and ethos of the schools in their practice area? Merely for a head to undertake to explain his school's objectives, organization and curriculum to his own and other probationers (in front of other professionals and on such neutral territory as a teacher centre) would help clarify them wonderfully in his own mind.

Certainly it seems vital that all probationary-year course organizers (i.e. including school-based tutors) should regularly meet with one another and with local college and school staff to help formulate the precise aims and to develop a body of knowledge and range of materials for their courses, bearing in mind the relevant constraints of time and money. For just as the lack of communication between the organizers of courses with closely similar functions but held by different LEAs is clearly apparent, so also is the lack of development of case study, video-tape, handbook and other induction materials, and so also are variations in the thoroughness with which probationer needs and wishes are evaluated before the course is planned.

The 1972 White Paper proposes that, from 1975, each probationary teacher should be released for not less than one-fifth of his first year for professional induction purposes. If this proposal is implemented then the dilemmas and problems about the aims, content, and structure of induction provision raised in this chapter, will be brought to a head. For example, one suspects that – however desirable – it may prove difficult in practice to avoid a situation in which the formal induction process is dominated either by the college, or by the LEA, or by the school. Again, the need to clarify and resolve the relationship between the induction and assessment of probationers (in terms of the criteria, personnel and roles involved) will become crucial. There therefore exists an obvious need for immediate short-term curriculum research and development in this field – quite apart from any later and longer term evaluative research. A large number of newly-appointed full-time 'professional tutors' who will be seeking specific curricula content and techniques as well as more general training to help them carry out their unfamiliar and difficult jobs. They may be based in professional centres (e.g. at universities, colleges, teacher centres, or large schools) but there also exists a clear and complementary need for at least some of these full-time specialized tutors to be visiting the probationer's school and sometimes working with him inside his classroom. For, as we have already emphasized, it is in the classroom that the probationer encounters his biggest problems and where his need is for immediate help geared to a specific teaching situation or problem.

Above all, however, in order to improve the professional standards and expectations of teachers in both their probationary and subsequent years, it is essential that the induction year must be seen as a bridging period between initial training and a comprehensive in-service programme during which established teachers and tutors are prepared to both guide and learn from beginning teachers. Only then will the first year of teaching begin to be less a period of trial and more a stage of continuous training and professional development.

# CHAPTER 16

## In-Service Training

### TOM HOLLINS

To mention 'teacher education' is to arouse an expectation that initial, or pre-service, training is to be discussed. This is because the money we spend and the institutions we have set up are nearly all devoted to pre-service education. And pre-service education is part of our system of higher education, whose function, scope, desirability and expense are continually in the forefront of our concern.

Nevertheless, a climate of opinion has been forming since the Second World War which sees education and vocational training as a lifelong process. A wealthier and more liberal society regards education as a good in itself and insists on more equal opportunities to acquire it. Rapid changes in technology and social attitudes quickly make knowledge and skills obsolete, and suggest that continuous retraining will be more and more necessary. In teaching, initial training is seen as inefficient in preparing students for the classroom, however good it may be as general education. In the last ten years, educationists have come to agree that in-service training is the answer. In-service training has not been seen narrowly as attendance at courses but as 'all those courses *and activities* in which a serving teacher may participate for the purpose of extending his professional knowledge, interest or skill' (Cane, 1969). It was therefore expected that when the Minister of State for Education and Science set up, in 1970, a committee of inquiry into 'the present arrangements for the education, training and probation of teachers in England and Wales' an increase in provision for in-service training would be a major recommendation. The Committee, under the chairmanship of Lord James of Rusholme, completed its work within a year, and its report has recently been published (James, 1972). In general, it has aroused sharp controversy, but there has been a wide welcome for its proposals on in-service training. It suggested that education and training should fall 'into three cycles: the first, personal education; the second, preservice training and induction; the third, in-service education and training', and that the second cycle is dependent on a comprehensive third-cycle system: 'A large expansion of third-cycle provision to give every teacher an entitlement to regular inservice education and training is an essential precondition of a more realistic and rational approach to initial training in the second cycle.'* But in-service education is welcomed for its own sake: 'The best education and training of teachers was that which is built upon and illuminated by growing maturity and experience', and 'a much expanded and properly co-ordinated programme of inservice education and training is essential to the future strength and development of the teaching profession.'† The James Committee puts forward proposals for this expansion, but these should be considered against the background of the present weaknesses in provision. This will now be outlined.

The situation will be described as it applies in England and Wales for which information seems more readily available; and a note on the Scottish and Northern Ireland systems will be added later. No exact figures are available, as they are in initial training, but the Department of Education and Science has estimated that some five- and-a-half million pounds is spent annually in England and Wales on courses for teachers in service (DES, 1970), and it is probable that a large part of this goes on replacements for teachers on full-time, one-year secondment. It is a negligible sum, compared with an annual expenditure of something like eighty million pounds on initial training. A survey undertaken for the DES 'indicated that in the period 1st September 1964 to 31st August 1967, the average time spent in courses was about 11 days per teacher; about one-third of teachers had attended no course and over 5 per cent had attended seven or more courses' (DES, 1970). As an example of regional variation, Cane reports (1969), in his survey of three countries, that thirty-one per cent. of Durham primary school teachers of more than three years' experience had not taken any in-service training, as compared with nineteen per cent. in Norfolk; the figures for secondary teachers were twenty-six per cent. and seventeen per cent. respectively.

There is no national policy or co-ordination, but that may be expected in a country proud of its decentralized educational arrangements. Until recently there was little in the way of regional co-ordination either, and even now under-provision or over-provision, duplication, overlap (of courses), competition and confusion are the hall-marks of most regional efforts, though, on the credit side, pockets of enthusiasm and worthwhile achievement are equally in evidence. An incoherent assemblage of courses is to be expected when they are provided by a multiplicity of agencies and a co-ordinating centre is lacking. Initial training is provided mainly by colleges of education and the departments of education of universities, and their work is co-ordinated by Area Training Organizations, regional bodies based almost entirely on universities. The local education authorities are

* P. 3.    † P. 5.

the biggest providers of in-service training, and they provide mainly short courses, often lasting only a half-day or a day, and seldom longer than a week. There are 162 local education authorities, all providing courses. The universities and many colleges of education will also be providing some short courses in the same areas, though these two agencies are also the main providers of the one-year full-time courses, usually leading to a 'supplementary' certificate or a diploma of a university. In the academic years 1966-7 it is estimated that more than 7,800 courses of all kinds were provided, attended by over 293,000 teachers (but this figure includes many teachers who attended more than one course); among these courses, there were about 150 one-year courses attended by approximately 1,500 teachers. (There would be about 350,000 full-time teachers in service in maintained schools at the time.) The Department of Education and Science, through its Inspectorate, also organizes short courses of high quality, often one-week residential vacation courses. These are the main providers, and their work is financed from public funds. But there are many other agencies, such as the teachers' professional associations, and the 'subject bodies', e.g. the National Association of Teachers of English, or the Mathematical Association, providing courses and conferences. H. E. R. Townsend, an officer of the National Foundation for Educational Research, estimated that there were over 500 separate organizations (including the 162 LEAs, providing in-service training courses for teachers (NFER, 1970), and stated that: 'there is . . . a considerable lack of co-ordination amongst these bodies. So that if something like Primary Mathematics then becomes the particular interest at the moment, there is nothing at all to stop most of these 500 bodies putting on courses in Primary Mathematics. . . .' This is substantially true, if slightly over-stated. There have been two fairly recent developments that promise to bring some order into the arrangements. One is that some of the smaller LEAs have been forming themselves into consortia, to keep themselves informed of each others' plans and to prevent overlap; and the other, even more important development, as it covers wider areas, is that some Area Training Organizations have been able to organize a committee representing all interests in their region, to co-ordinate the provision of in-service training. The DES is encouraging the latter development by making special grants to some ATOs.

The most promising element in current in-service training has been the establishment, mainly by LEAs, of teachers' centres. They are the by-product of the curriculum innovation programmes sponsored first by the Nuffield Foundation and then, from 1964 onwards, by the Schools Council. Curriculum innovations cannot be imposed on schools, and formal courses, while they arouse interest in a few teachers and schools, cannot sustain the effort needed to carry through the changes. The Schools Council has advocated the establishment of teachers' centres so that 'teachers should have regular opportunities to meet together and that they should look upon the initiation of thought, as well as the trial and assessment of new ideas and procedures drawn from other sources, as an integral part of their professional service to society' (Schools Council, 1967). The emphasis is on teachers working together rather than listening to experts all the time. Consequently the Schools Council commended workshops rather than lecture halls.

The accommodation provided for these specialised purposes has usually been of a workshop character, combining the facilities of a demonstration laboratory (whether for languages, mathematics, or science) with that of a practical preparation room. In addition to the workshop it was found convenient to provide in most cases an additional room for lectures and discussion.

A valuable result for the Schools Council, and other innovating bodies, has been 'feed-back' from teachers as to the practicability of their new schemes. The position of the college of education in in-service training is of special interest. These colleges have given pre-service training to most of our primary school teachers and a good number of the secondary. They are staffed by lecturers who have been specially selected for their scholarship and their successful experience as school-teachers. It would seem to follow that they should be leaders in the provision of courses for teachers in service. In fact, they provide few courses compared with the LEAs. In 1966-7 only 4·6 per cent. of courses were initiated by them, although 13·4 per cent. of the courses were located in colleges and, to be fair, both LEAs and universities invite individual lecturers to teach some of their courses. The reasons for this comparative neglect of what might well be a rich source of talent are perhaps threefold. First, the colleges' energies have been strained to the limit during the last fifteen years coping with a vast expansion, on limited resources, to provide initial training for a greatly increased number of teachers needed in a school system where there had been a shortage of teachers since the last war. Secondly, there was no climate of opinion in the country until recently to stress the importance of in-service training, and LEAs and the DES rather discouraged, through staffing and financial disincentives, the involvement of colleges in the work. This, as we have seen, is changing rapidly. Thirdly, there has been some distrust of colleges by teachers and their employers, the LEAs. Practising teachers tend to think that the colleges provide quite a good general education but that on the professional side they are insufficiently thorough, practical and down to earth. LEA organizers and head teachers sometimes see their job, with inexperienced staff, as making good the deficiencies of college teaching, helping probationers to cope with such things as class management and the teaching of reading. This kind of generalization does not apply everywhere. Some LEAs, for instance, when it came to the setting up of teachers' centres, turned to their colleges of education as the natural location for them. But most did not. Some LEAs have tried to make their colleges the natural base for all forms of in-service training. Essex, for instance, has appointed staff who are half-time organizers of in-service training and half-time lecturers in their two colleges of education. As a contrast, and to show what is likely to be a more character-istic state of affairs, one can refer to a report on in-service training in the West Riding of Yorkshire, one of the biggest and most progressive authorities, in educational terms, in the country. The authors, Hogan and Willcock (1967), outline the purpose of their authority's service and describe its well-deserved success. They are particularly proud of the development of Woolley Hall, as a specialized residential centre for short courses for teachers; and of the work of the Education Committee, their fourteen Inspectors and thirty-four specialist advisers. But their five colleges of education are not mentioned at all, though they do carry some in-service training. The colleges would doubtless be found admirable in another context, but it would seem to be a reasonable inference that the LEA officers do not readily think of them as part of the pattern of provision of courses for experienced teachers. This paradox will be referred to again when we come to consider the purposes of in-service training and the future.

Granted there is but a small and unsystematic provision of in-service training, does it give the teachers what they need, in the senses both of what teachers want and what it may be desirable they should have? Without decrying the valuable efforts of the providing bodies, particularly the LEAs, it can be said that improvements could be made. The NFER (1970) hints at a change in priorities:

> When the content of the courses is analysed, we find a heavy emphasis on *subject* courses (e.g. mathematics, physical education, art and craft); only one course in four deals with wider and more general aspects of education (e.g. infant education, counselling, courses for married women returners). Among the subject courses we find great stress on Physical Education, Art and Craft, and Music. This reflects not only the views of the McNair, Plowden and Gittins Reports, but also – and more fundamentally – the number of organizers of these subjects found in the L.E.A.s.

Brian Cane's research for the NFER (Cane, 1969) gives us one picture of what teachers would like. Six topics were requested by more than fifty per cent. of primary and secondary teachers in the three counties he sampled. These were:

1. Learning difficulties that any child might have, and methods of dealing with them;
2. Pros and cons of new methods of school/class organization;
3. Operation and application of new apparatus and equipment, with practice opportunities;
4. Recent findings of educational research in the teacher's area of teaching;
5. Planning and developing syllabuses in detail so that content is relevant to the modern child, and arranged in teachable units;
6. Description and demonstration of methods of teaching 'academic' subjects to 'non-academic' children.

Two other topics had sizeable support, mainly from primary teachers:

7. Methods of dealing with large classes of varied abilities with little equipment or space;
8. Practical details and aims of recently introduced schemes of work, and discussion of teaching results and demonstrations.

And one topic aroused no interest in primary teachers but was valued by more than half the secondary teachers:

9. Construction, marking, and interpretation of schools examinations and assessment tests.

Cane then gives a 'second list' of eleven topics desired by quite large minority groups. Five of these are practical, like the first list, such as the problem of ESN children and studies for prospective head teachers; but the other six are all concerned with study for degrees of further academic work. Teachers were also asked to choose one topic from a shorter list of general headings which they thought should be given priority by organizers. The topics chosen were all 'those that came under the headings "teaching methods, aids and materials", and "the development of new teaching schemes and programmes" '. It is also of interest to note that, as regards methods of teaching to be used at courses, teachers much prefer discussion and the like, which involve the participants in lively interaction, than formal lectures. County Inspectors and organizers were asked to analyse the courses they had provided in 1966–7 under these topic headings if they could. It appeared the topics best catered for were 'the practical details and aims of recently introduced schemes of work', and 'the recent findings of educational research', if 'educational research' is broadly defined to include 'curriculum development'. Four of the topics had scarcely any time allotted to them: new methods of school/class organization, methods of teaching 'academic' subjects to 'non-academic' children, methods of dealing with large classes of varied abilities, and, finally, school examinations and assessment methods.

No doubt criticisms could be made of this research. For instance, there must have been considerable semantic problems in keeping the topics clearly defined, unambiguous, not covering too much ground, and not overlapping; nor are these problems entirely resolved. The author himself draws attention to this difficulty. Again, although the teachers could not think of topics not covered by the questionnaires, they might have responded to other topics if suggested to them. This is borne out by another survey carried out by Townsend, when he was at Manchester University, for the DES (Townsend, 1970). He reports that the teachers surveyed in 1965–6 (9,822 questionnaires were sent out to a national sample of teachers) attended nearly 14,000 courses. Provision fell into two main groups: subject areas and those of a more general and theoretical education nature. The most popular courses fell mainly within the first group, and included primary maths; physical education; arts, crafts and music; secondary science and maths; initial teaching alphabet; and religious education. This is a result similar to Cane's survey. The results where teachers gave their own preferences were, however, rather different, presumably because they had a different check list (based on the provision mentioned above) before them. The most popular choices of course were, in order: B.Ed., primary maths, art and craft, the teaching of reading, audio-visual aids, school organization, the teaching of slow-learning pupils, infant education, comprehensive education and junior education. It is noticeable that only three of the preferences are subject courses. The most important difference between the two researches is Townsend's findings that so many teachers want to take a B.Ed. degree, while Cane found it important only to a minority group of teachers. Nevertheless, there is an overall similarity in the two groups of findings, especially in the three main generalizations we can draw from them: the lack of correlation between demand and provision; the relative lack of teacher interest in subject courses, and, apart from the interest in degrees, the overwhelmingly practical nature of teachers' preferences. The courses which teachers ask for seem to be on topics which providing agencies would also agree are important, so that if teachers are not having such courses, the difficulty is probably due to an absence of feed-back from teachers to providers. In Cane's survey, the majority of teachers complained that they were not consulted sufficiently about the planning and organization of in-service training.

A last and equally important finding to emerge from Cane's research is the lack of interest shown by most teachers towards in-service training and the reasons they give for this lack of interest. There may be few courses, but, with the exception of full-time one-year courses leading to a named award, and degree courses, the number of applications for course places seldom exceeds the number of course places provided by the LEA or university. Yet eighty per cent. of teachers in the survey 'declared positively

11—EOT  *  *

their need for in-service training'. This figure needs to be looked at sceptically for two reasons. One reason is that we almost all respond idealistically when a questioner asks us to choose a good or a bad course of action, though our actual conduct may be different. The other is that even when our intentions are good, we more often than not do not act on them. The implication is that even if more suitable courses were supplied it is not very likely that teachers would rush to join them; unless some deeper motivation than good will could be provided. This problem will also be considered later. Meanwhile, it is important to look at the reasons the teachers give for their lack of interest. These may be grouped into three classes. First, there are the reasons we have already considered, the poor provision and limited choice of courses; with these go the complaint that there is no proper information and advisory service to make it clear exactly what courses are offered, and the level of knowledge and skill needed to tackle the course successfully. Secondly, there are professional considerations; the knowledge that there is usually no replacement available if one goes off to a course, in which case extra work falls on a colleague; and the feeling that one is responsible for a certain group of pupils one knows well, so that there is a reluctance to hand them over to anyone else. And there is the question of promotion; many teachers feel that their employers take no account of attendance at courses and the good work that may be done there when considerations of promotion arise. Thirdly, there are personal reasons. Teachers feel the expenses allowed do not fully cover the cost of attending courses. Then they dislike travelling and residence away from home for any length of time. And family and domestic responsibilities, spare-time activities, and even simply tiredness are often inhibiting factors. Finally, if the replacement difficulty could be overcome they would prefer in-service training to take place in school time, though most were willing to attend courses during the evenings, and for half-days at weekends; and 'a high percentage of teachers were prepared to spend up to one week of their vacation attending a course at a local centre convenient for daily travel' (again good intentions have to be met with mild scepticism). It would appear that even one-year full-time courses on secondment, working for a qualification and usually entailing residence away from home, would be much more popular if they were held in local centres, where daily commuting was possible.

It may seem that the difficulties are much the same for all. But the picture is complicated by the inequity in provision of in-service training opportunities over the country. Some teachers live in a university town, near a college of education, in an LEA area with a rich in-service provision; they can usually get the course they want. Others, particularly teachers in sparsely populated rural areas, have little choice or have to depend on residential courses which they may not be allowed to attend in working time. LEAs vary markedly in the generosity they show to their teachers. Johnson (1971) notes that where the LEA is free to reimburse what proportion of a teacher's expenses it wishes, 'Some county treasurer, or chairman of a finance committee, or even LEA clerk will decide what proportion of tuition, travel, accommodation, and food should be paid to the teacher. . . . The result is that some teachers get next to nothing and some get nearly all their costs.' He points out that some LEAs are generous in supporting a teacher who wishes to attend a course outside the authority's area, and others insist on attendance at their own courses. There is a wide variation in attitudes towards regular absences from school to attend courses; and, of course, it is particularly difficult to get leave of absence in those areas where a bare minimum of teachers is employed. Finally, Johnson condemns 'the sanctions which some LEAs appear to apply when teachers seek secondment, i.e. that of requiring them to return to service for a period of one year or two years with the local authority sending them'.

A note must be added to this survey of provision in England and Wales to describe the position in Scotland and Northern Ireland. Not much can be said as there is little documentation; the most recent history of the training of teachers in Scotland, for instance, by Marjorie Cruickshank, which was published in 1970, makes only fleeting reference to in-service training as an activity of colleges of education; and the annual reports of the Scottish Education Department seldom give more than a page to the subject. Scottish ideas of training have strongly influenced Northern Ireland, so that they are quite similar in provision, and the organization is markedly different from that of England and Wales. The Scottish and Northern Irish systems have been marked by strong central control, and, in Scotland, by a well-organized regional provision of training, especially of initial training, in large non-residential colleges of education. Until fairly recently the colleges were solely responsible for in-service training, but growing demand has outstripped their resources, and increasingly the universities and LEAs are playing a part. The colleges still play the biggest role, however; and the importance of in-service training to the college, unlike the position in England and Wales, can be judged by the resources allocated to it. Sir Henry Wood writes of Jordanhill College of Education, Glasgow, for instance: 'The range and number of courses is such that Jordanhill now requires a vice-principal with five full-time lecturers, an administrative staff and a budget of £30,000 a year solely for in-service work. In addition all college tutors are expected to give appropriate help to the in-service department.' (Wood, 1970.)

The continuing grip of the central authority in Scotland, and its desire to have a clear, national and regional, co-ordinated system of training, is shown by the establishment in 1970 of a National Committee for the In-Service Training of Teachers 'with the three-fold task of identifying needs, of making recommendations on the general pattern of provision, and on the extent to which there should be regional co-ordinating machinery' (Scottish Education Department, 1967). The membership includes the colleges of education, the education authorities, representatives of the General Teaching Council, the teachers' associations, the universities, the central institutions and the Scottish Education Department. Two years later, the Department's Report shows how the organization has developed:

> The whole administrative structure of in-service training has been under close examination by the National Committee for the In-Service Training of Teachers. The National Committee found that in-service training would have to be planned on a more logical and systematic basis, and recommended to the Secretary of State the establishment of four regional co-ordinating committees representing education authorities, colleges of education, universities, central institutions and teacher associations and with responsibility for planning adequate programmes of in-service training in their areas. The Secretary of State has accepted these recommendations, and committees based on Jordanhill, Moray House, Dundee and Aberdeen Colleges of Education are now being established to serve the south-west, south-east, eastern and northern areas, respectively. While these committees will take the main responsibility for ensuring that adequate programmes are efficiently provided throughout the country, the National Committee will remain responsible for arrangements for courses of national interest. (Scottish Education Department, 1969)

Although the Scots score high marks for system and co-ordination, and, as in England and Wales, demand and provision increase year by year (over the four years 1967–70 the number of teachers attending courses increased from 16,834 to 20,066), it is likely that complaints similar to those made by English teachers about type of course and choice of topic would be made if the opinions of Scottish teachers were surveyed. As in the south, there is the same emphasis on fashionable topics such as primary mathematics, and on subjects, especially for secondary school teachers. Here is a summary of the programmes in 1969, as illustration:

> Courses in primary mathematics again attracted the greatest number of (primary) teachers and many were repeated during the year. Other courses which drew substantial enrolments were on science in the primary school, music, art and crafts, and teaching of infants and nursery school children.
>
> The main subjects studied [by secondary teachers] were art, biology, classics, commerce, English, geography, history, homecraft, mathematics, modern languages, modern studies, music and programmed

learning. Courses attracting a substantial number of teachers were held in arts and crafts, the language arts, sixth-year studies, field studies in geography, health, physics, the use of radioactive materials and in the alternative syllabuses of the Scottish Certificate of Education examinations in mathematics, physics, chemistry and biology. (Scottish Education Department, 1969)

Sir Henry Wood (Wood, 1970) stresses the involvement of all partners in in-service training – employers, tutors (at college and university) and 'most significant of all, the teachers themselves. . . . The teachers themselves must decide what is good for them'. An admirable sentiment, but it is unlikely that teachers have this right anywhere and even less likely in Scotland, where there is so much organization from above.

In Northern Ireland, centralization and systematic organization of in-service training have been possible because until recently the Ministry of Education itself has been the main provider, by means of short courses in regional centres and an annual two weeks' summer school.

The Ministry's provision, however, is no longer adequate for the multifarious needs arising from the far-reaching changes now taking place in basic educational psychology and practice. If schools are to derive the maximum benefit from the curricular projects and researches of bodies like the Schools Council, it is essential for teachers themselves to be intimately involved in the trial of new ideas, methods and materials. (Ministry of Education, Northern Ireland, 1968)

Help has therefore been found in the universities and the colleges of education, and professional bodies have made valuable contributions. The LEAs have provided short courses for a number of years, and the number of these increases all the time. It seems that most of these courses too are concerned with subject areas.

This survey of demand and provision has been critical and it may be thought that the providers merit censure. But it is rather the reverse. Until recently there was no climate of opinion in the world of education in which the pros and cons of in-service training could be debated. It was not indifference so much as a blank in educational thinking. Seen in this context, the small band of organizers in LEAs, universities, colleges and elsewhere who have seen the need for further training of teachers, who have had to fight hard for minimal resources and to overcome the indifference of schools, and who have shown such enthusiasm for improving the teaching of mathematics and so on, deserve congratulation. Nevertheless, the defects of a hand-to-mouth provision should be made good now that there is an awareness of the importance of the continuing education of teachers.

We can now consider the recommendations of the James Committee. In general, in-service training (the third cycle) is to be central and an expanded, properly articulated provision is envisaged, as we have stated in the introduction to this chapter. In detail, every teacher should be entitled to release from school with pay for one term every seven years at first, and later every five years; every school should have on its staff a 'professional tutor' to look after the training of its staff members; and a country-wide network of 'professional centres' (amalgamating the functions of the present professional institutions and the teachers' centres) should be set up. All teacher training would be under the control of national and regional co-ordinating bodies. The staffing of schools would have to be more generous, to allow for the extra training functions, and professional centres would need a full-time warden and probably other staff. All this would cost extra money – how much is not specified – though, in what is perhaps a warning note, the Committee says that to implement their report will depend 'more upon the better use of resources already committed than upon a diversion of additional resources from other desirable objectives in social and educational policy'.

A policy of national and regional co-ordination of training is clearly an advance, especially as the regional bodies are to control finance, rationalize provision, and approve centres and courses. It is also proposed to divide up the country into approximately equal regions, so that there would be an opportunity to bring in greater equity of provision than at present. But there would still be serious difficulties to resolve which are not touched on in the Report. One follows from the composition of the proposed Regional Councils. They would not be based on any one institution, but would represent all those bodies and institutions in the region having an interest in teacher training: the LEAs, universities, polytechnics, colleges of education, Open University, CNAA, and teachers; with DES assessors. The academic members would be in the majority, but as the LEAs would still have financial powers, and control over their own colleges, the tensions might become acute. The aim of the James Committee was to give the colleges more autonomy. At the moment, academic control of pre-service training in the colleges rests ultimately with the Area Training Authority which, with one exception, is based on universities; and the LEAs and universities are the two agencies which control the largest sectors of in-service training. James describes the universities' influence over the colleges as undesirable tutelage. But in the controversy following the publication of the Report, the teachers, at least, have made it clear that they wish to strengthen the connections of the profession with the universities rather than to weaken them. The other major professions are also strengthening their links with the universities and polytechnics. James has ignored the attraction of the university for the professions: it not only has high status but engenders respect for its concern for scholarship, standards and research, and for its impartiality. The university can be disinterested in a way that the LEA, responding to political pressures, would find difficult to emulate. There is an argument, therefore, for extending university responsibility for teacher training, not only for pre-service but for in-service training, and giving the ATO co-ordinating bodies the powers proposed for Regional Councils. This is not an argument in any way, of course, for cutting down LEA provision of courses, but for putting ultimate responsibility for the training programmes into the hands of the universities.

Another difficulty not discussed in the Report concerns the differences in outlook on teacher training between the LEAs and the colleges of education, and how these may be resolved. We have already described the tendency of the LEAs to leave pre-service education to the colleges but to try to make good their alleged deficiencies with in-service programmes in which the colleges, for the most part, have no say. The James Committee recommends that the professional institutions, which include the colleges of education and the university departments of education, should join with the LEAs and teachers' centres in planning a comprehensive system of in-service training under their regional bodies. But are colleges and university departments of education going simply to be concerned with the larger, more theoretical courses, and the LEAs with the severely practical, both parties in competition for teachers' patronage? No doubt this is a suitable role for the departments of education, but the college role is not so clear. Since 1960, when the two-year course of college teacher training was extended to three years, the colleges have attempted to establish themselves, with some success, as institutions of higher education comparable to minor universities, or at least liberal arts colleges. The universities have recognized this by instituting B.Ed. degrees in the colleges. Because the number of students training for teaching in the colleges is likely to fall in the 1980s, owing to the expansion of universities and polytechnics, the colleges have been pressing to be allowed to teach for degrees other than education. The James Report, which is as much a document about the higher education system as about teacher training, largely supports their claim. It is recommended that a few large colleges should teach B.A. and B.Sc. degrees, and that a much bigger group of colleges should teach a two-year course of general education, leading to a diploma in higher education, and open to students irrespective of vocation (first cycle), followed by a two-year course of professional education for intending teachers (second cycle) carrying with it the award of a B.A. in education. Degree study is associated with theory and analysis, so it may be thought appropriate that the college role in the third cycle, in-service training, should also be to teach at a highly theoretical level. But the James Committee's proposals for the second cycle cut across this trend. The second year of the second cycle is to be a reformed probationary year and will therefore be practical in nature. But the first year of the second cycle is also to be practical in nature. 'The second cycle should concentrate on preparation for work appropriate to a teacher at the beginning of his career, rather than on formal courses in educational theory'; and 'It is not suggested that educational studies . . . should be banished from the second cycle curriculum but only that their role should be seen as contributory to effective teaching'. Formal educational theory is to be studied in the first and third cycles. This will not be such a straightforward arrangement as it looks. At the moment, educationists in the colleges, following the higher education trend, are committed to the study of the formal disciplines of education. It is likely that they will carry this attitude into second-cycle work, and the course will not be as practical as teachers want. If they do develop practical units, these units will want to move into the practical work of the third cycle, and will be in competition with the LEAs and teachers' centres. This situation presents difficulties but it is not insoluble. How far in-service training should be aimed at the solution of practical problems is something that will be discussed later.

Shortage of money is likely to be a major stumbling block. Amid the general welcome for the James Committee's proposals on in-service training, a good deal of pessimism has been expressed as to whether the government will, or even can, meet a fraction of the cost. Teachers, who believe that educational reforms tend to lead to an increase in their work and their difficulties without a corresponding improvement in salary and conditions, are particularly pessimistic. It is true that resources are applied in a haphazard way in in-service training at the moment. Under-subscribed courses are fairly common, there is duplication and overlap; and, as James says, some of these resources could be reallocated. But the increase envisaged, with all teachers entitled to a release from school with pay for one term every seven years, entailing the replacement of up to three per cent. of the teaching force at any one time by full or part-time replacements, is likely to be very expensive. The James Report is a short document, devoted to polemic and persuasion, and unlike its illustrious predecessor of 1962, the Robbins Report on Higher Education, its arguments are not backed up with facts and figures. Until the Department of Education and Science publishes some forecasts, we do not know how much the increased service would cost. We do know, however, that the country is alarmed by the ever-increasing demands of the higher education sector and it is thought that, in fairness, more should be spent on schools, on buildings and resources, than on the further education of the teachers.

Even if the money is made available, there is likely to be resistance from teachers, particularly head teachers, to the suggestion that classes can be turned over regularly to part-time replacements. This objection has already been made to the recommendation of the James Committee that young teachers in the second year of the second cycle (probationers) should teach only four days a week and attend professional centres on the fifth. It is thought that children will become unsettled and their work will suffer in such a system. As an expression of the strong pastoral sense that is still found among teachers in Britain, the objection has its admirable side. However, as schools become larger, more bureaucratic, more specialized, and increasingly adopt educational technology and methods such as team teaching, such an attitude will be increasingly outmoded, except perhaps in infants' schools. And, of course, some of the continental educational systems have commonly made use of a pattern of teaching where one teacher may work part-time in several schools; and it seems to work. So it is to be hoped that this possible objection will not prevent the implementation of one of the more welcome proposals of the Committee. Teachers in the Cane and Townsend surveys objected to in-service training in their spare time; here is a recommendation which gives them what they asked for – further education during working hours. Of course, this recommendation refers to substantial periods of in-service training – the Report suggests that each should last at least four weeks full-time; it is expected that teachers will still be willing to attend short courses, conferences, and discussions outside school hours. Unfortunately, the full reimbursement of expenses by employers is still unlikely.

It is noteworthy that although the Report recommended that 'an entitlement to in-service training on the scale suggested should be included in every teacher's contract of service', it did not advocate that teachers should be compelled to take it; in fact it considered compulsion undesirable, 'at least initially'. No reasons were given, but this clause 'at least initially' suggests the Committee had no objection in principle to compulsion. Presumably they foresaw that there are not likely to be sufficient facilities available in the next few years to satisfy even the demands of teachers who do want in-service training. And they may wish the service to be spared the strong objections teachers would certainly have to compulsion, as attendance has been voluntary for so long. The case for compulsion rests on the general agreement that schools are provided for the benefit of the pupils. Schools must also satisfy the teachers in them, but in the end it is the teacher's duty to give up some of his autonomy if the interests of his pupils require it. Nevertheless, teaching and learning can only be satisfactory in the conviction that what goes on is worthwhile, and compulsion does not go with good motivation. It would be better if teachers could be brought to want in-service training. One incentive that will certainly be tried is the financial one. In many states in the United States tenure and increases in salary are tied to the successful completion of in-service training courses at stipulated levels. It is true that the system sometimes produces attendance for attendance's sake and some cynicism about the value of the courses taken, but on the whole American teachers are great believers in self-improvement, they accept in-service training as a natural part of professional life, and their teaching profits from it. Linked with the financial incentive is the allied one of promotion. Teachers in the Townsend survey said that attendance at substantial courses should count towards promotion. Linked with this is the teachers' desire that course-attendance should count towards the fulfilment of requirements for obtaining more advanced qualifications, especially degrees. Some universities and polytechnics are likely to experiment with substantial course-modules which can be taken both full- and part-time and would be added together to form a degree-course. This is something like the basis of the Open University degree structure; and clearly the Open University will play an increasing role in in-service training. It was perhaps this system the James Committee had in mind, as well as the longer one-year secondments for full-time study, in their conclusion that 'It would . . . be undesirable to offer direct financial incentives to take training courses, except insofar as these courses led to qualifications recognised by the Burnham Committee as justifying salary additions'.

Ideally the incentive for teachers to undertake in-service training should be the attractiveness of the courses. It is arguable that the courses provided for teachers at the moment are not very attractive. There is the small group of teachers who enjoy the one-year courses leading to advanced diplomas or degrees; another group, much larger, of enthusiastic teachers looking for new ideas or opportunities to try them out; another anxious to gain points for promotion; and another of professional course-attenders who will attend anything, and are not usually highly regarded in their schools. Altogether they are very much a minority. Michael Pollard, an educational journalist, lists some of the complaints of his teacher acquaintances.

There were complaints about tired ideas, incompetent or ill-informed speakers, and the constant re-tilling of well-ploughed ground. 'If I hear any more about Piaget, I'll walk out,' threatened one veteran course attender. Another teacher suspected that some trivial or frivolous courses were devised in order to fill up in-service programmes. (Pollard, 1971)

Pollard feels that the older teacher is particularly suspicious of in-service training. 'This view may be outdated, derived as it is from the time when in-service training for most teachers consisted of sitting in desks made for eight-year-olds at the fag-end of the day listening to second-hand advice from a speaker of probable low grade. . . .' But, in spite of these remarks, the tone of Pollard's article is optimistic. He believes that the answer is in the development of the teacher centres, where the emphasis is on discussion and the solution of problems in a workshop atmosphere, rather than attendance at courses. The James Committee, as we have already said, recommended the creation of a countrywide network of professional centres.

The give and take of ideas at teachers' centres suggests that co-operative work among teachers, at some problem they feel to be worthwhile, is an effective way of raising interest in in-service training among reluctant members of staff. Of course, from the schools' point of view, it may not be enough that teachers become interested in the newer approaches. One of the difficulties about carrying out curriculum development is that it is comparatively easy to interest teachers in it, but very difficult to get any changes made in school curricula, or at least more than temporary changes. The Schools Council has succeeded in arousing interest in its projects in teachers' centres, but it has not succeeded, on the whole, in getting them adopted in schools. Clearly a teacher, even a head teacher, who returns from a course or a centre with new ideas, tends to lose the will to put them into effect in his school if he meets with apathy or ridicule from his colleagues. This would be particularly so in a large secondary school, where the subject departments form a cluster of bureaucracies each anxious at least to preserve, and to extend if possible, the mystique and influence of the subject.

Nevertheless, the best hope for effective in-service training is to make the school, rather than the professional centre, the focus of curriculum development. A school staff setting out to examine their curriculum and methods produce a corporate spirit which arouses interest and determination to experiment, and provides the mutual support which carries its members through difficulties and temporary discouragement. Clearly this would be easier in a primary school, where the curriculum is undifferentiated, but it must be remembered that it is in the secondary school that teachers have mostly to meet the problems of children uninterested in learning, backwardness, and so on. To initiate and carry out this kind of activity is not easy, however. Eric Hoyle, in an article on curriculum change (Hoyle, 1969), reviews the literature which explores the possibilities and the difficulties. It emerges that three things are necessary if the co-operative activity is to be a success: that the atmosphere of the school has to be an 'open' one in which everyone can bring out ideas and feel they are welcomed; that the creation of an open, encouraging, yet none the less critical atmosphere depends very much on the quality of leadership of head teacher and senior staff; and that experts from outside have to be made welcome and their contributions used freely.

These considerations suggest various kinds of in-service training: courses located away from the school for the head teacher and certain kinds of departments, in which ideas about initiating changes can be discussed; short courses for staff, mainly of the workshop kind at professional centres, and which are based on attempted solutions to problems brought out in school; visits to the school by the teachers of courses, organizers and lecturers, who could be brought into staff discussions as outside experts; visits of expert heads and staff from other schools; and visits, throughout a region or locality, by members of staff, to each others' schools. Schemes like this will not be easy to carry through, however. In-service training is in such an undeveloped state that there will be few suitable courses and few experts available at first. One welcomes very much the James Committee's proposal that there should be a 'professional tutor' in every school, 'compiling and maintaining a training programme for the staff of the school', and that such tutors should be 'among the first to be admitted to third cycle courses, so that they could be trained for their new tasks'. But where are the suitable courses for such leaders, and even suitable courses he could recommend to his colleagues? However, the challenge does not present an insuperable task.

This suggestion for school-based in-service training has arisen out of discussion of the question of compulsory attendance for teachers. Of course, this is not to say that gaining teachers' interest is the major reason for undertaking schemes of curriculum development in schools. There is an urgent need to find out what schools should do and then how to implement what should be done. The carrying through of ideas is certainly best done in the schools themselves. But teaching is not like the other professions. Its materials – society, institutions, people, knowledge itself – make it an infinitely complex field of study and application. The education of teachers cannot therefore be limited to bread and butter concerns. It is true that the majority of teachers are impatient of training which is not practical and which does not appear to be solving their immediate problems. Therefore school-based work and work in professional centres will be preferred by most of them. But development in education will only come about through the interplay of theory and practice; and not simply the theory and practice of what to do in school and classroom. Courses of more abstract theory, usually leading to diplomas or degrees, are therefore important as the seed beds of the future, and the teachers who choose them, as much for interest as for promotion, are an important minority.

These are only some of the purposes and types of provision of in-service training. The James Report pointed to a whole spectrum of needs: the extension of knowledge and skills; the retraining of teachers for various purposes, including promotion and change of school; the special training for jobs such as counselling and school librarianship; research; purposes already discussed. The Committee was rightly concerned that in-service training should not be interpreted too literally; it should be able to comprehend the teacher who wants a spell in industry at one end, and the man who likes to sit in libraries and read, at the other. Refreshment is as important as edification.

CHAPTER 17

# Local Curriculum Development*

ALLAN RUDD

## An Exercise in Partnership

The James Report envisaged local curriculum development and evaluation as one important type of third-cycle activity through which teachers can extend their personal education, develop their professional competence and improve their understanding of educational principles and techniques. Such work (among other types) would go on in a network of professional centres, each under the leadership of a full-time professional warden who enjoyed an independent role. The work of these centres would involve bringing into partnership diverse agencies – schools, universities, polytechnics, colleges of education, advisory services, teachers' centres, resource centres and further education institutions – notably in helping to staff the professional centres. The basic principles of this proposal bear a marked resemblance to those on which local teachers' centres were established in north-west England in 1967, though the scale of activities now proposed is greatly in excess of that realized to date in these or other teachers' centres:

> There are two basic principles in which progress on curriculum development should be built: first, that motive power should come primarily from local groups of teachers accessible to one another; second, that there should be effective and close collaboration between teachers and all those who are able to offer co-operation. There is no hierarchy of initiative or control. The co-operative effort of each interest needs to be involved in equal partnerships, and all parties should be ready to give or to seek support.†

This paper presents a critique of some aspects of the North West Regional Curriculum Development Project, in terms of certain of the James principles.

* This paper was first presented on 4 July 1972 as part of a conference held at Leeds Institute of Education entitled *Inservice Education for Teachers: The Next Five Years.*

† Schools Council (1967), *Curriculum Development: Teachers' Groups and Centres (Working Paper 10)*, London, HMSO, para. 27.

But before beginning this I must affirm a basic belief on teacher education which shortage of space prevents me from attempting to justify. I believe that teachers learn in fundamentally the same manner as do their pupils. If we really expect them to adopt demonstrably better procedures in the classroom we must set up appropriate conditions for establishing and maintaining the new behaviours. Just as telling pupils how to carry through a task is not a sufficient condition for ensuring pupil mastery of that task, so merely telling teachers how to improve their teaching or presenting them with persuasive propaganda about the merits of particular techniques is unlikely by itself to lead to improved teaching. I regard it as axiomatic that the teacher who learns from his own (appropriate) experience understands in a way which is just not available to persons who merely try to follow the instructions of others or who seek to please their superiors. For experience-based innovation not only promotes increased pedagogical skill. From the manner in which the new skill is accumulated the teacher concurrently also learns the art of mastering new skills, and that confidence and sureness of touch which are the hallmarks of the full professional. In short, I see the local curriculum development group as a setting within which teachers can become the willing agents of their own continuing professional education.

## Task Orientation

The North West Project is a consortium of fifteen teachers' centres established and maintained by thirteen Local Education Authorities, most centres being supported jointly by two LEAs. The whole enterprise is co-ordinated through the University of Manchester Area Training Organization; but, except for major committees, all the project's work is carried on in one or other of the teachers' centres. When the project was launched early in 1967 few educationalists in the region (or elsewhere in the country) had many clearly developed ideas as to how such centres might run, and a good question was (and remains), 'Why should teachers take their professional concerns to local teachers' centres?'

The academic answer usually given is that such centres provide like-minded teachers with a local and relatively unstructured setting within which to discuss professional matters, often as a preliminary to proposing innovations within their own school setting. Yet five years later it has to be confessed that most such centres are still bedevilled by the problem of how to entice teachers into the centres for sustained bouts of professional work. Short in-service courses, exhibitions of teaching materials or of pupils' work, a reference library/resource centre, a workshop for making needed apparatus – all such are valuable services for a teachers' centre to offer. It has been our experience, however, that creative work in curriculum development provides much the strongest stimulus for schools' commitment to the work of teachers' centres. And in turn such commitment provides the teachers' centre with the life-space it needs if it is to function positively in its local area.

From our experience, the teachers' centre leader who wishes to stimulate creative work in curriculum planning would do well to concentrate attention on the critical areas of teacher concern, that is, pupil needs and interests and the demands which society makes on its young people. This is where commitment can begin; and it is only by dealing with the significant concerns of teachers that a professional centre can win recognition as a worthwhile focus for local professional effort.

The leader who succeeds in winning such life-space may well find that the issue which a group of teachers brings to his centre seems so vast, so complex and so basic that the working group despairs of its own capacity to contribute anything substantial to the problem's solution. In reply, the leader may argue that by pooling their knowledge, by drawing upon particular individual skills, and by extending their thought as they interact with other educationalists the group will achieve much more than could have been obtained by any one member working in isolation. Though teachers may be impressed they will not necessarily be convinced by such arguments; for they are, rightly, jealous of those demands upon professional time which interfere with their primary task, that of planning and guiding their pupils' learning. This implies that any professional centre's first development scheme must be, and must be seen to be, successful. The scheme need not be large, but it must deal with a real and urgent issue facing a definable group of teachers in the area, must appear from the outset to be well organized, must achieve its intermediate targets and must yield a product which demonstrates unequivocally the advantages of teachers co-operating for professional purposes.

The North West Project has derived much continued goodwill from teachers and LEAs in the region over a period of several years by focusing its effort on the RSLA problem, by maintaining several groups working in parallel (so that the anticipated total product would exceed the sum of its parts) and by meeting intermediate targets published before the project began.

There is, of course, no lack of suitable focal points for professional effort. Local schemes for combining two secondary schools into one comprehensive, for preparing pupils for examination under a new syllabus or for introducing counsellors into an authority's school are but three examples of situations where innovations initiated outside the school put strong pressure on identifiable groups of teachers to modify traditional practices. Less demanding of change, but no less stimulating towards innovation are the curriculum products published for the Schools Council, or the findings of research carried out by NFER or similar bodies. An alert professional centre leader will seek to grasp such 'teachable moments', and to fan a spark of passing interest into a steadily burning flame of commitment to inquiry, one capable of sustaining and directing effort over a period of time.

## Provision of Needed Resources

Once the development task has been given and accepted, adequate resources need to be provided for the work. These fall under three main headings: manpower, finance and support services. Only passing reference will be made here to questions of manpower, important as these are. It is a basic principle of local development work that teacher participation must be voluntary. Two implications of this principle are: that the dynamics and the climate of a working group must be constructive and satisfying rather than merely congenial, and that in an extended enterprise, such as the North West Project, regular opportunities have to be provided for group membership to change. Though in theory the latter implication might bring about dissipation of accumulating experience this circumstance has never arisen in the North West Project.

At no time has the project distinguished among types of teachers during recruitment of panel members. We have sought heterogeneous groups, whose members come from varying professional backgrounds. The enthusiasm and energy of the young have been as valued as the experience and wisdom of more mature teachers; and we have found that groups of such heterogeneity have ensured that a wide range of interests, ideas and suggestions is taken into account in reaching decisions. Now, near the end of the fifth year of development work, about one-quarter of current panel memberships consists of founder members, with another quarter having joined the project when field trials began and since remained with us.

Though it is a cardinal principle of the North West Project that all curriculum development work be controlled by teachers, such control could be absolute only if the teachers themselves were to underwrite project finances. In the early days the work was substantially, though not entirely, supported by finance from the Schools Council; but collectively the thirteen LEAs concerned have provided more than £200,000 of public money to support the project's work. Thus ways have had to be found to make possible the essential freedoms that development panels need, within the normal rules and practices of LEA financial administration.

For accounting purposes each projection team (of which there were seven) has been regarded as an educational unit with the panel chairman being cast in the role of headmaster. Estimates of proposed expenditure for the financial year 1969–70, for example, and forecasts for the year 1970–1, based upon discussions between panel chairman, panel members, and project director, were compiled according to the codes of expenditure in normal LEA use. Those familiar with LEA procedures will know that the financial year 1969–70 began in April 1969 and that, if the needed finance were to be available then, estimates would have to be submitted in October 1968 – just one month after the development panel had first met to plan and carry through its 1968–9 year's work. Thus each panel's first major activity involved making detailed predictions as to the form, content and extent of the field studies it was to undertake during the 1969–70 school year, since money for providing teaching kits to be used in these studies had to come from the funds then being estimated. Since the writing of a course worthy of field trials and the accumulation of a suitable teaching kit for this course were to be the focus of the year's panel work which was only then beginning, it is not difficult to appreciate the frustration among developers to which this demand might have given rise, however necessary this procedure was in the eyes of administrators.

The source of such possible irritation was removed, however, when the project's finance and general purposes committee agreed to group estimates into a small number of codes, and later to allow virement between codes and between years on each panel's account. These latter two provisions are believed to be outside the strict code of LEA rules, though within the discretionary powers available to administrators. The element of freedom introduced by these changes made it possible for panels to approach their development work at all times without any serious financial constraint on their planning.

This example illustrates beautifully the creative role which a liberal administration can play in local curriculum development work. However, if one is to generalize on the basis of this single example, two additional points must be made. First, that initiatives such as this are likely only when a basis of mutual trust and a sense of common purpose exist between developers and administrators. Secondly, that an important element in such trust is administrative competence on the part of the project executive, i.e. the professional centre leader; in particular, his ability to persuade panel chairmen to budget prudently and accurately in the first instance rather than to follow the common practice of submitting estimates greatly in excess of what the panel really needs, against the chance of across-the-board reductions before these estimates are approved.

Teacher control of local development work is a principle to which much thought has been given in the North West Project. Coupled with the need for adequate representation of all other interests involved in a wide-ranging and complex regional experiment, the principle inevitably implies a steering committee which is more effective as a reaction group than as a discussion group. Yet over the period under review the committee, far from degenerating into a mere 'talking shop', has proved a striking example of the processes of democratic control of a many-sided exercise. The fact is that at most meetings there have been serious matters for consideration, and discussion has never been cut short by the chairman. Papers on a great variety of topics have been presented for consideration, and have received the benefit of close scrutiny by a large number of people from different backgrounds.

Committee papers are prepared in the regional study group, an executive body comprising the project director, the deputy director and leaders of all fifteen teachers' centres. Anticipation of close scrutiny in committee, together with knowing that the decision eventually reached will have to be given effect by the executive, ensure careful planning in all matters. This organization also has the merit of keeping open three channels of communication between teachers and steering committee: via teachers' associations, via LEA administrations and via teachers' centre leaders (who are non-voting members of steering committee).

Without doubt the most notable feature of steering committees has been the relationship with its finance and general purposes committee. A school normally functions within a financial framework established by its LEA, one which generally bears little close relationship to the curricula proposed by the teaching staff of that school. In the North West Project, however, the finance and general purposes committee functions within a framework of general policy and curriculum proposals decided by a steering committee on which LEAs (even collectively) have only a minority representation. The novelty of this relationship and its success as a working organization provide striking evidence of the spirit of initiative and co-operation shown by both elected and professional LEA representatives throughout the life of the project.

## Support for Working Groups

An important asset of group work in local curriculum development centres is that each teacher brings to the group his own background of knowledge, skill and ability to think. These qualities offer great scope for studying curriculum problems because, when given the opportunity to think about his work, a teacher has greater potential than an outsider for promoting change, because he knows his own situation, its dynamics and the need for improvement. The problem under review has a personal meaning for him. However, this asset may turn into something of a liability should an emerging identity induce the group to adopt a narrow interpretation of its problem, and to become impervious to suggestions originating outside the group.

One way of avoiding this situation is to include teachers among the group in a way which crosses traditional lines of association and pockets of thinking. For example, it could have been very stimulating to have had a few teachers from primary schools among the membership of North West Project panels; but the pattern of release for panel work made this difficult to achieve. Another method, of which some but not enough use was made, was to include in each panel's programme events designed to extend professional insights, e.g. reviews of relevant literature or visits to schools where interesting work is taking place.

A third method, in which the project became very effective, was based on functions in which panel representatives met other teachers from schools in the region. Such meetings were almost always held for specific purposes, for example, to recruit teachers for panel work or schools for field trials; but this purpose was always set in the general context of reporting back to teachers with an outline of current plans, policies and proposed courses of action. Wherever possible these meetings were kept small, were held in teachers' centres and were led by members of the development panel concerned. Despite their informality, the challenge of presenting the panel's ideas to an informed and critical audience always put panel members on their mettle. Not every member welcomed the prospect of such meetings, but all prepared thoroughly for them. Afterwards many members admitted new insights from the encounter, and in the end felt delighted to realize their ability to hold and convince such an audience as to the value of the general thrust of their panel's work.

The regional study group has played a crucial role in supporting local development work. In the early days the discrepancy in leadership experience between the project director and the newly appointed leaders of local centres was vast. The latter had for the most part been recruited straight from the classroom, often to a temporary appointment; and they were given the task of establishing and maintaining centres for which few models then existed. At that time, therefore, the original study group became excessively director-centred, the local centre leaders being both professionally and emotionally over-dependent. Within a year, however, the professional confidence of local leaders began visibly to grow, as they realized their ability to describe (and where necessary to defend) the project's ideas to teachers in their areas, and as the centres themselves became increasingly acceptable as focal points for local as well as regional initiative. This proved to be a very difficult time in the regional study group as each local leader struggled to achieve more autonomy during discussions of both educational and administrative matters. Such struggles generally arose when individuals or subgroups invested great personal and professional capital in ideas which seemed to others unlikely to agree with the wider educational purposes of the project.

At such times it would have been very easy for the project director to have adopted either an excessively dominant or recessive style of leadership. Respectable arguments were not lacking to support either approach:

1. The project had been set up to carry out a specific programme of work within a given period of time, and it was important to work within these terms of reference.
2. The project had been established to study the feasibility of groups of teachers working as curriculum developers. Such groups had first to 'learn the trade'; and the short-term role of leadership was to teach the needed skills. If the project were to fail to demonstrate the competence of teacher groups for such work, the inhibiting effect of that failure upon curriculum development work within the region (and perhaps also elsewhere) might be very great indeed.
3. Where appointed leaders were unable to convince their groups of the wisdom of proposed courses of action each group should be allowed to go its own way, and to learn from its own – perhaps bitter – experience.

In the director's view, the project had to concern itself with all three of these major purposes (products, feasibility and training); and the result was that at this time regional study group meetings sometimes became very exhausting encounters indeed. It is therefore appropriate at this point to recognize the high degree of commitment and energy (both intellectual and emotional) which the local leaders brought to this work, from which they learned above all else how to create and maintain a humane yet purposeful climate for local development work.

Perhaps the most lasting problem with which the North West Project has struggled is that of making available to development panels the knowledge, wisdom and skill which specialist educationalists are anxious to place at panels' disposal. At an early stage in its life the project drew up and circulated extensive lists of such persons and institutions, leaving to panels themselves the initiative for seeking such support. It must be reported that these services have only very rarely been called for.

For much of its life morale in the panels, as well as among centre leaders, has been dominated by a feeling which might be expressed thus: 'For the first time groups of teachers have been given the opportunity to show what they can do as curriculum developers – and, by God, we're going to show them!' Even the project director, when visiting a panel, has occasionally been asked, half-jocularly, 'Have you come to tell us what to do?' The tone of voice in which the question is asked may indicate either resentment at the apparent suggestion that in any crisis leadership passes out of teachers' hands, or relief that in an emergency an authority figure is willing to come to the rescue. The question itself epitomizes the difficulties inherent in introducing outside consultants into local development panels.

This determination of teachers to throw off the (perceived) weight of imposed authority is one of the most pervasive features of the climate within which the project has operated. The source of perceived authority may vary, embracing, for example, the routine of traditional school practices, the force of new curriculum orthodoxies, the standpoint of traditional sources of wisdom and the thrust of advice given by those in positions of authority in the educational system. The response to the pressure from outside has always been the same: 'Why should we? We want to do it our way! Let us experiment for ourselves!' The parallels between this response and that of any young person discovering some new insight or developing some new skill are striking, and provide (at least for the project director) convincing evidence of the value of local curriculum development work as in-service education. Once more it is necessary to affirm a belief (for which the Project now has a good deal of supporting evidence) that teachers who learn by discovering and learn to discover are more likely to establish subsequently in their classrooms conditions in which their pupils can do likewise.

Nevertheless, a curriculum development project is concerned with products as well as with processes; and it would be a sign of increasing professional maturity when a panel felt sufficiently confident in itself to be able to state: 'As a panel we do not know enough about the problem with which we are trying to cope. Please come and give us your advice as to how we might best proceed.' It is encouraging to be able to report that in general panels in the North West Project have for the past year or so felt sufficiently mature to seek such support informally through their acquaintances, if not yet formally from available professional sources.

## A Humane Working Climate

Any professional centre leader finding himself in this position will give a great deal of his attention to creating in his centre circumstances likely to foster such emerging professional maturity. Experience in the North West Project suggests the importance for such outcomes of a humane working climate.

A humane working climate stems from many little actions and influences, too numerous to mention in detail. In the context of this paper, however, these may be summarized as follows:

1. Willingness on the part of the authorities to allow panels to work on problems which panel members and other teachers themselves perceive as real and worthy of attention;
2. Presence within the panel of able personnel in sufficient numbers to accomplish worthwhile tasks;

3. Freedom for panel members to express dissatisfaction with the current state of those affairs in schools, LEAs, or within the panel, in which the panel has a legitimate interest;
4. Willingness on the part of all panel members to work together to achieve common ends through agreed means;
5. Recognition that many kinds of educationalist can contribute to curriculum improvement;
6. An attitude of open-mindedness and healthy scepticism about both what is traditional and what is new;
7. Absence of undue pressure by those in authority (whether within or outside the project) about matters which properly fall within the panel's decision.

### The Professional Centre Leader

It will be apparent that if local curriculum development is to be successful the centre must enjoy competent professional leadership. In an age of specialists the centre leader needs to be a high-level general practitioner, able to understand and appreciate the concerns of class teacher, head teacher, LEA administrator, resources specialist, teacher trainer and higher education exponent. At the same time he needs to be good at establishing and maintaining productive and satisfying work relationships among persons drawn from several of these backgrounds but functioning as partners in a common task. To do this effectively he also needs a reasonable grounding in the several areas of academic study with which his centre's work is concerned.

To list these attributes is to invite two questions: 'Where are such masters of all the arts to come from?', and, 'Why should such persons go into, and remain in, professional centre leadership?' In the author's view the answer to the first question is deceptively simple. 'Since few such persons are currently available, we must set up leadership training programmes.' It is, of course, true that if the James proposals for professional centre leaders are to be adopted, courses need to be established through which potentially suitable applicants can accumulate the basic knowledge and the rudiments of the skills they need for this work. Essentially, however, it is in the field that the professional centre leader, as general practitioner, accumulates wisdom, finesse, judgement, sensitivity and imaginative flair. So what is deceptive about the response is that real, worthwhile and acceptable projects need to be maintained so that such journeymen can learn the arts and can experience the humane working conditions they must later seek to create elsewhere. And who is to lead *these* projects? Experience in the North West Project has shown the feasibility of university and LEA personnel working together on such a task. Once again, perhaps our most important finding has been that the centre leader who is a creative and enthusiastic member of a regional development panel is the one who induces in his centre a climate within which teachers working there can also capture the spirit of creative endeavour.

Finally, why should so well-qualified an exponent remain in professional centre work? It is obviously important to the education system that he should; for in sociological terms he is a change-agent, aiming to release more potential for innovation by promoting creative encounters among people interacting in flexible partnerships.

But he is also a person, often with a family and always with career prospects, living in a society which promotes specialists to high-status posts, even where the work done in those posts approximates more to general than to specialist practice. That the James Committee had considered this point is obvious from its recommendations that the leader be called a warden, that he be given an independent role and that he enjoy at least senior lecturer status. These may well be necessary conditions for the post; but in the experience of the North West Project they are not the chief considerations. These are that the leader's work also be emotionally and professionally satisfying, offering him the experience of personal growth and some evidence of the impact of his efforts upon schools. Because most of the project's centre leaders have experienced such rewards, I make bold to claim that there would be no shortage of able teachers eager to make careers as professional centre leaders. Accordingly, I conclude that the James proposals for a network of professional centres, each under the leadership of a full-time professional warden, were well conceived and merit the support of all proposed partners in third-cycle teacher education.

*Part 6*

# THE ECONOMICS OF TEACHER EDUCATION

CHAPTER 18

# The Scope for Economic Analysis

## KIETH DRAKE

The development of teacher education in Britain has largely been determined by a complex interplay of intuition, custom and accident. Ideally, decisions about investment in teacher education should be reached with the aid of some sort of critical logic, and, since economics is particularly concerned with the rational organization of scarce means to achieve specified ends, it would appear to be a useful contributory discipline. It is a restricted logic and can properly be employed only as an element in a multi-disciplinary approach. Often the economist reaches the frontier of his own dimension and, in the words of J. R. Hicks, 'wants to hand over the problem to some sociologist or other – if there is a sociologist waiting for him'.

The most optimistic agenda would centre on the calculation of social rates of return on different kinds of teacher education. These rates could be compared with alternative educational and non-educational investments to reveal whether there was under- or over-investment, and with each other to decide whether resources were being misallocated within teacher education. Some economists are optimistic about this approach (e.g. Lee Hansen, 1966); others are more reserved (e.g. Bowman, 1963; Morris and Ziderman, 1971). However, until it can be explored there are less ambitious investigations and analyses which may offer a worthwhile return.

This study* aims, first, to illustrate the range of problems to which economic analysis might be applied and so to sketch, albeit in a fragmentary and uneven way, an agenda for research into the economics of teacher education in Britain. Secondly, it reports a very preliminary investigation of productivity in colleges of education. Thirdly, it offers some analysis of relations between teacher education and the market for teachers.

* The author gratefully acknowledges the help of those who commented on an early draft, Dr Norman Lee, Raymond Ryba and Professor John Turner, while reserving to himself responsibility for those errors of omission and commission which remain.

## Some Limitations of Economics

The usefulness of an economic approach to the provision of teacher education depends as much on knowledge of its limitations, among users as well as among economists, as on the power of the discipline. Early attempts to calculate rates of return on education for teachers have been marked by a necessary, and, some would argue, still inadequate caution. Hinchliffe's estimates of the return to non-graduate teachers from an Open University degree course include a good deal of sensitivity analysis (Hinchliffe, 1971).

One problem is that maximizing behaviour has either been regarded as a rather low-status activity by British teacher educators, or has been completely ignored. The traditional concern of economics with maximization subject to constraints has been rated very low in comparison with activities leading to communication or creation. The degree to which the achievement of such desirable behaviours depends on unglamorous maximizing behaviour has not always been recognized, although one or two economists have tried to draw attention to the significance of the economic approach. Peston (1970), for instance, has posed a critical question which has profound implications for teacher education:

A higher average salary will enable better teachers to be recruited and trained, but for any given expenditure on salaries, pupil-teacher ratios must rise. I know of no research on the value of more teachers compared with better teachers, so, while the choice may be presented, the best decision is not obvious. Should we devote our marginal resources to raising standards or numbers?

Yet this failure to pursue maximization very far is combined with a general appreciation that teaching is not only a social service but also 'a bread and butter affair' (McNair, 1944). For instance, the General Teaching Council of Scotland recognized the importance of economic motivation when it ascribed the unsatisfactory quality of graduate recruitment to teacher education to inadequate student aid, 'another year of study on a relatively low standard of living, while graduates entering other professions may receive more competitive salaries' (Select Committee on Education and Science 1969–70).

What is required is far more than recognition of the significance of economic forces: it is an appreciation of the structure of economic thinking as it applies to teaching and to teacher education. Both the limitations and the explanatory power of applicability theorems which are derived from the engineering models of economics are related to the narrow-mindedness of this way of thinking. A. N. Whitehead (1948) put this very clearly when discussing the development of 'the science of political enconomy' as an example of modern scientific method. He argued that in the nineteenth century it was failure to observe the limitations of a set of abstractions which produced the de-humanizing effect, which is what so many teachers fear in economics:

> Its methodological procedure is exclusive and intolerant and rightly so. It fixes attention on a definite group of abstractions, neglects everything else, and elicits every scrap of information and theory which is relevant to what it has retained. This method is triumphant, provided that the abstractions are judicious. But, however triumphant, the triumph is within limits. The neglect of these limits leads to disastrous oversights.

At best economics can offer no more than probabilities, and often only agnosticism – though even this can prove a welcome antidote to some of the certainties of the received wisdom about teacher education. As an auxiliary discipline, preliminary to the decision on how to allocate scarce resources, economics cannot usurp the role of value judgements in the ultimate choice. But in teacher education so very little positive testable knowledge about its economics has been produced, so little knowledge of costs, benefits or productivity, that it is difficult to see why this usurpation has to occur.

It is true that cost-effectiveness exercises have, in the past, been related to widely-condemned policies, e.g. the notorious episode of payments-by-results in nineteenth-century Britain. In that instance, however, the pursuit of the measurable went hand in hand with disregard for the un-measured and for the unintended consequences of the form of measurement. Likewise, in contemporary education, the failure of performance contracting to measure adequately the side- and after-effects of a controlled educational process produces a feed-back mechanism which can be dangerously defective. The value of the control system may then be entirely offset by unintended detrimental effects. In either case, failure to appreciate the limitations of the cost-effectiveness operation has been critical. Such failure leads easily to a retreat from rationality so that positive issues concerning the allocation of resources, which may, with effort, be susceptible to testing through observation, measurement and experiment, are actually decided intuitively and on normative grounds. Not without some justification,

> Educators fear that the effort to increase efficiency will affect and change the goals of education because they suspect that economists will define 'efficiency' in solely financial terms and that concern about 'value for money' will inevitably lead to exclusive emphasis on immediately useful skills. (Woodhall and Blaug, 1968)

## A Critical Logic

Despite these dangers, the criteria derived from economics for determining the size and character of teacher education may have a considerable potential as aids to rationality. One approach is the calculation of marginal rates of return, social and private, on alternative investments in teacher education. The principle is straightforward and the calculation of forbidding complexity. Another approach, also employing the concept of teacher education as human capital formation, is to measure and analyse teacher productivity in order to concentrate training on those features of teaching which will raise teacher productivity. In practice the specification for teacher education has not even been derived from systematic job analysis, still less from an analysis of teacher productivity.

Pressure of numbers has dominated official thinking. Where short-term teacher-supply considerations have conflicted with what were thought to be important training considerations, the conflict has generally been resolved in favour of the former. The process has been facilitated by failure to develop indicators of teacher productivity which could provide concrete support in arguments on quality and so match the concreteness of the numbers game played by the DES. For instance, it has been pointed out by D. W. Humphreys (Taylor, 1969) that policy changes likely to affect the quality of teaching, such as the introduction of compulsory training for graduates in schools and diversification of colleges of education to abolish their monotechnic character, were for many years opposed on the ground that they would aggravate the supposed shortage of teachers. It is not possible to see how it was decided that the quality benefits would be outweighed by the consequences of the restriction on numbers. Only systematic investigation of the determinants of teacher productivity and the nature of the educational production function could provide a rational basis for this trade-off. The recent change of direction, which foresees the imminent end of teacher shortage, and therefore allows compulsory training at least in state schools, and consideration of college diversification, must be an example of circumstances altering cases. In practice DES forecasts of the demand for and supply of teachers are the principal determinant of the size and balance of the teacher education programme. No more than a minute fraction of the resources devoted to the forecasting operation have been used to investigate the potential of economic criteria.

The neglect is surprising, for in the notion of human capital formation economics offers a concept which provides a unifying principle for the investigation of many aspects of teacher education, off-the-job training and on-the-job training, teaching and learning, formal and informal, initial and in-service training. It may never be possible to describe teacher education very convincingly in the form of a set of equations, but it is possible to imagine greater rationality in calculating and prescribing the optimum length, timing and character of education for each kind of teacher – given current prices and technology.

For example, the cost of this investment was raised in the 1960s by extending the standard college course in England and Wales from two to three years and the course is again being lengthened, for increasing numbers of students, from three to four years with the introduction of B.Ed. courses. Student time is a very expensive input accounting for at least half of the total cost per student year in colleges of education in England and Wales (see Table 18.1). Yet in 1965 the Secretary of State inaugurated a campaign to raise productivity in the colleges of England and Wales largely by

Table 18.1

Costs[1] per Student Year in Colleges of Education in England and Wales Compared with Those in Advanced Full-time Further Education and Universities

| | Colleges | As percentage of costs in advanced full time further education | As percentage of costs in universities |
|---|---|---|---|
| Recurrent costs[2] | 395 | 66 | 34 |
| Annual capital costs[3] | 115 | 50 | 30 |
| Student earnings foregone | 665 | 96 | 84 |
| Total | 1,175 | 77 | 50 |

| | Colleges | Further Education | Universities |
|---|---|---|---|
| Student earnings foregone as percentage of total | 56 | 45 | 33 |

[1] Pounds per student year for 1967–8, adjusted to 1969 Public Expenditure Survey Prices rounded to the nearest five pounds.
[2] Publicly-borne student maintenance costs are excluded as transfer payments.
[3] Imputed rents and loan charges are excluded, capital costing being done on a marginal cost basis, i.e. an annual equivalent in pounds per student year for new teaching places (buildings and equipment). Except for some equipment, amortization is at ten per cent. over sixty years.

Source: Student Numbers in Higher Education in England and Wales (1970), Education Planning Paper No. 2, Table 14, p. 28, London. By permission of the Controller of Her Majesty's Stationery Office.

economizing the use of physical capital, which only accounts for about ten per cent. of the cost per student year. The cost of student time has been rising relative to the cost of other resources used in teacher education, with the possible exception of the cost of teaching staff. It is not immediately obvious why so little attention has been given to economizing the use of this most expensive input. Nor is it obvious that the rate of return on the marginal year of training, for example the fourth in the colleges, will be higher than the rate of return on some form of training at a later stage, that is, in-service training. All these decisions may be wise ones. What seems to be lacking is a coherent rationale which ties together spending only five per cent. of training expenditures on in-service courses, and extending the length of initial training while economizing the use of physical capital.

Until serious and sustained research has taken place over many years it is not possible to say whether useful knowledge of the optimum mix of resources required to achieve specified training objectives or the optimum mix of types of training, e.g. initial and in-service, can be gathered.

Decisions as to these mixes are taken meanwhile because such choices have to be made, but it is important to be clear how open to challenge they are. As this essay should demonstrate, the initial product of the process of defining problems and framing questions is a daunting pile of caveats and a greatly heightened awareness of a series of very mysterious relationships. It is, of course, impossible to predict whether the eventual outcome will be merely a despairing agnosticism or some usable guidelines for the rational allocation of resources in teacher education.

## Research Targets

Some of the more obvious targets for investigation are:

1. The life cycle of this particular type of human capital;
2. The economics of the training process or the training institutions;
3. The relationships between teacher training, teaching, the education system and the host society.

In this essay nearly all the evidence and analysis relates to teacher education in England and Wales, and in particular to initial training in the colleges of education. It is, therefore, concerned mostly with training for teaching in primary and secondary schools. But training in Scotland for Scottish schools or graduate teacher training in universities in England and Wales will in some respects be a significantly different operation, as will training for teaching in further or higher education anywhere in Britain. The study of teacher education for further or higher education is in most ways even more neglected than school-oriented training. Yet there are several colleges which specialize in training for further education and a considerable proportion of further education teachers have been trained for teaching or for research. Moreover, universities have for a good many years, especially in the natural sciences, invested very heavily in research training, notably Ph.D. programmes, a long, arduous and expensive process regarded by many as vital to the proper education of a university teacher. On the other hand, training which is not research-centred has been very rare in universities, and new recruits are even now offered only something like a voluntary two-week course and a very limited follow-up. This essay draws on only the most accessible and most commonly examined parts of a much wider area of study.

In the case of the first target, at least, the whole formal education of the teacher from reception class onwards is clearly relevant to the production of a trained teacher. It is, for instance, a commonplace of teacher education in Britain that the weakness of student teachers in number work is closely related to deficiencies in their early mathematical education and the difficulty of eradicating these before they start teaching as they themselves were taught. The efficiency of training will be affected not only by obvious variables like the natural ability of the student teacher but also by what might be termed the quality of a semi-manufactured good. The teacher training institution is only one unit in a line of vertically integrated skill factories, and the proper perspective of study ranges through the whole production process and on through the working life of the teacher.

Even the conventionally defined teacher education involves a number of quite different ways of learning how to teach, for instance learning-by-doing in contrast to the off-the-job and on-the-job training of an initial training course. Their economics have to be explained and compared, for instance, the difference between 'before' and 'after', the consequences of training graduates instead of relying on learning-by-doing and any casual teaching an untrained graduate might receive on the job. In further and higher education in Britain, and lingeringly in some secondary schools, there is still much sympathy for the view, so precisely expressed by R. M. Hutchins (1936), that 'all there is to teaching can be learned through a good education and being a teacher'. Presumably this view is based on the judgement that the cost-benefit ratio of this form of teacher education is more favourable than that on alternative programmes. Not only changes in the structure of initial training, but the return on the B.Ed. or on different forms of in-service training could in principle be assessed by comparing additional costs and additional benefits. Without some sort of comparative calculus, rational allocation of resources between the various options in teacher education is not possible.

In the study of the economics of those institutions which promote learning how to teach and what to teach pride of place in Britain will naturally

13—EOT * *

go to specialist institutions such as colleges of education or training departments in polytechnics and universities. But there are other bodies, such as the professional associations of teachers, which have a relatively neglected but possibly important role in teacher education. Since unpaid voluntary work is important in these associations, and exchequer subsidies are frequently enjoyed in the form of the tax advantages of charitable status, they probably account for a much larger investment in teacher education than the sum of their subscriptions and other income would indicate.

To analyse teacher education as a system leads quickly to its analysis as a sub-system of the whole education system and of the social and economic system of the country. There is, or should be, a clear relationship between the productivity of teachers in the education system and their experience in teacher education. There is even a more indirect relationship between teacher education and the productivity of the nation's economy, to be imputed back from the performance of trained teachers in the schools and the subsequent productivity of their pupils. As a sub-system British teacher education also appears to have additional objectives quite different from raising the effectiveness of teachers or promoting greater economic productivity.

For instance, teacher education certainly appears to share the general characteristics of British higher education in the areas of social role selection and income-redistribution. To borrow Jean Floud's terminology (Floud, 1967), teacher education is not structured to mobilize talent regardless of social class. Student aid provides an instructive example of this almost non-educational sub-system role of teacher education. A comprehensive study of a sub-system has to take account of all the costs and consequences of the sub-system, including social and economic side effects. Virtually all initial trainees in Britain are 'recognized', i.e. they receive awards. Maximum awards represent only a fraction of the direct cost of training a student, but the student-aid system has important social and economic consequences, apart from straightforward reduction of the private cost of training. No doubt some of the increasing interest now being shown in loan finance as an alternative to the present arrangements stems from a wish to reduce the effective demand for higher education. But there is an equity argument which provides an alternative base for this interest (for an early British loan scheme see Jones, 1924; for more recent foreign experience see Woodhall, 1970). Like other forms of higher education, teacher education in Britain is largely tax-financed and effectively distributes life chances and lifetime earnings. Many of those who receive this heavily-subsidized and privately beneficial training are already relatively privileged educationally, socially and economically. The social-class composition of student teachers is heavily skewed towards the middle and even upper income groups.

It is conceivable that the present arrangements for financing training so affect the private rate of return on training that, allied to other factors, such as the lack of student aid for the period between the end of compulsory schooling and entrance to training, they reinforce a marked tendency to social class bias in the provision of teacher education. The effects of this on income distribution would also repay investigation. On the face of it one effect would seem to be the distribution of benefits more or less in proportion to socio-economic advantage. This tendency to give more to those that have would appear to have several aspects. For example, the Open University, although chiefly designed as compensatory provision for those who had previously missed their chance of higher education, started life by recruiting almost one-third of its students from mainly non-graduate trained teachers. Very favourable exemptions, relative to those for people who have been educated in further education for example, led towards a second dose of subsidized higher education and a good chance to raise earnings substantially (Hinchliffe, 1971). But assessment of income-redistributory effects of the present arrangements would be a complex matter, for there are also contrary movements to be considered, for example the apparent long-term trend reduction in the pay of teachers relative to the pay of the less-educated (Routh, 1965). Certainly student aid can be studied adequately only within a complicated nexus of costs and benefits, and in the context of broad social as well as relatively narrow educational policies.

CHAPTER 19

# Productivity in Colleges of Education

KEITH DRAKE

## A Pilot Study: Productivity 1959-69

### 1. Input

An exploratory study of productivity in colleges of education in England
and Wales reveals a decline in measured output per unit of input at an
average annual rate of about 0·8 per cent. between 1959 and 1969.*

The input index used in this study is a crude measure. Until a single
composite index based on separate indices for wages and salaries, other
current expenditure, capital and cost of student time has been calculated
it is impossible to decide how good a proxy it is. The input data used for
Table 19.1† were calculated from current expenditures of maintained and

Table 19.1
Index of Real Current Expenditure, Colleges of Education
in England and Wales

|      |     |
| ---- | --- |
| 1959 | 100 |
| 1969 | 357 |

voluntary colleges, net of loan charges and capital outlay from revenue.
These expenditures were converted into constant terms, for want of specific
education-cost indices, using a retail price index adjusted to a fiscal year
basis. The fiscal year used was that of the maintained colleges and not that
of the voluntary colleges. Over the period chosen there is little to choose

* The author is indebted to Stephanie and Eric Twigg for carrying out most of
the data collection and calculations. Further details of the study are available
from the author at the Department of Education, Manchester University, on request.
    † Data for this table and for Table 19.3 based on *Statistics of Education* various.
Use of official statistics throughout this section, by kind permission of the Controller
of HMSO.

between the ordinary retail price index and a general price index of all goods and services in the British economy, so the former was employed because its monthly basis facilitated conversion to the fiscal year. Use of this deflator measures inputs in terms of opportunity costs, i.e. what the resources so employed might produce in an alternative employment. It can be argued that, compared with deflation by a specifically education index, this may slightly overstate the rise in real expenditures, the reason being that the alternative product of the high-level manpower which is so large a part of college inputs (see Table 19.2) rises in step with the growing productivity of the rest of the economy.

The final stage in calculating the input index was to calculate the output of each type of initial training course as a proportion of total student

Table 19.2

Composition of Public Expenditure 1959 and 1969, Colleges of Education in England and Wales

| | Percentage of total public expenditure from revenue | |
|---|---|---|
| | 1959 | 1969 |
| Teaching staff | 29·3 | 37·2 |
| Other staff | 21·1 | 16·5 |
| | 50·4 | 53·7 |
| Expenditure on premises | 17.7 | 12·8 |
| Books, stationery, and equipment and materials | 3·4 | 4·6 |
| Food | 10·7 | 6·3 |
| Other current expenditure | 8·6 | 12·8 |
| Loan charges | 7·5 | 9·1 |
| Capital expenditure from revenue | 1·5 | 0·7 |

Average number of students 1959 and 1969, Colleges of Education in England and Wales

| | Percentage of total | |
|---|---|---|
| | 1959 | 1969 |
| Resident in college | } 88 | 42 |
| Resident in approved lodgings | | 23 |
| Day students | 12 | 35 |

Source: *Statistics of Education 1969*, Vol. 5, Table 10.

numbers in each year during which the course students were in college. The same proportion of real current expenditure for each year was then attributed to the course output and summed to produce total real expenditure attributable to the production of the course students. Since the input index is based on the aggregate of all these attributed course inputs over several years, it is clearly very sensitive to the assumption that costs per completed student (counting those who failed first time as passes and ignoring drop-out) are equal between courses in any one year.

There are, of course, other important assumptions involved in the use of such a simple index. The deflation of current expenditure into constant pounds may, for instance, be less than satisfactory if the quality of college staffs does not vary directly with real expenditure on staff salaries. Other inputs, such as student time or capital, may vary in quality without this being accurately reflected in prices. On the input side the information system is seriously lacking except in the financial dimension, and even there it is often available in a form unsuitable for any purpose except auditing.

## 2. *Output*

On the output side the objectives of the colleges are generally diffuse and ill-defined, so only the crudest output indicator is available for a preliminary study, an indicator that has to stand proxy for the multiple outputs which characterize this educational process. The output index used in Table 19.3 was derived from data on students completing courses of initial training in colleges of education in England and Wales, 1959 and 1969.

Table 19.3
Index of Output, Colleges of Education in England and Wales

| | |
|---|---|
| 1959 | 100 |
| 1969 | 329 |

When institutions have multiple functions, e.g. initial training courses of different length and character, in-service training, research and publication, it is difficult to devise equivalent units of measurement by means of which the varied outputs can be combined in a composite measure. Moreover the major output, trained teachers, should obviously be assessed in terms of the teachers' productivity on the job. But assessment of that has scarcely begun. Indeed, the general difficulty of translating any of these outputs into either physical or market measures makes it easy to sympathize with the official habit of measuring output by input – and so enjoying constant productivity. Since all college output except that from initial training courses is ignored in this exercise, the accuracy of the output index is dependent on the extent to which the unmeasured output varies directly with the measured output, as well as the extent to which the weighting system employed deals with the problem of equivalency between different initial training courses.

The simplest output measure would probably have been an unweighted index of all students who completed an initial training course. However, such an index does not show quite so great an increase as an index using an elementary weighting system in which each successful student is weighted according to the length of course. The problem of unsuccessful students has sometimes been dealt with by weighting both successful and unsuccessful students by the average length of their course (Robbins, 1963, Appendices I and II). Woodhall and Blaug (1965) have pointed out that such a course length weighting system assumes constant educational returns over time, for which there is no evidence either way. This would be particularly relevant for a full-scale total factor productivity analysis, but in this crude and partial preliminary exercise the problem of unsuccessful students was handled merely by adding those who failed initially to those who passed and weighting them impartially by course length to produce a composite weighted index. This method ignores those who dropped out of a course, but that unmeasured output is partially compensated by treating all initial failures as passes, though there is an ultimate failure rate which is thought to be roughly half the initial failure rate. In this way, wastage, i.e. drop-out plus ultimate failure, is measured, but not at the same weight as success.

As with the input index, some large assumptions are made when this output index is used. Particularly important is the assumption that learning can be treated as if it were the product of teaching. When the raw material of the process, the student, is capable of virtually autonomous relevant change, great care has to be exercised in attributing additional learning to the resources devoted to teaching.

## 3. Productivity

Tables 19.1 and 19.3 indicate a fall in output per unit of input of the order of 0·8 per cent. per year between 1959 and 1969. However, this is only a fall in productivity if the quality of both inputs and outputs remained constant or at least changed insufficiently to wipe out the apparent decrease in productivity. Those quality indicators which are close to hand are fragile tools. Final examination standards may have changed between 1959 and 1969, or the reliability and validity of the examinations may have altered. The examination for the teacher's certificate may look like a criterion-referenced test, with its emphasis on practical teaching and criterion of 'good teaching'. But in practice it is arguably more like a norm-referenced test, with the appropriate susceptibility to change in standard without change in objectives. There is usually some grading in the examination, and the introduction of the B.Ed. qualification has recently provided an additional quality indicator. But it would only make the achievement measures slightly more complex to take these into account, whereas the ideal would be a value-added measure and not an achievement measure by itself. To develop a value-added measure it would, however, be necessary to know more about the measured ability of new students for the courses which completed in 1959 and 1969 and to be reasonably sure that variations in input quality were satisfactorily represented by, say, performance in GCE examinations.

Other British studies of educational productivity have recognized the problem of distinguishing between a rise in quality of output and a fall in productivity (Woodhall and Blaug, 1965). But this is a fair way from the common assumption in education that when more is put into a process more is got out. Productivity studies are desirable because it is difficult, in view of experience outside education, to see why in education a proportionate increase in output should necessarily follow an increase in input. No doubt that is the intention behind commitment of extra resources. This interpretative difficulty was one of the points on which H. G. Johnson (1965) criticized Woodhall and Blaug's study of British university productivity. Johnson argued that increased expenditure per student in universities, which was mostly expenditure on teaching staff, was designed to improve the quality of university education and that Woodhall and Blaug made 'the quality of education a constant by definition' so that increased unit costs were necessarily wasteful, i.e. diminished productivity. He argued that it would be as reasonable to adopt the assumption made in national income accounting that output varies directly with input (constant productivity) as it would be to adopt the constant quality assumption. The argument applies also to the colleges. Under the national income accounting assumption, if it appears to require 0·8 per cent. per year more input to produce a unit of output it follows that quality of output is rising by 0·8 per cent. per year. Under either assumption the output of certificated teachers per unit of input is falling. The question then is whether the teacher education system is producing teachers with higher productivity and so trading quantity for quality – and, a different question altogether, whether that is desirable. Alternatively, is the system simply becoming less cost-effective?

The possible flaws in this type of productivity measurement are obvious. But it should be compared with the pseudo-productivity measure so frequently employed in the past, which is the reciprocal of average cost per student. Since students are both input and output, and the student measure relates to students in training, not completed, this is not really a productivity measure at all: it is a ratio between two inputs, the other being goods and services measured by current expenditure, including some loan charges. Using this pseudo-productivity measure, colleges of education, with a rise in real cost per student of only two per cent. from 1963–4 to 1969–70, outperformed universities (a nine per cent. rise) and advanced further education (an eight per cent. rise) (*Social Trends*, 1971, Table 88). The DES appears to believe that this was due to the ability of colleges 'to exploit economies in regard to recurrent expenditures' (*Student Numbers*, 1970). If there are economies of scale the evidence is not well known, for in recent years there has been a notable lack of correlation between size and net tuition cost per student in colleges of education in England and Wales (*Costs per Student 1967–8 to 1970–1*). Presumably if the colleges had done just a little better and achieved an actual fall in unit costs it would have been possible to claim rising productivity. Some such claim would be necessary because college performance would look rather poor on the conventional assumption that the more education costs the better it is.

## Potential of the Input/Output Model

There are a number of more general points which can be made about the approach which treats teacher education rather as if it were a capital goods industry. The engineering model which is used is not, of course, the only possible model for the process of teacher education. Some might prefer to see a college as an organism in a state of ecological balance or, at times, of ecological disequilibrium. But an engineering model can open fresh lines of analysis. The only danger of such proven abstractions is that they can become intellectual prisons, can be endowed with a misplaced concreteness (Whitehead, 1948) and an exclusiveness which is false to their origins in a severe selection from experience.

With this proviso, how suggestive is the input/output model? To draw out the implications of the basic concepts is sometimes interesting by itself. For instance, the pattern of teacher education in Britain reveals an official belief that the capital formation which occurs in training is of a remarkable quality. This capital good is engineered to last: it is virtually free of obsolescence for its payback period of at least forty years. Only some five per cent. of training expenditure is on in-service training, the rest on initial training. This minute public provision for maintenance of capital, even when supplemented by the self-investment of teachers during their careers, suggests either a virtually stagnant technology, which is not expected to change, hence little depreciation of teacher capital, or that there is a wasteful allocation of resources between initial and in-service training.

### 1. *Input*

If the inputs into teacher education alone are considered it is clear that the process is managed in a curious fashion. The state has more or less complete control of the process. In the case of the most important agent, the colleges of education in England and Wales, the content and method of teacher education have been left very largely to the colleges and Area Training Organizations. But the DES effectively controls numbers, course length, material conditions and the balance of training, for instance, between men and women, between primary and secondary specialization. Logistic control is extremely thorough, and takes in staffing, building provision and recognition of in-service courses for grant as well as the structure of initial training. There is also a less direct control exercised through the ability of the DES to define the actual combination of resources used in public education and to specify, by implication, the optimum combination of resources. Through its control of the incidence of costs as between society and the student teacher and its dominating influence on the wage level and wage structure, it can significantly influence the private and social rates of return to teaching.

In this way the DES controls the demand for and opportunities open to teachers, and the attractiveness of teaching relative to other occupations. Both factors are critical for the rate of expansion of colleges and the quality of recruitment. This public power to influence private decisions on careers, although less direct than the more obvious controls on colleges, is at least as important as a regulatory device. Consider only the incomes policy for teachers pursued by successive British governments. In general, the DES has managed to maintain a nice equilibrium between the demand for and the supply of teachers, i.e. at the ruling price it has obtained the services of very nearly the precise number of teachers it was prepared to pay for. Given the scale of wastage from employment in schools and the size of the pool of inactive qualified teachers, the maintenance of a dynamic equilibrium is a tribute to shrewd management. The demand for teachers, despite fluctuations in school populations, can be controlled by varying staffing standards which are, ultimately, a function of the amount which governments are willing to spend on teacher salaries. The supply of teachers, despite fluctuations in wastage from employment, can be controlled through control of number of training places, and adjustment of demand to match supply.

With the level of salaries firmly within its control, the DES has been able to influence the private rate of return on teacher education and, therefore, its relative attractiveness. If the DES were to abandon its effort to maintain an equilibrium between demand and supply, for instance by raising staffing standards to a level which could not be met at current levels of output from colleges, then the only way of achieving required numbers would be by raising the relative pay of teachers. This would tend to draw in trained and (where still acceptable) untrained recruits not at present teaching. The private rate of return for all teachers would, other things being equal, be raised and, in particular, the private rate of return for initial trainees. In the long term, competition for training places would tend to rise and with it the quality of recruits. So the market power of the DES affects the quality of input to teacher education, and, since input is probably the main determinant of output, the quality of output also.

The precursor of a truly rational reconstruction of teacher education, where one set of hunches was not being replaced by another set, would be a definition of objectives. For the beginning of the process of costing inputs is to decide what is to be costed. Teacher effectiveness has been heavily if inconclusively investigated, but teacher cost-effectiveness, i.e. productivity, has been pointedly neglected. Presumably it is in the teacher's job and the functions of schools and other educational institutions that the objectives of teacher education are rooted. In practice these objectives, when stated, are so diffuse and ill-defined as to defy, in the preliminary study reached here, anything but the crudest attempt to cost them, i.e. the use of certification results as a proxy for the entire nexus of outputs.

It is no doubt significant that since 1963 the pioneering work of the Robbins Committee, though partially updated, has scarcely been advanced (Layard, King and Moser, 1969; *Student Numbers*, 1970; Brosan, Carter *et al.*, 1971). The Robbins Report illustrated very thoroughly the significance of the distinctions between costs borne by a student or his family, those borne by an institution, those borne by rate- and tax-payers, and those borne by society as a whole. The student thinks primarily of his private costs and largely ignores publicly-borne costs. The institution is pre-occupied with its own budget, but not with those public expenditures which do not pass through its budget, nor with non-financial costs like the cost of student time. The rate- and tax-payer is mostly aware of the taxation required to finance teacher education and it is certainly material to his interest that, when students are taken out of the labour force into full-time higher education, tax revenue is foregone – hence the extra taxes which tax-payers 'have to pay because the students do not pay income tax and national insurance contributions' (Robbins, 1963, Appendix IV, Annex E). For society, the cost of teacher education can be measured by what might be produced elsewhere in the economy with the resources committed to teacher education.

This sophisticated costing initiative of the Robbins Committee has remained unexploited, and it has, in its updated versions, retained its original orientation towards the incidence of costs. For the purposes of productivity analysis the cost-information system remains quite undeveloped. Some of the specific educational price indices which are essential would not be very difficult to construct, and from time to time throughout the 1960s economists have urged their construction. At the time of writing none has been published by the DES. The Robbins Report established for a wider public in Britain the notion of opportunity costing. Very little attempt seems to have been made to develop this, for example by considering the cost of achieving one objective in terms of lower achievement of another – for the multiple objectives of an educational process are not all (conveniently) complementary. The point about cost-minimization is that unless it is a matter of minimizing the cost of a specified output it is an exercise in public parsimony, not in the economic use of resources.

The consequences of this inadequate cost-information system are serious. To illustrate this, consider first the costing of a single input and, secondly, comparative costing. The single input is student time, accounting for roughly half of the total cost per student year on a full cost basis (see Table 18.1). As a social investment teacher education is, therefore, twice as expensive as the financial cost (which is much the best-known costing) would indicate. The fact that it is only within the last few years that this non-financial cost has been recognized at all widely helps to explain why in colleges, as elsewhere in higher education, the economical use of student time has not been considered an appropriate criterion in the selection of teaching methods.

This cost is also critical for private decision-making. There may be a group of potential student teachers for whom the size of net earnings foregone in order to train is critical because they have a different time preference rate from another group. That is to say, they value differently present as against future income. Such a divergence in time preference rates may help to explain why the same net earnings foregone by one student may weigh more heavily against training than they do for another student with a similar family income. The difference in time preference rates may have the same effect as foregoing more earnings, incurring a greater cost. It could be that this, along with the notorious aid gap between school leaving age and college entrance age, helps to explain the relatively poor representation of the working class among British teachers.

The inadequacies of the cost-information system are particularly obvious in most attempts at comparative costing, where failure to relate costs to objectives results in serious misunderstandings. Comparisons can be valuable. The investigations of the Robbins Committee, for instance, publicized the fact that the total capital cost per residential place in colleges of education was considerably less than that in universities (Robbins, 1963, Appendix II A, Part V). The justification for this was not clear and there is evidence that the differential is now disappearing (*Student Numbers*, 1970). But comparative costing derived from currently available data is far more useful for raising questions than settling them, simply because these costs are usually unit costs related to an input measure, e.g. cost per student year or per new teaching place, not to output measures.

Simple comparison of cost per student between institutions with differing

ing and multiple objectives can be very misleading. In 1971 the largest teacher union in Britain attacked the present allocation of resources in higher education, pointing out that in '1967–8 the cost per student in universities was £1,625, compared with £1,120 for students in advanced further education and £925 for college of education students' (NUT, 1971), quoting *Student Numbers*, 1970). If the students were following similar courses in each type of institution this would be alarming. But they are not.

The relation between cost and function shows clearly in university courses, which vary greatly in expense, a few of them costing two or three times as much to provide per student per year as other courses (*Selection of Unit Costs*, 1968, Table 13). Cost variations depend not only on the nature of the institution, but particularly on the amount of capital required. The latter is an obvious difference between university or advanced further education courses and those in colleges of education where relatively little science and technology is to be found. Partly for this reason, capital costs per student year in universities are three times and in advanced further education twice what they are in colleges of education (see Table 18.1). In addition, universities and, to a lesser extent, advanced further education, have major research functions not shared by the colleges. These differences in the mix of courses and in the balance of teaching and research are probably sufficient to account for much of the cost variation. Carter (1965) had no difficulty in demonstrating that the cost per full-time equivalent student, unweighted, in 1962–3 of teaching activities was much the same in humanities departments of universities and in colleges of education. Moreover, the average cost per full-time undergraduate is very similar in humanities and in university departments of education. Carter used data from the Robbins Report and the assumption that '41% of annual working time of university teachers of the humanities is attributable to research', and '10% of the time of staff of training college is so employed'.

There is a strong case for comparative costing, but not regardless of the objectives upon which these costs are incurred. There may be a good case for increasing expenditure on colleges at the expense of that of universities or even advanced further education, but it cannot be argued rationally in terms of a claim for parity of expenditure between institutions with disparate functions. Some students do require the expenditure of substantially less money than others. The rationale for altering the present allocation of resources within higher education in Britain has to reflect a comparative valuation of complex and varying functions in relation to their costs. Rate of return analysis is the most completely quantified version of this comparative calculus, but in the present state of the art less homogeneous measures, such as cost-effectiveness studies, may produce more useful results.

This is not to say that obvious eccentricities, such as historical differences in residential standards, should be ignored, or to deny the view of the NUT that wasteful duplication and misuse of resources in teacher education argues for some rationalization of provision in higher education. But inputs must be related to output as well as to each other. There are, for example, significant differences in staff-student ratios between colleges of education in England and Wales and those in Scotland, also between the colleges and university departments of education. But these differences cannot possibly be examined except in the context of the very different functions, or mix of functions, of the three kinds of institution.

## 2. Output

The antipathy of the teacher education sector to anything like a systems approach is most clearly revealed in the failure to develop output indicators, which turns on failure to specify objectives with sufficient precision and comprehension. Most British teachers are entrepreneurs rather than corporate planners, and the ethos of the training institutions emphasizes the good instinct approach rather than the systems approach. Management by objectives, like economics and a good deal of modern curriculum theory, is based on an engineering model and the assumption of an almost Newtonian educational universe. The argument should not be whether a purely individualistic or a mechanistic approach is appropriate, since either pole is patently absurd, but where in the spectrum is the right position for teacher education.

To take only one example of the advantages of a less intuitive and pragmatic approach: the way in which the output of teacher education is conceptualized is a vital matter. Much of the debate on teacher education reveals a steady confusion between concepts, especially between teacher education as consumption and as investment. As consumption it is a source of present pleasure, and, as a consumer durable, of future pleasure, as investment it is a source of future earnings and output. Systems analysis would require the objectives of the system and the status of its outputs to be clarified. At present students are educated as persons and trained as teachers concurrently in colleges and even, increasingly, in universities, though consecutive education and training is still the university norm. Despite the complementarity there probably is a distinction between education and training which is real and useful within limits. It is generality which characterizes education. It provides students with skills, knowledge and attitudes that will increase capacity for job-related instruction, but it is not itself job-related instruction. Moreover, education frequently provides both immediate and durable consumer benefits, i.e. the good life. Training, on the other hand, is particular, oriented toward a career, more work-applied and specific.

If good teachers need to be both well educated and well trained a nasty problem of costing separate products in joint supply might seem to have been avoided. Whether this is so depends on two quite different factors. One is the extent to which all the education provided is strictly necessary to produce a good teacher. There must be a cut-off point at which the return to be obtained from successive increases in general education for teachers falls below the return available on marginal resources in some other educational or non-educational employment. The second factor affecting the attempt to cost education as distinct from training is what happens after training. For, supposing that the mixture of education and training is regarded as optimal on other grounds, the subsequent career of a marriageable young woman might be thought highly relevant. Her rapid departure from teaching on marriage, and failure to return, might reclassify her course as simple consumption expenditure.

British governments have tended to regard the training of young women who then teach for only a very short while as simply a poor investment – hence Sir Edward Boyle's famous and revealing phrase concerning teacher supply, 'the economics of Passchendaele'. Indeed there have been times when expenditure on training men seems to have been regarded as investment and that on women as more of a consumption expenditure to be limited as far as possible in favour of investment.

The Robbins Committee talked about equality of access to higher education: 'The good society desires equality of opportunity for its citizens to become not merely good producers but also good men and women'. But the authentic official view is probably represented by the Ninth Report of the National Advisory Council on the Training and Supply of Teachers (1965), which advocated discrimination against women as an inferior investment to men. 'We regard supply considerations as paramount, and consider that the relative opportunities for boys and girls must be viewed in the context of higher education as a whole and not left for the teacher training system to remedy'.

This judgement contains a characteristic confusion of normative and positive elements. There is a positive judgement that training women as teachers is in future going to be an investment with a lower social return than training men – although some of that return, in the form of the quality of family life and of the early upbringing of children, is difficult to compare with the return from men teachers. There is a normative judgement that, in so far as training a woman who will do little teaching is a consumption expenditure, it is valued less than an alternative investment or consumption in an arts or social science faculty in a university, where the cost of educating the same young woman would be little more (*Selection of Unit Costs*, 1968, Tables 11 and 13). Like many economists, the state has tended to regard teacher education as a process with purely investment objectives, which is an extreme example of a widespread reluctance to consider education as consumption.

## 3. *Productivity*

When the study of both the inputs into and the output from a productive process are so undeveloped it is hardly surprising that existing ideas about factors which affect cost-effectiveness should be hazy. By way of example, official thinking has for years supported the idea that there is an optimum size at which cost per unit of output, (hopefully) specified in terms of quality as well as quantity, is minimized. The McNair Report in 1944 asserted that many colleges were 'too small for either effective staffing or economical management', and a similar refrain with recommendations for increase in size has continued ever since. It is suggested (*Student Numbers*, 1970) that there is a threshold of around 500 students beyond which economies of scale cease. In England and Wales nearly two-thirds of colleges have 500–1,000 students, twenty-four have over 1,000.

No work has been published, or possibly even done, on the large variations in unit costs between these expensive institutions, although a regression analysis of the kind done on independent schools by Glennerster and Wilson (1970, Appendix C) would seem possible. The DES may have resigned itself to operating beyond the cost optimum and to acceptance of a rough equality between average and marginal recurrent unit costs (*Student Numbers*, 1970). The Robbins Report was also unable to support its predilection for greater size except by assertion as to the relationship between size, effectiveness and academic status. It did, however, document a conflict concerning optimum size (Robbins Report, 1963, and Appendix II A). There is no particular reason why the optimum size of college for economic operation, i.e. achieving specified educational objectives at least cost, should be produced by a convenient co-incidence of the net tuition cost optimum, the optimum size for provision of teaching practice places without recourse to boarding away, the optimum size for adequate laboratory and library provision and the optimum size for staffing an adequate range of options.

Productivity studies, despite their difficulty, are too important to be neglected in the way they have been. It is well known that public expenditure on education has been rising at an extraordinary rate in Britain in recent times, and teacher training current and capital expenditure accounted for 4·6 per cent. of total educational expenditure in the United Kingdom in 1970–1, compared with 2·2 per cent in 1951–2 (*Social Trends* 1971, Table 138). There is some prima facie evidence that more and more resources are needed to produce one unit of college output, whereas productivity in the economy as a whole moves in the opposite direction. So teacher education costs may have been rising not only absolutely but relatively in the sense that the opportunity cost of producing a unit of output has risen, i.e. the cost in terms of other goods and services which might have been produced with the resources. If the resources needed to produce a specified output of non-educational goods and services remained constant year to year, then the opportunity cost of college output would change in inverse ratio to changes in college productivity. But with the amount of resources needed to produce non-educational goods and services falling year by year, the opportunity cost of college output may be rising at a rate which is a compound of the apparent rate of decline in college productivity and the rate of increase in non-educational productivity. However, teacher education is only absorbing an increasing share of national resources per unit of output if its productivity is negative, or positive and less than that of the whole economy.

The analysis of college productivity supports Blaug's contention (1970) that 'measurement never explains anything; it only tells us what there is to explain'. It reveals how misleading are the ersatz productivity measures currently employed, and how necessary it is to investigate the technology of teacher education. For instance, there is a considerable pressure for small group work, as in other areas of British higher education, and for maintenance, even for lowering, of staff-student ratios. The idea is to raise the quality of teacher education, but it is rare for anyone to wonder whether such a strategy actually delivers greater quality and whether, if it does, this quality improvement is worth the cost, bearing in mind the quality improvement which might be obtained from a different use of marginal resources. Teacher education is both teacher and student intensive. Yet, despite the fuss about CCTV and such developments, astonishingly little research and development work has gone into substituting cheaper for dearer labour, teacher time for student time, capital for labour, cheaper for dearer capital. It is traditional to employ very expensive lecturing staff for clerical and low-level technical and administrative work in preference to cheaper clerical or para-educational staff. That sort of investigation can only proceed hand in hand with the effort to identify and measure quantitative and qualitative changes in input and output and to sort out the productive process.

There are other reasons besides a crude and preliminary productivity analysis for thinking that such micro-economic research into teacher education is overdue. For instance, Vaizey and Sheehan (1968) have shown that since at least the First World War British education in general has become less labour-intensive, i.e. the proportion of total costs represented by teachers' salaries has decreased. There appears to be a long-term process of substitution of capital, and possibly of cheaper labour for the resource which is becoming increasingly expensive relative to other resources: teachers. By contrast the trend in colleges of education in England and

## Table 19.4
### Indices of Real Current and Capital Expenditures by Maintained and Voluntary Colleges of Education in England and Wales 1961-9

| | 1. Teaching Staff Salaries | 2. Other Salaries | 3. Total Salaries | 4. Other Current Expenditure | 5. Total Current Expenditure | 6. Loan Charges | Capital Expenditure from Revenue 7. Maintained Colleges | 8. Voluntary Colleges | 9. Total Capital Expenditure from Revenue | 10. Loan capital | 11. Total Public Expenditure from Revenue |
|---|---|---|---|---|---|---|---|---|---|---|---|
| 1961 | 100 | 100 | 100 | 100 | 100 | 100 | 100 | 100 | 100 | 100 | 100 |
| 1962 | 113 | 108 | 111 | 106 | 109 | 129 | 68 | 255 | 212 | 242 | 120 |
| 1963 | 143 | 123 | 135 | 135 | 135 | 176 | 81 | 251 | 212 | 294 | 145 |
| 1964 | 162 | 143 | 155 | 150 | 153 | 229 | 94 | 180 | 160 | 169 | 159 |
| 1965 | 192 | 147 | 175 | 179 | 176 | 252 | 130 | 173 | 163 | 193 | 184 |
| 1966 | 235 | 173 | 211 | 205 | 208 | 296 | 103 | 174 | 158 | 154 | 209 |
| 1967 | 268 | 195 | 240 | 238 | 239 | 323 | 108 | 143 | 135 | 171 | 235 |
| 1968 | 311 | 220 | 276 | 268 | 273 | 341 | 90 | 140 | 129 | 167 | 264 |
| 1969 | 333 | 235 | 295 | 273 | 286 | 364 | 95 | 148 | 136 | 142 | 277 |

Sources: *Statistics of Education*, 1968 and 1969, Volume 5: *Annual Abstract of Statistics*, 1969

Expenditure data for colleges relates to financial years ending on 31 March for maintained colleges and 31 July for voluntary colleges of the year cited, and was converted to constant pounds. An index for each column, on a 1960-1 base, was then constructed. Conversion to constant pounds calculated by applying an index of weekly wage rates for columns 1. and 2., a retail price index for columns 4. and 6. and a new construction index for columns 7., 8. and 10. In each case 1969 was the base year of the index.

Column 1. data included salaries, superannuation and national insurance. National insurance contributions were attributed between teaching and other staff by estimation for 1961 to 1968.

Column 3. = Column 1. + Column 2.

Column 5. = Column 3. + Column 4.

Column 6. relates only to colleges maintained by local education authorities. Official data excludes any loan charges arising from capital expenditure by voluntary bodies because such charges are not eligible for grant under Regulation 7 of the Training of Teachers (Grant) Regulations 1959.

Column 8. comprises DES grants to voluntary colleges.

Column 9. = Column 7. + Column 8.

Column 10. relates to capital expenditure from loans by maintained colleges only.

Column 11. = Column 5. + Column 6. + Column 9.

Wales between 1961 and 1969 appears to have been quite the opposite. Indeed, as Table 19.4 shows, the index of expenditures on teaching salaries rose by 233 per cent. compared with a rise of 177 per cent. in total public expenditure from revenue. In order to understand such patterns of resource use it will be necessary to disaggregate by institution and by course. The product mix is likely to be important, certain courses or subjects being more input intensive than others, with special resource combinations. It might then become possible, for instance, to see whether changes in productivity or quality were due to across-the-board changes or to alterations in the relative importance of courses or subjects.

CHAPTER 20

# Teacher Education and the Market for Teachers

KEITH DRAKE

## A Misused Proxy

### The Optimum Resource Combination

There is a vital distinction to be made between productivity, the subject
of the previous chapter, and efficiency. In education, as in other forms of
production, there is a spectrum of possible relations between input and
output which covers all feasible permutations within which resources can
be combined. The boundaries of this spectrum are determined by the
current technology, the limits of substitution between the resources used
in the teaching process.

For each resource combination there will be a maximum feasible output.
At current prices, there will be one combination of inputs which can produce
the specified output at a lower cost per unit of input than any other, and
this least-cost combination is the optimum resource combination. It may be
changed by technological developments or by alterations in the price of
inputs. Technological change alters the optimum resource combination
through the input/output ratios associated with each possible combination
of resources, i.e. it alters the maximum feasible productivity of resources.
Price change, by altering the price relationships between resources, may,
without any technological changes, shift the optimum resource combination,
the permutation with the least-cost per unit of output.

### The Staff-pupil Ratio as a Proxy

In Britain the DES uses a sophisticated computer programme to assist the
process of calculating the demand for and supply of teachers and, therefore,
what requirements are to be placed on the system of teacher education
(*Study on Teachers*, 1969). On the demand side there are variables such
as size and structure of school population and staffing standards; on the
supply side the nature of the existing teacher force, its age, sex and specialist
composition, incidence of wastage rates and rates of return to teaching and
intake of new teachers from the training sector. Staffing standards (strictly

teacher–pupil ratios) are a critical variable in the sense that their 'improvement' tends to be a central objective of planning and an important influence on the size and character of investment in initial training.

Very little effort has been made to explore the optimum resource combination for any particular educational process, but in the absence of knowledge a drastic assumption is often made which has powerful quantitative and qualitative consequences for teacher education. This assumption is that staffing ratios can be treated as a proxy for resource combinations – though they may not be particularly good ones since the same staffing ratios could be associated with rather different resource combinations according to the internal organization of schools. A staff-pupil ratio only expresses approximately a ratio between two resources, staff time and pupil time. It is often assumed that as school staffing ratios fall the optimum resource combination is approached. In other words, quality of provision is seen to be largely a matter of staffing ratios: the lower the ratio the better the quality. Actually it is conceivable that, within the range of ratios found in many British primary and secondary schools, the lowering of the ratio in a particular school would represent a 'worsening', a movement away from the optimum resource combination in the sense that the marginal resources used to lower the teacher–pupil ratio would have been more productive of pupil learning if devoted to increased use of other resources, e.g. auxiliary staff and equipment.

The ideal or optimum ratio is not stated, but it clearly exists by implication because educational planning treats most existing ratios as suboptimal and regards a lowering of ratios as improvement. Little is known about the relationship between the full and the proxy optimum resource combination, and the proxy is clearly determined bureaucratically and culturally, i.e. by the DES and the teachers. It is not technically determined. Moreover, it is treated for planning purposes as if there was a single, stable and homogeneous relationship between quality of provision and the ratio. Blaug's scepticism about treating quality as a function of class size in this way still applies, even though overall staffing ratios have tended to replace class size as the proxy:

> ... the functional relationship is probably not a monotonic one but rather a discontinuous step-function with more than one maximum and one minimum, varying with the nature of the subject, the type of teaching method and the age and ability of students. No single generalization could cover all the different situations in which quality sometimes rises and sometimes falls with variations in class size. (Blaug, 1970)

The demand for new teachers is a heavily administered demand. It is a function not merely of school populations and the existing teacher force, but also of the target staffing ratio (related to some optimum ratio), tempered as the movement towards the optimum ratio is by the availability of public money to pay salaries. In the planning of investment in teacher education the manpower requirements approach has been predominant, sensitive as that is to the optimum staffing ratio. Little account has been taken of the possibilities of manipulating the labour market by altering the relative net advantages of teaching and so, for instance, drawing more heavily on the pool of inactive qualified teachers. Little account has been taken of the danger of extrapolating existing mal-utilization of teachers. Within the limits of existing technology, ignoring possible innovations in the teaching process, there may be scope for optimizing substitutions between resources beyond those implicit in a steady lowering of staffing ratios. However, when the size and character of the pupil and teacher populations have been taken into consideration, this misconceived proxy for the optimum resource combination is left as a prime determinant of investment in teacher education.

This over-simple view of the determination of educational quality has serious consequences for teacher education. The nature of the proxy, cast as it is in terms of staff numbers per pupil, leads to a persistent tendency for marginal resources to be pre-empted for the production of sheer numbers of teachers. The numbers priority (not to say obsession) has a powerful prescriptive influence on the training sector, with consequences for job specification as well as for size of investment in training places.

Research on class size has been rather inconclusive as to the benefits of further reducing class sizes as they usually exist in the British school system. Yet official and teacher opinion still believes, for the most part, that the path to more productive schooling lies along a downward gradient of staff-pupil ratios. It has not been demonstrated that this strategy will raise teacher productivity faster than spending on other resources the money that is required to train and support the extra teachers. The consequences of spending extra money that way would be to reduce investment in training places and to alter the role of the teacher.

If the numbers obsession has led to or is leading towards over-manning of British schools the corollary is under-investment in other productive resources, e.g. under-capitalization. Over-manning would probably lead to the training of teachers with an inappropriate skill mix, one which is suitable for a very teacher-intensive production process but not for a more managerial role. Conceivably, the optimum resource combination would involve a retreat by teachers from jobs which machines or para-educational personnel could perform more efficiently, with concentration on management of the learning process and on those tasks which can only be carried out effectively by the most thoroughly and expensively trained educational personnel. Indeed, it might involve a retreat by teachers from jobs which they could perform more efficiently than machines or para-educational personnel. If, in the time saved by delegating a job to a slower or otherwise less efficient auxiliary worker, the teacher could perform a task which was very demanding, which only he could tackle (or one in which the productivity differential between himself and an auxiliary was still greater) then the substitution of one resource for another still represents a gain for the productivity of all the resources combined.

The misconception of the staff–pupil ratio extends further. The ratio is, after all, susceptible to alteration on the pupil as well as on the staff side. It really stands for a staff time–pupil time ratio and there is probably ample scope for economizing pupil time and effectively lowering the ratio without altering the number of staff. The role of staff, and therefore appropriate training, would again be altered. Because it has no budgetary costs, except transfer payments (student grants), attached to it, student time has been relatively ignored as an input into the production process. Many teachers are prodigal with it, treating it as if it was a free good. Teacher training has done nothing to correct this misapprehension, although in the colleges themselves the cost of staff time (salaries) represents something under one-fifth of the cost per student year on a full costing, whereas the cost of student time (net earnings foregone) is something over half of the total cost per student year.

## Elements of an Economic Theory of Teacher Training

When so little is known about the optimum combination of teachers with other resources, at current prices and with the existing technology, it is hardly surprising that so little systematic thought has been devoted to the relationship between teacher training and the market for teachers. However, the elements of an economic theory of teacher training do exist in labour economics and can, at least, be illustrated, in the hope that they will be suggestive of further analysis and investigation.

An efficient market for teachers would be one which distributed teachers so that the use of their specialized skills was optimized. A standard analysis (Hunter and Robertson, 1969) of the sort of factors upon which the efficient operation of such a market depends identifies them as: 1. the 'powers and processes of adjustment of the price (or wage) structure'; 2. 'the adequacy and balance of initial training'; 3. 'the availability of retraining and other means of adjusting the occupational structure'; 4. 'the ease or difficulty of moving workers from one location to another'; 5. 'the adequacy, accuracy and use of information'. As a framework for analysis this is probably least useful when its application is most general, but even at a high level of generality it serves to emphasize the significance of interconnections, like those between training and the wage structure, which are frequently and misleadingly ignored, for instance, by the James Report (*Teacher Education and Training*, 1972).

It is not clear whether tutors have gone far enough in promoting flexibility and readiness to innovate among young teachers, although, in general, tutors may be more alive to the possibilities of current technology than many school teachers. The predominant conservatism of teaching may tend to nullify the productivity of initial training. Combined with the acknowledged inadequacy of in-service training it may well be responsible for some of the serious rigidities and inefficiencies of the labour market. Assuming that the effect of initial and in-service training is broadly to improve the efficiency of the market, working against them are institutionalized conservatism, a poor information system and a wage structure so rigid that it cannot correct any significant shortage or surplus of teachers which it is beyond the capacity of the training system to eliminate.

In recent years there have been fruitful developments in the economic theory of training, for instance, Becker's use of the distinction between general and specific skills (Becker, 1964). To simplify what is in Becker a refined and complex theory: general training can be defined as training which provides skills useful in organizations other than that which provides the training, in this case outside the state education system. General training raises the marginal productivity of the trainee equally inside and outside the training organizations. Training costs are thus borne chiefly by workers in the form of earnings foregone, and workers hope to recoup these costs from rather high lifetime earnings. By contrast, specific training equips the trainee only with skills applicable within the training organization. That organization may be prepared to bear a very large proportion of training costs in the expectation of recouping them while paying workers less than the enhanced value of their marginal product.

The labour market for teachers is, in a sense, a series of inter-related markets for teachers. Some teachers, for example, really able university graduates, may be in demand in the private sector of education, in the armed forces or company training schemes, or quite outside education. On the other hand, infant teaching is probably more specific because the market is that much narrower, indeed, apart from a tiny private sector, there is only one possible buyer, the state school system. These labour-market subdivisions and related elasticities of substitution might repay investigation. For instance, Becker (1964) suggested that a really strong monopsonist (a single buyer) might have to cope with very little poaching of trained workers and so training investments would be highly specific. The degree of monopsony and therefore of specificity will clearly vary between sub-markets. According to the theory, it might be expected that to the extent that trainee teachers have received a specific training they will not be very well paid after training. Or, if the private costs of training vary between different types of teacher, as they surely do, the private rate of return on teacher training will vary in the same way. Bearing in mind that the power of the monopsonist is heavily determined by the degree of elasticity of substitution of the trained manpower, it would be worth following up Becker's aside that a 'relatively large difference between marginal product and wages in monopsonies might measure, therefore, the combined effect of economic power and a relatively large investment in employees' (Becker, 1964).

Consideration of the wage level and structure in relation to teacher training and supply is extraordinarily neglected in Britain, as is consideration of the cost of training. It is another example of that neglect of prices which is the traditional Achilles' heel of the manpower requirements approach to educational planning. Despite the formidable array of controls at the command of the DES, and the less blatant but still powerful influence which it can exert, lack of control of some variables, like student preferences or wastage from teaching, and the length of the lead time of college output, allows specific short-term imbalances between supply of and demand for teachers to develop. There are even long-term imbalances which are resistant to corrective measures. Mathematics teachers are a case in point.

To some extent, the case of mathematics teachers is a dramatic instance of reaction to the occupational squeeze in which British teachers have been caught for some decades. The reduction of income differentials between teachers and non-white collar workers is not unrelated to the impressive expansion of education and of the communications media, which has tended to devalue one of their prime assets, the scarcity and inaccessibility of knowledge. Their position is in one important respect analogous to the classic case of the clerks. As Hunter and Robertson (1969) pointed out, the extension of education 'removed obstacles to entry to clerical employment, so that despite a major expansion of demand the relative wage position of the clerical worker has fallen vis-à-vis the average manual worker'.

In the case of teachers, because the DES has decreed the end of teacher shortage in the 1970s (on unrevealed evidence), even the accustomed growth in demand for teachers may disappear. The squeeze on differentials appears to have affected recruitment of mathematics teachers so severely that only a very substantial differential in their favour, of a size impossible to achieve within the present wage structure, could hope to attract sufficient recruits – of an adequate quality – to overcome the national shortage of mathematics teachers. In its highly revealing advertising the DES recognizes (but does not say) that the earnings differentials which are paid to mathematics teachers in British schools are inadequate to secure an adequate supply of trained mathematics teachers. It recognizes that career prospects and above all the low and early pay ceiling common to all British school teachers are critical handicaps to recruitment with or without training. Advertising therefore stresses the possibilities for mathematics teaching in terms of reaching the career ceiling more quickly than the average teacher and then, key attraction, the opportunity to reach higher levels of pay by leaving teaching and being 'promoted' to administration, inspection and so forth. To regard the level and structure of pay as more or less given, as the DES does, reduces its otherwise formidable power to control teacher supply. In the face of really contrary market forces, physical control of training is not an effective mechanism for securing an adequate supply of teachers – of a given quality.

Nor is the disparity in quantity and quality of recruitment to different specialities the only example of the consequences of the self-denying ordinance whereby the DES so rarely manipulates the wage structure as a supply control. For instance, in the 1960s it was thought advisable (*Ninth Report*, 1965) to try to alter the balance of the sexes in training in favour of men, in the belief, presumably, that men were a better investment and that non-vocational education of women was not the job of the colleges, at least not to the extent to which it was occurring. In the event, indicative rationing of places, the manpower requirements approach (literally) was seen to be very limited. For the relative pay of men and women was markedly different, even where their earnings were equal. As Routh (1965) was able to show, using scale averages rather than earnings, women teachers have tended to do better than men in the sense that 'the 1960 average for qualified teachers was 589 per cent of 1913 for men and 778 for women'. When the effect of the advent of equal pay for women teachers is combined with the severe restriction on the occupational choice of women compared with men, it will be seen that a policy of altering the sex ratio against women was working directly against the grain of the labour market. Little progress could be expected without imbalancing even further the quality differential between male and female recruits to training.

The planning of teacher supply and teacher training in Britain has generally taken account of need rather than demand, the need for teachers being calculated with little regard to the price of teachers in relation to the price of other kinds of skilled manpower, whereas demand is a matter of prices and quantities. Yet changes in relative pay and employment conditions have always been an important determinant of the quality as well as the quantity of recruits to teaching and to teacher training. Unfortunately, economists have not discovered how to remedy this general defect of manpower planning as it applies to the demand for teacher training or for education in general. As Schultz (1968) remarked rather brutally:

    ... there is as yet no satisfactory theory which connects ex post rates
    of increase in the demands for the satisfactions and earnings that accrue

to college and university students with future rates of increase in these demands. Projections, of course, abound, but they are in principle as naïve as exponential population projections. You can take your choice, and if you happen to be correct, it will not be because of reason but because of luck. Manpower studies do not provide the answer, nor are the sophisticated programming models as yet providing an answer.

The DES plans teacher training as part of its forward planning on teacher supply, which is turn premised to a significant extent upon an implied optimum combination of resources, represented by the staff which schools 'need'. It can do little, and does less, about the movements of relative input prices, yet, even if the technology remains stable, these prices must be critical determinants of an optimum resource combination.

Although not incorporated openly into teacher training plans, it has long been recognized how important are the responses of potential teachers to the complex of hidden and explicit prices, psychic income, relative pay and employment conditions. In 1924 Lance Jones quoted the 1912–13 Report of the Board of Education: 'The number of young persons adopting the profession of a teacher will ultimately be determined by its attractiveness in respect of emoluments, immediate and prospective, status and security.' The stress laid by Jones on the relative attractiveness of teaching could be illustrated in the 1960s with reference to the quality and number of recruits in mathematics or physics, or of men to train in colleges. In British teaching there have been examples, fortunately few, of a diseconomy of low wages, which produces what might be called the Macaulay effect, i.e. teachers became 'the refuse of other callings' (Macaulay's speech in House of Commons, 19 April 1847, quoted by Lance Jones, 1924). Poor quality in teaching may be a function of poor relative pay rather than poor training, for teacher training, like any other form of education, depends heavily on the quality of its input for the quality of its output.

In a fragmentary and intuitive way the intending teacher no doubt takes far more than relative pay into account, estimating private costs as well as private benefits, a view supported by august educational opinion, for example, the General Teaching Council for Scotland in its Memorandum for the Select Committee on Education and Science (Select Committee 1969–70). The General Teaching Council clearly believed that the quality of entrants to teacher training is a direct function not only of lifetime earnings, but also of the extent to which the opportunity cost of training is offset. It ascribed the unsatisfactory quality of graduate recruits to training to 'another year of study on a relatively low standard of living, while graduates entering other professions may receive more competitive salaries'. It argued for training grants 'equivalent in value to commencing salaries on the national scales' and cited in support Home Office advertising for graduates willing to train as probation officers which stated that 'during training they will be treated as trainee employees – and paid a salary of not less than £930'.

To assess the net advantages of teaching relative to those of alternative employments is a task of daunting complexity. Yet an understanding and manipulation of relative net advantages may be as important for the quality of teachers produced by the training system as all the re-jigging of the machinery which so concerned the James Committee on Teacher Education and Training. Wage factors, such as the size, security and lifetime profile of prospective earnings, and non-wage factors, such as working conditions, holidays, pensions, promotion possibilities and status, have to be measured in some common unit and compared between different jobs. But relative net advantages have been little investigated, except by or for interested parties such as teacher unions and associations, whose exercises are marred by special pleading, and excepting occasional solo efforts (e.g. Norris, 1971).

It could be that appropriate adjustments to the relative net advantages of teaching would, in some instances, secure changes in the quality and quantity of newly-trained teachers more cheaply and easily than altering training. Norris offers some evidence that non-wage factors are becoming less important for teachers in relation to wage factors. He has attempted to qualify some of the more quantifiable non-monetary benefits of teaching, especially the abnormally long holidays. He decided that all these non-monetary benefits were now only slightly larger for teachers than for comparable occupational groups. The balance of relative net advantage might, therefore, be swinging against teachers in the matter of non-wage factors just as the balance of monetary advantage appears to have been swinging for a long time against the lower professional groups as a whole.

To take into account only certain factors, e.g. wage factors, could be seriously misleading. What matters is the nexus of advantages and disadvantages in teaching and in competing occupations, and the comparison of net advantages. The complexity of the accounting can be illustrated in terms of relative pay. On first employment a trained honours graduate in teaching is paid a rate which compares favourably with the starting salary in almost any competing occupation. But as the years go by his relative position changes and the rather peculiar lifetime earnings profile of British teachers becomes significant. The range of earnings in teaching has been rather smaller than in occupations with similar training and qualifications. In particular, for men and for women, the ratio of the earnings of the upper decile of salary earners to those of the lower decile has been lower than in any comparable occupational group or even for all full-time workers (Norris, 1971, Table 1). This is an example of one of the disadvantages of teaching which has to be set off against advantages, other disadvantages being the non-transferability of non-graduate training, poor pensions, low status, very constricted promotion prospects beyond a certain level, setting in rapidly for women, and limited scope for sidestepping into other occupations later in life.

The options which have been mentioned are important in this sort of accounting, but quite as difficult to value as the job satisfaction which can count for so much. When the subjectivity of valuing status and psychic benefits is brought into the accounting the game might seem to be lost. But with regard to consequences for recruitment to and therefore output from training, as well as wastage among trained teachers, this is not so. There are severe limits on the degree to which benefits are regarded as substitutes for each other. In certain cases, for example, some university teachers, status and psychic benefits are substitutes for monetary income. They may be able to command considerably higher incomes in other jobs with inferior net advantages, and the difference between their actual earnings in university work and their transfer earnings is a minimum measure of the residual balance of advantage. But there is an economic man inside each teacher, who knows well that mortgages are not paid with psychic income. To act upon the net advantages of teaching requires an appreciation of the scope for and limitations on substitution, for it is on specific advantages or disadvantages that action is taken, while the decision of the would-be teacher is based on the final balance which is struck.

It will be seen, even from this fragmentary and merely illustrative discussion of the significance of costs and prices for recruitment to training, that there are two different concepts of teacher shortage. One relates to an optimum physical resource combination (i.e. regardless of price) and the other is a market measure. The first is not shortage at a price; the second is. The first is defined in relation to a staffing ratio which is lower than the existing ratio, and the shortage is the number of extra teachers who would be needed, but are not actually being demanded, to achieve that ratio. At the moment the shortage is said to exist, neither the money nor the training places exist to eliminate it. This shortage is an aspect of the general economic problem that resources are limited in relation to our wants, that scarcity exists. Its existence says little more than that there is a scarcity of productive resources for education.

On the other hand, a market shortage might be expected to raise teacher pay and provoke an increase in recruits for training. At the ruling price (the wage level) this shortage, crudely defined, would mean that effective demand exceeded numbers offering themselves for teaching, a situation experienced only with one or two categories of teachers in some areas or schools. The first, a manpower shortage, is, as Bowman (1963) has argued, an absolute measure. She cites, as an example of the way such absolute manpower shortages can appear overnight, the case of the first sputnik, which 'created the image, if not the reality, of a large shortage of technical manpower in the United States'.

The image of a technical manpower shortage in British schools posited by the DES is of a similar character. It too appears like a deus ex machina whose interventions in the action provide a convenient, if ill-founded, premise for official policy. In a frank footnote Bowman (1963), writing about manpower forecasts in general, put her finger on an important limitation of the sort of teacher manpower forecasting which is the basis of investment in teacher training in Britain. She remarked that 'though increasingly sophisticated in presentation, procedures nevertheless remain essentially ad hoc, without foundations in analytical delineation of current or prospective shortage or excess'. The absolute type of shortage is founded on a hypothesis about the basic parameters of the teaching-learning process, especially the optimum use of teaching time in combination with other resources. The whole process is so little understood that it does not require much pessimism to believe that the chance of actually using teachers efficiently at what are supposed to be optimum staffing ratios is little better than random.

On the other hand, the relative measure of shortage describes a situation of failure to clear the market, where employers cannot hire as many teachers of specified quality at current prices as they are willing to pay for. Presumably the missing manpower is attracted by the superior net advantages of other employments. This type of market shortage has not been apparent in Britain in general, though the lack of information about the quality of teachers could mean that equilibrium between effective demand for and supply of teachers has been achieved at the expense of quality, i.e. if quality was held constant a true market shortage would be apparent.

An obvious criterion for market shortage is relative pay changes, and a more refined one is changes in relative net advantages. If there was a general, serious and long-term market shortage of teachers, then, even in the sticky and rather uncompetitive labour market, teacher pay might be expected to rise more than those of most other groups. Teacher pay having, if anything, risen less than pay of other groups in recent decades, then, assuming no change in quality, either a pre-existent shortage has been ameliorated, a shortage has turned into excess, or an excess has been aggravated. Unless changes in relative pay are significantly disproportionate to changes in relative net advantages these are the options.

In theory there is one criterion of market shortage more sophisticated than movements in relative pay or relative net advantages, which is the comparative rate of return. Its superiority lies in the fact that it takes into account costs and relates them to benefits, which is what the private decision-makers, potential teachers, do. In theory the efficient allocation of resources between teacher education, other educational investments and non-educational investments should be determined by comparison of marginal rates of return, and resources should be reallocated between competing investments until marginal returns on expenditure are equal on all investments.

Unfortunately, the measurement of such social rates of return is highly problematic. Given the wage structure for British teachers, the differences between the lifetime earnings streams of teachers with different educations may reflect with some accuracy these educational differences, but the assumed connection between earnings and educational differentials is less likely to hold outside teaching, though sensitivity analysis can do something to mitigate this difficulty. However, it is harder to see a way round the objection that rate of return analysis cannot safely ignore the consumption benefits of education or the objection that a teacher's earnings can only be very remotely connected to his contribution to the national product and are not, therefore, an accurate measure of that contribution.

One obvious reason why teacher earnings will be a poor measure of contribution to the national product is that the external productivity of teachers must, in some unfathomed way, be derived from the productivity of their pupils. Since the external productivity of pupil and of teacher and the inter-relationship are impossibly difficult to measure and attribute it is difficult to see how, even in competitive markets (and labour markets are notoriously uncompetitive), pupil and teacher earnings could reflect marginal productivities. In sum, many of the returns are not measurable within the system of prices and so by an internal rate of return. Finally, in order to use the rate of return approach to decide investment policy it would, as usual, be necessary to go on to make some daring connections between observed behaviour and future behaviour.

It is, however, quite clear that in the market for teachers in Britain the predominant force is the employer, who provides teacher training and enjoys the power of a single buyer, a monopsonist. In the provision of education the state has built up an immensely powerful monopoly position over the last century, so that the teacher has little or no alternative to employment with the state on conditions of training and wages prescribed by the employer. Consumers, whether parents or pupils, have little influence over the nature of educational provision and, therefore, over the sort of training given to teachers, which aims to fit them to provide what the state prefers.

The curious case of Risinghill, or discussion of voucher systems and deschooling proposals, is symptomatic of some discontent with the sort of education provided by the monopolist and prescribed, through the house training system, for teachers. The proposals of the James Report, under a verbal smokescreen about increased teacher participation, advocated a more homogeneous and tightly controlled teacher training system. It was to be wrested from the influence of the relatively autonomous universities, topped off by a body directly financed and appointed by the DES, and clearly aimed to continue the process of eliminating the remaining sources of independent initiative in the training system.

The reality of workers' (i.e. teachers') control of the school system is little greater than the reality of consumer sovereignty (e.g. parental choice). The essentials of professional autonomy, of which one is control of training, lie within the power of the employer, the state. It is the employer, not educators, who determines the requirements needed to practise. Certification is a function of the employer. It is not difficult to imagine some of the consequences of the professionalization of teaching if the employer allowed it. Standards of training might easily be raised more quickly than has been the case in the past, and compulsory certification would spread more quickly into further and higher education and into the private sector. In the short run, until relative pay had shifted in favour of the teachers, this could create a general market shortage of teachers and would raise the quality of recruitment to training.

In practice, the employer has moved only with slow and grudging steps towards a trained teacher force throughout the British education system. If the requirement to train endangers the supply as well as the quality of recruits, then, instead of improving the relative net advantages of teaching sufficiently to overcome the disincentive effect of training, the state has always tended to exempt from or water down training and, therefore, presumably the quality of teaching. No doubt the James Report, with its suggestions for drastically reduced training for scarce categories of recruits (*Teacher Education and Training*, 1972) and merely voluntary in-service training, accurately interpreted the predisposition of an employer whose monopoly position allows considerable adulteration of the product.

Some of the objectives of professional groups, for example, the quiet life and security of employment, have been granted by the employer, but not other objectives such as high incomes and status, both of which would probably require independent powers to restrict entry and control training. Control of access to teaching, which in the state school sector means access to training from 1973 onwards, is a critical power for professionalization. Control of access is a critical power for other effective labour monopolies in Britain, such as those operated by dockers and printers as well as doctors and architects. In British education this power belongs to the employer.

British school teachers, like American ones, are clearly not members of a profession in the normal sense of the word. They suffer non-professional restrictions on the autonomy of the individual practitioner and of the occupational group as a whole, and notably lack, as do American teachers, a 'comprehensive self-governing organization of practitioners' (Lieberman, 1956). At best, British teachers have had to settle for the form without the substance. Thus Scottish teachers, no doubt aware of the General Medical Council, have a General Teaching Council, a statutory body to advise on the training and supply of teachers, with considerable power over training but, significantly, subject in the last resort to the Secretary of State for Scotland (Select Committee on Education and Science 1969–70). This Council reviews 'standards of education, training and fitness to teach appropriate to persons entering the teaching profession'. It has 'statutory responsibilities in advising the Secretary of State about the length and nature of courses of instruction. The advice the Council tenders on the supply of teachers must, under the Act, exclude reference to salaries and conditions of service' (Select Committee). It is only an advisory body, an ersatz for professional autonomy and control of training and entry, with power to expel.

As salaried employees of the state (technically, in general, of pseudo-employers, local education authorities), British teachers are controlled by laymen and administrators, not by their peers. This is not to argue, one way or another, whether education is too important to be left to educators. It is merely to describe a situation. The quality of their services is not the responsibility of the teachers themselves to anything like the extent that it is for lawyers or doctors, whose training, though heavily subsidized by the state, is not strictly controlled by it, and whose services are not inspected by local and central government.

A significant proportion of teacher time is spent on activities for which training to teach is hardly necessary. As Lieberman (1956) has argued in an American context, if teachers concentrated on teaching and delegated other jobs to educational sub-professions there would develop the sort of hierarchy of function and of professional competence which is to be found in medicine. Such increased specialization would undoubtedly feed back into training, for many British teachers expect the training system to promote the existing degree of despecialization. Well-trained and highly experienced teachers spend an important amount of their time on tasks for which a much shorter and cheaper training would be adequate, and in criticism of newly trained teachers by experienced teachers particular prominence is given to their incompetence at keeping registers, counting dinner money and a host of other sub-professional tasks. If there was increased job specialization, training for education would become more closely related to the scarcity of particular abilities and skills, and teacher training would top off a hierarchy of educational training programmes in the same way as the training of doctors relates to its penumbra of sub-professional training programmes for nurses, technicians, radiotherapists, administrators and so forth. Specialization, besides raising efficiency, might also change the role of teachers, putting them in a better position to control their own destiny.

It has to be emphasized that such specialization need not increase the specificity of teacher training; indeed, it might well reduce it. It has been suggested that the elasticity of substitution, which measures the specificity and generality of teacher training, is particularly related to the type of training institution. Taylor (1968) has argued that modern technology is

. . . in a sense less specialised in its educational demands . . . [it] alters the elasticity of substitution of people with different qualifications, and this may come to affect what happens to the output of colleges of education. It has been a commonplace for years in the United States that a substantial proportion of those graduating in education never teach. Some of those in this country who defended the retention of teacher education in single purpose institutions thought that this might protect the sources of supply, but inadequate attention seems to have been given to changes in the market for highly educated manpower. It used to be said that training as a teacher disqualified a person for any other kind of useful work. We now have to face up to the consequences of a situation in which this is becoming less and less true.

Taylor's analysis is suggestive, but without further detailing at certain points it is difficult to be quite sure of the line of argument. Whether teachers train in monotechnic or polytechnic institutions is not, in itself, a significant determinant of the specificity of their training. What matters is the nature of the specialization, whether the particular mix of knowledge, skills and attitudes characteristic of the trained teacher has a market value outside the education system. What matters also is the quality of the person who has so specialized. Lawyers, classicists, engineers and accountants are frequently found in the civil service or business management, but not employed specifically, i.e. for their original skills. The fact that so high a proportion of trained teachers are women immediately explains, to some degree, the greater specificity of teacher training. The nature of the training and the quality of those who are trained, in relation to the entire market for high-level manpower, might explain most of the remaining differences in specificity between trained teachers and those with different vocational training.

Narrowly conceived, the interest of a monopsonist might be held to be the maintenance of a tame teacher force whose bargaining power is weakened by maximizing the specificity of training. A relatively despecialized teacher force, with entry qualifications below the norm for higher education and inferior final qualifications (even if the James Report proposals were to be implemented) would fit this strategy. The interest of pupils and students might be better served by raising the quality of teachers, and quality costs money. In Britain that money means rates and taxation, which in turn means votes won or lost. However, the economics of British politics, though relevant, is a different story.

*Part 7*

RESEARCH IN TEACHER EDUCATION

CHAPTER 21

# An Introduction to Research in Teacher Education

## Donald Lomax

The earlier chapters of this book have clearly revealed that the history of teacher training is relatively short. The development of research into teacher education is of even more recent origin. For most of the time since teacher training began, researchers have taken little interest in the problems which have confronted the colleges and departments of education. Taylor (1969 b) has argued that there are three main links between teacher training and educational research. First, it is necessary that the teacher training curriculum should reflect our increased understanding of how learning takes place. Studies of the learning processes have rapidly extended our knowledge during this century and a glance at recent work suggests that our understanding is steadily increasing (Adams and Bray, 1970; Anderson and Myrow, 1971; Boruth, 1970; Bruce and Crowley, 1970; Crothers, 1970; Meyer, 1970; Olson, 1970; Rothkopf, 1970). The application of this newly acquired knowledge will continue to be a challenge to teachers. The second link which Taylor sees is the influence of research, undertaken by individuals or groups in teacher training institutions, on the development of teacher education. Unfortunately little influential research has been done by lecturers in colleges of education and the output from university departments has been more restricted than might have been expected. The third link, he claims, is that between studies of the process of teacher education and the determination of policy. It is fair to say that the impact of such research has not been great.

It may be argued that the chief purpose of research into the education of teachers is to improve the programmes of teacher preparation which are provided in university departments and colleges of education. In recent times, however, more stress has been placed on increasing the numbers of students in training than on improving the processes by which they are educated. As, by the end of the twentieth century we shall need half a million teachers to satisfy the needs of the ten million children who will then be in our schools (Wilson, 1969), it seems probable that questions concerning the demand for, and the supply of, efficient teachers will continually require consideration. It is the realization that we are unlikely to have enough competent teachers within the foreseeable future that has led to the conclusion that we must make the best use of our limited resources, and must therefore seriously question the efficiency of our present programmes of teacher education. These programmes have been developed mainly during the last hundred years, on the basis of an increased knowledge of general psychological principles, an inadequate understanding gained from the practical experience of teachers, and the growth of studies in the social sciences and philosophy (Smith, 1971). Those who have been involved in research in teacher education have therefore found it necessary to seek greater understanding of teaching behaviour and greater knowledge of its influence on pupil learning. At the present time we may be only cautiously optimistic, for the attainment of such knowledge and understanding would still leave us with the task of modifying our institutions and their teacher education courses – a task which Othanel Smith has likened to that of rebuilding vehicles while they are in motion. Unfortunately, until relatively recent times, there has been little rigorous British research into teacher education, and although American studies may now be counted by the thousand (Barr, 1929, 1948, 1952, 1961; Gage, 1963; Biddle and Ellena, 1964; Simon and Boyer, 1967; Smith, 1969; Flanders, 1970) it remains true that we still have a serious lack of dependable knowledge upon which to base our training procedures.

Smith (1971) has pointed out that an adequate course of teacher education must include 1. training in skills; 2. teaching of pedagogical concepts and principles; 3. the creation of relevant attitudes; 4. teaching the subject matter of instruction. The first three of these have usually been described as professional training while the fourth has usually been considered to be personal academic education. This distinction between academic and professional education has provided matter for considerable argument over the years. Reference to these discussions and to their influence on curriculum structure and educational administration has been frequently made in earlier chapters of the present volume. The James Report has rekindled the long-standing fiery debates on the virtues and weaknesses of concurrent and consecutive courses. There are strong demands for more evidence to reinforce the arguments. It therefore seems that teacher education and research into its problems matter. It seems that the social, economic and technological needs of our society now demand that research activity should be extended. Fortunately, during the last decade there has been a great increase in the amount of research undertaken and a steady increase also in the amount of money which has been made available for research purposes.

The arrangements for stimulating educational research in Britain tend to be based on a loose network of organizations, which may be broadly divided into two categories. In the first of these categories are found organizations which are generally concerned with examining research applications with a view to financing suitable projects, while the second category contains institutions which are mainly concerned with the implementation of research projects, using finance provided by other bodies. These categories are not, however, mutually exclusive, and there are many overlapping areas of interest. The main funding bodies include the Department of Education and Science and a number of research councils which separately administer the funds which they receive from the central government. As far as teacher education is concerned, the Social Science Research Council is of foremost importance. This Research Council came into operation in 1966 at a time when advancements in the social sciences clearly indicated the need for greater financial support for new studies. In 1968–9 the budget for this body was £1·5 million; in 1969–70 £2·25 million; and in 1970–1 £3·4 million. The main research interests of the Council's Educational Research Board are teacher education and utilization; nursery and pre-school education; minority groups; further education; and the evaluation of new approaches to education.

The Schools Council for Curriculum and Examinations which was founded in 1964 is financed by the Department of Education and Science and by local education authorities. The Council's income for research and development was £775,000 in 1968–9; £675,000 in 1969–70; and £709,000 in 1970–1. Although this body does not yet participate in initial teacher training, its local teachers' centres help to promote curriculum development. As there is to be strongly increased future emphasis on in-service training then this council may have an important role to play. The Council's present research policy is to commission other institutions – such as university departments or the National Foundation for Educational Research, to carry out the investigations in which it is particularly interested. The Director of the Schools Council has pointed out that increasing thought is now being given to the problem of liaising with colleges of education with regard to the work undertaken in the training of teachers (Wrigley, 1970). The Council is aware that the teacher education curriculum is now providing the focus for a lively debate.

The National Council for Educational Technology was founded in 1967 and is financed directly by the Department of Education and Science, the Ministry of Education in Northern Ireland, and the Scottish Education Department. Its aim is to promote the development, application and evaluation of those systems, techniques and aids which are essential to the improvement of the processes of human learning. This work is obviously of great relevance to teacher education. The Council's budget (only £22,000 in 1967–8) is relatively limited, but some large-scale projects are at the planning stage. The Council is currently engaged upon work in both the initial and in-service sectors of teacher education.

In addition to the institutions briefly described above there are a number of other foundations which give some support to projects having relevance for teacher education. The Nuffield, Rowntree, Wolfson, Gulbenkian and Leverhulme foundations have all supported work in British universities.

The main institution responsible for carrying out educational research, apart from the universities, is the National Foundation for Educational Research which was founded in 1946. The NFER receives support from both the DES, and from local education authorities. Its total budget was £467,000 in 1968–9; £477,000 in 1969–70 and £528,000 in 1970–1. Although the Foundation was not originally directly concerned with the training of teachers, many of its projects have been of great relevance to teacher education. More recently, however, projects have been undertaken in the teacher training sector. In Chapter 16 of this volume, Hollins has already referred to Cane's (1969) investigation into in-service training, which demonstrated the gap existing between the needs of teachers for in-service training and the present available provisions. Pidgeon (1970) has given brief interesting descriptions of two other recent investigations ('Educational Research and the Teacher' and 'The Teaching Day Project'), which are of special interest to the teaching profession.

It will be clear from this brief outline of the existing arrangements for the promotion of research in Britain that most of the grant-giving institutions are of recent origin, and have budgets which are modest by American standards. By 1970 two million pounds were being invested in empirical research in education. Although this is only one-tenth of one per cent. of the total expenditure on education, it marks a vast improvement on the level of support for research that obtained in past decades. Wrigley (1970) believes that future prospects are bright, and sees the main shortage to be not one of money but rather of qualified and competent research workers. Recently the Council of Europe (1971) has produced a Survey of Educational Research in Europe which provides full details of educational research policy and activities in a large number of countries. British researchers who seek a broader perspective will find these publications extremely helpful.

It is not unusual for reviews of research in teacher education to begin by explaining the great difficulties which face the author who attempts to impose some form of classification upon the varied assortment of recent studies. Here a systems approach (Astin, 1966; Oxtoby, 1967; Taylor, 1969 b; Lomax, 1972a) will be adopted, in which attention will be directed towards contextual variables, input variables, process variables and output variables. The assignment of studies under these general headings will often be arbitrary, but the work discussed in the following chapters will cover some important problem areas.

As Taylor (1969 a) has pointed out, it is hardly possible to understand the present problems and achievements of colleges and departments of education without some knowledge of their development during the last 130 years. In the earlier chapters of this book, Ross (Chapter 8) has traced the development of colleges as institutions of higher education offering professional courses of study, and has analysed the unresolved dichotomy between professional and general education, while Turner (Chapter 9) has described the creation and the development of the Area Training Organizations in a penetrating analysis of their structure, difficulties and aspirations. Studies of the historical development of university departments of education have been provided by Tuck (Chapters 5 and 6) in papers which contain an abundance of fascinating detail. The comparative studies of Scotland (James Scotland, Chapter 3), Europe and the United States of America (Holmes, Chapter 2) widen the perspective and produce an interesting background against which to evaluate recent changes in British teacher training procedures.

One of the important characteristics of the teaching profession is its size (Vaizey, 1969). The fact that teachers are such a large body means that numerically they resemble such other occupational groups as shop assistants or nurses rather than the smaller, more exclusive professional groups. Etzioni (1969) classifies teaching in the same category as nursing and social work, and regards these as 'semi-professions', whose members are trained within a relatively short period and thus acquire a less specialized body of knowledge. Hence they have lower status and weaker authority than the smaller elite groups. Further insights into the historical development of the teaching profession have been given by Sir Ronald Gould (Chapter 4). Another perspective emerges from the various histories of individual colleges (Fuller, 1966; Warwick, 1966) and one of the most interesting of these is also one of the most colourful (Body and Frangopulo, 1970). Collier (Chapter 10) traces some of the historical background of his own college and then goes on to provide a fascinating picture of part of the administrative structure upon which teacher training is based.

Much useful background information has been produced for researchers by various official reports. Amongst these the McNair Report (1944) deserves special mention, while the Robbins Report (1962) has become compulsory reading for all those with a serious interest in higher education. The Weaver Report (1966) is of particular interest to those who wish to understand administrative developments in colleges of education. In this book several chapters (Holmes, Chapter 2; Tuck, Chapter 6; Ross, Chapter 8; Turner, Chapter 9) give critical accounts of various sections of the James Report (1972).

A major contextual variable which has had profound effects upon the development of teacher education is society's demand for well-educated teachers (Taylor, 1969 b). This demand may be interpreted as a function of the national birth rate, the population age distribution and Britain's current stage of technological development. Taylor (1969 a) has outlined the effects of these influences on teacher supply and has discussed the desirability of a more structurally differentiated teaching force. A further source of useful information for researchers is provided by the statistics of education which the DES produces annually. These reports include detailed analyses of the costs of various sectors of the system and thus produce useful data for both the educationalist and the economist. In theory, economics should provide a useful paradigm for rational decision-making, but as Drake (Chapter 18) points out, little is known about costs and benefits of training in any occupation. Although it is possible to analyse the publicly-borne costs of teacher education, or the relationship between teacher education and the labour market, other aspects of the current situation, such as the task of measuring private and social rates of return on teacher education, present severe difficulties, which indicate the need for cautious planning and serious research efforts. Valuable studies of the economics of education have been produced by Blaug (1967, 1968, 1969 and 1970) and Woodhall (1970). As Maureen Woodhall points out, much research in economics evolves from two basic questions. First, it is necessary to consider the nature of the interaction between the nation's economy and the system of education, and secondly, to enquire whether the traditional tools and techniques of the economist help to produce more efficient administration and planning of education. Research is continuing into the methodology of cost-benefit analysis of education and the use of manpower forecasting in educational planning.

The studies briefly discussed above have described the development of teacher education and the economics and administration of its current provision. This is the context within which the following chapters will examine the input variables, the process variables and the output variables.

In Chapter 22, Cohen examines some important input variables in describing college of education students in terms of their social origins, attainments, attitudes and personal characteristics. These variables are identified as those which both qualify the range and content of the training course and affect the quality of its outputs. In his selective review of the literature he produces evidence that the majority of college students have been recruited from the upper working and lower middle classes. Although the 1960s brought a massive expansion in student teacher numbers, there is no evidence to indicate that this led to a decline in academic standards. In general, however when judged in terms of intelligence test scores or their performance at the Advanced Level GCE, the college students are shown to be inferior to their university contemporaries. Those students who originally sought unsuccessfully to gain university entrance, and thereafter accepted a college of education place as a second-best alternative, devoted their energies mainly to those academic subjects in which they had already experienced success. It seems, however, that many other students chose teaching as a genuine expression of their liking for children. They looked for a socially useful and satisfying vocation which gave opportunities to work with people rather than with objects. The evidence suggests that, as a group, student teachers are diverse in their personality characteristics, although there is some support for the view that successful teaching is associated with qualities of stability and extraversion. Most students evaluate college courses in terms of practical utility rather than in terms of intellectual content. The wide variation found in the personal characteristics of students indicates that the impact made by college courses is likely to be equally varied. In Chapter 23, therefore, Cohen directs his attention towards studies which have attempted to assess the impact of the college course. After discussing the complexity of the definitional and methodological problems involved, he goes on to review studies which have been designed to identify changes in students' academic and practical teaching capabilities during the training period. He then engages in a comprehensive review of researches concerned with the measurement of attitudinal changes in student teachers and usefully summarizes some general findings. In the second part of his chapter Cohen discusses in greater detail a recent British study, which was designed to investigate some of the complex effects of structural and personal variables upon the attitudes and values of students. The discussion of the preliminary results of this study (Marsland, 1969) forms a link with the research reported by McLeish in the following chapter. The work of both Marsland and McLeish emphasizes the value of studies which are sufficiently sophisticated in design to encompass key variables in the complex processes of teacher socialization.

In Chapter 24 McLeish begins by extensively reviewing previous efforts to measure the impact of college environments upon students. He finds that the outcome of research into colleges from various standpoints reveals, firstly, that a number of instruments and conceptual schemes have been made available which serve to illuminate problems associated with sub-group differences. Secondly, he suggests that major dimensions of variations between colleges have been identified in these studies. Finally, he points out that the considerable variations which exist often cut across many of the commonly accepted classifications. In the second section of his chapter McLeish describes in detail a major longitudinal study of changes in students' attitudes, which was conducted over a period of three years in ten colleges of education in a single institute of education area. The characteristics of the training process are insightfully discussed in the light of extremely complex problems, which require a sophisticated research design and instruments of established reliability and validity. The papers of Renshaw (Chapter 12) and Collier (Chapter 10) also throw light on some aspects of the problem discussed by McLeish. In summarizing researches which have met the stringent requirements he has described, McLeish outlines the effects of college education which these studies have revealed.

In Chapter 25 Garner reviews research on the nature of teaching and the effectiveness of teachers. The output of colleges may be described in terms of both quantity and quality. Descriptions of the quantitative output of colleges are relatively simple to provide, but descriptions of the qualitative output are far more difficult to achieve. Garner suggests that any study which attempts to make statements about teaching ability or teacher effectiveness should also include a statement as to what kind of teacher-produced effects are thought to be desirable, followed by a statement about the extent to which these valued effects were deemed to have occurred. After critically assessing various experimental designs he concludes that there is an urgent need to explore the relationships existing between classroom behaviour and learning outcomes, for knowledge of these is necessary for the evaluation of teacher effectiveness and the creation of satisfactory teacher training programmes. It is essential that we study the interactions between methods of presentation and styles of classroom management in the attainment of objectives.

The various studies which are discussed in the following chapters suggest that the education of teachers ought to be logically determined by the nature of the job which awaits them in the community. The rigorous development of a concept of teaching is therefore a prerequisite for the creation of teacher education processes. Unfortunately we know too little about the relationship between teacher behaviour in the classroom and the changes which occur in children as a consequence of this behaviour. If teacher education programmes are to be demonstrably valid, then we must try to establish relationships between the courses we provide in colleges and departments of education and later criteria of successful performance in the profession. If these criteria of successful professional performance are also to be considered valid, they will need to be associated with the learning of children.

CHAPTER 22

# Student Characteristics and Attitudes in Colleges of Education

LOUIS COHEN

## Social Origins of Student Teachers

Traditionally teaching has offered an opportunity for social advancement to aspirants of lower social class origins and while in comparison with elite professions its recruits are still of more 'modest social class origin' (Leggatt, 1970) there are indications of change in recruitment patterns within certain segments of the teaching profession. A study undertaken in 1955 (Floud and Scott, 1958) identified significant changes in the social class backgrounds of teachers by comparing recruitment statistics in prewar and postwar years. In the period 1947–51 following the Second World War there was a significant proportional decrease in working-class entrants to teaching. Discussing overall changes in the period from 1920 onwards, Floud and Scott observe that in all types of school the majority of teachers are now drawn from non-manual family backgrounds.

The Committee on Higher Education (Robbins Report, 1963) is a source of comparatively recent statistics on the social origins of teachers. In 1961–2 ninety-two per cent. of the student teachers who entered colleges of education in England and Wales came from selective secondary schools, in particular, from maintained grammar schools. The great majority of those students (eighty-eight per cent.) had remained at school until eighteen years of age or older. Not unexpectedly in the light of reported social class differences in attainment as children grow older students tended to come from middle-class (fifty-four per cent.) or upper working-class (twenty-eight per cent.) home backgrounds.* Only eleven per cent. of the students had fathers who were engaged in semi-skilled or unskilled manual work as compared with forty per cent. whose fathers were in professional or managerial positions. Almost fifty-nine per cent. of the student teachers had at least one parent who had attended a selective secondary school. Only

* Robbins Report, Appendix 1, Part 2.

thirteen per cent. had a parent who had either graduated or had obtained a teacher's certificate.

There are important implications in any change in the 'pull' that teaching might have upon eligible students from middle-class and working-class backgrounds. Kelsall's observations are apt: 'It would be paradoxical if, at a time when, with the impending raising of the school leaving age and other related changes, the proportion of pupils from working class families was rising, the proportion of teachers from such families should show a tendency to decline instead of increasing' (Kelsall and Kelsall, 1969).

## Religious Beliefs and Political Affiliations

One of the most comprehensive investigations of student teachers undertaken in Great Britain was reported by McLeish (1970). The study, longitudinal in design, sampled some 1,671 students in ten colleges of education. The inclusion of 'controls' (students not attending colleges of education) permitted observation of changes taking place in student teacher groups that could be attributed to the effects of the college experience itself. The reported changes are discussed by McLeish in Chapter 24. The test battery employed, *The Cambridge Survey of Educational Opinions*, consisted of personality and attitudinal measures adapted from published and unpublished sources.*

McLeish's sample, though not representative of student teachers as a whole,† nevertheless includes a sufficiently large number of teacher trainees to warrant a close inspection of their reported religious beliefs and political affiliations.

### Political Affiliations

McLeish shows the student teachers in his sample to be considerably more Conservative than the population at large. Table 22.1 compares the political affiliations of both groups.

### Religious Affiliations

The religious affiliation of fifty-seven per cent. of the sample was indicated as Church of England, while only sixteen per cent. declared a lack of any religious connections. Table 22.2 shows the percentage distribution of declared religious affiliations.

---

* The battery included tests of anxiety (Crown, 1952). Social attitudes (Eysenck, 1947), the MPI (Eysenck, 1959), attitudes towards corporal punishment (Kissack, 1956), attitudes towards classroom methods and organization (Stern, 1960), personal values (Wickert, 1940), opinions about education (Butcher, 1959), and educational values (Higson, 1951).

† The sample was predominantly female (males 130, females 1,541).

Table 22.1
Percentage Comparison of Political Affiliations of Student Teachers
with the General Population

|  | Student Teachers | General Election 1966 | By-Elections 1966–8 |
|---|---|---|---|
| Conservative | 45 | 32 | 29 |
| Liberal | 13 | 6 | 6 |
| Labour | 19 | 32 | 23 |
| Other parties | 0 | 1 | 8 |
| Not voting | 23 | 29 | 34 |
| Total | 100 | 100 | 100 |

Source: adapted from McLeish (1970), p. 64.

Table 22.2
Percentage Distribution according to Religious Affiliation

| | |
|---|---|
| Church of England | 57 |
| Non-conformists | 21 |
| Roman Catholic | 5 |
| Other | 1 |
| No religious affiliation | 16 |
| Total | 100 |

Source: adapted from McLeish (1970), p. 59.

A disproportionate number of student teachers who were politically Conservative were also members of the Established Church. More Labour supporters than might be expected by coincidence declared themselves to be atheists or agnostics; more Liberals than might be expected by chance were affiliated with non-conformist sects.

These data on students' declared political and religious affiliations illuminate studies and discussion of the teacher stereotype as perceived by potential entrants to the profession. (Morton-Williams et al., 1966; Kelsall and Kelsall, 1969).

## School Qualifications and Academic Ability

Official surveys (as well as independent ad hoc researches), Central Register and Clearing House statistics, and the findings of a recent large-scale comparative study of teacher education (Dickson, 1965), permit both an examination of the changing quality of school-leaving qualifications among student teachers and a comparison of their academic ability with under-graduates in Great Britain and the United States.

## ˙A' Level Qualifications

When performance is measured by the quality of 'A' level examination results, universities have traditionally creamed-off the better-qualified sixth formers at the expense of other institutions of higher education. In 1961–2, eighty-three per cent. of university entrants in England and Wales had earned three or more 'A' levels as compared with only fourteen per cent. who, similarly qualified, entered colleges of education (Robbins Report, 1963). This latter figure has changed little over ten years. Of 37,384 students accepted by colleges in the autumn of 1970, only thirteen per cent. had obtained three or more 'A' levels (Central Register and Clearing House, 1970). Land's (1960) inquiry in twenty-one representative colleges through-out England and Wales had similarly reported thirteen per cent. of the entrants with three or more 'A' levels.

A survey conducted in a number of universities, polytechnics and colleges of education confirms the continuing disparity in the 'A' level attainments of those entering teachers' colleges when compared with university entrants (Entwistle et al., 1970). Almost sixty-nine per cent. of the university students in this latter survey had 'A' level grades equivalent to three Cs. The com-parable percentage among college of education students was less than eight per cent.*

There is evidence of a continuing growth in the number of well-qualified sixth formers entering colleges of education. The recent enquiry by the University of London Institute of Education (1971) which sampled 3,000 second-year students in colleges within its Area Training Organization re-ported that seventy-five per cent. of them in addition to their five 'O' levels had obtained at least one 'A' level and that forty per cent. had two or more 'A' levels. On a national basis, Table 22.3 shows the continuing growth in the quality of 'A' level qualifications over the past fifteen years.

## Academic Ability

College of education students have been compared with university under-graduates on academic criteria other than 'A' level results. Entwistle (1970), using the Test of Academic Aptitude (Verbal and Numerical), divided the range of scores obtained by university and college of education students into five categories. Forty-four per cent. of the university sample scored in

* When considering minimum university entry qualifications, however, there is a greater overlap in the 'A' level qualifications of student teachers and under-graduates (Robbin's Report, 1963, Appendix 2B, Tables 85 and 86).

Table 22.3

Percentage of Entrants to Colleges of Education in England and Wales having 'A' Level Qualifications

|  | Year | Two or More 'A' Levels | One 'A' Level |
|---|---|---|---|
| Men | 1955 | 16 | 10 |
|  | 1960 | 34 | 24 |
|  | 1967 | 37 | 25 |
|  | 1970 | 38 | 27 |
| Women | 1955 | 19 | 16 |
|  | 1960 | 32 | 23 |
|  | 1967 | 35 | 24 |
|  | 1970 | 39 | 26·5 |

Sources: *Higher Education*, Appendix One, Table 17. HMSO London, 1963. *Annual Report Central Register and Clearing House*, 1970. Layard, King and Moser, *The Impact of Robbins*, Table 16, Penguin, 1969. Reproduced by permission of Penguin Books.

the top two categories as compared with less than eleven per cent. of the college students. Only four per cent. of the university students' scores fell in the lowest ability category. The comparable percentage of college of education students' scores was twenty-four per cent.

Evans (1964) differentiated between university and college of education students in respect of reasoning ability (Valentine's Reasoning Tests and Heim's AH5), the university group scoring significantly higher on both tests. There were no differences between the two groups on the Nufferno Speed and Accuracy Tests (GIS. 14. E36). Moreover, some twenty per cent. of the college of education group (mainly women) obtained better scores than the university students on the reasoning tests. Discussing these findings, Evans queried why such able college of education students had not gained higher academic distinction at school and proceeded to university studies.

As part of the large-scale international study Dickson (1965) compared the scores of some 1,311 college of education students on tests of academic achievement, general mental ability and teacher attitudes with those of 857*

* Within the university graduate group Dickson included a number of college of education students whose professional training lay in the 'secondary' rather than elementary (junior) sector. In comparing the two British samples, therefore (the college of education group v. the university graduate group) the tendency is to *underestimate* the differences between them. The battery of tests included the Comprehensive College Tests (ETS 1965); Co-operative General Culture Test; Mathematics Form A; Culture Fair Intelligence Test, Scale 3, Form A; Teacher Education Examination Program (ETS, 1962); Teacher Characteristics Schedule (Ryans, 1960); MTAI Form A.

university graduates enrolled in postgraduate certificate courses in university departments of education throughout Great Britain. The mean score of the university graduates group exceeded that of the college of education sample on all but one of the tests of intelligence and academic achievement.

In the same study the British college of education student was found to compare very favourably with his American counterpart typically following a four-year undergraduate course of teacher education. Mean scores on intelligence and English attainment were significantly higher in the British sample.

In summary, while the university undergraduate's superiority over the college of education entrant in IQ, academic ability and attainment is well-established, there is evidence both of a continuing improvement in the school-leaving qualifications of those sixth formers intent upon careers in teaching and of a considerable overlap in the qualifications of many college entrants with those of university undergraduates. Both groups, it should be remembered, represent a top ten per cent. 'cream' of the total age group which has remained in secondary education until the age of eighteen.


## Choice of Teaching as a Career


Occupational choice is a complicated process, the outcome of a succession of sequential stages which begin with an individual's inborn potentialities which set limits upon his subsequent performance and end with his eventual location in a particular field of employment (Butler, 1968).

Such complexity is not likely to be unravelled by the simple techniques of interview and questionnaire that have typically been used to examine motivation in the career choices of teachers and other occupational groups.

British research from Austin (1931), Valentine (1934), Vernon (1937) and Tudhope (1944) onwards is largely based upon interview and questionnaire. It has analysed the reasons volunteered by students as explanations of their motivation to teach. To what extent those reasons are coloured by the personalities of the respondents is largely unknown.

Earlier studies reflect the direct influence of teachers and relatives upon students' choice as well as the strong attraction of a secure job during times of unemployment (Austin, 1931; Tudhope, 1944). The influence of the school upon choice of teaching as a career is suggested in Evans' study (1952). Pupils whose interests were academic and who had favourable attitudes towards school in general were more likely to hold favourable attitudes towards teaching as a career. More recent studies show that once the decision to teach has been made, the school and older fellow students become important sources of information influencing the choice of particular colleges of education made by intending teachers (Simons, 1965; Shipman, 1966). In a study of the transition from sixth form to higher education (or employment) Morris (1969) found the head teacher to be the most influential person in advising pupils on their choice of colleges of education. The pupils themselves reported that the factor 'interesting work' was by far the most important reason for their choice of a particular institution. Notwithstanding college brochures and prospectuses and the availability of advice from head teachers, almost half the sixth formers contacted by Morris claimed to have made their final short-list of colleges unassisted.

A recurring theme in the majority of studies from the earlier work of Austin (1931) to the later investigations of Bewsher (1965), Derricott (1968) and Ashley et al. (1970), is the expression by student teachers of a fondness for children and a desire to work with them. In Bewsher's analysis of the anonymous essays of 303 teacher trainees, the two most important reasons given for choice of teaching were 'opportunity to influence children', and 'a liking for children'. This people-orientation, revealed by a desire to do socially-useful work involving people rather than things is a common and consistent expression of intending teachers in undergraduate groups (Morton Williams, 1966), mature entrants to the profession (Altman, 1967) and 'committed' as opposed to 'reluctant' students in colleges of education (Smithers and Carlisle, 1970). Less favourable images of children and teaching serve to distinguish sixth formers and undergraduates not intending to teach (Clarke, 1968; Morton Williams et al., 1966).

A different approach to the analysis of reasons given by students for their choice of teaching is reported by Ashley and his associates (1967 a, 1967 b, 1970). By factor analytical techniques they developed a paradigm of student motivation based upon the extent to which students showed themselves to be attracted to three distinct roles associated with teaching, namely, the teacher as educator, the teacher as worker, and the teacher as person. Different groups of students were shown to give distinctive emphases to these various role elements. For example, young women teachers following a course of study leading to a diploma qualification more strongly emphasized child-centred reasons loading on 'the teacher as a person' factor than did graduate men teachers.

For an unknown number of more able college of education students, choice of teaching may be a matter of 'hedging one's bets' against the possibility of failure to gain admission to a university.

The Robbins Report showed that eighty-five per cent. of the students in colleges who had applied to enter a university would have preferred to go there rather than to the college where they were then located. For many better-qualified students, the college of education may therefore be a second-best institution, albeit one which enables them to continue to work in those areas of academic study in which they have experienced 'A' level success. For some of those students the professional training elements in the college course may be of secondary importance and interest (Rolls and Goble, 1971).

Central Register and Clearing House statistics on withdrawal by acceptable candidates from places already offered them by colleges show that the most usual reasons given are 'acceptance by' or 'application to a university'. Out of 5,534 withdrawals in 1970 no less than 2,479 (forty-five per cent.) were because of acceptance (or hope of acceptance) by a university. Only 591 (ten per cent.) of the withdrawing candidates alluded to a 'wrong choice of career' as an explanation of their non-acceptance of available places.

## Personality Characteristics of Student Teachers

Given the large number of students entering colleges of education each year and the wide variation in their abilities, attainments and interests, it would be surprising if they were not as diverse in their personalities as any other occupational group (Vernon, 1953).

Yet there is little empirical evidence to date to show how student teachers' personalities compare with those of other young adults outside or inside full-time higher education (Taylor, 1969; McLeish, 1970; Morrison and McIntyre, 1969; Lomax, 1969). What research has been undertaken has more often been concerned with identifying those aspects of personality which are associated with scholastic attainment and teaching success. In general these attempted predictions have been far from conclusive (Warburton et al., 1963).

The distinction between students' personality characteristics and their attitudes and values, to which we turn in the next section, is at best arbitrary. Personality characteristics may be thought of as 'more basic or fundamental [than attitudes] in that they tend to influence much other psychological behaviour' (McConnell and Heist, 1962). Neuroticism, for example, is likely to influence both the student teacher's relationships with his fellows and his attitudes towards a variety of social events and objects. In discussing students' personalities, attitudes and values one is, strictly speaking, dealing with their non-intellective characteristics. It is appropriate, however, to begin with a number of studies which have been concerned with the predictive ability of measures of intellect upon students' subsequent performance.

Intelligence appears to be a poor predictor of teaching ability. Studies of English student teachers (Cortis, 1966; Solomon, 1967; Morgan, 1969), Scottish student teachers (Herbert and Turnbull, 1963) and Irish student teachers (Tarpey, 1965) have reported few significant correlations between intelligence and teaching practice marks. Where significant correlations have been shown (Lomax, 1969; Crocker, 1968) they are low, not an unexpected finding considering the highly-selected nature of student teachers when compared with unselected groups, and the complexity of the criterion itself. Crocker suggests that once a minimum level of intelligence is surpassed (and the majority of students in colleges are well above that minimum), IQ has no measurable effect upon teaching ability.

Studies which have attempted to relate the personality dimensions intro-version/extraversion, neuroticism/stability to student teachers' academic attainment have reported inconsistent findings. Whereas Gibbons and Savage (1965), Cortis (1966) and Solomon (1967) have shown stability/extraversion to be associated with scholastic attainment, Evans (1964) reported significant positive correlations between introversion and academic attainment, and Entwistle, Percy and Nisbet (1970) significant negative correlations between extraversion and academic performance in male college of education students.

Stability has generally been shown to correlate positively with academic performance in college of education groups (Warburton and Hadley, 1960; Helliwell, 1963; Cortis, 1966; Solomon, 1967) though a 'moderate level of anxiety [on entry to college] seems to pay off in examination success three years late' (McLeish, 1970). On the other hand there is evidence that neuroticism in undergraduate student populations is positively associated with academic success (Warburton, 1962) and stability (in conjunction with extraversion) with academic failure (Furneaux, 1962; Cohen and Child, 1969). Some inconsistencies in the reported research findings arise out of the failure to differentiate between university and college of education groups.

Other personal correlates of teaching ability that have been identified are skill in interpersonal relationships with fellow students (Cornwall, 1958), flexibility (Crocker, 1968) and social sensitivity (Meldon, 1968; Davis and Slatterly, 1969; Morgan, 1969). A number of studies have examined the relationship between academic motivation and academic performance in college of education groups.

Using a motivation questionnaire with 118 college of education students Entwistle and Entwistle (1970) showed a significant positive correlation between motivation and performance. Gallop (1970) developed a n'ach scale from one originally used by Robinson (1964) and reported higher need for achievement in a stratified sample of fifty B.Ed. students as compared with fifty certificate of education students.

Cohen, Reid and Boothroyd (1972), employing anglicized versions of n'ach scales developed by Mehrabian (1968, 1969) for separate use with male and female students, are currently examining differing need for achievement levels among student teachers who have identified themselves as 'committed' and 'non-committed' to a career in teaching. A parallel investigation of matched groups of B.Ed. and certificate students is also in progress (Cohen and Reid, 1972).

## Sex and Personality Differences in Student Teachers

McLeish's study (1970) identified wide ranging personality differences between male and female student teachers, differences that variously mediate the impact of the college course in complex and, as yet, unknown ways. Female students, for example, on entry to college were significantly more tenderminded than males. Moreover, students preparing to teach in infant and lower junior classrooms (predominantly the choices of females) were found to score significantly higher on naturalism than those oriented towards upper junior and secondary classes. In the light of such differences it seems reasonable to hypothesize that the 'child-centredness' of the college (Taylor, 1969) will have a significantly different impact upon those female students whose personality dispositions are already congruent with a major element in the prevailing belief system than upon more toughminded, idealistic males.

As distinct from identifying aspects of personality associated with teaching ability and academic attainment, other studies have focused upon student personality 'inputs' which relate to their preferences both for styles of interpersonal relationships with college tutors and for the behaviour of children in school practice classrooms. Students exhibiting low self-esteem (Rosenberg, 1965) and high dogmatism (Rokeach, 1954, 1960) are reported to prefer passive as opposed to active relationships with college staff in the planning and conduct of their academic studies* (Cohen, 1971). Mature student teachers, identified as highly dogmatic, describe the 'ideal' junior pupil on school practice as passive, obedient, accepting, significantly more often than fellow students scoring low on the Rokeach scale (Cohen, 1971).

A longitudinal study currently in progress and based upon the whole first-year intake of a college of education has employed the Cattell 16 PF Personality Inventory and the Mooney Problem Checklists to explore the relationship between personality and persisting problems throughout the period of college course (Cohen, 1971). Preliminary analyses show that students as a whole reveal a wide spectra of personal problems on entry to college. This is particularly the case in respect of the anxious, introverted student teacher. By the end of the first year in college, while there is a

---

* Similarly McLeish (1968) found student teachers who preferred lectures to discussion periods also placed high value on toughmindedness, formalism, submission, and workmanship.

significant reduction in the overall incidence of reported problems, for certain students (the anxious, the introverted, the passive) problems in social relationships persist.

McLeish's study also identified a number of personality correlates of students' political and religious affiliations and their social attitudes. For example, in both male and female groups (but particularly among males) the absence of religious affiliation was associated with high levels of anxiety. There were, moreover, highly significant differences in extraversion between the various religious denominations, Roman Catholic and Church of England members being more extravert than non-conformists and those denying any religious affiliation. Students, grouped by their religious and political affiliations were also found to differ substantially in their educational values.

Studies of the personality characteristics of teacher trainees as they begin their college courses seek a fuller understanding of students as persons. Such understanding is essential if the complex interplay of psychological and social variables that constitutes professional socialization is to be better comprehended.

### Attitudes towards College and Professional Training

A number of studies of individual colleges have been concerned with student attitudes towards various aspects of college life. Differing degrees of dissatisfaction with rules and regulations governing the social activities of college are identified in studies by Bewsher (1965), Shipman (1966), Phillips (1967) and Derricott (1968). Phillips' study is of particular interest in showing how within the total student body particular sub-groups identified by year, social-class and religious or non-religious affiliation respond with varying degrees of favourability to college discipline.

There is considerable evidence that students, by and large, evaluate the college course in terms of its practical usefulness to them as future teachers rather than its ability to stimulate their intellectual appetites (Williams, 1963; Clark and Nisbet, 1963; McLeish, 1970). A recent study based upon a stratified sample of 216 students in six colleges of education identified the degree to which students believed that their professional college courses fell short of practical relevance and value to the classroom situation they would eventually face (Eason and Cross, 1971). Table 22.4 highlights some of the major findings.

The Robbins Committee reported the views of a large representative sample of student teachers concerning the balance of their studies, the teaching arrangements, and the extent of supervision and personal guidance provided by the colleges. A very high proportion (seventy-eight per cent.)

Table 22.4
Students' Assessments of the College Course

*Does, and should, the college try to develop your real understanding of children?*

| | Percentage | | Percentage |
|---|---|---|---|
| Should try a little | 2 | Does try a little | 47 |
| Should try a lot | 87 | Does try a lot | 47 |

*Does, and should, the college in your opinion develop your understanding of the classroom teaching situation?*

| | | | |
|---|---|---|---|
| Should try a little | 5 | Does try a little | 59 |
| Should try a lot | 85 | Does try a lot | 21 |

Adapted from Eason and Croll, *Staff and Student Attitudes in Colleges of Education*, (1971), p. 64, a National Foundation for Educational Research publication.

of those contacted wanted changes in existing arrangements. They were anxious to see a greater amount of time devoted to those aspects of the college course which promoted their competence as teachers, in particular their main subject work and teaching practice. They were less happy about the time given over to theoretical education studies. On curriculum course studies students were more evenly divided, twenty-one per cent. wanting more time, twenty-six per cent. less time, and fifty-one per cent. being content with existing arrangements. A more recent survey, however (London Institute of Education, 1971), reported that the large majority of the 3,000 students contacted felt that too little emphasis was placed on curriculum studies and teaching methods, in short, on the practical elements in the professional studies course.

While no exact comparison is possible between teaching methods in colleges of education and universities, the evidence discussed by Collier in Chapter 14 suggests that student teachers experience a greater number of staff-student contact hours per week than university undergraduates and that contact is mainly in the form of lectures and small-group discussion periods. Tutorials, as commonly conceived in university, are rare in colleges of education. Both student teachers and undergraduates call for more informal methods of teaching, more seminars and fewer lectures (Robbins Report 1963, 2B, Part IV, Table 55). To what extent college of education students regard the small group discussion periods referred to above as 'informal methods of teaching' is not known. That this type of contact between a tutor and ten or so students serves an important function has been noted both by King (1969) and Taylor (1969). The 'mother-hen principle' according to King, is an 'attempt to generate emotional bonds in the hope that understandings will be reached that are based on affectivity rather than objective facts or scientific theories of social behaviour'. Less caustically though no less pointedly, Taylor sees this method as 'manipulative socialization', a means by which 'the college is able to bring influence to bear upon its students in the direction of commitment to "professional" values'.

Not unexpectedly in the light of the additional 'professional' elements in the teacher training course requiring curriculum studies and teaching practices, student teachers spend considerably fewer hours per week than undergraduates in private study. Entwistle *et al.* (1970) report the comparable hours as seventeen per week in colleges of education and twenty-three in the universities (the Robbins figures were sixteen hours in colleges and twenty-three in universities).

There may also be differences in the patterns of private study pursued in colleges and universities. Most undergraduates undertake a greater amount of study as they approach their final year examinations (Robbins Report, 1963, 2B, Part IV, Table 23). A recent investigation of study habits in a college of education, however, reported an opposite trend (Davis, 1967). An examination of students' diaries showed that significantly less time was devoted to academic studies as students progressed through the three-year course and significantly more time to 'spontaneous recreational activities'. How typical this finding is of colleges in general is as yet unknown.

## Summary

The purpose of this chapter has been to describe college of education students in terms of their social origins, their abilities and their attitudes. To that end, a selective review has been undertaken of the many surveys and research studies reported in the literature.

The majority of student teachers come from lower middle-class and upper working-class backgrounds. Politically they have been described as more Conservative than the population at large although the evidence is based upon the views of a largely female sample and is unrepresentative of student teachers as a whole.

While college of education students have continually fallen short of university undergraduates in their 'A' level achievements and in their performance on objective tests of intelligence there is no evidence to suggest that there has been any decline in the academic quality of student teachers despite the enormous increase in the college of education population during the past ten or fifteen years.

Many sixth formers choose to teach because they are genuinely fond of children and look for a socially useful, satisfying occupation working with people rather than things. For others, particularly those who initially aspired to university places, college may be a second best and teaching an inevitable consequence of three years spent pursuing academic study in those areas where success had been previously experienced.

There is no evidence that teaching recruits a certain type of individual who can be differentiated in terms of personality or attitudes from his fellows. There is however some support for the view that it is the stable, extrovert student who is the more likely to exhibit teaching ability and to enjoy teaching success. The majority of students tend to evaluate the college course in terms of its practical utility to them as future classroom practitioners rather than its ability to stimulate them intellectually.

Because college of education students vary widely in their abilities, personalities and interests the impact that the college course makes upon them is likely to be equally varied. It is to a number of studies of college impact that attention is directed in the chapter that follows.

# CHAPTER 23

# The Impact of the College Course

LOUIS COHEN

## Introduction

The primary purpose of the college of education course is to prepare men and women to act as capable and responsible classroom teachers.

'Capability' refers to the possession by the teacher of requisite academic and professional knowledge; 'responsibility' to his or her acceptance of a set of beliefs and values about education and the learning process that serve to translate this academic/professional expertise into appropriate classroom behaviour.

The impact that the college course has upon student teachers has generally been conceived of in terms of the changes that take place in students' knowledge, behaviour, and beliefs both during and after the three-year period of training. The measurement of such changes however raises a number of problems.* Indeed as Taylor (1969) observes, the dearth of empirical British studies of college influence upon students is indicative of the bewildering complexity of the definitional and methodological difficulties involved.

The problem of defining and operationalizing 'requisite professional knowledge' and 'appropriate classroom behaviour' clearly subsumes the discussion of methodological difficulties in the design of investigations of college impact which follows.

First, it is generally the case that studies of change in college of education students have failed to provide adequate controls in the form of non-student groups matched by age, qualifications, personality characteristics, etc, in order to examine the possibility that such changes which do occur may be due to maturational factors rather than to the effects of the college course.

Secondly, the majority of studies of change are cross-sectional rather than longitudinal in design. That is to say they make comparisons between students grouped by year of training or professional course rather than within groups as they progress through the three-year training course.

* For a recent technical dicussion see Feldman, 1970.

Unlike the longitudinal study, the cross-sectional design makes assumptions about the homogeneity of the various subgroups within the total college population, and these assumptions may not be warranted.

Thirdly, until recently few studies have taken into account in their designs the many situational factors in the college environment which McLeish (Chapter 24) suggests may be potent sources of influence in the structuring and the changing of students' beliefs and behaviour. The majority of studies employing personality and attitudinal measures, moreover, have sought to explore the single rather than the multi-relational effects of those predictors upon academic attainment, teaching ability or role conceptions. Few studies as yet have been designed to tease out the interaction of situational and psychological factors upon such criteria (McLeish, 1970; Marsland, 1969).

Finally there is the problem of differentiating between the transitory and the lasting effects of the college upon its students. There is a small but growing literature on the short-term attitudinal and behavioural changes taking place during and immediately after college. What the lasting effects of the college course are have yet to be identified.

## Changes in Academic and Professional Knowledge

Surprisingly little work has been directed towards identifying changes in students' academic capabilities during the course of the three-year training period. A recent comparative study, however (Dickson et al., 1965), provides data on the academic attainment and professional attitudes of British and American teacher education students. The study is cross-sectional in design and the results are reported in terms of the mean scores (without standard deviations) of various student groups. Although Dickson shows significant differences between British and American students on several academic and attitudinal measures it is unfortunate for present purposes that we are not able to examine differences within the British sample by tests of significance. Nevertheless there are a number of discernible trends.

## British and American Student Teachers Compared

*Academic Attainment*

Scores on general intelligence and verbal understanding were consistently found to favour British over American students. This was particularly the case when college of education students training for primary school work were compared with American undergraduates following elementary education courses. On tests of mathematics, literature and fine arts British students again were superior to their American counterparts. The reverse, however, was true in respect of biological and physical sciences. Here, American elementary teacher education students were consistently better than British primary student teachers.

## Professional Knowledge

On measures of professional knowledge (including child development, educational psychology, guidance and measurement) British and American mean scores in both primary and secondary groups were very similar, American students tending to score higher than British.

## Year of Training

In general, whereas the mean scores of American students on academic attainment measures showed a downward turn in direction from the first year onwards, British student teachers tended to improve their mean scores. There were some reversals, however, particularly in mathematics and the sciences among primary student-trainees (see Table 23.1). The pattern of

Table 23.1

Mean Scores of British Primary and Secondary Student Teachers on Academic Achievement, Cattell Culture-Fair IQ Test (IPAT), and Professional Knowledge

| Measure | Primary | | | Secondary | | |
|---|---|---|---|---|---|---|
| | First Year | Second Year | Third Year | First Year | Second Year | Third Year |
| IPAT | 113·3 | 113·7 | 112·1 | 115·0 | 115·3 | 115·4 |
| English Composition | 58·2 | 59·1 | 58·3 | 57·0 | 58·1 | 59·8 |
| Biological Science | 20·8 | 21·5 | 20·7 | 22·9 | 24·4 | 25·1 |
| Physical Science | 16·7 | 17·4 | 16·1 | 21·8 | 21·6 | 21·6 |
| Total Natural Science | 37·5 | 39·0 | 36·9 | 44·7 | 46·0 | 46·8 |
| Fine Arts | 23·8 | 24·8 | 25·3 | 23·4 | 24·0 | 25·1 |
| Literature | 25·0 | 26·0 | 25·9 | 24·4 | 24·5 | 25·5 |
| Total Humanities | 46·5 | 48·5 | 47·9 | 45·3 | 45·7 | 47·6 |
| Mathematics | 19·3 | 19·8 | 17·7 | 25·8 | 26·6 | 25·1 |
| Child Development | 18·7 | 19·8 | 19·9 | 18·2 | 18·9 | 19·6 |
| Guidance and Measurement | 14·2 | 15·8 | 16·0 | 14·3 | 16·1 | 17·0 |
| Instructional Methods | 17·3 | 18·2 | 18·7 | 17·4 | 17·4 | 19·0 |
| Elementary Education | 57·0 | 59·9 | 59·9 | — | — | — |

Source: Dickson *et al.* (1965) Appendix H, Tables 33–44.

incremental gain in students' mean scores over the three years was more consistent in the area of professional knowledge than academic attainment. Exactly what these incremental gains represent is more difficult to judge given the cross-sectional design of the study and the absence of significance tests applied to the mean scores of the various year groups.

### Changes in Teaching Ability and Classroom Practices

The assessment of the impact of the college in terms of increasing teaching ability and skill in classroom procedures as students progress through the college course is virtually unexplored in Great Britain. The dearth of British studies of students' teaching ability is, in part, attributable to the difficulty of developing valid and reliable methods of observing and recording classroom behaviour. Work currently in progress at Exeter (Wragg, 1971) and Stirling (Duthie, 1970) in connection with the identification and classification of teachers' classroom behaviour is indicative of the increasing attention that is being paid to classroom practices and procedures by ecologically-oriented researchers. American evidence suggests that this is a promising area of enquiry for those concerned with evaluating the effects of professional course work upon students' classroom performances. Turner (1963), for example, has identified not only increments in student teachers' ability to deal with problematic aspects of classroom teaching as they progress through their course of training but has associated the development of such professional skills both with teaching practice and with the instruction received in method classes.

### Changes in Students' Attitudes during the College Course

We turn now to review a representative selection of the large number of studies that have been concerned with changes in the attitudes of student teachers both during and after their course of training. In an earlier discussion we distinguished between students' personality characteristics and their attitudes, suggesting that personality might be seen as more basic or fundamental, and that attitudes are in part a consequence of personality functioning. Our separation of the discussion of student personality and student attitudes into two chapters serves also to distinguish between what appear to be differing foci of personality and attitudinal studies extant in the literature.

By and large, studies of student personality characteristics are concerned to describe student groups, to distinguish between such groups, and to identify various correlates of the personality measures they employ. Studies of student attitudes, in addition to describing groups, distinguishing between them and identifying various attitudinal correlates, more usually attempt to map the direction and the intensity of changes occurring in those attitudes during the course of professional training. These differing foci derive to no small extent from the distinction drawn earlier between basic personality structures and their manifestation in the form of attitudes. As McLeish (1970) has commented, personality dimensions and basic personal values probably belong to similar relatively intractable areas that will be little affected by the experience of college, whereas one might expect educational and social attitudes to be 'more amenable to the processes of persuasion, rational analysis and ideological indoctrination which go on during the... years in college'. Indeed, some studies of attitude change discuss their findings in terms of just such an on-going process of professional socialization.

We begin by examining a number of studies, both longitudinal and latitudinal in design, which have employed various attitudinal measures and role inventories to study changes in the beliefs and values of student teachers. In the final section of the review, a small number of recent studies, more sophisticated in their examination of the interaction of specific sociological and psychological variables, are discussed in greater detail.

Despite its shortcomings (Evans, 1958; Oliver and Butcher, 1962), the Minnesota Teacher Attitude Inventory has been used to examine the growth and development of student teacher attitudes (Herbert and Turnbull, 1963; Dickson et al., 1965; Evans, 1967). The MTAI consists of some 150 statements about pupils, classroom practices and educational views towards which respondents indicate their agreement or disagreement on a five-point rating scale. Higher scores are held to be indicative of more favourable attitudes.

Other investigators have used the Allport, Vernon and Lindzey (1950) scale of values to describe student teachers on entry to college and/or to map changes occurring during the college course (Evans, 1967, 1969; Warburton, Butcher, Forrest, 1963; Lomax, 1969; Gallop, 1970). The Allport, Vernon and Lindzey scale measures an individual's values in six broad areas of cultural activity – theoretical, aesthetic, social, political, religious and economic.

The most commonly-used inventory employed in the analysis of student teachers' educational beliefs and attitudes is the Manchester Opinion Scales in Education (Oliver and Butcher, 1962). It consists of three scales of naturalism, radicalism, and tendermindedness, and has been used in studies of English and Scottish student teachers, graduates following diploma courses and serving teachers (Butcher, 1959; 1965; McIntyre and Morrison, 1967; Morrison and McIntyre, 1967; Lomax, 1969; Wain, 1971).

A number of researchers have developed their own attitudinal measures (Kissack, 1956; Steele, 1958; Starr, 1967), some based upon semantic differential techniques (Kitchen, 1965; Manion, 1969), others in the form of role inventories (Cohen, 1965; Finlayson and Cohen, 1967; Camplin, 1970).

By and large the British findings summarized below support those reported in the American literature which suggest that students become increasingly progressive in their attitudes during the course of their college education but move in the opposite direction towards more traditional beliefs when they experience the impact of full-time teaching. This general statement of the overall dynamics of attitude change must however be qualified in several important ways in the light of the findings of some of the research.

## Attitude Change: Some General Findings

1. Significant increases in scores on the Minnesota Teacher Attitude Inventory among second- and third-year students as compared with first-year groups are reported by Herbert and Turnbull (1963), and by Dickson et al. (1965) in respect of students training for primary school classrooms.
2. Gains in social values scores on the Allport, Vernon and Lindzey Scale during the college course are reported as a feature common to teacher training groups (Evans, 1967, 1969).
3. There is a consistent tendency for naturalism, tendermindedness, and radicalism scores (the Manchester Opinion Scales in Education) to increase during the period of the college course (Butcher, 1965; McIntyre and Morrison, 1967; McLeish, 1970).
4. Students, as a whole, become more utilitarian in outlook and more concerned with the practicalities of teaching as they progress through the course of training (Kitchen, 1965; McLeish, 1970; Cohen, 1969).
5. There is a consistent tendency for gains in naturalism, tendermindedness and radicalism to be followed by changes in the opposite direction when students take up their first teaching posts. Such reversals do not cancel out all the gains made during the period of training (Steele, 1958; Butcher, 1965; McIntyre and Morrison, 1967; Morrison and McIntyre, 1967).

However, differences in the degree (and in some cases the direction) of attitude change are reported when students are differentiated by their professional training group (Steele, 1958; Cohen, 1965), year cohort (Finlayson and Cohen, 1967), sex (Manion, 1969; McLeish, 1970), and personality (McLeish, 1970). Such findings urge caution in interpreting results and generalizing from studies where adequate controls have not been incorporated in research designs. They highlight the need for investigations designed to identify more of the crucial variables involved in student attitude formation and change and to map the complex interactions among these variables.

In this second section of the current chapter we examine in greater detail a recent British study of a college of education population (Marsland, 1969). The study is designed to tease out some of the complex, inter-related effects of personal and structural variables upon students' attitudes and values.*

## An Exploration of Professional Socialization

One of the most thorough, on-going studies of the professional socialization of student teachers is reported by Marsland (1969). His 'systems' approach is shown in Figure 23.1.

### Figure 23.1
### The System of Independent Variables in Professional Socialization

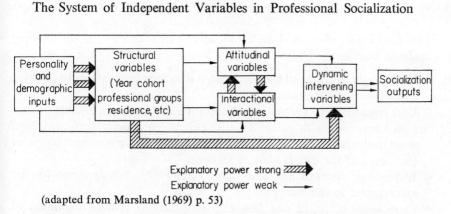

Explanatory power strong
Explanatory power weak

(adapted from Marsland (1969) p. 53)

Marsland views teacher training as a social system, a complex of inter-actions between individuals and various aspects of their college culture, a social system moreover, which provides the crucial learning environment for students as they pass through the three-year course. His study of one large, mixed, metropolitan college is longitudinal rather than latitudinal in design, thus avoiding difficulties in interpreting data which assume stability in the recruitment patterns of yearly college intakes. His dependent variables (including students' educational/academic orientations, their organizational commitment/detachment, their educational philosophies and their role conceptions) are measured by eleven summated rating scales. Various in-dependent variables are specified, for example, demographic variables (age, sex, social class), personality variables (authoritarianism, extroversion), attitudinal variables, interactional variables (the degree to which students

* See also the study by McLeish described in Chapter 24.

participate in the social system), structural variables (indices of students' location in the social system of the college – their year cohort, type of residential accommodation, their professional course group, etc.), and dynamic variables, described by Marsland as a set of variables specifically appropriate to the exploration of professional socialization, and composed of attitudinal and interactional elements.

The aim of the study is to identify the source, the strength, and the multifarious interconnections between the various influences upon students' attitude change and emerging conceptions of the teacher's role as they progress through the college course. In this first report of his preliminary analyses, Marsland details the degree and direction of changes occurring in the dependent variables together with some correlations between those changes and certain of the independent variables.

### Changes in Students' Attitudes

Marsland's data show that during the course of their professional training students become:

1. Increasingly educational and less academic in their orientations to teaching and classroom behaviour;
2. Less committed to the school organization and its requirements;
3. Less concerned with career (status, income, promotion) prospects and more concerned with vocation (commitment to the worthwhileness of teaching and the satisfaction of service);
4. Increasingly modern and less traditional in their beliefs about teacher involvement in the community;
5. Increasingly affective and less affectively-neutral in their definition of the teacher's role vis à vis others;
6. Increasingly progressive and less traditional in their educational philosophy and methods;
7. Increasingly specific and less diffuse in their teacher role definitions.

### Correlates of Students' Attitude Change

Certain of the independent variables are reported to be strongly associated with the major attitudinal changes referred to above. For example, among the demographic variables, whereas age is not significantly associated with attitude change, sex is; male students tending to remain more academic and less educational than female students and less inclined to change towards affective definitions of the teacher's role. Socio-economic status is associated with only one of the eleven change measures, the working-class student tending to become more favourable toward the prospect of teaching as a career than his fellow students from different social class backgrounds. Although personality variables apparently play a larger part in attitudinal change than demographic factors they are nevertheless limited in their degree of association with the criterion variables. Authoritarianism is shown to be negatively correlated with a modern conception of the teacher's involvement in the community; extraversion correlates positively with an increased educational as opposed to academic orientation.

One of the most important findings reported by Marsland is the strong association between informal staff-student interaction and student attitude change. Both increasingly favourable commitment to teaching and growing educational professionalism on the part of students is substantially associated with greater contact with the academic staff of the college. A second finding is concerned with the association between student peer group interaction and attitude change. Marsland shows that greater involvement among the students in discussions of teaching is associated with increasing career commitment and progressive attitudes. A third finding refers to the complex effects in the teachers' socialization process resulting from the students' membership of main subject departments and professional training groups (infant, junior, secondary).

## Conclusions

In conclusion it may be said that the work of McLeish* and Marsland has emphasized the potentially rich rewards in terms of research findings that can accrue from studies sufficiently sophisticated in their initial design to encompass some of the key variables in the complex processes of teacher socialization.

Broadly, the McLeish and Marsland studies substantiate the already well-documented changes towards radicalism and progressivism in students' educational ideas occurring during the course of their college experience. Specifically, both studies point to the strong association between student attitude change and certain sub-environments within the college. In particular the association of student teachers with college of education staff and with their fellow students within subject and professional training groups appear to be potent sources of influence. Marsland's study in particular, with its tentative models of differing routes to professional identification among student teachers, enumerates some key conditions and mechanisms of teacher socialization which could be re-examined in future studies involving other colleges of education and other student populations. Replication

* See Chapter 24.

of Marsland's major findings would provide empirical evidence on which to base policy decisions in teacher education. For example, support for his distinction between professional and apprentice socialization would raise immediate practical issues concerning the recruitment and selection of student teachers, the content of their college course, and the organization of the three-year course itself.

# CHAPTER 24

# College Environment and Student Characteristics

JOHN MCLEISH

For we would not have our guardians reared among images of evil as in a foul pasture, and there day by day and little by little gather many impressions from all that surrounds them, taking them all in until at last a great mass of evil gathers in their inmost souls, and they know it not. Plato, *Republic*, Book 3, *401*

Evil communications corrupt good manners.    *I Corinthians*, XV, *33*

## College Environment Measures: State of the Art

In a famous report, Jacob (1957) demonstrated that in social science departments in American universities no significant changes in students' attitudes or values could be attributed to the curriculum, the methods of teaching, or the quality of the teaching. This was true of the great mass of students. In exceptional cases, and in a limited number of colleges, some teachers seemed to be capable of exerting a profound influence on some students. This effect seemed to be associated with a distinctive climate of unhurried, relaxed, frequent and adult encounters between teachers and students, where the teacher behaved habitually in a warm, out-going manner, clearly expressing his own value-commitments.

Attention was thus drawn sharply to the 'college environment', this being interpreted primarily in terms of the interpersonal relations, social climate, the psychological qualities and intellectual emphasis which prevailed in the college, some regard being paid also to the physical facilities and amenities. Barton (1959, 1961, 1963) conceptualized the college as a system of interacting elements, composed not only of students, but of faculty and administration as well as external sources of control and support. He indicated a vast range of problems and inter-relations within this systems model which cried out for investigation before meaningful statements could be made about students, about their perceptions of college life and structure, about the impact of college on their characteristics, beliefs and values, about the real sources of influence which operated.

The first objective measuring instrument for studying college environments was the *College Characteristics Index* of Pace and Stern (1958). This 300-item questionnaire sought to identify the 'press' of the environment according to H. A. Murray's theory of thirty personality needs, of which the various environmental 'presses' are counterparts. The Stern *Activities Index* (1958) sought to provide a parallel form which would identify congruent events, conditions and practices to be found on college campuses which would be significant for students and their teachers. The relations between the CCI and AI have been clarified by McFee (1961), more recently by Stern (1970). The parallelism between these measures has *not* been demonstrated: each gives rise to its own factors. In the case of CCI these have been identified (Stern, 1965) as: vocational climate, intellectual climate, aspiration level, student dignity, self-expression, group life and social form. The scores from these, or similar factors (Pace, 1962; Stern, 1963) can be used to compare colleges, or groups of colleges, and to relate environment differences to 'productivity' of scholars, Ph.D.s, attitude changes, student 'sub-cultures', and other variables. A form of the Pace and Stern *College Characteristics Index*, suited to English colleges of education, was devised by McLeish (1970), who sought to relate changes in students' attitudes and beliefs over a three-year period to the quality of their environment. Another version of this instrument devised by Ann Sutherland has been used in the Manchester group of colleges, under the guidance of the late Stephen Wiseman.

The CCI is based on the collective perception, or consensus of students on the specific features of their college. Several other instruments have been devised on this basis of discovering what constitutes the college 'image'. Some, like Pace's *College and University Environment Scales* (CUES, 1963) and Thistlethwaite's *Factored Scales* (Nunnally and Thistlethwaite, 1963) are based on the CCI. Pervin (1967, 1968) has devised a *Transactional Analysis of Personality and Environment* (TAPE) by means of which students provide data which throw light on the integration among students, faculty and administration. A semantic differential technique reveals accord or discrepancy between the student's perception of himself, his college, other students, the faculty, the administration and the ideal college. A sample of three thousand students from twenty-one colleges rated these concepts on fifty-two scales, using an eleven-point scale. The scales have shown their usefulness in relation to the problem of student 'drop-outs': large perceived discrepancies between the student and college are associated with dissatisfaction ratings and the intention to terminate.

Other workers take the view that the types of students who enrol in a college provide one of the most salient features of the environment. This is the assumption underlying Astin's work in this area (Astin and Holland, 1961; Astin, 1962, 1963, 1964, 1965). His *Environmental Assessment Technique* takes account of college size, the intelligence level of the students and their personal characteristics as shown by their vocational choice. Adapting Holland's classification of vocations in six categories (realistic, intellectual, social, conventional, enterprising and artistic) to the major fields of study, and calculating the proportions of students in each category, it is possible to differentiate college environments in terms of their salient emphasis. Astin (1965) has demonstrated that classroom environments reflect systematic differences according to the various fields of studies. The instructor's personal style and classroom behaviour, the students' attitudes to knowledge, to the instructor and to the kind of evaluation used are related to the subject area. For example, students in English and Political Science tend to argue more with the instructor and other students than do those in Chemistry and Biology. Instructors in French and Spanish are more likely to know their students by name than are those in Sociology and Psychology. In a sense, the field of study represents a crude personality test, and constitutes a guide to possible behaviour patterns. According to this view, these behaviour patterns of students and instructors are essential, differentiated features of the college environment. The great advantage of the EAT technique is that, at least in the United States, the necessary data on colleges can be obtained from public sources, thus eliminating the need for reliance on informants in the institutions being investigated. The validity of the method has been checked (Astin, 1963) by correlating the public data against questionnaire responses made by selected students from seventy-six colleges and universities.

More recently, Astin (1968) has conducted a survey of students, National Merit Scholarship winners located in 246 institutions. The objective was to identify patterns of environmental stimuli which could be used to differentiate between colleges. Factor analyses were carried out on the student peer environment, the classroom environment, the administrative environment, and the physical environment. Beginning with a list of 275 'stimuli' (defined as any behaviour, event, or other observable characteristic of the institution capable of changing the student's sensory input), Astin discovered twenty-seven which differentiate between institutions. In addition, seventy-five items dealing with the student's impressions of his college environment yielded eight more measures of the college 'image'. The study is too complex to summarize adequately, but the flavour can be conveyed from the characterization of teacher education colleges. The peer environment is typically feminine, a large amount of leisure is associated with regular sleeping habits and frequent use of automobiles. Students show less independence and are more decisive about their career plans than students in other institutions. Students and instructors are deeply involved in the classroom; there is little familiarity with the instructor; there is little verbal aggressiveness. Students are relatively passive. The administrators are very harsh towards student aggressiveness although relatively permissive about cheating. There is a very low degree of academic competitiveness and school spirit is low. Interesting differences were also detected between religious and secular colleges, negro and integrated colleges, single sex and co-educational colleges.

A third approach to measuring the college environment was used by Astin (1962). This consisted of analysing thirty-three pieces of objective data, from directories and other published sources, for 335 colleges. The data consisted of major attributes such as financial resources, denominational affiliation, student and faculty orientations and characteristics as well as the EAT materials previously mentioned. The six dimensions along which colleges seemed to vary were identified as: wealth, size, private versus public, masculinity versus femininity, technical emphasis and homogeneity. The most important of these factors turned out to be affluence in that it accounted for, or was associated with, nearly a quarter of the measured differences between these colleges (variance). In a study of high-ability students who give up their college courses Astin (1964) found no association between these environmental variables and the student's decision to discontinue, except that the chances of a female student 'dropping out' are increased if the college contains a high proportion of men.

The fourth technique for analysing environments is the study of student and faculty behaviour, with special reference to the concept of 'sub-cultures'. Trow (1960, 1962) identifies four broad patterns of response or orientation towards colleges: *the collegiate* (football, fraternities, dates, cars and drinking, campus fun), *the vocational* (courses, credits, student placement, a job), *the academic* (knowledge, libraries, laboratories, seminars, scholarship) and *the non-conformist* (verbal aggressiveness, ambivalence towards faculty, critical detachment, hostility to administrators, alienation, pursuit of an 'identity'). In the *College Student Questionnaire* (Educational Testing Service, 1965) descriptions of these life-styles are presented, the student respondent being invited to indicate which description comes closest to his own values, interests and attitudes, ranking the other three as well. The environment can then be characterized in terms of the prevailing sub-cultures by totalling the numbers in the four categories (Adams, 1966). In reflections on 'the troubles at Berkeley', Trow (in Dennis and Kauffman, 1966) remarks:

> Berkeley is not an academic community, despite all the rhetoric; it is a collection of communities and aggregates of students. At least some of our difficulties have arisen out of our indifference to the nature of the complex society that these constitute.

One of the ways in which conflict develops in this situation of institutional complexity, as Trow points out, is that administrators are oriented towards infractions of discipline by the relatively immature 'collegiate' subcultural group and are not equipped by habit or training to deal with the organized political activists belonging to the 'non-conformist' sub-culture.

Becker and his associates (in Sanford, 1962), using a more direct method of participating observers, studied the behaviour of students and student groups in the University of Kansas Medical School. The theoretical framework used was to consider student sub-cultures as differentiated responses to a common set of environmental pressures. The most important factor in the development of student culture is the formation of groups of a small and intimate kind (Boyer, 1965). These generate common understandings, norms of behaviour, agreements about what constitutes 'academic crud' and the 'straight griffin' (to use a Yorkshire expression). Student culture, so generated, consists of a set of perspectives and practical recipes for dealing with the problems imposed by the continuous, unremitting pressures of clinical work and the question of how to select from the faculty 'offerings' what the group believes to be relevant to their future day to day work in medicine. For example, laboratory work, blood counts and urinalyses are regarded as a time-wasting imposition as students believe they will never be called upon to carry out these procedures as established physicians. The student culture is in many ways a mechanism for institutionalizing deviance from the formal rules and values of the medical school. At the same time it is a mode of adaptation to the pressures of the curriculum. It provides a rationale for coping with what would otherwise be a totally unrealistic demand on their time and energies.

These four different approaches to the definition and measurement of the environment are not mutually exclusive. Indeed, each is open to criticism on methodological grounds of various kinds* which can best be muted by an attempt to make use of all four methods of evaluation (McLeish, 1970). In other words the techniques and theoretical approaches can be considered as complementary, possibly subsumed in the concept of the college as a miniature social system. As Barton (1961) says:

Organizations are made up of individual people, but they are more than mere collections of individuals. The people are interacting; their interactions are governed by informal expectations and formal rules which are agreed upon to varying degrees; the members have attitudes and beliefs about the organization which may form a common culture or a set of conflicting subcultures; and the organization as a whole possesses common facilities and symbolic objects, such as its plant, its budget, and its constitution. The measurement of organizational char-

* See *Review of Educational Research*, 1965, 35, 258–9.

acteristics must take into account these complex relationships, groupings and common properties.

The net outcome of research on colleges from these various standpoints
may be summarized: firstly, a number of instruments and conceptual
schemes have been made available to administrators, teachers and research
workers which can throw a bright light on a number of problems of adjustment to the realities of sub-group differences (between colleges, between
teachers and students, between administrators and other sectional interests,
etc); secondly, major dimensions of variations between colleges have been
recognized (intellectual, humanistic-vocational, friendliness, and propriety);
thirdly, that considerable variation exists, cutting across many of the commonly accepted classifications (liberal arts versus teacher education; secular
versus denominational; co-educational versus single-sex; regional or rural
versus urban; residential versus non-residential, etc).

### English Colleges of Education: Environments and Student Characteristics

In a longitudinal study of changes in students' attitudes over a period of
three years in ten colleges of education in a single institute of education area,
McLeish (1970) used a *College Environment Index* based on Pace and
Stern's *Inventory*. The attempt was made to relate the students' image of
their environment to objectively determined features of the academic community as well as to their examination results, attitude and personality
changes, and values of a personal, social and religious kind. A complete
sample ($\eta = 1,247$) of the student intake was tested on entry and retested on
exit. Ten dimensions of college environment were established – student
energy, concern for individuality, social commitment, staff image, intellectual
climate, clarity and system of courses, student loyalty to college, humane
regulations, group participation and lack of tension. It was found that the
colleges differed very significantly across all ten dimensions and that the
differences were meaningfully associated with the more public aspects of
the colleges, for example, their physical environments (situation, facilities,
aesthetic value), local authority in contrast to private colleges, rural/urban,
co-educational/single sex, size and composition of the student body.

The *College Environment Index* was also related to thirty attitude and
personality variables, to students' final examination results, to attitudes to
three teaching methods and to twenty-three indices drawn from returns
made by colleges to the Ministry of Education. These objective indices
of environment were grouped under four headings: size, character of
college, nature of the courses provided, and staff preparation.

The relationship between the various dimensions of the *College Environ-*

*ment Index* was examined by factor-analysis. Two main factors were considered, the first being a general approval factor, the second a bipolar factor which contrasted student response to staff competence (see Figure 24.1). Further analyses, including the thirty variables of students' attitudes on completion of their courses, indicated that scores on the environment index were closely related to professional attitudes to teaching as a career (Figure 24.2) rather than to authoritarianism, expressiveness or social utility. This is consoling news, especially in view of the remarkably unflattering estimate of the colleges of education given by these students on the *College Environment Index* (McLeish, 1970).

In an earlier study of a random sample of University of Reading students (McLeish, 1968) a typology had been erected on the basis of students' expressed attitudes to the methods of lecture, seminar and tutorial. The nine student types revealed by this classification were clearly distinguishable in terms of social, political and vocational attitudes, as well as in terms of personality variables. Almost precisely the same distribution of types was discovered in the college of education sample, using extreme scores on one or other of the teaching method attitude scores as identifying 'tags'. Students who are 'naturalistic' in their philosophy of education, who are radical in politics and independent in their thinking tend to take an unfavourable view of the college environment and of the lecture method. Older, conservative students who believe in formal methods, who are stable, submissive to expert opinion, scoring high on religious value and relatively unsure of their own views tend to have a favourable attitude to the college environ-

Figure 24.1

The Inter-relations of the Ten Dimensions of the College Environment Index

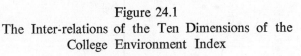

Factor 1: General Approval

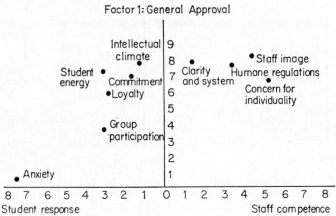

**Figure 24.2**

Plot of College Environment Index with Other Attitudinal and Personality Measures

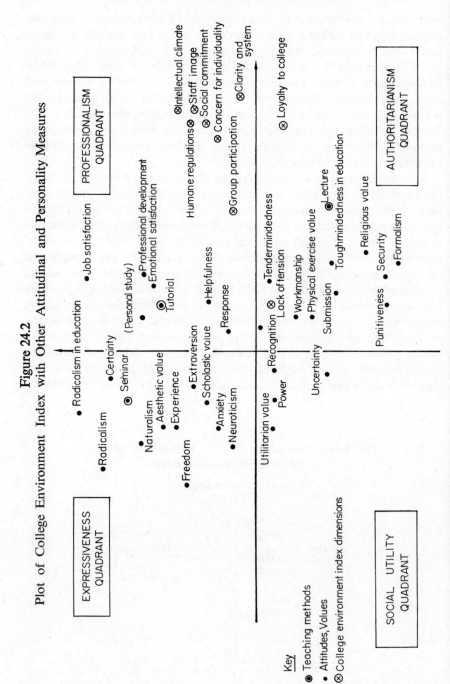

ment and the lecture method. Similar relationships are found with regard to the seminar and tutorial methods. Factor analysis of this sample verified the student typology: rebels versus enthusiasts, oracular versus participatory, tutor-centred versus student-centred, group-oriented versus individually-oriented, and quietists – developed previously (McLeish, 1970 a).

The students in this study were also classified in terms of their main ('non-vocationally oriented') subject, college by college. Striking differences appear between students in the different subject areas, these of course determine a large part of the differences between colleges of different emphases and point to the existence and nature of kinds of student 'sub-culture' other than those given by the earlier typology. Using 'humanities' students as the criterion group, since they are the most numerous, it is manifest that students taking divinity or physical education or sociology or home economics subjects, as well as those who fail their main subject, are distinctive in terms of their attitudes and values at the time of the examination, as well as differing markedly on entry. The differences are clarified in Table 24.1.

Differences between students classified by main subjects are not as great as the differences between the students as a group and the college lecturers as a group. The latter are, to begin with, older, they are considerably more radical, are much more certain of their opinions, are more naturalistic and less punitive. In addition, they are much more stable and introverted, they are less religious, they disbelieve in formal methods of instruction in schools. The lecturers, classified according to subject area, differ from each other even more than the corresponding student groups. This means that the student must accommodate himself not only to the academic staff as a group, in terms of their different norms, aspirations, attitudes and expectations; they confront also the varying emphases of subject specialists, as well as their individual qualities. The fact that the students themselves fall into various sub-groupings in terms of basic social, educational and professional attitudes as well as in their approach to the college experience no doubt assists each individual student to adjust to the environment in his own unique way during this period of professional development. Each student can draw the necessary support from the appropriate peer groups in his struggle to accommodate to the pressures to which he is subjected.

## Impact of the College Environment

The main outcome of colleges of education in this particular sample is that students, over a period of three years, change in the direction of the lecturers' and tutors' views in so far as they tend to move from a religious conservatism towards a secular humanism. This is associated with greater radicalism, a greater emphasis on spontaneity in child development, a dis-

Table 24.1
Differences in Main Course Students
('Humanities' Students as Criterion Group)

| | $\eta = 76$ | $\eta = 27$ | $\eta = 32$ | $\eta = 71$ | $\eta = 28$ | $\eta = 365$ |
|---|---|---|---|---|---|---|
| Attitude or Value | Divinity | P.E. | Sociology | Home Ec. | Failures | Humanities |
| Radicalism | low | — | — | — | — | average |
| Tenderminded | high | — | — | — | very low | average |
| Formalism | — | — | — | high | high | average |
| Helpfulness | high | — | — | — | — | average |
| Experience | low | — | — | — | low | average |
| Power need | low | high | — | high | — | average |
| Recognition | — | — | high | — | very high | average |
| Naturalism | — | low | low | low | — | average |
| Uncertainty | — | high | high | — | — | average |
| Physical value | — | very high | — | low | — | average |
| Aesthetic value | low | very low | — | — | — | average |
| Scholastic value | — | low | low | low | — | average |
| Religious value | high | low | — | — | — | average |
| Job satisfaction | — | — | low | — | low | average |
| Individuality, College concern for | — | low | very low | very low | low | average |
| College intellectual climate | — | low | — | very low | low | average |
| Anxiety | — | — | — | very low | — | average |

enchantment with traditional teaching methods and the development of a less punitive attitude towards disciplinary offences.

The most surprising outcome of the investigation is that the change towards social and secular radicalism seems closely related to two main influences. There is a direct relationship between the educational quality of the environment and the amount of change which takes place in students – the better the college, the greater the change. Of equal influence is the question whether the college objectives are framed within a matrix of liberal theology and assumptions or in a secular, local-authority framework. The religious colleges of liberal persuasion 'push' their students further towards non-commitment to a religious confession than do the secular colleges. The less liberal the religious college, the less is the change towards secular radicalism. Quality of environment and religious 'liberalism' have approximately the same value as far as general outcome is concerned.

The two main predictors of change were found to be *emphasis on science* and *democratic climate*. Combining college scores on these two predictors provided a multiple correlation of 0.73 with regard to change towards radical humanism in the student body. The inter-relationships are shown in Figure 24.3.

The direction of change is in line with the results of other studies, in

Figure 24.3
Predictors of Outcome in Ten Colleges

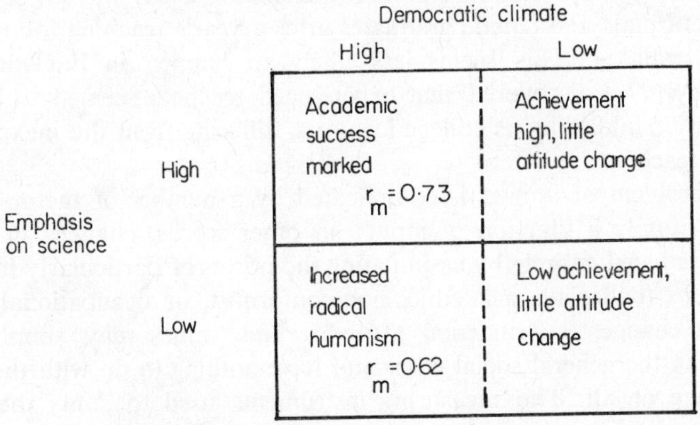

Democratic climate

|  | | High | Low |
|---|---|---|---|
| **Emphasis on science** | High | Academic success marked $r_m = 0.73$ | Achievement high, little attitude change |
|  | Low | Increased radical humanism $r_m = 0.62$ | Low achievement, little attitude change |

Britain as well as in the United States. Webster and his associates (Sanford, 1962) has summarized the research on personality and other changes in college students in America. In contrast to Jacob's findings (1957), Webster *et al.* assert that students in this period, as in the 1930s and 1940s, become more 'liberal' in their attitudes, more sophisticated and independent in their thinking, more tolerant of ethnic differences. This is a result of their college years. In England K. M. Evans (1967) found marked changes after one year's training on the *Minnesota Teacher Attitude Inventory*; on the other hand there were virtually no changes on the Allport, Vernon and Lindzey *Study of Values* with the same group. Newcomb and Feldman (1969), reviewing about 1,500 studies carried out over a forty-year period, discovered consistent patterns of change in students' values and attitudes in general agreement with the findings set out above. The pattern of change in the 1960s as a result of college experience can be characterized as a tendency to lose faith in religion, and to develop radical viewpoints. Attitudes to war, communism, patriotism, censorship, civil rights, labour and government are affected: these changes are attested to by well-designed studies which follow groups of students through their college years. There are, of course, differences in the rate of change as between men and women, Catholics, Protestants and Jews, different colleges and universities. But the general line of change is leftwards and towards atheism and agnosticism, against the Establishment. Authoritarianism also declines; students tend to become less dogmatic and less conventional.

Morrison and McIntyre (1967) working in Edinburgh, discovered that Scottish student teachers became less toughminded about education, more radical in their views about desirable changes in the school system, and more inclined to naturalism as an educational philosophy after three years of teacher training. However, after one year of actual teaching they reverted to their original position. A similar 'backlash' effect was discovered in samples of male and female graduates after a year's teaching following one year of training. This seems less likely to happen in England, where McLeish (1970) discovered that experienced teachers seemed to have the same basic philosophy as college lecturers, differing from the inexperienced student teachers.

The problem of impact is complicated by a number of factors. Output may be simply a function of input: in other words, changes in students may be induced entirely by assimilating the norms of particularly influential sub-groups (collegiate, academic, non-conformist, or occupational). Alternatively, changes in students' attitudes and values may simply reflect changes in the general social ethos and have nothing to do with the college experience at all. The measuring instruments used to study the college environment may be so crude or inappropriate in relation to the objectives of college education, or the criterion tests for measuring change may be so irrelevant that the real causal associations may be obscured rather than revealed by their use. Different departments certainly maintain different pressures on students (and on faculty); different personality types react differently to similar aspirations and similar pressures. Where there is a congruency between personality, press, sub-culture aspirations, faculty objectives, administrative provision and societal demands we can assume maximum impact. As Pace (1969) has proposed, there is probably a law of mass-action operating in this area. The more massive, cumulative and congruent with each other the input stimuli are, the greater the impact they will have on students. Perhaps cross-cultural studies would be the experimental area within which such a law might be demonstrated. But we are dealing with an extremely complex problem where a research design is necessary in which students are tested on entry to college with instruments of proven validity and reliability, and retested with the same instruments on completion of their training (Harris, 1963). A control group design is also mandatory to discover what extra-college influences affect students in general during the period being investigated and which are specifically associated with the college environment. It is also desirable to deal with complete groups (to resolve the problem posed by 'drop-outs' from the programme), rather than with 'volunteers' or with other kinds of supposedly 'random samples'.

Those investigations which meet these rather stringent research desiderata (McLeish, 1970, summarizes these), uniformly suggest that the effects of college education are to produce an increased open-mindedness, a growing awareness of the realities of individual experience, a developing aesthetic sense and a declining commitment to a fundamentalist and institutionalized religion. In many cases there is also an increased interest in intellectual matters. In personal development a greater independence of judgement is manifested, there is also an increased confidence and a greater expressiveness. Students are less dominated by conventional habit patterns and more ready to deal with the emotional and other aspects of the real situation.

Some colleges are more successful in generating these changes than others: how they do it is the question.

# CHAPTER 25

## The Nature of Teaching and the Effectiveness of Teachers

JOHN GARNER

The period from 1969 to 1972 has seen a series of enquiries into the state of teacher education in Britain of which one of the more striking features has been the absence of evidence on fairly crucial issues. Directly or indirectly the debate has been about the quality of the output of the teacher education sector of higher education, since discussions concerning the form or content of teacher education provision inevitably make assumptions about the relative effectiveness of any proposed variations. Similarly the discussions that take place within the colleges about the mix between 'academic' and 'professional' studies, the content of syllabuses, the mode of teaching practice organization, and the place of in-service provision make these same assumptions. Such enquiries and discussions are very welcome signs of an interest in, and concern with, teacher education, but what is needed if these various debates are to be anything more than exchanges of opinion (however informed) are some measures of the achievements of training institutions. Basically the output of colleges can be described in terms of both quantity and quality. The latter can be described in terms of intellectual achievements and what is often called 'suitability for teaching' or 'potential for effective teaching'. Description of the quantitative output of colleges is relatively simple; description of the qualitative output is far more difficult, especially in the case of 'suitability for teaching'. To reiterate, it is hard to see how discussions about the effectiveness of different patterns of organization can be more than mere exchanges of opinion until such time as acceptable measures are available. In their absence it is not too surprising to find that organizational problems are being approached and decided in terms other than those of their effectiveness in producing teachers of high quality.

In view of the importance of the description of 'teacher quality' it is disappointing to find that most of the reviewers of the vast teacher effectiveness literature conclude that little of utility has been discovered, and to find that so little British research effort has been directly concerned with the problem. This chapter represents an attempt to understand why the state of knowledge about teacher effectiveness is so unsatisfactory, and to point to potentially more promising methods of enquiry. [Those readers seeking a comprehensive review of research into teacher effectiveness are referred to articles by Evans (1961), Taylor (1969) and Lomax (1972a) for British research, and to Flanders and Simon (1970) and Mueller (1971) for American research.]

Until recently British research has been dominated by studies attempting to predict teacher effectiveness from the personal characteristics of students in training, and has been carried out in an attempt to improve the procedures by which students are selected for entry into teacher training programmes. A typical study is that carried out by Cortis (1968) who administered a substantial battery of tests, including measures of intelligence, personality, vocabulary, creativity and self images, to 259 students drawn from three colleges of education, and related these scores to criterion measures derived from the teachers' certificate examination. The data analysis produced some 2,000 correlation coefficients (between the forty-seven test scores, twelve biographical details and six criterion measures) which were then subjected to a factor analysis. The levels of relationship between the many variables were almost all uniformly low, and only one predictor, naturalism in education, was related to the practical teaching mark. In this instance the correlation was only $+.182$, a value which hardly warrants discussion. Other studies have been a little more fortunate: Warburton, Butcher and Forrest (1963) found seven variables that correlated between $+.220$ and $+.276$ with teaching marks; Start (1966) found seven personality variables that discriminated between teachers rated highly on practical ability and their less successful colleagues; Davis and Satterly (1969) found four variables that fulfilled a similar discriminating function, but the magnitude of the relationships could not be estimated because of the techniques of data analysis that were used. What would seem to be the ultimate in studies of this kind is that of Lomax (1969) who included 278 predictor variables and fourteen criterion variables in his study of sixty-eight college of education students. The analyses of the data illustrated the complexity of the criterion problem and focused attention on the width of the range of variables which may be important determinants of success. Taken together these studies appear to substantiate Vernon's comment that 'teachers are as diverse in their psychological traits as any other occupational group', and that 'it is fallacious to talk of teaching personality as something distinct and consistent' (1953).

Although the intentions behind these studies can be appreciated, it is less easy to appreciate the assumptions that underlie this kind of research. On the methodological side all the authors mentioned above express reservations about the criterion measure of teaching ability. Davis and Satterly (1969) note that 'in an attempt to ensure consistent evaluation of teaching ability, four experienced tutors were relieved of supervisory duties to act as moderators', and leave the matter at that. Start (1966) notes that 'Studies relying on the subjective opinion of a variety of judges – often head teachers – are bedevilled by the problem of multiple and different criteria. In the present study an attempt was made to circumvent the difficulty by having one rater and hence one set of criteria to contend with'. The problem referred to by Start is highlighted to an even greater extent by Wiseman and Start (1965) who, after finding no relationship between college teaching grades and head teachers' ratings five years later, remarked, "It may be that the colleges and headmasters are using different criteria in assessing teaching ability'. All three quotations indicate that different raters will be likely to differ in their assessments but, from the evidence provided in the studies, it is impossible to decide whether this likely disagreement stems from differing conceptions of good teaching or from differences in perception, given that all the raters are looking for the same things.

The important point to be noted here is that the concept of good (or bad) teaching is a value concept, a point made very clearly by Rabinowitz and Travers (1953) when they state, 'The effective teacher does not exist pure and serene, available for scientific scrutiny, but is instead a fiction in the minds of men. No teacher is more effective than another except as someone so decides and designates.' If this point is accepted then it becomes apparent that the criteria of teaching ability used in studies such as that of Davis and Satterly were value judgements, and it would be interesting to know if the process of moderation consisted of a discussion of the desirability of certain teacher effects, followed by a discussion of the extent to which the various students produced these effects, or whether their moderation was in a more global and less explicit style. In the light of this discussion it is therefore suggested that any study of teaching ability or teacher effectiveness should state what kind of teacher-produced effects are thought to be desirable, and describe the extent to which these valued effects were deemed to have occurred. In this way at least some of the uncertainty involved in these studies would be resolved.

The importance of the first stage in this proposed approach varies somewhat according to the purposes to which any particular enquiry is directed, being more of a problem in certification exercises than in research investigations. It is becoming increasingly customary in researches into teaching to avoid the evaluative problem by describing the events within the classrooms of teachers possessing various personality attributes or kinds of training, rather than by rating their performance on some scale of excellence. A rare British example of this approach is provided by Wragg (1971) using the Flanders Interaction Category System (Flanders, 1960). In this system the verbal events of a classroom can be described in either of ten ways (e.g. teachers asking questions, encouraging children, using their ideas or criticizing them, and pupils expressing their ideas or responding to the teacher). The data analysis yields statements about the relative frequencies of different sequences of classroom talk. In Wragg's study teachers were observed before and after an in-service training course, and the statements about the effects of the course were made in terms of the changes in the frequencies of certain behaviour sequences: the reader was left to decide whether or not the changes were in desirable directions. Although this kind of approach appears to sidestep neatly the values question it should be noted that it does not avoid it completely, since each system for describing classroom behaviour is the embodiment of a set of values. Gallagher and Aschner (1963), for example, have devised a system that describes the sorts of thinking that are used by teachers and pupils, using categories such as divergent, convergent, cognitive, memory, etc. (based on Guildford's (1959) model of the intellect), and its use assumes that an enquiry into children's thinking is a legitimate activity. Although there would be few who would argue that the development of different modes of thinking is not a legitimate aim of the educational process, it is still the case that the decision to abstract this particular aspect of the life of the classroom is based on a system of values.

In the case of the assessment of teachers for certification purposes the problem cannot be sidestepped in this way. As one of the functions of the certification process is that of determining the desirability of an intending teacher's values, it would appear that the evaluators of teaching perform- ance must come to grips with the question as to whose values are to be accepted in the description of desirable teacher effects. In attempting to solve the problem it might be useful to distinguish between 'successful' and 'effective' teaching by analogy with Bass's model of leadership behaviour (1961). In that model he distinguishes between successful leader- ship, defined as an attempt at producing change in the behaviour of others in a direction determined by the one making the attempt, and effective leadership, where such changes are also desired by those at whom the attempt is directed. In the case of teaching, successful teaching will be defined as that where the teacher achieves the effects that he is seeking, and effective teaching as that where the teacher achieves effects that are thought to be desirable by those who are in the evaluative role. On this view there would thus be four basic categories of teaching: that which was successful but ineffective, unsuccessful and ineffective, successful and effective, and unsuccessful but effective. Although examples of the last category might be expected to be rare, it is possible to imagine a teacher attempting to inculcate racial prejudices, and succeeding only in producing a culturally- approved liberality of view as a reaction against his own teaching. The value of making these distinctions is that it underlines the separation between the valuator's values and the teacher's performance, and enables separate statements to be made about degrees of competence (a possibly better term than success) and degrees of effectiveness, the one requiring behavioural skills and the other requiring certain values to be held.

The preceding paragraphs have been attempting to clarify not only what is meant by 'effective' but also what is meant by the term 'teaching'. The point is that it is at least a two-part activity, the one concerned with selecting desirable effects, the other concerned with those teacher behaviours that will be employed in attempts to achieve such effects. Possibly more order can be brought into this discussion if further elements are introduced, and a four-phase definition of teaching is proposed. Firstly, already mentioned, to select aims and formulate objectives. Secondly, to select strategies that will lead to the attainment of the objectives. Thirdly, to translate the preceding phases into action. Finally, to evaluate the extent to which the action was successful in attaining the objectives specified in the first phase. This particular four-phase definition of teaching is apparently very widely accepted since it is an explicit statement of the definition implicit in a vast number of teaching practice files, past, present and doubtless future. Thus it is usual for a student teacher's lesson notes to include a statement of aims and/or objectives for the lesson, a statement of the methods or strategies to be employed in their achievement, the actual teaching behaviour in the classroom, and finally a set of comments on the way the lesson went.

If this definition of teaching were to be explicitly accepted it would imply that the evaluation of teaching should become a four-phase activity, in that separate measures would be made for each phase, leading to the production of a teaching profile. For the teacher trainer such a refinement would be expected to lead to improved diagnostic techniques and subsequent prescriptions, since the four phases correspond roughly to courses in the philosophy of education, educational psychology, the practice of teaching, and the observation of teaching and educational measurement. It might also have implications for those research studies that attempt to evaluate the effects of training course alterations (e.g. McNamara, 1971), in that it suggests at which phase of the teaching process any proposed innovation might be expected to produce some effect.

To return to the research studies from which this discussion started, a rather puzzling feature has been the lack of explicit theorizing about the relationships that would be expected between teacher characteristics and teaching quality. The model of teaching behaviour that seems to be implicit in these studies is extremely simple – that teaching behaviour is a function of qualities of the teacher. Occasionally it seems to be assumed that the nature of the function might vary with the type of school in which the teaching takes place, as evidenced by Davis and Satterly's separate analyses by primary and secondary school levels (1969), and by Wiseman and Start's division of their sample into grammar, secondary modern, and primary school teachers (1965). This functional model is in interesting contrast to the early psychological models of human behaviour put forward by the behaviourists in the 1920s, where it was assumed that behaviour was a function of the situation in which the person was to be found. However, it was soon found necessary to assert that behaviour was a function of both the situation and the person in the situation, and recent years have seen quite complex models intended to represent the nature of these interactions. Social psychology in particular has been forced to acknowledge that the determinants of behaviour in social settings are of a complex nature. All that can be said on the evidence available to date is that the simple model that has been adopted is inadequate; if there were some single direct relationships between personal characteristics and teacher performance – given the difficulties associated with measuring such performance – it might have been expected that some consistent findings would have emerged, but, alas, they have not. This model stands in sharp contrast with some of the models of teacher behaviour discussed by Gage (1963), which seem to do more justice to research findings. One feature of all these models is that to varying extents they assume that the teacher's behaviour is in part determined by the children being taught, an assumption that allows for a difference in a teacher's behaviour when he teaches a docile first form and a rebellious fourth form, so that he might be competent with one and incompetent with the other. One such model, produced by Ryans (1960) in his painstaking study of the characteristics of teachers, places the personality characteristics of teachers at some considerable 'distance' from their teaching behaviour. Thus the basic personality traits of individuals will interact with the kind of teacher education that they will receive (the views of children, society, and subject matter to which they are exposed) to produce certain teaching styles, such as understanding or aloof classroom behaviour, businesslike or slipshod classroom organization, and so on. These styles will in turn be affected by the conventions of the particular school and the particular subject matter that is to be taught. The resultant of this interaction will be the generally-observed behaviour of the teacher in the classroom – whether the teacher is kind or harsh, original or unimaginative. At the final level of specificity this general classroom style will be varied from pupil to pupil, and from moment to moment, depending on the interactions between the characteristics of specific pupils, specific problems that arise or specific kinds of activities being undertaken. The main implication of this model for the predictive studies with which we are concerned is that the power of personality measures as predictors of teacher behaviour will be greatest when the interacting conditions are held constant for the sample of teachers about whom the predictions are to be made. If the teachers had the same 'social origins', had attended the same courses in college, and taught the same topics to the same children, then it would follow from the model that personality measures should have a reasonable predictive power. Such a situation is an 'ideal type' of course, but this ideal has implications for the design of studies of the predictive kind in several ways. It follows from this that predictive studies might be best conducted within the same institutions, and within the same courses in those institutions. It also follows that since the characteristics of children interact with the teachers' characteristics, then the prediction should be stronger when the teaching behaviour measures relate to the teaching of kinds of children rather than children in general, a point that has already been confirmed. Thus Washburne and Heil (1960) classified teachers as either 'turbulent', 'self-controlled' or 'fearful' and then proceeded to show that the amount of pupil achievement and satisfaction that they produced depended on whether the child was a 'striver', an 'opposer' or a 'waverer', while Amidon and Flanders (1961) found an interaction between teaching style and the achievements of 'dependent-prone' students learning geometry.

The Ryans model also has implications for a second theme in British research into teachers and teaching, that concerned with the effects of colleges on students' attitudes. These studies would seem to be concerned with the second stage in the model in which the basic personality traits of the teacher interact with the kind of teacher education that they receive to produce 'teaching styles'.

The earliest attempt to produce a scale of attitudes towards education and teaching was the American Minnesota Teacher Attitude Inventory but it has been little used in Britain, although Herbert and Turnbull (1963) found that their students became more 'progressively' oriented through their college course, and that 'MTAI' scores served as useful predictors of both teaching practice grades and education theory marks. Rather more widespread have been studies using the Manchester 'Survey of Opinions about Education', developed by Oliver and Butcher (1962). These scales yield scores on three independent factors labelled as naturalism, radicalism and tendermindedness, and the results that have been obtained so far can be held to demonstrate the utility of Ryans' model. Butcher (1965), for example, administered the scales to experienced teachers, graduates in training, and to small samples of students in two colleges of education. A subsequent administration of the scales to the trainee teachers enabled statements to be made about attitude changes as a result of their courses, the most interesting feature of which was that one of the colleges showed an increase in radicalism only, while the university department of education and the second college showed increases in all three factors. Referring to this Butcher notes, '... It is also possible that the lack of significant change on the naturalism and tendermindedness scales represents a genuine difference between contrasting types of training college', and indeed the direction of the differences is consistent with the differences in emphasis which the two colleges displayed at that time. That these attitudes were influenced by more general considerations in serving teachers was demonstrated by Oliver and Butcher (1968) who found differences on all three scales between teachers having different religious and political affiliations, and on the naturalism and tendermindedness scales between teachers in different kinds of schools. McIntyre and Morrison (1967) carried out a study similar to to that of Butcher (1965) and found that although there were increases on all scales for both men and women students, these were greater in the case of the women. In a follow-up study Morrison and McIntyre (1967) found a decrease on the scales for women but not for men during their first year of teaching, but more interestingly found negative correlations between the decrease in scores on the scales and the rated 'progressiveness' of the schools in which the teachers were placed. The correlation cofficients for the 'R', 'T' and 'N' scales were $-.19$, $-.30$, and $-.26$ respectively, and although only the value for the 'T' scale is significant it remains interesting that the other two relationships are in the same direction. To relate these studies to Ryans' model there is evidence that these attitudes towards teaching (mental 'teaching styles') are influenced by the attitudinal milieu in which the student or the teacher finds himself, and that changes of milieu lead to changes in attitude. Unfortunately, however, there have been no attempts to see if attitudinal influences interact with more basic personality traits to produce a variety of attitudinal outcomes, although the sex differences reported by McIntyre and Morrison could be held to come into this category. Further, contrary to expectations derived from the model, the Manchester Opinion Scales do not predict teaching grades, although as Morrison and McIntyre (1969 a) have noted, this could have been due to the unreliability of teaching grades, to the behaviours reflected by the attitudes not being thought important by the raters, or to the trainee teachers not possessing the teaching skills necessary to allow their attitudes to teaching to be expressed in actual behaviour. They favour the latter reason on the grounds that American studies have found consistent relationships between Minnesota Teacher Attitude Inventory scores and pupil ratings with experienced teachers, while being unable to do so with inexperienced teachers. Obviously much remains to be done, and it is suggested that models of expected influence patterns should be adopted to guide the kind of research that is done; in particular the Ryans model is commended since it directs the researcher to asking specific rather than global questions about such patterns.

To summarize some of what has been said so far, and to draw attention to further problems and research areas, a model for research into teaching will be presented (Figure 25.1). The arrows are intended to indicate the

## Figure 25.1
## A Model of Teaching

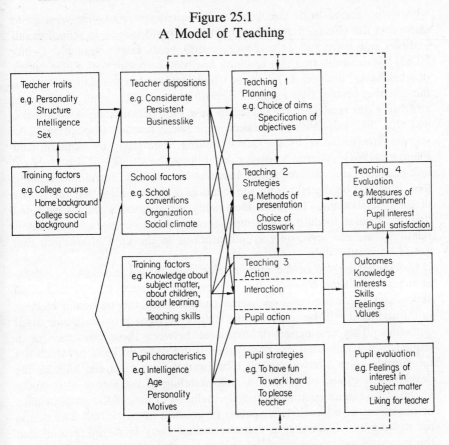

direction of influences, while broken lines indicate 'feed-back' influences. Before examining the model in some detail two features should be noted. The first is that some of the patterns of influence that are displayed are probable, but not necessary (e.g. the school might be permissive towards its teachers, and exert no constraints on a teacher's choice of aims and objectives, or the teacher's choice of methods for presenting subject matter might take no account of the characteristics of the pupils). The second is that the patterns of influence have been kept to a minimum since, as it is, the complexity raises doubts on the feasibility of research into teaching.

It should also be noted that most of the suggested influence patterns are supported by research findings. For example, the relationship between school factors, pupil characteristics, pupil actions and outcomes has been traced with considerable ingenuity and skill by Himmelweit and Swift (1971). They found that the effects of streaming by ability differentially affected the attitudes towards school and the behaviour in school of children who were deemed to be intelligent or less intelligent, and then went on to show that the effects of streaming influenced performance in school examinations and were still in evidence several years later. Similarly Turner (1965) has demonstrated that teaching involves the performance of a variety of work tasks, the precise nature of which depends on the setting in which the teaching occurs, that teachers' dispositions and their abiilty to produce and carry out strategies are related to how they perform these work tasks, and that the relationships between strategies, teacher dispositions, and success are mediated by the school setting. The study by Amidon and Flanders (1961), referred to earlier, establishes the validity of the proposed link between pupil characteristics, teaching 'actions' and learning outcomes. Lest it should be thought from the mention of such studies that the nature of these relationships has been thoroughly investigated it should be noted that the studies to date have simply scratched the surface of these interrelationships, and serve only as indicators as to the kind of research that would be worth while.

Unfortunately one of the most glaring gaps in the knowledge available at the present time concerns the relationships between teacher and pupil action and interaction, and outcomes. In examining this particular element in the model it will be useful to distinguish between proximate and distal outcomes. This distinction differentiates between those outcomes of a sequence of actions that are observable in the situation itself or which are measurable soon afterwards, and those longer-term outcomes such as the development of sets of values, an understanding of the nature of scientific methods, and other such items usually included in lists of the goals or aims or objectives of education in general or courses in particular. The reason for making this distinction is that the further away from the 'action' that the measures are, the more difficult it is to attribute the one to the other (except possibly in fairly standardized experimental or quasi-experimental situations), while for both research and teacher evaluation purposes the most useful measures would be events that occurred in classrooms that are known to bear relationships to the more distant goals. An example of this approach is provided by Garner (1972) who related the incidence of certain teacher behaviours to the amount of time that children spent attending to tasks that the teacher had specified, on the rationale that attention was necessary before learning – hence more distal outcomes – could occur. Some support for that assumption has been provided by Lahaderne (1967), who related 'classroom attention' and learning outcomes with encouraging results. Given this kind of detailed research to discover the relationships between classroom action and longer-term outcomes, then the problem of criterion measures becomes more tractable. A good deal of effort has been expended on this kind of problem by Flanders and others using his system of classroom observation, and the results obtained so far suggest that this is a fruitful kind of activity. Since he has recently summarized his findings (Flanders, 1970) only a brief outline will be given here. Flanders quotes some twenty-three studies, most of which show a consistent relationship between what is called 'indirect' teaching (a preponderance of teacher talk which 'accepts feelings', praises or encourages', 'accepts ideas of pupils' and 'asks questions', over 'lecturing', 'giving directions' or 'criticising') and positive pupil attitudes and pupil achievements. One of these studies (Soar, 1966) is especially worthy of note since it provides very detailed information about the precise nature of this relationship for different kinds of task. His study involved fifty-four classes at four age levels, and each class gains on tests of creativity, vocabulary and reading skill were related to the 'indirectness' of their teachers. The results are shown in Figure 25.2, where the

Figure 25.2

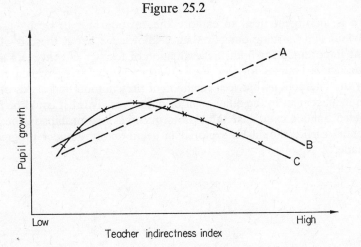

curves marked A, B and C represent the gains for creativity, vocabulary and reading skill. These results are most interesting since they suggest that different kinds of teacher behaviour are required to optimize different kinds of pupil growth, and are precisely the kind of results that are so badly needed if the study of effective teaching is to make progress. Given this sort of information, studies such as Wragg's, referred to earlier, become much more meaningful. Wragg demonstrated that certain kinds of in-service courses led to certain kinds of changes in their teaching behaviour, and the effects of these changes can be inferred from the Flanders group's studies.

Again in America there are a growing number of researchers looking at the kinds of explanations that teachers use, and relating these to pupil thinking (Smith and Meux, 1970; Perkins, 1964 and 1965; Wright, 1967; Gallagher and Aschner, 1963), which will again further knowledge as to what certain sequences of teacher behaviour imply for the attainment of different kinds of objectives. Such studies are most encouraging, and although this sort of research has to contend with many problems – not all of which are overcome – the development of knowledge about classroom behaviour and its consequences is at last beginning to give an air of promise to the study of teacher effectiveness. It is equally encouraging to note that there is a growing number of research projects in Britain that are concerned with classrooms, noticeably those of Wragg, Worthington, Burgess, Adelman and Walker – all separately studying the effects of different kinds of classroom groupings – and of Duthie and McIntyre, who are examining the kinds of skills that are needed for effective classroom functioning.

## Conclusion

There is an urgent need to explore the relationships between classroom behaviour and learning outcomes since knowledge about these is of paramount importance for both the evaluation of teacher effectiveness and for the design of courses for the preparation of teachers. There is a need to study the interactions between methods of presentation and styles of classroom management in the attainment of objectives. This list could be further extended but indicates that the close sequential relationships in the model presented earlier should be explored in detail before grander progress can be made.

# References

Adams, D. V. (1966) 'An analysis of student subcultures at Michigan State University'. *Dissertation Abstracts,* **27** (3–A), 595–6.

Adams, J. A., and Bray, N. W. (1970) 'A closed-loop theory of paired-associate learning'. *Psychological Review,* **77**, 385–405.

Allen, D. W., and Ryan, K. A. (1969) *Micro Teaching.* Reading, Mass.

Altman, E. (1967) 'The mature student teacher'. *New Society,* 28 December.

Amidon, E. J., and Flanders, N. A. (1961) 'The effects of direct and indirect teacher influence on dependent-prone students learning geometry'. *J. Educ. Psychol.,* **52**, 286–91.

Amidon, E. J., and Hough, J. B. (eds.) (1967) *Interaction analysis: theory, research and application.* New York, Addison-Wesley.

Anderson, A. W. (1962) 'The teaching profession: an example of diversity in training and function' in Henry, N. B., (ed.) *Education for the Professions. The Sixty-first Yearbook of the National Society for the Study of Education.* Chicago, NSSE.

Anderson, H. H. (1937) 'Domination and integration in the social behaviour of young children in an experimental play situation'. *Genet Psch. Monog.,* **19**, 341–408.

Anderson, R. C., and Myrow, D. L. (1971) 'Retroactive inhibitions of meaningful discourse'. *Journal of Education Psychology Monograph,* **62**, 81–94.

Archambault, R. D. (ed.) (1965) *Philosophical Analysis and Education.* London, Routledge & Kegan Paul.

Ashley, B., Cohen, H., and Slatter, R. (1967 a) 'Social classifications: relevance to the teacher'. *Times Educational Supplement* (Scotland) 17 March.

Ashley, B., Cohen, H., and Slatter, R. (1967 b) 'Why we are teachers'. *Times Educational Supplement* (Scotland) 12 May.

Ashley, B., Cohen, H., McIntyre, D., and Slatter, R. (1970) 'A sociological analysis of students' reasons for becoming teachers'. *Sociological Review,* **18**, 1, 53–69.

Astin, A. W., and Holland, J. L. (1961) 'The environmental assessment technique: a way to measure college environments'. *J. Educ. Psychol.,* **52**, 308–16.

Astin, A. W. (1962) 'An experimental characterization of higher educational institutions'. *J. Educ. Psychol.,* **53**, 224–35.

Astin, A. W. (1963) 'Further validation of the environmental assessment technique'. *J. Educ. Psychol.,* **54**, 217–26.

Astin, A. W. (1964) 'Personal and environmental factors associated with college drop-outs among high aptitude students'. *J. Educ. Psychol.,* **55**, 219–27.

Astin, A. W. (1965) 'Classroom environment in different fields of study'. *J. Educ. Psychol.,* **56**, 275–82.

Astin, A. W. (1968) *The college environment.* Washington, D. C, American Council on Education.

Astin, A. W., Panos, R. J., and Creager, J. A. (1966) 'A programme of longitudinal research on the higher education system'. *American Council on Education Research Reports No. 1.*

ATCDE (1970) *Higher Education and Preparation for Teaching. A Policy for Colleges of Education.* London, ATCDE.

ATCDE (1971) *The Professional Education of Teachers.* London, ATCDE.

ATCDE (1971) *Handbook of Colleges and Departments of Education 1972.* London, Lund Humphries.

Ayer, A. J. (1956) *The Problem of Knowledge.* Harmondsworth, Penguin Books.

Baker, R. (1966) 'A comparative study of perceptions of a university environment between honor and non-honor freshmen groups'. *Educ. & Psychol., Measurement,* **26,** 973–6.

Baker, J. R. A. (1967) 'A teacher co-tutor scheme'. *Ed. for Teaching,* **73,** 25–30.

Bales, R. F. (1950) *Interaction Process Analysis: a method for the study of small groups.* Addison Wesley, Reading, Mass.

Barnard, H. C. (1961) *A History of English Education from 1760.* London, University of London Press.

Barr, A. S. (1929) *Characteristic Differences in the Teaching Performance of Good and Poor Teachers of the Social Studies.* Bloomington, Illinois, Public School Publishing Co.

Barr, A. S. (1948) 'The measurement and prediction of teaching efficiency. A summary of investigations'. *J. Exp. Educ.,* **16,** 203–83.

Barr, A. S., *et al.* (1952) 'Report of the Committee on the Criteria of Teacher Effectiveness'. *Revue of Educational Research,* **22,** 233–63.

Barr, A. S., *et al.* (1961) 'Wisconsin studies of measurement of teacher effectiveness: A summary of investigation'. *J. Exp. Educ.,* **30,** 5–156.

Barton, A. H. (1959) *Studying the effects of college education: a methodological examination of changing values in college.* New Haven, Edward W. Hazen Foundation.

Barton, A. H. (1961) *Organizational measurement and its bearing on the study of college environments.* College Entrance Examination Board Research. Monographs No. 2, NY CEBB.

Barton, A. H. (1963) 'The college as a social organization'. *College Admissions,* 10: *The Behavioral Sciences and Education.* College Entrance Examination Board, NY, 31–45.

Bass, B. M. (1961) *Leadership, psychology and organizational behaviour.* Harper & Row, New York.

Battle, Haron, J. (1957) 'Relation between personal values and scholastic achievement'. *J. Exp. Educ.* 1957, **26,** 27–41.

Becker, G. S. (1964) *Human Capital. A Theoretical and Empirical Analysis with Special Reference to Education.* New York, University Press, Princeton.

Becker, H. S. (1962) 'The Nature of a Profession' in Henry, N. B., (ed.) *Education for the Professions. The Sixty-first Yearbook of the National Society for the Study of Education.* Chicago, NSSE.

Becker, H. S., and Carper, J. (1956) 'The elements of identification with an occupation'. *American Sociological Review,* **81.** 341–8.

Bell, J. (1966) 'Learning their job in a comprehensive', *Times Ed. Supplement,* 14 Oct, 849.

Benn, S. I., and Peters, R. S. (1959) *Social Principals and the Democratic State.* London, George Allen & Unwin.

Bereday, G. Z. F., and Lauwerys, J. A. (eds.) (1963) 'The education and training of teachers'. *The Year Book of Education 1963*. London, Evans Brothers.

Bereiter, C. (1971) 'Education and the Pursuit of Reality'. *Interchange*.Vol. 2, No. 1, 46.

Berger, P. L., and Luckmann, T. (1969) *The Social Construction of Reality*, London, Allen Lane, The Penguin Press.

Bernstein, B. (1971) 'On the Classification and Framing of Educational Knowledge' in Young, M. F. D. (ed.) *Knowledge and Control*. London, Collier-Macmillan.

Bewsher, L. G. (1965) 'A study of attitudes and incentives among a group of students training to be teachers'. M. A. Dissertation, University of London.

Biddle, B. J., and Ellena, W. J. (1964) *Contemporary Research on Teacher Effectiveness*. New York, Holt, Rinehart & Winston.

Binns, H. B. (1908) *A Century of Education*. London, Dent.

Blaug, M. (1967) 'Approaches to educational planning'. *Economic Journal*. 262–88.

Blaug, M. (1968) *Economics of Education: Selected Readings. Vol. 1*. London, Penguin.

Blaug, M. (1969) *Economics of Education: Selected Readings. Vol. 2*. London, Penguin.

Blaug, M. (1970) *The Economics of Education: A Selected Annotated Bibliography*. London, Pergamon.

Blaug, M. (1970) *An Introduction to the Economics of Education*. London, Allen Lane, The Penguin Press.

Bloom, S. W. (1959) 'The role of the sociologist in medical education'. *Journal of Medical Education*. No. XXXIV, July, 667–73.

Bloom, B. S., and Webster, H. (1960) 'The outcomes of colleges'. *Rev. Educ. Res.*, 30, 321–33.

Board of Education (1925) Report of the Departmental Committee on the Training of Teachers for Public Elementary Schools. HMSO.

Board of Education (1944) Teachers and Youth Leaders. Report of the Committee appointed by the President of the Board of Education to consider the Supply, Recruitment and Training of Teachers and Youth Leaders. HMSO.

Board of Education Special Committee (1944) *Teachers and Youth Leaders* (McNair Report). London, HMSO. 78.

Body, A. H., and Frangopulo, N. J. (1970) *The Silver Jubilee*. Didsbury, Morten.

Bolam, R. (1970) 'Guidance for probationer teachers'. *Trends in Education*. No. 21. University of Bristol.

Boruth, J. R. (1970) *On the Theory of Achievement Test Items*. Chicago, University of Chicago Press.

Bowles, F. (1965) *Access to Higher Education*. Vols. I & II. UNESCO and IAU. Paris.

Bowman, M. J. (1963) 'Educational shortage and excess'. *The Canadian Journal of Economics and Political Science*, 4, 454–8.

Bowyer, C. H. (1970) *Philosophical Perspectives for Education*. Glenview, Illinois, Scott Foresman & Co.

Boyer, R. K. (1967) 'The student peer group: Its effect on college performance'. *Dissert. Abstracts*, 27 (7-A), 2193.

Brandt, R. B. (1959) *Ethical Theory: The Problems of Normative and Critical Ethics*. Englewood Cliffs, N. J., Prentice-Hall International.

Brosan, G., Carter, C., Layard, R., Venables, P., and Williams, G. (1971) *Patterns and Policies in Higher Education*. London, Penguin.

Brown, N. C. (1961) *Orientation to college learning—a reappraisal*. Washington, D.C: American Council on Education.

Brown, Roberta D. (1966) 'Student characteristics in relation to adjustment in two different college environments'. *Dissertation Abstracts*, **27** (3–A), 596–7.

Browne, J. D. (1969) 'The balance of studies in colleges of education' in Taylor, W. (ed.) *Towards a Policy for the Education of Teachers*. London, Butterworth, 99–109.

Browne, J. D. (1971) 'The Curriculum' in Hewett, S. (ed.) *The Training of Teachers. A Factual Survey*. University of London Press, 81–92.

Bruce, D., and Crowley, J. J. (1970), 'Acoustic similarity effects on retrieval from secondary memory'. *Quarterly Journal of Experimental Psychology*, **9**, 190–6.

Burgess, T. (ed.) (1971) *Dear Lord James*. London, Penguin Books.

Burns, T., and Stalker, G. M. (1961) *The Management of Innovation*. Tavistock.

Butcher, H. J. (1959) 'The opinions of teachers and student teachers about education'. Unpublished Ph.D. Thesis, University of Manchester.

Butcher, H. J. (1965) 'The attitudes of student teachers to education'. *Brit. J. Soc. Clin. Psychol.*, **4**, 17–24.

Butler, J. R. (1968) *Occupational Choice*, Science Policy Studies No. 2 Department of Education and Science. London.

Butterfield, H. (1945) *The Englishman and his History*. London, Cambridge UP.

Camplin, K. (1970) 'Role transition and the development of a professional self image in student teachers'. M.Ed. dissertation. University of Newcastle.

Cane, B. (1969) *In-Service Training*. National Foundation for Educational Research, Slough.

Carter, C. F. (1965) 'The Economics of Higher Education'. *Manchester School*, XXXIII, 1, 6.

Case, D. (1968) 'First Year Out. A Survey of Probationary Teachers in Black Country Schools'. University of Keele.

Caspari, I. E., and Eggleston, J. (1965) 'A New Approach to Supervision of Teaching Practice'. *Education for Teaching*, No. 68, November, 42–52.

Chambers, P. (1971) 'The Study of Education in the Colleges. Harking Back!'. Tibble, J. W. (ed.) *The Future of Teacher Education*. London, Routledge & Kegan Paul.

Clarke, F. (1948) *Freedom in the educative society*. London, ULP.

Clark, R. P., and Nisbet, J. D. (1963) 'The first two years of teaching'. Aberdeen College of Education. (Mimeograph.)

Clarke, J. H. (1968) 'The image of the teacher'. *Brit. J. Educ. Psychol.* 280–5.

Cogan, M. L. (1953) 'Toward a Definition of Profession'. *Harvard Educational Review*, Vol. 23, Winter.

Cohen, L. (1965) 'An exploratory study of the teachers' role as perceived by head-teachers, tutors, and students in a training college'. M.Ed. dissertation. University of Liverpool.

Cohen, L., and Child, D. (1969) 'Some sociological and psychological factors in university failure'. *Durham Research Review*, **22**, 365–72.

Cohen, L. (1969) 'Students' perceptions of the school practice period'. *Research in Education*, **2**, 52–8.

Cohen, L. (1971) 'Active versus passive relationships with college tutors: some differing correlates of the preferences of general course and specialist course student teachers. *Papers in Education*', **4**, 21–25.

Cohen, L. (1971) 'Dogmatism and views of the ideal pupil: a study of mature student-teachers'. *Educational Review*, **24**, 3–10.

Cohen, L. (1971) 'Personality, school experience, and preference for tutor-student relationships in colleges of education'. *Human Relations*, **24**, 5, 349–58.

Cohen, L. (1971) 'Personality and changing problems among first year college of education students'. *Durham Research Review*, **6**, 28, 617–22.

Cohen, L., and Boothroyd, K. (1972) 'Need for achievement in "committed" and "reluctant" teachers'. School of Research in Education, University of Bradford. (Mimeographed.)

Cohen, L., and Reid, I. (1972) 'Need for achievement in B.Ed. and Certificate Students'. School of Research in Education, University of Bradford. (Mimeographed.)

Collier, L. G. (1969) 'School and college link in training teachers', *Education*, March, 412–44.

Collier, K. G. (1969) *New Dimensions in Higher Education*. London, Longmans.

Collier, K. G., Hodge, H. P. R., Horton, T., and Rathborn, M. (1971) *Colleges of Education Learning Programmes; a Proposal*. Working Paper No. 5. National Council for Educational Technology, Councils and Education Press.

Collins, M. (1969) *Students into Teachers*. London, Routledge & Kegan Paul.

Committee on Higher Education (1963) *Higher Education*. Report of the Committee appointed by the Prime Minister under the chairmanship of Lord Robbins (1961–63). HMSO.

Conant, J. B. (1963) *The Education of American Teachers*. New York, McGraw Hill.

Coombes, A. W. (1969) Florida Studies in the Helping Professions. *Univ. of Florida Monog.*, Social Sciences No. 37.

Cope, E. (1971 a) *School Experience in Teacher Education*. University of Bristol.

Cope, E. (1971 b) *A Study of a School Supervised Practice*. University of Bristol.

Corey, J. L. (1955) Values of future teachers. N.Y. Bureau of Publs. Teacher's College Columbia University.

Cornwell, J., *et al.* (1965) 'The Probationary Year'. Report published privately by University of Birmingham Institute of Education.

Cortis, G. A. (1966) 'The prediction of student performance in colleges of education'. M.Ed. thesis. University of Manchester.

Cortis, G. A. (1968) 'Predicting student performance in colleges of education'. *Brit. J. Educ. Psychol.*, **38**, 115–22.

Craft, M. (1967) 'Education and Social Work'. Pedley, F. H., (ed.) *Education and Social Work*. London, Pergamon.

Craft, M. (1970) 'Developments in interprofessional training' in *Higher Education Journal*, Vol. 17, No. 3.

Craft, M. (1971) 'A broader role for colleges of education'. Tibble, J. W. (ed.) *The Future of Teacher Education*. London, Routledge & Kegan Paul.

Crothers, E. J. (1970) *The Psycholinguistic Structure of Knowledge. Studies in Mathematical Learning Theory and Psycholinguistics*. Boulder, University of Colorado.

Crown, S. (1952) 'The Word Connection List as a diagnostic test: norms and validation'. *Brit. J. Psychol.*, **43**, 103–12.

Curtis, S. J. (1967) *History of Education in Great Britain*. London, Dakers.

Davie, J. S. (1958) 'Satisfaction and the college experience' *Psychosocial Problems of College Men*. B. M. Wedge (ed.) New Haven, Yale, UP, 1958, 15–42.

Davie, J. S., and Rust, R. M. (1962) 'Studying students as students: a case sample'. *J. Psychol.*, **53**, 161–82.

Davies, G. D. (1967) 'A study of attitudes and behaviour patterns among students at a college of education'. M.Ed. dissertation. University of Birmingham.

Davis, F., and Olesen, V. (1963) 'Initiation into a women's profession: Identity problems in the status transition of co-ed. to student nurse'. *Sociometry*, **26**, 1, 59–101.

Davis, T., and Satterly, D. J. (1969) 'Personality profiles of student teachers'. *Brit. J. Educ. Psychol.*, 39, 183–7.

Davis, W. R. (1967) 'An analysis of certain relationships between student needs, college environment, and academic achievement'. *Dissertation Abstract*, 1967, **27** (3–A), 2722–3.

Dearden, R. F. (1968) *The Philosophy of Primary Education*. London, Routledge & Kegan Paul.

Dennis, L. E., and Kauffman, J. P. (eds.) (1966) *The College and the Student*. Washington, DC, American Council on Education.

Denham, E. C. (1966) 'The prediction of college success with biographical data and self-ratings'. *Dissertation Abstracts*. 1966, 27 (3–A), 599.

Dent, H. C. (1963) *The Educational System of England and Wales*. London, ULP.

Dent, H. C. (1971) 'An Historical Perspective'. Hewett, S., (ed.) *The Training of Teachers*. London, ULP.

Department of Education & Science (1966) Report of the Study Group on the Government of Colleges of Education. HMSO.

Department of Education & Science (1970) Memorandum to the Select Committee, *Teacher Training*, Vol. 1. HMSO, London.

Department of Education & Science (1972) *Teacher Education and Training*. A Report by a Committee of Inquiry appointed by the Secretary of State for Education & Science under the chairmanship of Lord James of Rusholme. London, HMSO.

Derricott, R. (1968) 'The attitudes of education students to aspects of their course of training'. M.Ed. Dissertation. University of Nottingham.

Dewey, J. (1904) 'The Relation of Theory to Practice in Education' *Third Year Book of the National Society for the Scientific Study of Education*, (ed.) C. A. MacMurray, Bloomington, Indiana, Public School Publishing Co. Quoted in Taylor, W. (1969) *Society and the Education of Teachers*. Faber & Faber, 149.

Dickson, G. E., and Wiersma, W. (1966) 'Student-teachers—American and British', *New Society*, 4 Aug., **201**, 187–91.

Domas, S. J., and Tiedeman, D. (1950) 'Teacher competence: in annotated bibliography'. *J. Exp. Educ.*, **19**, 101–218.

Downes, L. W., and Shaw, K. E. (1968) 'Innovations in Teaching Practice,' *Trends in Education*, 42–5.

Duggan, E. P., and Stewart, W. A. C. (1970) 'The Choice of Work Area of Teachers'. *Keele Sociological Review Monograph*.

Duthie, J. H. (1970) *Primary School Survey: A Study of the Teacher's Day*. Edinburgh, HMSO.

Eason, T. W. (1971) 'Main Subject Courses'. Tibble, J. W. (ed.) *The Future of Teacher Education*. London, Routledge & Kegan Paul.

Eason, T. W., and Croll, E. J. (1971) *Staff and Student Attitudes in Colleges of Education*. Slough. NFER.

Eddy, E. D. (1959) *The college influence on student character*. Washington, DC, American Council on Education.

Education Authorities Directory and Annual, The (1971) School Government Publishing Co., 1971.

Edwards, A. (1957) The Social Desirability Variable in Personality Assessment and Research. New York, Dryden Press.

Elam, S. (ed.) (1964) *Education and the Structure of Knowledge.* Chicago, Rand MacNally.

Entwistle, H. (1970) *Education Work and Leisure.* London, Routledge & Kegan Paul.

Entwistle, N. J., *et al.* (1971) *Educational Objectives and Academic Performance in Higher Education,* Department of Educational Research, Lancaster.

Entwistle, N., and Entwistle, D. (1970) 'The relationship between personality, study methods and academic performance'. *Brit. J. Educ. Psychol.,* **40**, 2, 132–41.

Entwistle, N. J., Percy, K. A., and Nisbett, J. B. (1970) Summary of the Preliminary Report to the Joseph Rowntree Memorial Trust on 'Social Implications of Educational Change'. Department of Educational Research, University of Lancaster. (Mimeographed.)

Etzioni, A. (1961) *A Comparative Analysis of Complex Organizations.* New York, Free Press of Glencoe.

Etzioni, A. (ed.) (1969) *The Semi-Professions and Their Organization.* New York, The Free Press.

Evans, E. G. S. (1964) 'Reasoning ability and personality differences among student teachers'. *Brit. J. Educ. Psychol.,* **34**, 3, 305–14.

Evans, K. M. (1958) 'An examination of the Minnesota Teacher Attitude Inventory'. *Brit. J. Educ. Psychol.,* **28**, 374–84.

Evans, K. M. (1961) 'An annotated bibliography of British research on teaching and teaching ability. *Educ. Res.,* **4**.

Evans, K. M. (1965) *Attitudes and Interests in Education.* London, Routledge & Kegan Paul.

Evans, K. M. (1967) 'Teacher training courses and students' personal qualities'. *Educ. Res.,* **10**, 1, 72–7.

Eysenck, H. J. (1947) 'Primary social attitudes: I. The organisation and measurement of social attitudes'. *International Journal of Opinion and Attitude Research,* **1**, 49–84.

Eysenck, H. J. (1959) *Manual of the Maudsley Personality Inventory.* London, ULP.

Fagan, B. M. (1971) *Experiment and Innovation.* Vol. 4, University of California.

Feldman, K. A. (1969) 'Studying the impact of colleges on students'. *Sociology of Education,* **42**, 207–37.

Feldman, K. A. (1970) 'Some methods for assessing college impacts'. *Sociology of Education,* **44**, 133–50.

Feldman, K. A. (1971a) 'Measuring college environments: some uses of path analysis'. *AERA Journal,* **7**, 51–70.

Feldman, K. A. (1971b ) Some methods for assessing college impacts. *Sociology of Education,* **44**.

Finlayson, D. S., and Cohen, L. (1967) 'The teacher's role: a comparative study of the conceptions of college of education students and head teachers'. *Brit. J. Educ. Psychol.,* **37**, 1, 22–31.

Flanders, N. A. (1960) 'Teacher influence, pupil attitudes and achievement' Monograph No. 12. USOE, CRP 397. University of Minnesota.

Flanders, N. A. (1970) *Analysing Classroom Behaviour.* New York, Addison-Wesley.

Flanders, N. A. (1970) *Analysing Teaching Behaviour.* Reading, Mass., Addison-Wesley.

Flanders, N. A., and Simon, A. (1970) 'Teaching effectiveness: a review of research 1960–1966'. R. L. Ebel (ed.) *Encyclopedia of Educational Research*. Chicago, Rand McNally.

Floud, J., and Scott, W. (1961) 'Recruitment to teaching in England and Wales'. Halsey, A. H., Floud, J., and Scott, W., (eds.) *Education, Economy and Society*. Glencoe, Free Press, 527–44.

Floud, J. (1967) *Educational Planning*. London, Evans.

Ford, G. W., and Pugno, L. (eds.) (1964) *Structure of Knowledge and the Curriculum*. Chicago, Rand McNally.

Freedman, M. B. (1967) *The College Experience*. San Francisco, Jossey-Bass Inc.

Freire, P. (1970) *Pedagogy of the Oppressed*. New York, Herder and Herder.

Fuller, F. (1966) *The Founding of St. Luke's College Exeter*. Exeter. The College.

Fuller, F. F. (1969) 'Concerns of teachers: A development conceptualisation' in *American Educational Research Journal*. Vol. VI, No. 2, March, 208–11.

Furneaux, W. D. (1962) 'The psychologist and the university'. *Universities Quarterly*, **44**, 95–106.

Gage, N. L. (1963) *Handbook of Research on Teaching*. Chicago, Rand McNally.

Gage, N. L. (1963) 'Paradigms for research on teaching'. Gage, N. L. (ed). *Handbook of Research on Teaching*. Chicago, Rand McNally.

Gallagher, J. J., and Aschner, M. J. (1963) 'A preliminary report on analyses of classroom interaction'. *Merrill-Palmer Quarterly*, **9**, 183–94.

Gallop, R. (1969) 'A study of the B.Ed. student'. M.Sc. dissertation, School of Research in Education, University of Bradford.

Gallop, R. (1970) 'A study of the B.Ed. student'. *Brit. J. Educ. Psychol.*, **40**, 2, 220.

Garner, J. (1972) 'Some aspects of behaviour in infant classrooms'. *Research in Education*, (In press.)

Getzels, J. W., and Jackson, P. W. (1963) 'The teacher's personality and characteristics'. Gage, N. L. (ed.) *Handbook of Research on Teaching*. Chicago, Rand McNally.

Gibbons, K. C., and Savage, R. D. (1965) 'Intelligence, study habits, and personality factors in academic success'. *Durham Research Review*, **5**, 8–12.

Glennerster, H., and Wilson, G. (1970) *Paying for Private Schools*. London, Allen Lane, The Penguin Press.

Goldhammer, R. (1969) *Clinical Supervision*. New York, Holt, Rinehart & Winston Inc.

Goldsen, R. K., et al. (1960) *What College Students Think*. Princeton, N. J., Van Nostrand.

Goode, W. J. (1969) 'The Theoretical Limits of Professionalization' in Etzioni, A. (ed.) *The Semi-Professions and Their Organisation*. New York, The Free Press.

Gottleib, D., and Hodgkins, B. (1963) 'College student subcultures: Their structure and characteristics in relation to student attitude change'. *School Review*, **71**, 266–89.

Greenwood, E. (1966) 'The Elements of Professionalization' in Vollmer, H. M. and Mills, D. L. (eds.) *Professionalization*. Englewood Cliffs, New Jersey, Prentice-Hall.

Gribble, J. W. (1969) *Introduction to the Philosophy of Education*. Boston, Allyn and Bacon.

Guilford, J. P. (1959) 'Three faces of intellect'. *American Psychologist*, **14**, 469–79.

Hall, R. H., Hans, N., and Laywerys, J. A. (eds.) (1953) *The Year Book of Education 1953*. London, Evans Brothers.

Halliwell, K. (1965) 'An investigation into the validity of methods of student selection for teacher training in a training college'. Ph.D. thesis. University of Sheffield.

Hannam, C., Smyth, P., and Stephenson, N. (1971) *Young Teachers and Reluctant Learners*. London, Penguin.

Hansen, W. Lee (1966) 'Human Capital Requirements for Educational Expansion: Teacher Shortages and Teacher Supply'. Anderson, C. A. and Bowman, M. J. (eds.) *Education and Economic Development*, London, Cass.

Harris, C. W. (ed.) (1963) *Problems in measuring change*. Madison, Univ. Wisconsin Press.

Hassenger, R., and Weiss, R. (1966) 'The Catholic college climate'. *School Review*, **74**, 417–45.

Hatch, S. (1968) *Student Residence*. London, Society for Research into Higher Education.

Headmasters' Association and the Headmasters' Conference Joint Working Party, The (1970) 'Our Schools and the Preparation of Teachers'.

Heath, D. H. (1968) *Growing up in College*. San Francisco, Jossey-Bass.

Heist, P. (1960) 'Diversity in college student characteristics'. *J. Educ. Sociol.*, **33**, 279–91.

Herbert, N., and Turnbull, G. H. (1963) Personality factors and effective progress in teaching'. *Educational Review*, **16**, 24–31.

Hewett, S. (1970) 'Changing Roles for Colleges of Education' in *Univ. Qu.*, Vol. 25, No. 1, Winter.

Hewett, S. (1971) *The Training of Teachers*, London, ULP.

Higginbotham, P. J. (1969). 'The Concept of Professional and Academic Studies in Relation to Courses in Institutions of Higher Education (particularly Colleges of Education)' in *Brit. J. Educ. Studs.*, Vol. XXII, No. 1, February.

Higher Education (1963) The report of the Committee appointed by the Prime Minister 1961–1963. (The Robbins Report), HMSO.

Higson, F. G. (1951) 'An enquiry into the interests in education of teachers in training'. Unpublished M.Ed. thesis. University of Manchester.

Hilliard, F. H. (1968–69) 'Universities and the Education of Teachers' in *Educational Review*, Vol. 21, 89.

Hilliard, F. H. (1971) 'Theory and Practice in Teacher Education' in Hilliard, F. H., (ed.) *Teaching the Teachers*, London, George Allen & Unwin.

Himmelweit, H. H., and Swift, B. (1971) 'The class as a reference group'. Paper read at the British Psychological Society Annual Conference, Exeter.

Hinchcliffe, K. (1971) 'Teachers, the Open University and the Rate of Return', *Higher Education Review*, **3**, 3.

Hirst, P. H., and Peters, R. S. (1970) *The Logic of Education*. London, Routledge & Kegan Paul.

HMA, and HMC (1970) *Our Schools and the Preparation of Teachers*. December.

Hogan, J. M., and Willcock, (1967) In-Service Training of Teachers. *Trends in Education*, **8**, HMSO, London.

Hollins, T. H. B. (1969) *Another Look at Teacher Training*. Leeds University Press, 18–19.

Hollins, T. H. B. (1971) 'Desirable Changes in the Structure of Courses' in Hilliard, F. H., (ed.) *Teaching and Teachers*. London, George Allen & Unwin.

Holmes, B. (1971) 'The Future of Teacher Education in England and Wales'. *Education for Teaching*.

Holmes, B., and Scanlon, D. (eds.) (1971) *Higher Education in a Changing World, The World Year Book of Education* 1971/72. London, Evans.

Hoyle, E. (1969, Nov.) 'How does the Curriculum Change?—2: Systems and Strategies'. *Journal of Curriculum Studies*, 1, 3, 230.

Hunter, L. C., and Robertson, D. J. (1969) *Economics of Wages and Labour*. Macmillan, London.

Hutchins, R. M. (1936) *The Higher Learning in America*. New Haven, Yale University Press.

Illich, I. (1970) 'The Need for a Cultural Revolution'. *The Great Ideas Today*. Chicago, Encyclopaedia Britannica Inc.

Illich, I. (1971) *De-schooling Society*. London, Calder & Boyars.

Jacob, P. E. (1957) *Changing Values in College: An Exploratory Study of the Impact of College Teaching*. New York, Harper & Row.

James Report (1972) Teacher Education and Training. Department of Education and Science. London, HMSO.

Jervis, F. M., and Congdon, R. G. (1958) 'Student and faculty perceptions of educational values'. *Amer. Psychol.*, 13, 464–66.

Johnston, J. (1971) *Teachers' In-Service Education*. Oxford and NY, Pergamon Press.

Jones, L. G. E. (1924) *The Training of Teachers in England and Wales: A Critical Survey*. London, OUP.

Judges, A. V. (1952) *Pioneers of English Education*. London, Faber.

Kay, J. P., and Tufnell, E. C. (1841) 'The Training School at Battersea'. *Report on the Training of Pauper Children*. HMSO 201–342.

Kearney, D. L., Nolan, C., and Rocchio, D. (1956) 'The effect of teacher education on the teacher's attitude'. *J. Educ. Res.*, 49, 703–8.

Kelsall, R. K. (1963) *Women and Teaching*. London, HMSO.

Kelsall, R. K., and Kelsall, H. M. (1969) *The School Teacher in England and the United States*. London, Pergamon Press.

Kissack, M. (1956) 'The attitudes of training college towards corporal punishment'. Unpublished M.Ed. thesis. University of Manchester.

Kitchen, R. D. (1965) 'An investigation into the attitudes of first year and third year students in a training college using the semantic differential technique'. M.Ed. thesis. University of Birmingham.

Komisar, T. and MacMillan, J. (eds.) (1967) *Psychological Concepts in Education*. Chicago, Rand McNally.

Koos, L. V. (1970) *The Community College Student*. University of Florida Press, Gainesville.

Lahaderne, H. M. (1967) 'Attitudinal and intellectual correlates of attention'. Report in Jackson, P. W., '*Life in Classrooms*'. New York, Holt, Rinehart and Winston.

Land, F. W. (1960) *Recruits to Teaching: A Study of the attainments, qualifications and attitudes of students entering training colleges*. Liverpool University Press.

Lauwerys, J. A., and Bereday, G. Z. F. (eds.) (1963) *The Education and Training of Teachers*. The Year Book of Education 1963. London, Evans.

Layard, R., King, J., and Moser, C. A. (1969) *The Impact of Robbins*. London, Penguin.

Legatt, T. (1970) 'Teaching as a Profession'. Jackson, *Professions and Professionalization*. CUP 155–77.

Lieberman, M. (1956) *Education as a Profession*. Prentice-Hall, Englewood Cliffs, New Jersey.

Lomax, D. E. (1969) 'The characteristics of successful students'. Ph.D. thesis, University of Manchester.

Lomax, D. E. (1970) 'An analysis of success and failure in the education of teachers'. Social Science Research Council Report No. HR 273.

Lomax, D. E. (1971) 'Focus on the student teachers'. Burgess, T. (ed.) *Dear Lord James*. London, Penguin.

Lomax, D. E. (1972a) 'British research in teacher education'. *Review of Educational Research*.

Lomax, D. E. (1972b) 'The nature of student difficulties'. *School of Education Gazette*. **17**, 8–12. University of Manchester.

Lomax, D. E. (1973) 'Student anxiety'. *School of Education Gazette*, **18**, 16–23. University of Manchester.

Lortie, D. C. (1969) 'The balance of control and autonomy in elementary school teaching'. Etzioni, A. (ed.) *The Semi-Professions and their Organization*. New York, The Free Press.

Ludeman, W. W. (1956) 'Qualities of the ideal and effective college student: A study of student evaluation'. *J. Educ. Res.*, **50**, 151–3.

Lunneborg, P. W., and Lunneborg, C. E. (1966) 'The differential prediction of college grades from biographic information'. *Educ. & Psychol. Measurement*, **26** (4), 917–25.

Lynn, R. (1969) 'An achievement motivation questionnaire'. *Brit. J. Psychol.*, **60**, 4, 529–34.

Maden, M. (1971) 'The teaching profession and the training of teachers'. Burgess, T. (ed.) *Dear Lord James*. London, Penguin.

Manion, L. (1969) 'Attitude change in college of education students during their first year'. M.Sc. dissertation, University of Bradford.

Marks, E. (1967) 'Student perceptions of college persistence, and their intellective, personality and performance correlates'. *J. Educ. Psychol.*, **58**, 210–21.

Marsland, D. (1969) 'An exploration of professional socialization: the college of education and the teacher's role'. London, SRHE 5th Annual Conference 45–78.

Mason, W. S. (1961) *The Beginning Teacher* N. S. Department of Health, Education and Welfare, Washington Circular No. 644.

McConnell, T. R., Anderson, G. L., and Hunter, P. (1962) 'The University and Professional Education'. Henry, N. B. (ed.) *Education for the Professions. The Sixty-first Yearbook of the National Society for the Study of Education*. Chicago, NSSE.

McConnell, T. R., and Heist, P. (1962) 'The diverse college student population' Sanford, N. (ed.) *The American College*. N.Y. Wiley & Sons, 225–52.

McFee, A. (1961) 'The relation of students' needs to their perceptions of college environment'. *J. Educ. Psychol.*, **52**, 25–9.

McGrath, E. J. (1962) 'The ideal education for the professional man' in Henry, N. B. (ed.) *Education for the Professions. The Sixty-first Yearbook of the National Society for the Study of Education*. Chicago, NSSE.

McIntyre, D., and Morrison, A. (1967) 'The educational opinions of teachers in training'. *Brit. J. Soc. Clin. Psychol.*, **6**, 32–7.

McIntyre, D. (1971) 'Micro Teaching', Discussion Paper for Ed. Section, British Psychological Society Conference, York.

McLeish, J. (1968) 'Lecture, tutorial, seminar: The student's view'. *Education for Teaching*, **75**, 21–17.

McLeish, J. (1968) *The Lecture Method*. Cambridge Monographs on Teaching Methods, No. 1.

McLeish, J. (1969) *Teacher's Attitudes: A Study of National and other Differences*. Cambridge Institute of Education.

McLeish, J. (1970) *Students' Attitudes and College Environments*. Cambridge Institute of Education.

McLeish, J. (1970 a) 'Students' Attitudes to Teaching Methods'. *Alberta Journal of Educational Research*, **16**, 179–87.

McNair Report (1944), *Teachers and Youth Leaders*. London, HMSO.

McNamara, D. R. (1971) 'The evaluation of an innovatory course in applied education in colleges of education'. Paper read at the Conference for Research into Teacher Education, Whitelands College, London.

Mehrabian, A. (1968) 'Male and female scales of the tendency to achieve'. *Educational and Psychological Measurement*, **28**, 493–502.

Mehrabian, A. (1969) 'Measures of achieving tendency'. *Educational and Psychological Measurement*, **29**, 445–51.

Meyer, D. E. (1970) 'On the representation and retrieval of stored semantic information'. *Cognitive Psychology*, **1**, 242–300.

Ministry of Education (1957) Pamphlet No. 34. *The Training of Teachers: Suggestions for a three-year training college course*, 12–13.

Ministry of Education for Northern Ireland (1968) *Education in Northern Ireland in 1968*. HMSO, Belfast.

Mooney, R. L., and Gordon, L. V. (1950) *The Mooney Problem Checklists*. NY, The Psychological Corporation.

Morgan, C. (1969) 'Predicting academic and practical teaching success in a college of education'. M.Ed. thesis, University of Manchester.

Morrill, W. H. (1966) 'The relationship of student personality, area of concentration and college environment'. *Dissertation Abstracts*, **27** (4–A), 961.

Morris, R. N. (1969) *The Sixth Form and College Entrance*. London, Routledge & Kegan Paul.

Morris, V., and Ziderman, A. (1971) 'The economic return on investment in higher education in England and Wales'. *Economic Trends*, **211**, XXI.

Morrison, A., and McIntyre, D. (1967) 'Changes in opinions about education during the first year of teaching.' *Brit. J. Soc. Clin. Psychol.*, **6**, 161–3.

Morrison, A., and McIntyre, D. (1969) *Teachers and Teaching*. London, Penguin Books.

Morton-Williams, R., Finch, S., and Poll, C. (1966) *Undergraduates' Attitudes to school teaching as a career (England and Wales)*. Central Office of Information: Social Survey for Ministry of Education. SS 354, April.

Mosher, R., and Purpel, D. (1972) *Supervision: the Reluctant Profession*. Houghton Mifflin Co., Mass. 113–48.

Mueller, D. G. (1971) 'How to evaluate teaching'. *Journal of Teacher Education*, **22**, 229–43.

Musgrove, F. (1968) 'Curriculum Objectives'. *J. Curric. Studies*, Vol. 1, No. 1, November.

National Advisory Council (1957) *6th Report on the Training and Supply of Teachers*, p. 8, p. 5.

National Foundation for Educational Research (1970) Evidence to the Select Committee. *Teacher Training*, Vol. 1, London, HMSO.

National Union of Teachers and the Association of Teachers in Colleges and Departments of Education (1961) *Teachers in their First Posts*. London, NUT.

National Union of Teachers (1970) *Teacher Education: The Way Ahead*. A discussion document. London, NUT.

National Union of Teachers (1971) 'The Probationary Year'. A report prepared by a sub-committee of the National Young Teachers Advisory Committee of the NUT, for submission to the National Young Teachers Conference, Bradford.

National Union of Teachers (1971) *The Reform of Teacher Education*. London, NUT, 55–9.

Ninth Report of the National Advisory Council on the Training and Supply of Teachers (1965) *The Demand for and Supply of Teachers 1963-1986.*

Newcomb, T. B., *et al.* (1967) *Persistance and change: Bunnington College and its students after twenty-five years.* London & New York, John Wiley & Sons.

Newcomb, T. M., and Feldman, K. A. (1969) *The impacts of college on students.* San Francisco, Jossey-Boss, 2 Vols.

Newcombe, I. M. (1943) *Personality and social change: Attitude formation in a student community.* New York, Dryden Press.

Newcombe, I. M., and Wilson, E. K. (eds.) (1966) *College peer groups: problems and prospects for research.* Chicago, Aldine.

Nichols, R. C. (1967) 'Personality change and the college'. *Amer. Educ. Res. J.,* **4,** 173–90.

Nosow, S. (1958) 'Educational value—orientations of college students'. *J. Educ. Res.,* **52,** 123–8.

Nunnally, J. C., Thistlethwaite, D. L., and Wolfe, S. (1963) 'Factored scales for measuring characteristics of college environments'. *Educ. Psychol. Measurement.* **23,** 239–48.

OECD (1969) *Development of Secondary Education Trends and Implications.* OECD.

OECD (1971 a) *Développement de l'enseignment supérieur 1950–1967.* OECD, Paris.

OECD (1971 b) *Towards New Structures of Post-secondary Education.* OECD, Paris.

Ofchur, L. T., and Gnagey, W. I. (1963) 'Factors related to the shift of professional attitudes of students in teacher education'. *J. Educ. Psychol.,* **54,** 149–53.

Olesen, V., and Whitaker, E. (1969) *The Silent Dialogue.* San Francisco, Jossey-Bass.

Oliver, R. A. C. (1953) 'Attitudes to education'. *Brit. J. Educ. Studs.,* **2,** 31–41.

Oliver, R. A. C., and Butcher, H. J. (1962) 'Teachers' attitudes to education—the structure of educational attitudes'. *Brit. J. Soc. Clin. Psychol.,* **1,** 56–69.

Oliver, R. A. C., and Butcher, H. J. (1968) 'Teachers' attitudes to education'. *Brit. J. Educ. Psychol.,* **38,** 38–44.

Olson, D. R. (1970) 'Language and thought: Aspects of a cognitive theory of semantics'. *Psychological Review,* **77,** 257–73.

Ormrod Report (1971) Report of the Committee on Legal Education. Cmnd. 4595. London, HMSO.

Osborne, G. S. (1966) *Scottish and English Schools.* London, Longman.

Oxtoby, R. (1967) 'Reform and resistance in higher education: A critique of current research'. *Educational Research,* **10,** 1, 38–50.

Pace, C. R. (1960) 'Five college environments'. *College Bd. Rev.,* **41,** 24–8.

Pace, C. R., and McFee, A. (1960) 'The college environment'. *Rev. Educ. Res.,* **30,** 311–20.

Pace, C. R., and Stern, G. G. (1958) 'An approach to the measurement of psychological characteristics of college environment'. *J. Educ. Psychol.,* **49,** 269–77.

Pace, C. R. (1962) 'Methods of describing college cultures'. *Teachers College Record,* **63,** 267–77.

Pace, C. R. (1969) 'College environments'. *Enc. of Educ. Res.,* 169–73.

Peirson, E. G. (1971) Chairman's Address: ATCDE, December, 1970. 'At the Cross roads'. *Education for Teaching,* No. 84, Spring. 1971.

Perkins, H. V. (1964) 'A procedure for assessing the classroom behaviour of students and teachers'. *American Educational Research Journal,* **1,** 249–60.

Perkins, H. V. (1965) 'Classroom behaviour and underachievement'. *American Educational Research Journal,* **2,** 1–12.

Pervin, L. A. (1967) 'The college as a social system: a fresh look at three critical problems in higher education'. *Journal of Higher Education*, **38**, 317–22.

Pervin, L. A. (1968) 'The college as a social system: student perception of students, faculty and administration'. *J. Educ. Res.*, **61**, 281–4.

Peston, M. (1970) 'High peaks or safe lowlands'. *The Times Educational Supplement*, 20 February, p. 4.

Peters, R. S. (ed.) (1966) *Ethics and Education*. London, George Allen & Unwin.

Peters, R. S. (ed.) (1967) *The Concept of Education*. London, Routledge & Kegan Paul.

Phenix, P. H. (1964) *Realms of Meaning*. New York, McGraw Hill.

Phillips, D. J. (1967) 'A study of the attitudes of students in a college of education to college discipline'. M.A. thesis, University of Wales.

Pidgeon, D. (1970) 'The National Foundation for Educational Research in England and Wales'. Butcher, H. J., and Pont, H. B., (eds.) *Educational Research in Britain 2*. London, ULP.

Plowden Report (1967) Department of Education and Science, 'Children and their Primary Schools'. A Report of the Central Advisory Council for Education (England), Vols, 1 and 2. HMSO.

Pollard, H. M. (1956) *Pioneers of Popular Education*. London, Murray.

Pollard, M. (1971) 'In-service training'. B. Kemble (ed.) *Fit to Teach*. London, Hutchinson Educational.

Poppleton, P. K. (1968) 'The assessment of teaching practice: what criteria do we use'? *Education for Teaching*, **75**, 59–64.

Rabinowitz, W., and Travers, R. M. W. (1953) 'Problems of defining and as essing teaching effectiveness'. *Educational Theory*, **3**, 212–19.

Reimer, E. (1971) 'An essay on alternatives in education'. *Interchange*, Vol. 2, No. 1.

Renshaw, P. (1969) 'A concept of a college of education'. Unpubl. M. Phil. thesis, University of London.

Renshaw, P. (1971) 'The objectives and structure of the college curriculum'. Tibble, J. W. (ed.) *The Future of Teacher Education*. London, Routledge & Kegan Paul.

Renshaw, P. (1971) 'A Curriculum for Teacher Education'. Burgess, T. (ed.) *Dear Lord James. A Critique of Teacher Education*. London, Penguin.

Rich, R. W. (1933) *The Training of Teachers in England and Wales during the Nineteenth Century*. London, CUP.

Richardson, C. A., Brûlé, H., and Snyder, H. E. (1953) *The Education of Teachers in England, France and the U.S.A.* Paris, UNESCO.

Richardson, J. E. (1967) *Group Study for Teachers*. London, Routledge & Kegan Paul.

Robbins Report (1963) Committee on Higher Education, *Higher Education*. London, HMSO.

Robinson, E. E. (1971) 'Degrees for teachers'. Burgess, T., (ed.) *Dear Lord James: A Critique of Teacher Education*. London, Penguin.

Robinson, W. P. (1961) 'The measurement of achievement motivation'. D.Phil. thesis. University of Oxford.

Robinson, W. P. (1964) 'The achievement motive, academic success and intelligence test scores'. *Brit. J. Soc. Clin. Psychol.*, **4**, 2, 98–103.

Rokeach, M. (1954) 'The nature and meaning of dogmatism'. *Psychological Review*, **61**, 194–204.

Rokeach, M. (1960) *The open and closed mind*. NY, Basic Books.

Rolls, I. F., and Goble, P. M. (1971) 'Future teacher or uncommitted student?' *Sociological Review*, **19**, 2, 229–32.

Rosenberg, M. (1965) *Society and the Adolescent Self-Image.* Princeton, Princeton University Press.

Rothkopf, E. Z. (1970) 'The concept of mathemagenic activities'. *Review of Educational Research,* **40,** 325–36.

Routh, G. (1965) *Occupation and Pay in Great Britain 1906–60.* National Institute for Economic and Social Research, London, CUP.

Rudd, W. G. A., and Wiseman, S. (1962) 'Sources of dissatisfaction among a group of teachers'. *Brit. J. Educ. Psychol.,* **32,** 275–91.

Ryans, D. G. (1960) 'Characteristics of teachers'. *American Council on Education,* Washington DC.

Ryle, G. (1949) *The Concept of Mind.* London, Hutchinson.

Sandgren, D. L., and Schmidt, L. G. (1956) 'Does practice teaching change attitudes toward teaching?' *J. Educ. Res.,* **49,** 673–80.

Sanford, R. N. (ed.) (1956) 'Personality development during the college years'. *J. Soc. Issues,* **12,** 1–72.

Sanford, R. N. (ed.) (1962) *The American college: a psychological interpretation of the higher learning.* NY, Wiley.

Scheffler, I. (1960) *Language of Education.* Springfield Ill., Charles C. Thomas.

Scheffler, I. (1965) *Conditions of Knowledge.* Glenview Illinois, Scott Foresman & Co.

Schwab, J. J. (1969) *College curriculum and student protest.* Chicago University Press.

Schools Council, The (1967) *Curriculum Development: Teachers' Groups and Centres.* Working Paper No. 10, London, HMSO.

Schultz, T. W. (1968) 'Resources for higher education: An economist's view'. *Journal of Political Economy,* **76,** 3, 334.

Scotland, J. (1969) *The History of Scottish Education.* London.

Scott, W. (1957) 'The fertility of teachers in England and Wales'. *Population Studies,* **11,** 1.

Scott, W. (1958) 'Fertility and mobility among teachers'. *Population Studies,* **11,** 3.

Scottish Education Department (1967) *Education in Scotland in 1967.* Edinburgh, HMSO.

Scottish Education Department (1969) *Education in Scotland in 1969.* Edinburgh, HMSO.

Seebohm Report (1968) Report of the Committee on Local Authority and Allied Personal Social Services. Cmnd. 3703. London, HMSO.

Select Committee on Education & Science, Scottish Sub-Committee (1969–70) *Teacher Training.* Vol. 11, London, HMSO.

Shipman, M. D. (1966) 'Personal and social influences on the work of a teacher's training college'. Ph.D. thesis. University of London.

Shipman, M. D. (1969) *Participation and staff-student relations.* London, Society for Research into Higher Education.

Simons, M. (1965) 'Intercollegiate differences between students entering three-year courses of training for teaching'. M.Ed. thesis. University of Durham.

Simon, A., and Boyer, E. G. (1967) *Mirrors for Behaviour. An Anthology of Observation Instruments.* Philadelphia: Research for Better Schools, Regional Educational Laboratory.

Smith, B. O. (1969) *Teachers for the Real World.* Washington, DC, American Association of Colleges for Teacher Education.

Smith, B. O. (1971) *Research in Teacher Education.* Englewood Cliffs, New Jersey.

Smith, F. (1923) *The Life and Work of Sir James Kay Shuttleworth*. London, Murray.

Smith, and Ennis (eds.) (1961) *Language and Concepts in Education*. Chicago, Rand McNally.

Smith, B. O., and Meux, M. O. (1970) *A Study of the Logic of Teaching*. Illinois, University of Illinois Press.

Smith, B., Othanel and Ennis, R. H. (1961) *Language and Concepts in Education*. New York, Rand McNally.

Smithers, A. G., and Carlisle, S. (1970) 'Reluctant teachers'. *New Society*, 5 March, **15**, 391–2.

Soar, R. S. (1966) 'An integrative approach to classroom learning'. Final report, PHS, Grant No. 5–RII MH 01096 to University of South Carolina.

Solomon, E. (1967) 'Personality factors and attitudes of mature training college students'. *Brit. J. Educ. Psychol.*, **37**, 1, 140–2.

Starr, J. W. (1967) 'The attitudes of a group of student teachers to the use of corporal punishment in schools'. *Educational Review*, **19**, 214–24.

Start, K. B. (1966) 'The relation of teaching ability to measure of personality'. *Brit. J. Educ. Psychol.*, **36**, 158–65.

Steele, M. (1958) 'Changes in attitude among training college students towards education in junior schools'. M.Ed. dissertation. University of Manchester.

Stern, G. G. (1960) 'Congruence and dissonance in the ecology of college students'. *Student Medicine*, **8**, 304–39. American College Health Association.

Stern, G. G. (1962) 'The measurement of psychological characteristics of students and learning environments'. Messick S. and Ross, John (eds.) *Measurement in Personality and Cognition*. (ed.) New York, Wiley, pp. 27–68.

Stern, G. G. (1962) 'Environments for learning'. Sanford, N. (ed.) *The American College*, New York, Wiley, 690–730.

Stern, G. G. (1963) 'Characteristics of the intellectual climate in college environments'. *Harvard Educational Review*, **33**, 5–41.

Stern, G. G. (1965) 'Student ecology and college environment'. *Research in Higher Education: Guide to Institutional Decision*. New York, College Entrance Examination Board, 35–52.

Stern, G. G. (1965) 'Student ecology and the college environment'. *Journal Medical Education*, **40**, 132–54.

Stern, G. G. (1970) *People in Context: Measuring Person—Environment Congruence in Education and Industry*. New York, Wiley.

Sternberg, C. (1955) 'Personality trait patterns of college students majoring in different fields'. *Psychol. Monographs*, **69**, No. 403.

Stevenson, C. L. (1944) *Ethics and Language*. New Haven, Connecticut, Yale University Press.

Strauss, A., Schatzman, L., Bucher, R., Erlich, D., and Sabhin, M. (1964) *Psychiatric Ideologies and Institutions*. New York, Free Press.

Stricker, G. (1967) 'Interrelationships of Activities Index and College Characteristic Index scores.' *J. Counselling Psychol.*, **14**, 368–70.

Study on teachers: Germany, Belgium, United Kingdom (1969) OECD, Paris.

Sutherland, R. L., *et al.* (eds.) (1962) *Personality factors on the college campus: review of a symposium*. Hogg Foundation. Austin, Texas, University of Texas.

Symposium (1960) 'Aims of methods of teacher training'. *New Era*, **41**, 21–39.

Taba, H. (1962) *Curriculum Development: Theory and Practice*. New York, Harcourt, Brace & World.

Tarpey, M. S. (1965) 'Personality factors in teacher trainee selection'. *Brit. J. Educ. Psychol.*, **35**, 2, 140–9.

Taylor, J. K., Dale, I. R., and Brimer, M. A. (1971) 'A survey of teachers in their first year of service'. University of Bristol.

Taylor, P. W. (1961) *Normative Discourse*. Englewood-Cliffs, N. J., Prentice-Hall International.

Taylor, W. (1967) 'The social and regional origins of college of education students'. University of Bristol.

Taylor, W. (1968) *Half a Million Teachers*. University of Bristol Institute of Education, Lyndale House Papers.

Taylor, W. (1969) *Society and the Education of Teachers*. London, Faber.

Taylor, W. (1969) 'Recent Research on the Education of Teachers'. Taylor, W. (ed.) *Towards a Policy for the Education of Teachers: Proceedings of the Twentieth Symposium of the Colston Research. Society* London, Butterworth, 223–55.

Taylor, W. (1969 b) 'Recent research on the education of teachers: An overview'. *Towards a Policy for the Education of Teachers*. London, Butterworth, 222–55.

Tibble, J. W. (1966) 'Practical work training in the education of teachers'. *Education for Teaching*. No. 70, May, 49–54.

Tibble, J. W. (1967) 'Interprofessional training'. Craft, M., Raynor, J. M., and Cohen, L., *Linking Home and School*. London, Longman.

Tibble, J. W. (1971) 'The Universities'. Hewettt, S., *The Training of Teachers*. London, ULP.

Tibble, J. (1972) *Future of Teacher Education*. London, Routledge & Kegan Paul.

Tizard, J. (1970) 'New trends in developmental psychology'. *Brit. J. Educ. Psychol.*, **40**, 1–7.

Todd Report (1968) Report of the Royal Commission on Medical Education Cmnd. 3569. London, HMSO.

Townsend, H. E. R. (1970) 'The In-Service Training of Teachers in Primary and Secondary Schools. Department of Education and Science, Survey of In-Service Training of Teachers. *Statistics of Education, Special Series No. 2*. London, HMSO.

Tropp, A. (1957) *The School Teachers*. London, Heinemann.

Trow, M. (1960) 'The campus viewed as a culture'. *Research on College Students*. Boulder, Colorado; Western Interstate Commission on Higher Education, 105–23.

Trow, M. (1962) 'Student cultures and administrative action'. Sutherland, Holtzman, Koile, and Smith (eds.). *Personality Factors on the College Campus: Review of a Symposium*. Austin, Texas, Hogg Foundation for Mental Health.

Tudhope, W. B. (1944) 'Motives for the choice of the teaching profession by training college students'. *Brit. J. Educ. Psychol.*, **14**, 129–41.

Turner, R. L. (1965) 'Characteristics of beginning teachers: their differential linkage with school system types'. *School Review*, **73**, 48–58.

Turner, R. L. (1967) 'Pupil influence in teacher behaviour'. *Classroom Interaction Newsletter*, 3, No. 1, 5–8.

Universities Council for the Education of Teachers (1971) *The Education of Teachers: Looking to the Future*. London, UCET.

University of London Institute of Education (1971) *The Education and Training of Teachers*. An interim report. April. 22, 29.

Vaizey, J. (1969) 'Demography and economics of teacher education'. Taylor, W., (ed.) *Towards a Policy for the Education of Teachers*. London, Butterworth.

Vaizey, J., and Sheehan, J. (1968) *Resources for Education*. London, Allen & Unwin.

Vernon, M. D. (1937) 'The drives which determine the choice of a career'. *Brit. J. Educ. Psychol*, **7**, 302–16.

Vernon, M. D. (1938) 'The drives which determine the choice of a career'. *Brit. J. Educ. Psychol.*, **8**, 1–15.

Vernon, P. E. (1953) 'The psychological traits of teachers'. *Yearbook of education*, 51–75.

Committee of Vice-Chancellors and Principals of the United Kingdom (1970) *University Development in the 1970s*. London.

Wain, G. T. (1971) 'The attitudes of first-year college of education students'. M.Sc. (dissertation), University of Bradford.

Warburton, F. (1955) *The selection of students in a University Department of Education*. London, Organisation Mondiale pour l'education prescolaire.

Warburton, F. W. (1962) 'Measurement of personality'. *Educational Research*, **4**, 3, 193–206.

Warburton, F. W., Butcher, H. J., and Forrest, G. M. (1963) 'Predicting student performance in a university department of education'. *Brit. J. Educ. Psychol.*, **33**, 68–79.

Warburton, F. W., and Hadley, S. T. (1960) 'Predicting the achievement in teacher training courses of college students studying to be teachers'. Institute of Personality and Ability Testing, Champaign. Illinois. Bulletin, No. 4.

Warburton, F. W., and Southgate, V. S. (1969) *i.t.a.: an independent evaluation*. London, Chambers and Murray.

Warwick, D. W. (1966) 'The Colleges of St. Mark and St. John: Their History as Illustrating the Development of Teacher Training in this Country'. Unpublished, M. A. thesis, University of London.

Washburne, C., and Heil, L. M. (1960) 'What characteristics of teachers affect children's growth'. *School Review*, **68**, 420–8.

Werts, C. E. (1967) 'The study of college environments using path analysis'. *National Merit Scholarship Corp. Research Reports*, **3**, 40.

Werts, C. E., and Watley, D. J. (1968) 'Analysing college effects: correlation vs. regression'. *A. & R. A. Journal*, **4**, 585–98.

Werts, C. E., and Liner, R. L. (1970) 'Path analysis: psychological examples'. *Psychol. Bull.*, **74**, 193–212.

Wheeler, R. G. (1971) 'Academic and professional studies in a college of education: The case of history'. *Education for Teaching*. No. 84. Spring, 55–61.

Whitehead, A. N. (1946) *The Aims of Education*. London, Williams & Norgate, (1st. ed., 4th impression).

Whitehead, A. N. (1948) *Science and the Modern World*. New York, Mentor.

Wickert, F. (1940) 'A test of personal goal-values'. *J. Soc. Psychol.*, **11**, 259–74.

Willey, F. T., and Maddison, R. E. (1971) *An Enquiry into Teacher Training*. London, ULP.

Williams, R. H. (1963) 'Professional studies in teacher training'. *Education for Teaching*, **61**, 29–33.

Wilson, R. (1969) 'Unity and diversity in the education of teachers'. Taylor, W., (ed.) *Towards a Policy for the Education of Teachers*. London, Butterworth.

Wilson, W. C., and Goethals, G. W. (1960) 'The relation between teachers' backgrounds and their educational values'. *J. Educ. Psychol.*, **51**, 292–8.

Wiseman, S. (1964) *Education and Environment*. Manchester University Press.

Wiseman, S., and Start, K. B. (1965) 'A follow up of teachers five years after completing their training'. *Brit. J. Educ. Psychol.*, **35**, 342–61.

Withall, J. (1951) 'The development of a climate index'. *Journal of Ed. Research*, **45**, 93–99.

Wood, Sir Henry, (1970) 'The in-service training of teachers in Scotland'. *Developments in the In-Service Training of Teachers*, Barr. F. ed. *Advancement of Science*, **129**, 265.

Woodhall, M. (1970) *Student Loans: A Review of Experience in Scandanavia and Elsewhere*. London, Harrap.

Woodhall, M. (1970) 'The economics of education'. Butcher, H. J., and Pont, H. B., *Educational Research in Britain 2*. London, ULP.

Woodhall, M., and Blaug, M. (1965) 'Productivity trends in British university education, 1938–62'. *Minerva*, Summer, 489–95.

Woodhall, M., and Blaug, M. (1968) 'Productivity trends in British secondary education, 1950–63'. *Sociology of Education*, **41**, 1, 4.

Wragg, E. C. (1970) 'Interaction analysis as a feedback system for student teachers'. *Education for Teaching*, **81**, Spring, 38–47.

Wragg, E. C. (1971) 'Interaction Analysis in Great Britain', Department of Education, University of Exeter. (Mimeographed).

Wragg, E. C. (1971) 'The influence of feedback on teachers' performance'. *Educational Research*, **13**, 218–21.

Wright, M. J. (1967) 'Teacher—pupil interaction in the mathematics classroom'. *Technical Report 67–85*. Minnesota National Laboratory, Minnesota State Department of Education.

Wrigley, J. (1970) 'The Schools Council'. Butcher, H. J., and Pont, H. B., (eds.) *Educational Research in Britain*, 2. London, ULP.

Young, M. F. D. (1971) 'An approach to the study of curricula as socially organised knowledge'. Young, M. F. D. (ed.) *Knowledge and Control*. London, Collier-MacMillan.

# Author Index

# Subject Index